Fodor's®

Moscow and St. Petersburg

The complete guide, thoroughly up-to-date

Packed with details that will make your trip

The must-see sights, off and on the beaten path

What to see, what to skip

Mix-and-match vacation itineraries

City strolls, countryside adventures

Smart lodging and dining options

Essential local do's and taboos

Transportation tips, distances and directions

Key contacts, savvy travel tips

When to go, what to pack

Clear, accurate, easy-to-use maps

Background essay

Fodor's Travel Publications, Inc.
New York • Toronto • London • Sydney • Auckland
www.fodors.com

Fodor's Moscow and St. Peterburg

EDITOR: Robert I. C. Fisher

Editorial Contributors: Stephanie Adler, Catherine Belonogoff, David Brown, Lauri del Commune, Sam Lardner, Mary MacVean, Pierre Noel, Kevin O'Flynn, Paul E. Richardson, Helayne Schiff, Katherine Semler, Julia Solovyova, Natalya Tolstoya

Editorial Production: Tom Holton

Maps: David Lindroth, *cartographer*; Steven Amsterdam and Bob Blake, *map editors*

Design: Fabrizio La Rocca, *creative director*; Guido Caroti, *associate art director*; Jolie Novak, *photo editor*

Production/Manufacturing: Mike Costa

Cover Photograph: Jeffrey Aaronson/Network Aspen

Copyright

Special Sales

CONTENTS

ON THE ROAD WITH FODOR'S

WHEN I PLAN A VACATION, the first thing I do is cast around among my friends and colleagues to find someone who's just been where I'm going. That's because there's no substitute for a recommendation from a good friend who knows your tastes, your budget, and your circumstances, someone who's just been there. Unfortunately, such friends are few and far between. So it's nice to know that there's Fodor's *Moscow and St. Petersburg*.

In the first place, this book won't stay home when you hit the road. It will accompany you every step of the way, steering you away from wrong turns and wrong choices and never expecting a thing in return. Most important of all, it's written and assiduously updated by the kind of people you *would* hit up for travel tips if you knew them. They're as choosy as your pickiest friend, except they've probably seen a lot more of these two magnificent Russian cities. In these pages, they don't send you chasing down every town and sight in Moscow and St. Petersburg but have instead selected the best ones, the ones that are worthy of your time and money. To make it easy for you to put it all together in the time you have, they've created itineraries and neighborhood walks that you can mix and match in a snap. Will this be the vacation of your dreams? We hope so.

About Our Writers

Our success in helping to make your trip the best of all possible vacations is a credit to the hard work of our extraordinary writers.

Born, raised, and educated in San Francisco, **Catherine Belonogoff** received her degree in Comparative Literature at UC Berkeley and thereafter moved to Vilnius, Lithuania to become editor-in-chief of a travel magazine series. Since then, Catherine has helped write Fodor's UpClose Los Angeles guide and updated various Fodor editions, including the Baltic States guide and the Exploring Moscow section in this book. Though living in Eastern Europe at the moment, Catherine yearns for Moscow and its inimitable people. She adores their

hostile kindness, ability to make vague directions even more so, and people's complete lack of respect for personal space. Even so, she's currently scheming ways to work exclusively on spa destinations in sunny places.

Author of the Moscow and St. Petersburg chapters, **Laura del Commune** lived in Russia for much of the past decade. Today, she's back in New York City working for the international department of Alfred A. Knopf in New York.

Mary MacVean is a writer and editor who has lived in Moscow since 1997. A former food writer for the Associated Press, she has written extensively about food and travel, and is the editor of several cookbooks and restaurant guides. She first visited Moscow on a graduate student fellowship in 1983, arriving without a word of Russian—and without her luggage, which was lost. Helpful Intourist officials directed her to the giant GUM department store, where she found mostly bare shelves and virtually no clothing in her size (happily, her luggage eventually arrived). Years later, GUM became a viable shopping option. Among the pages she updated for this edition are the Lodging and Outdoor Activities sections in the Moscow chapter.

Pierre Noel, a Belgian national, made his first trip to Russia in 1981, at the age of 18. Since then, he has marked his Russian adventure with historic signposts, such as the state funerals of three consecutive Secretaries-Generals of the Communist Party and the last speech by Gorby December 25, 1991. He now follows the story of Czar Boris from his St. Petersburg residence. An interpreter at the United Nations from 1989 to 1994, he works as a both an interpreter and journalist, leaving him just enough time to update this book's St. Petersburg chapter.

Dining critics for the Moscow chapter, **Kevin O'Flynn** and **Julia Solovyova** are both journalists with the *Moscow Times*. Kevin arrived in Moscow in 1995 after stints as an English Language teacher in Moldova and Uzbekistan. After a brief period at the *Moscow News* he switched to the capital's other leading English-language newspaper, where he has been sports, travel, and arts editor before working as a feature journalist and restaurant reviewer. Julia came to Moscow from her hometown of Perm in the Urals in 1994. She worked to help raise funds for the restoration of the Bolshoi Theater before joining the *Times* in 1996 where she is currently a news reporter.

Paul Richardson was bitten by the Russian bug nearly twenty years ago and has almost never looked back. He ran one of the first Western joint ventures in Russia in 1989-90 and has been author (through seven editions) of the leading guide to business travel to Russia, *Russia Survival Guide: Business & Travel.* He is presently publisher and editor of *Russian Life* magazine and travels to Russia from his home in Vermont as often as his wife and two young children will allow. For this book, he updated the Smart Travel Tips chapter, the Shopping section in the Moscow chapter, and rewrote many parts of the new Golden Ring chapter and the book's introductory chapter, for which he also provided a new scene-setting essay, "The Russian Conundrum."

Writer **Natalya Tolstaya** was born in St. Petersburg. She has a Ph.D. in Scandinavian and Russian literature and is an associate professor at St. Petersburg University. She is author of short stories and a book, *St. Petersburg: City of White Nights,* a history of the city that includes essays on contemporary life there.

Connections

We're pleased that the American Society of Travel Agents continues to endorse Fodor's as its guidebook of choice. ASTA is the world's largest and most influential travel trade association, operating in more than 170 countries, with 27,000 members pledged to adhere to a strict code of ethics reflecting the Society's motto, "Integrity in Travel." ASTA shares Fodor's devotion to providing smart, honest travel information and advice to travelers, and we've long recommended that our readers—even those who have guidebooks and traveling friends—consult ASTA member agents for the experience and professionalism they bring to your vacation planning.

On Fodor's Web site (www.fodors.com), check out the new Resource Center, an on-line companion to the Gold Guide section of this book, complete with useful hot links to related sites. In our forums, you can also get lively advice from other travelers and more great tips from Fodor's experts worldwide.

How to Use This Book

Organization

Up front is the **Gold Guide,** officially called Smart Travel Tips A to Z, an easy-to-use section arranged alphabetically by topic. Under each listing you'll find tips and information that will help you accomplish what you need to in Moscow and St. Petersburg. You'll also find addresses and telephone numbers of organizations and companies that offer destination-related services and detailed information and publications.

The first chapter in the guide, Destination: Moscow and St. Petersburg, helps get you in the mood for your trip. New and Noteworthy cues you in on trends and happenings, What's Where gets you oriented, Pleasures and Pastimes describes the activities and sights that make these two Russian cities unique, Fodor's Choice showcases our top picks, and Festivals and Seasonal Events alerts you to special events you'll want to seek out.

Each city chapter begins with Exploring information, which is divided into neighborhood sections; each recommends a walking and then lists sights in alphabetical order. The regional chapter on the Golden Ring and Moscow environs is covered by town in logical geographical order; within town sections, all restaurants and lodgings are grouped. To help you decide what to visit in the time you have, all chapters begin with our recommended itineraries. The A to Z section that ends all chapters covers getting there and getting around. It also provides helpful contacts and resources. At the end of the book you'll find the Portrait chapter, which contains a wonderful essay by Stephen Drucker.

Icons and Symbols

★   Our special recommendations
✕   Restaurant
⌂   Lodging establishment
☺   Good for kids (rubber duck)
☞   Sends you to another section of the guide for more information
✉   Address

☎   Telephone number
🕐   Opening and closing times
🎟   Admission prices (those we give apply to adults; substantially reduced fees are almost always available for children, students, and senior citizens); note that because of the current ruble crisis in Russia, prices are generally given in dollars (approximately 6.5 rubles to the dollar). For complete information, ☞ Money *in* Smart Travel Tips A to Z.

Numbers in white and black circles (e.g., ③ ❸) that appear on the maps, in the margins, and within the tours correspond to one another.

Dining and Lodging

The restaurants and lodgings we list are the cream of the crop in each price range. Price charts appear in the Dining and Lodging sections of each city chapter, and in the Pleasures and Pastimes section of the Golden Ring chapter.

Hotel Facilities

We always list the facilities that are available—but we don't specify whether you'll be charged extra to use them: When pricing accommodations, always ask what's included. In addition, assume that all rooms have private baths unless noted otherwise. In addition, when you book a room, be sure to mention if you have a disability or are traveling with children, if you prefer a private bath or a certain type of bed, or if you have specific dietary needs or other concerns.

Assume that most hotels operate on the **European Plan** (with no meals). More and more hotels, however, are now offering breakfast included with the room rate; check when making reservations.

Restaurant Reservations and Dress Codes

Reservations are always a good idea in any country—particularly so in Russia, where dining out is still considered a special occasion. In our restaurant listings, we mention reservations only when they're essential or are not accepted. Unless otherwise noted, the restaurants listed are open daily for lunch and dinner. We mention dress only when men are required to wear a jacket or a jacket and tie. Look for an overview of local dining-out habits in the Gold Guide and in the Pleasures and Pastimes section that follows each chapter introduction.

Credit Cards

The following abbreviations are used: **AE,** American Express; **DC,** Diners Club; **MC,** MasterCard; and **V,** Visa.

Don't Forget to Write

You can use this book in the confidence that all prices and opening times are based on information supplied to us at press time; Fodor's cannot accept responsibility for any errors. Time inevitably brings changes, so always confirm information when it matters—especially if you're making a detour to visit a specific place.

Were the restaurants we recommended as described? Did our hotel picks exceed your expectations? Did you find a museum we recommended a waste of time? Keeping a travel guide fresh and up-to-date is a big job, and we welcome your feedback, positive *and* negative. If you have complaints, we'll look into them and revise our entries when the facts warrant it. If you've discovered a special place that we haven't included, we'll pass the information along to our correspondents and have them check it out. So send us your thoughts via e-mail at editors@fodors.com (specifying the name of the book on the subject line) or on paper in care of the Moscow/St. Petersburg editor at Fodor's, 201 East 50th Street, New York, New York 10022. In the meantime, have a wonderful trip!

Karen Cure

Karen Cure
Editorial Director

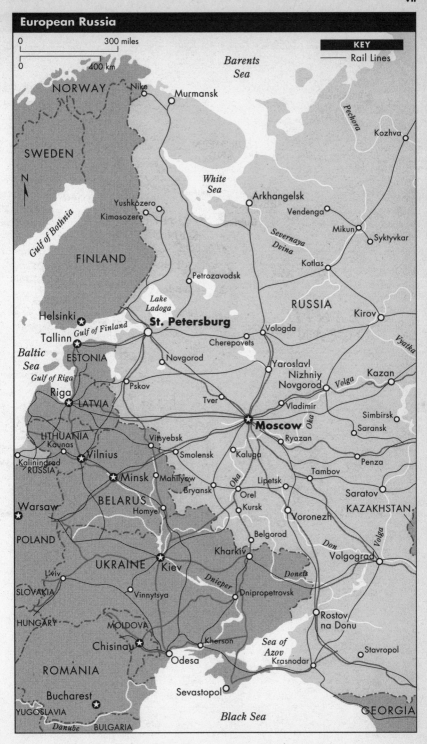

European Russia

0 — 300 miles
0 — 400 km

KEY
— Rail Lines

Barents Sea

NORWAY
Nike
Murmansk

SWEDEN

White Sea

Pechora
Kozhva

Yushkozero
Kimasozero

FINLAND

Arkhangelsk
Vendenga
Mikun
Syktyvkar

Severnaya Dvina

Kotlas

Petrozavodsk

RUSSIA

Gulf of Bothnia

Helsinki

Lake Ladoga

St. Petersburg

Kirov

Tallinn
Gulf of Finland

Vologda
Cherepovets

Vyatka

Baltic Sea

ESTONIA

Novgorod

Yaroslavl
Nizhniy Novgorod

Kazan

Gulf of Riga

Pskov

Volga

Riga
LATVIA

Tver

Vladimir

Simbirsk
Saransk

LITHUANIA
Kaunas

Vitsyebsk

Moscow

Oka

Kaliningrad
RUSSIA

Vilnius

Smolensk

Kaluga

Ryazan

Penza

Warsaw

Minsk
Mahilyow
Bryansk

Oka

Lipetsk

Tambov

Saratov

BELARUS
Homyel

Orel
Kursk

Voronezh

KAZAKHSTAN

POLAND

Belgorod

Don

Volga

Lviv

UKRAINE
Kiev

Kharkiv

Volgograd

SLOVAKIA

Vinnytsya

Dnieper

Donets

HUNGARY

Dnipropetrovsk

Rostov na Donu

MOLDOVA

Kherson

Sea of Azov

Stavropol

Chisinau

Odesa

Krasnodar

ROMANIA

Sevastopol

GEORGIA

Bucharest

YUGOSLAVIA

Danube
BULGARIA

Black Sea

SMART TRAVEL TIPS A TO Z

Basic Information on Traveling in Moscow and St. Petersburg, Savvy Tips to Make Your Trip a Breeze, and Companies and Organizations to Contact

AIR TRAVEL

BOOKING YOUR FLIGHT

Price is just one factor to consider when booking a flight: Frequency of service and even a carrier's safety record are often just as important. Major airlines offer the greatest number of departures. Smaller airlines—including regional and no-frills airlines—usually have a limited number of flights daily. On the other hand, so-called low-cost airlines usually are cheaper, and their fares impose fewer restrictions, such as advance-purchase requirements. Safety-wise, low-cost carriers as a group have a good history—about equal to that of major carriers.

Nonstop flights from the United States are available only to Moscow, originating in New York or Los Angeles. To St. Petersburg, either a direct flight, which requires at least one stop, or a connecting flight, which requires a change of airplanes, will be your only choice. Some flights, especially nonstops, may be scheduled only on certain days of the week. Depending upon your destination and originating city, you may need to make more than one connection. Your best bet is to use Helsinki or Frankfurt, which have the greatest number of connecting flights. Helsinki is less than an hour from St. Petersburg and less than two hours from Moscow. From Frankfurt, Lufthansa offers direct flights to Russian cities other than Moscow or St. Petersburg.

Ask your airline if it offers electronic ticketing, which eliminates all paperwork. There's no ticket to pick up or misplace. You go directly to the gate and give the agent your confirmation number. There's no worry about waiting in line at the airport while precious minutes tick by.

CARRIERS

When flying internationally, you must usually choose between a domestic carrier, the national flag carrier of the country you are visiting, and a foreign carrier from a third country. You may, for example, choose to fly Aeroflot to Moscow or St. Petersburg. National flag carriers have the greatest number of nonstops. Domestic carriers may have better connections to your home town and serve a greater number of gateway cities. Third-party carriers may have a price advantage.

➤ MAJOR AIRLINES: **Aeroflot** (✉ 630 5th Ave., New York, NY 10011, ☎ 800/995–5555 in the U.S.; 095/155–5045 or 095/753–8030 in Moscow; 812/104–3444 in St. Petersburg). **Air France** (☎ 800/237–2747 in the U.S.; 095/234–3377 in Moscow; 812/325–8832 in St. Petersburg). **British Airways** (☎ 800/247–9297 in the U.S.; 095/258–2492 in Moscow; 812/329–2565 or 812/329–2566 in St. Petersburg). **Delta** (☎ 800/241–4141 in the U.S.; 095/258–1288 in Moscow; 812/311–5819 or 812/311–5820 in St. Petersburg). **Finnair** (☎ 800/950–5000 in the U.S.; 095/292–8788 in Moscow; 812/315–9736 or 812/314–3645 in St. Petersburg). **KLM** (☎ 800/374–7747 in the U.S.; 095/258–3600 in Moscow; 812/325–8989 in St. Petersburg). **Lufthansa** (☎ 800/645–3880 in the U.S.; 095/975–2501 in Moscow; 812/314–4979 or 812/314–5917 in St. Petersburg). **SAS** (☎ 800/221–2350 in the U.S.; 095/925–4747 in Moscow; 812/325–3255 in St. Petersburg). **Swissair** (☎ 800/221–4750 in the U.S.; 095/258–1888 in Moscow; 812/325–3250 in St. Petersburg).

➤ SMALLER AIRLINES: **Czech Airlines** (☎ 212/765–6545 in the U.S.; 095/973–1847 or 095/973–2120 in Moscow). **Transaero** (☎ 212/582–0505 or 312/917–3200 in the U.S.;

095/241–7676 in Moscow; 812/279–1974 or 812/279–6463 in St. Petersburg).

CHECK IN & BOARDING

Airlines routinely overbook planes, assuming that not everyone with a ticket will show up, but sometimes everyone does. When that happens, airlines ask for volunteers to give up their seats. In return these volunteers usually get a certificate for a free flight and are rebooked on the next flight out. If there are not enough volunteers, the airline must choose who will be denied boarding. The first to get bumped are passengers who checked in late and those flying on discounted tickets, so **get to the gate and check in as early as possible,** especially during peak periods.

Although the trend on international flights is to drop reconfirmation requirements, many airlines still ask you to reconfirm each leg of your international itinerary. Failure to do so may result in your reservation being canceled.

Always **bring a government-issued photo ID to the airport.** You may be asked to show it before you are allowed to check in.

CONSOLIDATORS

Consolidators buy tickets for scheduled international flights at reduced rates from the airlines, then sell them at prices that beat the best fare available directly from the airlines, usually without restrictions. Sometimes you can even get your money back if you need to return the ticket. Carefully read the fine print detailing penalties for changes and cancellations, and **confirm your consolidator reservation with the airline.**

➤ CONSOLIDATORS: **Cheap Tickets** (☎ 800/377–1000). **Discount Travel Network** (☎ 800/576–1600). **Unitravel** (☎ 800/325–2222). **Up & Away Travel** (☎ 212/889–2345). **World Travel Network** (☎ 800/409–6753).

COURIERS

When you fly as a courier, you trade your checked-luggage space for a ticket deeply subsidized by a courier service. It's all perfectly legitimate, but

there are restrictions: You can usually book your flight only a week or two in advance, your length of stay may be set for a certain number of days, and you probably won't be able to book a companion on the same flight.

CUTTING COSTS

The least expensive airfares to Moscow and St. Petersburg are priced for round-trip travel and usually must be purchased in advance. It's smart to **call a number of airlines, and when you are quoted a good price, book it on the spot**—the same fare may not be available the next day. Airlines generally allow you to change your return date for a fee. If you don't use your ticket, you can apply the cost toward the purchase of a new ticket, again for a small charge. However, most low-fare tickets are nonrefundable. To get the lowest airfare, **check different routings.** Compare prices of flights to and from different airports if your destination or home city has more than one gateway. Also price off-peak flights, which may be significantly less expensive.

Travel agents, especially those who specialize in finding the lowest fares (☞ Discounts & Deals, *below*), can be especially helpful when booking a plane ticket. When you're quoted a price, **ask your agent if the price is likely to get any lower.** Good agents know the seasonal fluctuations of airfares and can usually anticipate a sale or fare war. However, waiting can be risky: The fare could go *up* as seats become scarce, and you may wait so long that your preferred flight sells out. A wait-and-see strategy works best if your plans are flexible. If you must arrive and depart on certain dates, don't delay.

DISCOUNT PASSES

If you plan to make more than one stopover on your way to or from Moscow or St. Petersburg, **look for a "European Multi-Coupon Airpass,"** which is good for discounted flights between points within Europe, including Russia. Each flight generally costs $175–$200, depending on the season and length of the flight. Often, you can use the pass on more than one airline within Europe. Some passes require that your transatlantic carrier be one of the participating carriers, but not all—so ask.

Single-coupon discounted flights may also be available to travelers with an international air ticket. You can purchase these in the United States or in Europe. However, **it's best to compare the cost of a single ticket versus multiple tickets before leaving home.** Sometimes, a single fare that includes all stopovers is the better deal.

ENJOYING THE FLIGHT

For better service, **fly smaller or regional carriers,** which often have higher passenger-satisfaction ratings. Sometimes you'll find leather seats, more legroom, and better food.

For more legroom, **request an emergency-aisle seat.** Don't sit in the row in front of the emergency aisle or in front of a bulkhead, where seats may not recline.

If you don't like airline food, **ask for special meals when booking.** These can be vegetarian, low-cholesterol, or kosher, for example.

When flying internationally, try to maintain a normal routine, to help fight jet lag. At night, **get some sleep.** By day, **eat light meals, drink water (not alcohol), and move around the cabin** to stretch your legs.

Many carriers have prohibited smoking on all of their international flights; others allow smoking only on certain routes or certain departures, so **contact your carrier regarding its smoking policy.**

FLYING TIMES

Flying time is 8½ hours from New York, 10–11 hours from Chicago, and 12 hours from Los Angeles.

HOW TO COMPLAIN

If your baggage goes astray or your flight goes awry, complain right away. Most carriers require that you **file a claim immediately.**

➤ AIRLINE COMPLAINTS: U.S. Department of Transportation **Aviation Consumer Protection Division** (✉ C-75, Room 4107, Washington, DC 20590, ☎ 202/366–2220). **Federal Aviation Administration Consumer Hotline** (☎ 800/322–7873).

WITHIN RUSSIA

The airline industry in the former Soviet Union is in a state of flux. Aeroflot, once the Soviet Union's only airline, was broken up into Aeroflot-Russian International Airlines (RIA) and a bunch of smaller, regional airlines (often called "Babyflots"). The former offers good international service between Russia and some 200 destinations, plus it is starting to move into some domestic routes. The latter are generally poorly maintained, offer unpredictable service, and should be avoided. One exception, however, is Transaero, which flies to all the major destinations within Russia and the CIS (or the Commonwealth of Independent States, a quasi-confederation of states including most of the former Soviet Union) as well as to major cities in Western Europe and the United States. Flying only Boeing aircraft (as opposed to Russian-made Ilyushin planes) and reportedly refusing to hire anyone who previously worked for the old Soviet Aeroflot, Transaero is establishing new standards for safety and service on flights within the old Soviet territory.

Since the collapse of the Soviet Union, many routes have been abandoned, smaller airports have been closed permanently, and the scheduled flights that remain are often canceled due to fuel shortages. Because of unpredictable service, many tour operators are now chartering flights for their groups. Seasoned business travelers frequently choose to fly circuitous routes on international carriers (e.g., Moscow–Helsinki–Kiev), which often proves faster and certainly more reliable than flying direct on a Babyflot.

If you are flying as an independent traveler within the CIS, **it's best to purchase your ticket with a credit card via an agent in your home country or a reputable one in Russia.** This will allow you the best chance for refunds if your flight is canceled. Be forewarned, however, that delays and outright cancellations are common. If you book from abroad, you should reconfirm your booking in person as soon as you arrive in the country.

On the day of your departure, **get to the airport early to avoid being bumped.** Bring some snacks and beverages with you—on some domestic flights (Aeroflot-RIA and Transaero excepted), there is little or no in-flight food service. On flights shorter than four hours the only refreshment served is vile-tasting mineral water. Planes are usually boarded with no regard for assigned seats; passengers either take a bus or walk en masse across the runway to their waiting plane and then push and shove their way aboard. If you are traveling with a group of foreign tourists, you may be granted the courtesy of boarding ahead of the Russian passengers. If you are traveling independently, it is likely that you will be completely ignored and left to your own defenses.

The rules regulating carry-on luggage are strict but often disregarded. Since checked luggage is frequently lost and/or pilfered, **pack as much as you can in your carry-on, including all of your valuables.** Many airports have a special section set aside for foreign travelers, a holdover from the days when foreigners received preferential treatment by Soviet authorities. These sections are usually more comfortable and often have a shop or café where you can buy snacks and refreshments.

AIRPORTS

The major international airports are **Sheremetyevo II Airport** in Moscow and **Pulkovo II Airport** in St. Petersburg.

For domestic travel, Moscow has three airports aside from Sheremetyevo II. They are **Sheremetyevo I** (for flights to the north and west), **Domodedovo** (for eastern destinations), and **Vnukovo** (for southern destinations). In St. Petersburg, there is one airport other than Pulkovo II: **Pulkovo I**, which handles domestic flights. Needless to say, even though the departing or arriving airport may be printed on your ticket, double-verify this information with your local travel agent.

➤ AIRPORT INFORMATION: **Domodedovo Airport** (☎ 095/323–8565). **Pulkovo I Airport** (☎ 095/104–

3822). **Pulkovo II Airport** (☎ 095/104–3444).

Sheremetyevo I Airport (☎ 095/578–2372). **Sheremetyevo II Airport** (☎ 095/956–4666 or 095/578–0101). **Vnukovo Airport** (☎ 095/436–2813 or 095/436–7112).

BUS TRAVEL

Traveling by bus can be a bit daunting in Russia if you do not speak the language. But for some smaller towns and to suburban destinations, this may be the only way to travel. And it is generally cheaper than travel by train. Take note, however, that shrinking city budgets have made all surface transport less reliable, and when you can, you should travel by train or suburban train (*elektrichka*). You will typically purchase your ticket at a ticket office before departing, where handwritten seating charts and tickets are the norm. But seats, even for longer rides, are sold even when there are no places left, leading to some very crowded conditions (and, on hot days, quite stuffy situations, as these buses, while reasonably comfortable, do not have air-conditioning). You can buy advance tickets for peak travel days—Friday, Saturday, and Sunday—and that is recommended.

BUSINESS HOURS

Erratic business opening/closing times and lunch hours, to say nothing of inexplicable all-day shutdowns, irritating holdovers from Soviet times, are slowly beginning to disappear. Most shops will be open from 10 to 4, with many open longer hours, particularly "Western-style" shops. Most shops are open six days a week and very little is open on Sundays, although it is getting increasingly easy to find restaurants and shopping arcades open on Sunday.

CAMERAS & COMPUTERS

EQUIPMENT PRECAUTIONS

Always **keep your film, tape, or computer disks out of the sun.** Carry an extra supply of batteries, and **be prepared to turn on your camera, camcorder, or laptop** to prove to security personnel that the device is real. Always **ask for hand inspection of film,** which becomes clouded after successive exposure to airport X-ray machines, and **keep videotapes and computer disks away from metal detectors.**

ONLINE ON THE ROAD

Checking your e-mail or surfing the Web can sometimes be done in the business centers of major hotels, which usually charge an hourly rate. Web access is also available at many fax and copy centers, many of which are open 24 hours and on weekends. During business hours and in Moscow and St. Petersburg, local Internet Service Providers often allow hourly-rate e-mail access at their offices. Whether you have e-mail at home or not, you can **arrange to have a free temporary e-mail address** from several services, www.hotmail.com, www.yahoo.com, or www.excite.com (the sites explain how to apply for an address).

TRAVEL PHOTOGRAPHY

➤ PHOTO HELP: **Kodak Information Center** (☎ 800/242–2424). *Kodak Guide to Shooting Great Travel Pictures,* available in bookstores or from Fodor's Travel Publications (☎ 800/ 533–6478; $16.50 plus $4 shipping).

CAR RENTAL

If you want to explore parts of Moscow and St. Petersburg that are out of the way, or most easily visit nearby towns in the warmer seasons, renting a car can be a good option, but very expensive. You must be comfortable driving on roads that are marked only with Cyrillic and international road signs, not mind dealing with the bribe-hungry GAI (traffic inspectors), and be a bit adventurous. You can also hire a car with driver for about $15–$35 per hour. Some local tour companies like Patriarshy Dom Tours or Western travel agents specializing in independent travel, like Mir Corporation can arrange daily-rate car and driver options, which are less expensive.

Car-rental rates are all over the map for Russia, but if you shop around, you should be able to get rates of as low as $80 a day and $500–$600 a week for a Russian car with at least 100 free km (60 mi) per day (manual,

without air). Foreign cars, automatic, and air-conditioning add a premium. These prices usually include tax on car rentals, which is 20%. Travelers renting a car in Russia should purchase mandatory insurance if your own car coverage does not extend to international rentals. Russian rentals usually include the cost of insurance, which is roughly 10% of the rental price.

➤ MAJOR AGENCIES: **Budget** (☎ 800/ 527–0700, 0800/181181 in the U.K.). **Dollar** (☎ 800/800–4000; 0990/565656 in the U.K., where it is known as Eurodollar). **Hertz** (☎ 800/ 654–3001, 800/263–0600 in Canada, 0345/555888 in the U.K., 03/9222–2523 in Australia, 03/358– 6777 in New Zealand). **National InterRent** (☎ 800/227–3876; 0345/ 222525 in the U.K., where it is known as Europcar InterRent).

➤ TOUR COMPANIES: **Mir Corporation** (☎ 800/424–7289). **Patriarshy Dom Tours** (☎ 095/795–0927 in Moscow; email: alanskaya@co.ru).

CUTTING COSTS

To get the best deal, **book through a travel agent who is willing to shop around.**

Also **ask your travel agent about a company's customer-service record.** How has the company responded to late plane arrivals and vehicle mishaps? Are there often lines at the rental counter? If you're traveling during a holiday period, does a confirmed reservation guarantee you a car?

Be sure to **look into wholesalers,** companies that do not own fleets but rent in bulk from those that do and often offer better rates than traditional car-rental operations. Prices are best during off-peak periods. Rentals booked through wholesalers must be paid for before you leave the United States.

Rental Wholesalers: AUTO EUROPE (☎ 207/842–2000 OR 800/223– 5555, FAX 800/235–6321).

INSURANCE

When driving a rented car you are generally responsible for any damage to or loss of the vehicle. Before you rent, **see what coverage you already have** under the terms of your personal auto-insurance policy and credit cards.

Collision policies that car-rental companies sell for European rentals typically do not cover stolen vehicles. Before you buy additional coverage for theft, check with your credit-card company and personal auto insurance—you may already be covered.

REQUIREMENTS

Your own driver's license is not acceptable in Russia. An International Driver's Permit is necessary; it's available from the American or Canadian automobile association, and, in the United Kingdom, from the Automobile Association or Royal Automobile Club.

SURCHARGES

Before you pick up a car in one city and leave it in another, **ask about drop-off charges or one-way service fees,** which can be substantial. Note, too, that some rental agencies charge extra if you return the car before the time specified in your contract. To avoid a hefty refueling fee, **fill the tank just before you turn in the car,** but be aware that gas stations near the rental outlet may overcharge.

CAR TRAVEL

Due to poor and sometimes even dangerous conditions, you should **avoid driving in Russia.** Even the main highways are potholed and in poor condition. Repair stations are few and far between, and there are many places selling bad gasoline. In addition, you should not underestimate the risk of crime: Highway robbery and car theft are on the rise, and foreign drivers are number-one targets. Russian drivers routinely remove their windshield-wiper blades, side mirrors, and anything else removable when parking their car for the evening, since theft of these items is common. Also, you should **never leave anything of value inside your car.**

Traffic control in Russia is exercised by traffic inspectors (GAI), who are stationed at permanent posts; they also patrol in cars and on motorcycles and like to sit in ambush. They may

stop you for no apparent reason other than simply to check your documentation. In this event, you are not required to exit your vehicle, just to show documentation. Information on rules and road conditions can be obtained from them; they will also supply directions to motels, campsites, restaurants, and filling and service stations.

If you do decide to drive in country, be sure to get adequate road and street atlases (sold on major streets along with other books) and plan your travel out ahead of time. Road signs, where extant, are in Cyrillic and/or use international symbology.

Tourists driving in Russia will need an international driver's license and an international certificate of registration of the car in the country of departure. You will also need a certificate of obligation if you have driving it in over the border. This should be registered with customs at the point of entry.

EMERGENCY SERVICES

Since repair stations are few and poorly stocked, tourists are advised to bring a complete emergency repair kit, including a set of tools, a towing cable, a pressure gauge, a pump, a spare tire, a repair outfit for tubeless tires, a good jack and one or two tire levers, a gasoline can, a spare fan belt, spare windshield-wiper blades, and spark plugs. You should also have a set of headlight bulbs and fuses, a set of contact-breaker points for the ignition distributor, a spare condenser, a box of tire valve interiors, and a roll of insulating tape.

GASOLINE

Because of sporadic business hours and unpredictable station locations, you should fill up your tank at every opportunity. Gasoline is no longer inexpensive (comparable to U.S., but not yet European prices). Out-of-the-way locations can be subject to local shortages, so many drivers, on longer trips, will employ the patently unsafe practice of filling up metal gas canisters and packing them in the trunk. It is very difficult to find unleaded gasoline and foreign cars should only be filled with 95 octane gas (cost:

FOR RELATED INFO ON THE WEB VISIT **WWW.FODORS.COM/RESOURCE**

THE GOLD GUIDE / SMART TRAVEL TIPS

about 43 cents a liter in late 1998, or $1.60 a gallon), now available at most locations. Russian-made cars run on 92 octane (about 35 cents a liter, or $1.30 per gallon).

ROAD CONDITIONS

Most all the regions covered in this guide are served by paved roads. But most of Russia's roads are not paved with asphalt. Russia's dirt roads offer very sticky driving in spring and dangerously slippery driving in winter.

ROAD MAPS

Good street atlases of Moscow and St. Petersburg, as well as decent road atlases of the surrounding regions, are easily available at major bookstores in Moscow and St. Petersburg, or at sidewalk bookselling stalls.

RULES OF THE ROAD

Driving regulations are strict, but they are often broken by local drivers; a good rule of thumb is to drive defensively. Traffic keeps to the right. The speed limit on highways is 90 kph (56 mph); in towns and populated areas it is 60 kph (37 mph), although on the wide streets of Moscow few people observe this rule. You can proceed at traffic lights only when the light is green—this includes left and right turns. You must wait for a signal—an arrow—permitting the turn, and give way to pedestrians crossing. Wearing front seat belts is compulsory; driving while intoxicated carries very heavy fines, including imprisonment. Do not consume any alcohol at all if you plan to drive. You should also **keep your car clean**—drivers can be fined for having a dirty car.

CHILDREN & TRAVEL

CHILDREN IN MOSCOW & ST. PETERSBURG

Moscow and St. Petersburg have plenty of museums, parks, and recreation facilities that are kid-friendly (and often offer free admission for children). Both cities have great circuses (ask your hotel concierge or service bureau to get tickets for you) and great riverboat rides.

Due to recent outbreaks of some common infectious diseases, and the fact that children can be more susceptible to these diseases, you should make sure all immunizations are up to date. Specifically, children (and adults) should be immunized against diptheria, measles, mumps, rubella, and polio, as well as hepatitis A and typhus. A flu shot is also recommended for winter travel.

Be sure to plan ahead and **involve your youngsters** as you outline your trip. When packing, include things to keep them busy en route. On sightseeing days try to schedule activities of special interest to your children. If you are renting a car don't forget to **arrange for a car seat** when you reserve.

GROUP TRAVEL

When planning to take your kids on a tour, look for companies that specialize in family travel.

➤ FAMILY-FRIENDLY TOUR OPERATORS: **Families Welcome!** (✉ 92 N. Main St., Ashland, OR 97520, ☎ 541/482–6121 or 800/326–0724, FAX 541/482–0660). **Mir Corporation** (✉ 85 S. Washington St., Suite 210, Seattle, WA 98104, ☎ 800/424–7289, FAX 206/624–7360).

HOTELS

Most hotels in Moscow and St. Petersburg allow children under a certain age to stay in their parents' room at no extra charge, but others charge them as extra adults; be sure to **ask about the cutoff age for children's discounts.**

CONSUMER PROTECTION

Whenever possible, **pay with a major credit card** so you can cancel payment or get reimbursed if there's a problem, provided that you can provide documentation. This is the best way to pay, whether you're buying travel arrangements before your trip or shopping at your destination.

If you're doing business with a particular company for the first time, **contact your local Better Business Bureau and the attorney general's offices** in your state and the company's home state, as well. Have any complaints been filed?

Finally, if you're buying a package or tour, always **consider travel insurance** that includes default coverage (☞ Insurance, *below*).

➤ LOCAL BBBs: Council of Better Business Bureaus (✉ 4200 Wilson Blvd., Suite 800, Arlington, VA 22203, ☎ 703/276–0100, FAX 703/525–8277).

CUSTOMS & DUTIES

When shopping, **keep receipts** for all of your purchases. Upon reentering the country, **be ready to show customs officials what you've bought.** If you feel a duty is incorrect, appeal the assessment. If you object to the way your clearance was handled, get the inspector's badge number. In either case, first ask to see a supervisor, then write to the appropriate authorities, beginning with the port director at your point of entry.

IN RUSSIA

Upon arrival in Russia, you first pass through passport control, where a border guard will carefully examine your passport and visa, and retain one sheet of your Russian visa. You can speed your transit through Passport Control by bringing along a photocopy of your visa and handing this, along with the original, to the border guard.

After retrieving your luggage, you fill out a customs form that you must keep until departure, when you will be asked to present it again (along with a second, identical form noting any changes). You may import free of duty and without special license any articles intended for personal use, including clothing, food, tobacco and cigarettes, alcoholic drinks, perfume, sports equipment, and camera. One video camera and one laptop computer per person are allowed. Importing weapons and ammunition, as well as opium, hashish, and pipes for smoking them, is prohibited. The punishment for carrying illegal substances is severe. You should write down on the customs form the exact amount of currency you are carrying (in cash as well as traveler's checks); you may enter the country with any amount of money, but you cannot leave the country with more money than you had when you entered. You should also **include on your customs form any jewelry (particularly silver, gold, and amber) as well as any electronic goods (cameras, personal tape recorders, computers, etc.) you have.** It is important to include any valuable items on the form to ensure that you will be allowed to export them, but be aware that you are expected to take them with you, so you cannot leave them behind as gifts. If an item included on your customs form is stolen, you should obtain a police report to avoid being questioned upon departure. (You are allowed to bring into the country up to $2,000 of consumer items for personal use and gifts. But customs at the airport has been enforcing this rule sporadically at best, and will not likely challenge you on this front unless you have an excessive amount of luggage.)

IN AUSTRALIA

Australia residents who are 18 or older may bring back A$400 worth of souvenirs and gifts (including jewelry), 250 cigarettes or 250 grams of tobacco, and 1,125 ml of alcohol (including wine, beer, and spirits). Residents under 18 may bring back A$200 worth of goods.

➤ INFORMATION: **Australian Customs Service** (Regional Director, ✉ Box 8, Sydney, NSW 2001, ☎ 02/9213–2000, FAX 02/9213–4000).

IN CANADA

Canadian residents who have been out of Canada for at least seven days may bring in C$500 worth of goods duty-free. If you've been away less than seven days but more than 48 hours, the duty-free allowance drops to C$200; if your trip lasts 24–48 hours, the allowance is C$50. You may not pool allowances with family members. Goods claimed under the C$500 exemption may follow you by mail; those claimed under the lesser exemptions must accompany you. Alcohol and tobacco products may be included in the seven-day and 48-hour exemptions but not in the 24-hour exemption. If you meet the age requirements of the province or territory through which you reenter Canada, you may bring in, duty-free, 1.14 liters (40 imperial ounces) of wine or liquor *or* 24 12-ounce cans or bottles of beer or ale. If you are 16 or older you may bring in, duty-free, 200 cigarettes and 50 cigars.

THE GOLD GUIDE / SMART TRAVEL TIPS

You may send an unlimited number of gifts worth up to C$60 each duty-free to Canada. Label the package UNSOLICITED GIFT—VALUE UNDER $60. Alcohol and tobacco are excluded.

➤ INFORMATION: **Revenue Canada** (⊠ 2265 St. Laurent Blvd. S, Ottawa, Ontario K1G 4K3, ☎ 613/993–0534, 800/461–9999 in Canada).

IN NEW ZEALAND

Although greeted with a "Haere Mai" ("Welcome to New Zealand"), home-ward-bound residents with goods to declare must present themselves for inspection. If you're 17 or older, you may bring back $700 worth of souvenirs and gifts. Your duty-free allowance also includes 4.5 liters of wine or beer; one 1,125-ml bottle of spirits; and either 200 cigarettes, 250 grams of tobacco, 50 cigars, or a combo of all three up to 250 grams.

➤ INFORMATION: **New Zealand Customs** (Custom House, ⊠ 50 Anzac Ave., Box 29, Auckland, New Zealand, ☎ 09/359–6655, ☎ 09/309–2978).

IN THE UNITED KINGDOM

From countries outside the EU, including Russia, you may import, duty-free, 200 cigarettes or 50 cigars; 1 liter of spirits or 2 liters of fortified or sparkling wine or liqueurs; 2 liters of still table wine; 60 milliliters of perfume; 250 milliliters of toilet water; plus £136 worth of other goods, including gifts and souvenirs.

➤ INFORMATION: **HM Customs and Excise** (Dorset House, ⊠ Stamford St., London SE1 9NG, ☎ 0171/202–4227).

IN THE UNITED STATES

U.S. residents may bring home $400 worth of foreign goods duty-free if they've been out of the country for at least 48 hours (and if they haven't used the $400 allowance or any part of it in the past 30 days).

U.S. residents 21 and older may bring back 1 liter of alcohol duty-free. In addition, regardless of your age, you are allowed 200 cigarettes and 100 non-Cuban cigars. Antiques, which the U.S. Customs Service defines as objects more than 100 years old, enter

duty-free, as do original works of art done entirely by hand, including paintings, drawings, and sculptures.

You may also send packages home duty-free: up to $200 worth of goods for personal use, with a limit of one parcel per addressee per day (and no alcohol or tobacco products or perfume worth more than $5); label the package PERSONAL USE, and attach a list of its contents and their retail value. Do not label the package UNSOLICITED GIFT, or your duty-free exemption will drop to $100. Mailed items do not affect your duty-free allowance on your return.

➤ INFORMATION: **U.S. Customs Service** (Inquiries, ⊠ Box 7407, Washington, DC 20044, ☎ 202/927–6724; complaints, Office of Regulations and Rulings, ⊠ 1301 Constitution Ave. NW, Washington, DC 20229; registration of equipment, Resource Management, ⊠ 1301 Constitution Ave. NW, Washington, DC 20229, ☎ 202/927–0540).

DINING

If you are traveling on an organized tour, you can expect your hotel meals to be hearty and ample but far from gourmet (except, of course, in fine four- and five-star hotels). If you depend on coffee to wake you up in the morning, **bring a small jar of instant coffee with you**; sometimes only tea is available in the morning and often hotel restaurants use "coffee-flavored drink" instead of genuine coffee.

When you tire of the traditional hotel cuisine, you can explore the many new private restaurants that have recently opened in Moscow and St. Petersburg. You should try to make reservations in advance for upscale restaurants. Be prepared to set aside an entire evening for your restaurant meal; Russians consider dining out to be a form of entertainment, and table turnover is virtually an unknown concept in more traditional restaurants (this is, needless to say, not the case with the newer, fast-food type restaurants).

Drinks are normally ordered by grams (100 or 200) or by the bottle. An average bottle holds about three-

quarters of a liter. In upscale establishments you will often find an
impressive wine list with imported
wine and foreign liquors, but many
hotel restaurants and smaller restaurants usually have only vodka and
wine available. Georgian wine is
excellent, although supplies have
become limited (distribution has been
disrupted by the ongoing ethnic strife
in that country). Wine and spirit
counterfeiting has become an increasingly untenable problem, so you are
best advised to order well-known
Western and Russian brands of wines
and spirits.

Getting a quick snack on the go is
getting easier to do in all three cities.
Though some of the old state-run
cafés and stolovayas (cafeterias) are
still open, they're being steadily
replaced by new chains of fast-food
restaurants (Russian- and foreign-
owned) that offer a much more appe-
tizing variety of sandwiches, snacks,
light meals, and beverages at fairly
inexpensive prices.

DISABILITIES & ACCESSIBILITY

ACCESS IN MOSCOW AND ST. PETERSBURG

Provisions for disabled travelers in
Russia are extremely limited. Traveling with a nondisabled companion is
probably the best solution. Some of
the new, foreign-built hotels in
Moscow offer wheelchair-accessible
rooms, but beyond that, special
facilities at public buildings are rare.
Public transportation is especially
difficult for the disabled traveler to
maneuver.

MAKING RESERVATIONS

When discussing accessibility with an
operator or reservations agent, **ask
hard questions.** Are there any stairs,
inside *or* out? Are there grab bars
next to the toilet *and* in the
shower/tub? How wide is the doorway to the room? To the bathroom?
For the most extensive facilities
meeting the latest legal specifications,
opt for newer accommodations, which
are more likely to have been designed
with access in mind. Older buildings
or ships may have more limited
facilities. Be sure to **discuss your
needs before booking.**

TRANSPORTATION

➤ COMPLAINTS: **Disability Rights
Section** (U.S. Department of Justice,
Civil Rights Division, ✉ Box 66738,
Washington, DC 20035–6738,
☎ 202/514–0301 or 800/514–0301,
TTY 202/514–0383 or 800/514–
0383, FAX 202/307–1198) for general
complaints. **Aviation Consumer
Protection Division** (☞ Air Travel,
above) for airline-related problems.
Civil Rights Office (U.S. Department
of Transportation, Departmental
Office of Civil Rights, S-30, ✉ 400
7th St. SW, Room 10215, Washington, DC 20590, ☎ 202/366–4648,
FAX 202/366–9371) for problems with
surface transportation.

TRAVEL AGENCIES & TOUR OPERATORS

As a whole, the travel industry has
become more aware of the needs of
travelers with disabilities. In the
United States, the Americans with
Disabilities Act requires that travel
firms serve the needs of all travelers.
Note, though, that some agencies and
operators specialize in making travel
arrangements for individuals and
groups with disabilities.

➤ TRAVELERS WITH MOBILITY PROB-
LEMS: **Access Adventures** (✉ 206
Chestnut Ridge Rd., Rochester, NY
14624, ☎ 716/889–9096), run by a
former physical-rehabilitation counselor. **Flying Wheels Travel** (✉ 143
W. Bridge St., Box 382, Owatonna,
MN 55060, ☎ 507/451–5005 or
800/535–6790, FAX 507/451–1685),
a travel agency specializing in cus-
tomized tours and itineraries worldwide. **Hinsdale Travel Service** (✉ 201
E. Ogden Ave., Suite 100, Hinsdale,
IL 60521, ☎ 630/325–1335), a
travel agency that benefits from the
advice of wheelchair traveler Janice
Perkins.

DISCOUNTS & DEALS

Be a smart shopper and **compare all
your options** before making any
choice. A plane ticket bought with a
promotional coupon may not be
cheaper than the least expensive fare
from a discount ticket agency. For
high-price travel purchases, such as
packages or tours, keep in mind that
what you get is just as important as
what you save. Just because some-

thing is cheap doesn't mean it's a bargain.

CLUBS & COUPONS

Many companies sell discounts in the form of travel clubs and coupon books, but these cost money. You must use participating advertisers to get a deal, and only after you recoup the initial membership cost or book price do you begin to save. If you plan to use the club or coupons frequently, you may save considerably. Before signing up, find out what discounts you get for free.

➤ DISCOUNT CLUBS: **Entertainment Travel Editions** (✉ 2125 Butterfield Rd., Troy, MI 48084, ☎ 800/445–4137; $20–$51, depending on destination). **Great American Traveler** (✉ Box 27965, Salt Lake City, UT 84127, ☎ 801/974–3033 or 800/548–2812; $49.95 per year). **Moment's Notice Discount Travel Club** (✉ 7301 New Utrecht Ave., Brooklyn, NY 11204, ☎ 718/234–6295; $25 per year, single or family). **Privilege Card International** (✉ 237 E. Front St., Youngstown, OH 44503, ☎ 330/746–5211 or 800/236–9732; $74.95 per year). **Sears's Mature Outlook** (✉ Box 9390, Des Moines, IA 50306, ☎ 800/336–6330; $19.95 per year). **Travelers Advantage** (CUC Travel Service, ✉ 3033 S. Parker Rd., Suite 1000, Aurora, CO 80014, ☎ 800/548–1116 or 800/648–4037; $59.95 per year, single or family). **Worldwide Discount Travel Club** Ð(✉ 1674 Meridian Ave., Miami Beach, FL 33139, ☎ 305/534–2082; $50 per year family, $40 single).

CREDIT-CARD BENEFITS

When you use your credit card to make travel purchases you may get free travel-accident insurance, collision-damage insurance, and medical or legal assistance, depending on the card and the bank that issued it. American Express, MasterCard, and Visa provide one or more of these services, so **get a copy of your credit card's travel-benefits policy.** If you are a member of an auto club, always **ask hotel and car-rental reservations agents about auto-club discounts.** Some clubs offer additional discounts on tours, cruises, and admission to attractions.

DISCOUNT RESERVATIONS

To save money, **look into discount-reservations services** with toll-free numbers, which use their buying power to get a better price on hotels, airline tickets, even car rentals. When booking a room, always **call the hotel's local toll-free number** (if one is available) rather than the central reservations number—you'll often get a better price. Always ask about special packages or corporate rates.

When shopping for the best deal on hotels and car rentals, **look for guaranteed exchange rates,** which protect you against a falling dollar. With your rate locked in, you won't pay more, even if the price goes up in the local currency.

➤ AIRLINE TICKETS: ☎ **800/FLY–4–LESS.**

➤ HOTEL ROOMS: **Hotels Plus** (☎ 800/235–0909). **International Marketing & Travel Concepts** (☎ 800/790–4682). **Steigenberger Reservation Service** (☎ 800/223–5652). **Travel Interlink** (☎ 800/888–5898).

PACKAGE DEALS

Packages and guided tours can save you money, but don't confuse the two. When you buy a package, your travel remains independent, just as though you had planned and booked the trip yourself. Fly/drive packages, which combine airfare and car rental, are often a good deal. In cities, ask the local visitor's bureau about hotel packages. These often include tickets to major museum exhibits and other special events.

ELECTRICITY

To use your U.S.-purchased electric-powered equipment, **bring a converter and adapter.** The electrical current in Russia is 220 volts, 50 cycles alternating current (AC); wall outlets take continental-type plugs, with two round prongs.

If your appliances are dual-voltage, you'll need only an adapter. Don't use 110-volt outlets, marked FOR SHAVERS ONLY, for high-wattage appliances such as blow-dryers. Most laptops operate equally well on 110 and 220 volts and so require only an adapter.

EMBASSIES

See Embassies *under* Moscow A to Z *in* Chapter 2 *and* St. Petersburg A to Z *in* Chapter 4.

EMERGENCIES

See Emergencies *under* Moscow A to Z *in* Chapter 2 *and* St. Petersburg A to Z *in* Chapter 4.

➤ DOCTORS & DENTISTS: *See* Hospital and Clinics *under* Moscow A to Z *in* Chapter 2 *and* St. Petersburg A to Z *in* Chapter 4.

➤ EMERGENCIES: **Militia–Police** (☎ 02). **Fire Department** (☎ 01).

➤ HOSPITALS: **Ambulance services** (☎ 03). For additional services, ☞ listings for Doctors & Dentists, *above.*

➤ 24-HOUR PHARMACIES: See Late-Night Pharmacies *under* Moscow A to Z *in* Chapter 2 *and* St. Petersburg A to Z *in* Chapter 4.

GAY & LESBIAN TRAVEL

One carryover from the Soviet era—when homosexuality was officially banned—is that there is little social and cultural acceptance of gay persons in Russia today. This translates, even now, to few openly gay service providers or establishments. Your best bet is to contact some of the international organizations below for the latest news and information.

➤ LOCAL RESOURCES: Two organizations in Moscow serve as clearinghouses for information about gay life in Russia: the **International Gay and Lesbian Human Rights Commission** (✉ 21/15 Bolshevistskaya ul., ☎ 095/252–3316) and the **Rainbow Foundation** (✉ 4 Malomoskovskaya ul., ☎ 095/489–2543).

➤ GAY- AND LESBIAN-FRIENDLY TRAVEL AGENCIES: **Corniche Travel** (✉ 8721 Sunset Blvd., Suite 200, West Hollywood, CA 90069, ☎ 310/854–6000 or 800/429–8747, FAX 310/659–7441). **Islanders Kennedy Travel** (✉ 183 W. 10th St., New York, NY 10014, ☎ 212/242–3222 or 800/988–1181, FAX 212/929–8530). **Now Voyager** (✉ 4406 18th St., San Francisco, CA 94114, ☎ 415/626–1169 or 800/255–6951, FAX 415/626–

8626). **Yellowbrick Road** (✉ 1500 W. Balmoral Ave., Chicago, IL 60640, ☎ 773/561–1800 or 800/642–2488, FAX 773/561–4497). **Skylink Travel and Tour** (✉ 3577 Moorland Ave., Santa Rosa, CA 95407, ☎ 707/585–8355 or 800/225–5759, FAX 707/584–5637), serving lesbian travelers.

HEALTH

The Russian medical system is far below world standards. Anyone visiting these countries runs the risk of encountering the horrors of their medical facilities, and individuals in frail health and those who suffer from a chronic medical condition should take this risk into careful consideration. You may want to **purchase traveler's health insurance,** which would cover medical evacuation. Sometimes even minor conditions cannot be treated adequately in country due to the severe and chronic shortage of basic medicines and medical equipment.

These warnings aside, as long as you don't get sick, a visit to Russia poses no special health risk.

FOOD & DRINK

You should **drink only boiled or bottled water.** The water supply in St. Petersburg is thought to contain an intestinal parasite called Giardia lamblia, which causes diarrhea, stomach cramps, and nausea. The gestation period is two–three weeks, so that symptoms usually arise after the traveler has already returned home. The condition is easily treatable, but be sure to let your doctor know that you may have been exposed to this parasite. Avoid ice cubes and use bottled water to brush your teeth. In Moscow and St. Petersburg, imported, bottled water is freely available in shops. It is good practice to buy a liter of this water whenever you can. Hotel floor attendants always have a samovar in their offices and will provide boiled water if asked.

Food poisoning is common in Russia, so **be wary of dairy products and ice cream that may not be fresh.** The *pirozhki* (meat- and cabbage-filled pies) sold everywhere on the streets are cheap and tasty, but they can give you a nasty stomachache.

THE GOLD GUIDE / SMART TRAVEL TIPS

MEDICAL PLANS

No one plans to get sick while traveling, but it happens, so **consider signing up with a medical-assistance company.** Members get doctor referrals, emergency evacuation or repatriation, 24-hour telephone hot lines for medical consultation, cash for emergencies, and other personal and legal assistance. Coverage varies by plan, so **review the benefits of each carefully.**

➤ MEDICAL-ASSISTANCE COMPANIES: **International SOS Assistance** (✉ 8 Neshaminy Interplex, Suite 207, Trevose, PA 19053, ☎ 215/245–4707 or 800/523–6586, FAX 215/244–9617; ✉ 12 Chemin Riantbosson, 1217 Meyrin 1, Geneva, Switzerland, ☎ 4122/785–6464, FAX 4122/785–6424; ✉ 10 Anson Rd., 14-07/08 International Plaza, Singapore 079903, ☎ 65/226–3936, FAX 65/226–3937).

SHOTS & MEDICATIONS

Foreigners traveling to Russia are often advised to be vaccinated against diphtheria—not so long ago, both Moscow and St. Petersburg had outbreaks of this disease, along with cases of cholera. In particular, children should be immunized against diphtheria, measles, mumps, rubella, and polio, as well as hepatitis A and typhus. A flu shot is also recommended for winter travel for all travelers.

INSURANCE

Travel insurance is the best way to **protect yourself against financial loss.** The most useful plan is a comprehensive policy that includes coverage for trip cancellation and interruption, default, trip delay, and medical expenses (with a waiver for preexisting conditions).

Without insurance, you will lose all or most of your money if you cancel your trip, regardless of the reason. Default insurance covers you if your tour operator, airline, or cruise line goes out of business. Trip-delay covers unforeseen expenses that you may incur due to bad weather or mechanical delays. It's important to compare the fine print regarding trip-delay coverage when comparing policies.

For overseas travel, one of the most important components of travel insurance is its medical coverage. Supplemental health insurance will pick up the cost of your medical bills should you get sick or injured while traveling. U.S. residents should note that Medicare generally does not cover health-care costs outside the United States, nor do many privately issued policies. Residents of the United Kingdom can buy an annual travel-insurance policy valid for most vacations taken during the year in which the coverage is purchased. If you are pregnant or have a preexisting condition, make sure you're covered. British citizens should buy extra medical coverage when traveling overseas, according to the Association of British Insurers. Australian travelers should buy travel insurance, including extra medical coverage, whenever they go abroad, according to the Insurance Council of Australia.

Always **buy travel insurance directly from the insurance company;** if you buy it from a cruise line, airline, or tour operator that goes out of business you probably will not be covered for the agency or operator's default, a major risk. Before you make any purchase, **review your existing health and home-owner's policies** to find out whether they cover expenses incurred while traveling.

➤ TRAVEL INSURERS: In the U.S., **Access America** (✉ 6600 W. Broad St., Richmond, VA 23230, ☎ 804/285–3300 or 800/284–8300). **Travel Guard International** (✉ 1145 Clark St., Stevens Point, WI 54481, ☎ 715/345–0505 or 800/826–1300). In Canada, **Mutual of Omaha** (Travel Division, ✉ 500 University Ave., Toronto, Ontario M5G 1V8, ☎ 416/598–4083, 800/268–8825 in Canada).

➤ INSURANCE INFORMATION: In the U.K., **Association of British Insurers** (✉ 51 Gresham St., London EC2V 7HQ, ☎ 0171/600–3333). In Australia, the **Insurance Council of Australia** (☎ 613/9614–1077, FAX 613/9614–7924).

LANGUAGE

If you make an effort to learn the Russian (Cyrillic) alphabet, you will be able to decipher many words; with just a rudimentary knowledge of the alphabet you will be able to navigate the streets and subways on your own. You may want to learn a few basic words, but don't expect to become conversant overnight. Hotel staff almost always speak good English, and the many restaurants and shops catering to foreigners are also staffed with English-speakers. Outside these places a good grasp of English is uncommon, though most people know at least a few words and phrases since they all took English in grade school. German is the second most common language.

LODGING

Detailed information about the hotels available can be found in the individual city chapters. In most instances you can book reservations (and request visa support for your Russian visa) directly with the hotel (in the past, all hotel reservations had to be made through Intourist, the official state tourist agency of the Soviet Union). But it can be difficult to communicate with Russia. In addition to the language barrier, placing a call to Russia can be time-consuming. International telephone lines are occasionally overloaded and once you get through, you may find that no one answers the phone. To save time and avoid language problems, book your hotel through a travel agent or sign on for an organized tour.

Many hotels have key attendants on each floor to whom you are supposed to relinquish your room key every time you leave the hotel. Since only one key is given out for a double room, you may find this a convenient system. But the key attendant often leaves the key unattended (in an open box on the desk in front of the stairwell), so if you can coordinate your schedule with your roommate, you're better off "attending" to the key yourself. The key attendants—usually rather stern elderly women—can be quite friendly and helpful, however. They can provide extra blankets or help get a leaky faucet fixed. They almost always have a samovar in their office and will provide hot water for tea or coffee.

Accommodations at Sputnik hotels vary tremendously but are often just as good as the more expensive Intourist hotels. Rooms are usually doubles or triples with only the basic necessities provided (bath and bed but little else). Sputnik hotels are most commonly found on the city outskirts.

HOSTELS

No matter what your age, you can **save on lodging costs by staying at hostels.** In some 5,000 locations in more than 70 countries around the world, Hostelling International (HI), the umbrella group for a number of national youth hostel associations, offers single-sex, dorm-style beds and, at many hostels, "couples" rooms and family accommodations. Membership in any HI national hostel association, open to travelers of all ages, allows you to stay in HI-affiliated hostels at member rates (one-year membership is about $25 for adults; hostels run about $10–$25 per night). Members also have priority if the hostel is full; they're eligible for discounts around the world, even on rail and bus travel in some countries.

➤ HOSTEL ORGANIZATIONS: **Hostelling International–American Youth Hostels** (✉ 733 15th St. NW, Suite 840, Washington, DC 20005, ☎ 202/783–6161, ℻ 202/783–6171). **Hostelling International—Canada** (✉ 400-205 Catherine St., Ottawa, Ontario K2P 1C3, ☎ 613/237–7884, ℻ 613/237–7868). **Youth Hostel Association of England and Wales** (Trevelyan House, ✉ 8 St. Stephen's Hill, St. Albans, Hertfordshire AL1 2DY, ☎ 01727/855215 or 01727/845047, ℻ 01727/844126; membership in the U.S. $25, in Canada C$26.75, in the U.K. £9.30).

MAIL

Postal rates are roughly equivalent to U.S. rates. You can buy international envelopes and postcards at post offices and in hotel-lobby kiosks. Beware that the postal system in all parts of Russia is notoriously inefficient and mail is often lost. DHL and Federal Express have offices in Moscow and St. Petersburg if you need to send something important back home. Postcards generally have a better chance of reaching their destination than letters.

RECEIVING MAIL

Mail from outside Russia takes approximately four weeks to arrive, sometimes longer, and sometimes it never arrives at all. If you absolutely must receive something from home during your trip, consider using an express-mail service, such as DHL or Federal Express.

MONEY

COSTS

Russians talk about prices in much the same way Americans talk about weather. The inflation rate is mind-boggling, but so far the exchange rate via-à-vis the dollar has kept pace. In November 1989, when the Soviet government relaxed the strict regulations controlling exchange rates, one ruble was worth approximately $1.50; today, it has climbed to the usual conversion rate of about 6 rubles to the dollar. For information about the current ruble devaluation crisis, ☞ Currency, *below.*

Goods and services aimed at foreigners are as expensive as anywhere in Western Europe. A cup of coffee in a foreign-run hotel will cost around $3; in a stand-up café around 50¢. A ride on the metro is about 35¢ and a pass for the entire month costs around $15, but there is no need to make that commitment—you can now buy a 20-ride pass (a card with magnetic strip, usable in any metro station) for about $3.50. Taxi rates are generally fairly low, but as soon as the driver realizes that you are a foreigner, the rate goes up. In general, it's best only to deal with taxis that have been ordered for you by the staff of your hotel. Some museums, such as the Armory Palace in the Kremlin and St. Basil's Cathedral on Red Square, have instituted special, higher fees for foreign tourists, whereas tickets for Russians are incredibly inexpensive. It is no longer inexpensive to spend a night at a concert or play—expect to pay $15–$50 per person for name performances.

CREDIT & DEBIT CARDS

Because of the economic crisis concerning the ruble devaluation, the major credit-card companies have become leery of extending card privileges throughout Russia. While this guide book lists the credit cards accepted at many hotels and restaurants, keep in mind this situation is changing on a monthly basis, and credit-card courtesies once extended in the past have been curtailed at many places in Moscow and St. Petersburg. If you can continue to use your credit card or a debit card, the benefits are several. A credit card allows you to delay payment and gives you certain rights as a consumer (☞ Consumer Protection, *above*). A debit card, also known as a check card, deducts funds directly from your checking account and helps you stay within your budget. When you want to rent a car, though, you may still need an old-fashioned credit card. Although you can always *pay* for your car with a debit card, some agencies will not allow you to *reserve* a car with a debit card.

Otherwise, the two types of plastic are virtually the same. Both will get you cash advances at ATMs worldwide if your card is properly programmed with your personal identification number (PIN). (For use in Russia, your PIN must be four digits long.) Both offer excellent, wholesale exchange rates, and both protect you against unauthorized use if the card is lost or stolen. Your liability is limited to $50, as long as you report the card missing.

➤ ATM LOCATIONS: **Cirrus** (☎ 800/424–7787). **Plus** (☎ 800/843–7587) for locations, or visit your local bank.

➤ REPORTING LOST CARDS: To report lost or stolen credit cards, call the following toll-free numbers: **American Express** (☎ 800/327–2177); **Discover Card** (☎ 800/347–2683); **Diners Club** (☎ 800/234–6377); **Master-Card** (☎ 800/307–7309); and **Visa** (☎ 800/847–2911).

CURRENCY

The national currency in Russia is the ruble. On January 1, 1998, Russian currency was re-denominated, losing three zeroes (the 1,000 ruble was replaced by the 1 ruble note, etc.). There are paper notes of 5, 10, 50,

100, and 500 and there are 1-, 2-, and 5-ruble coins. There are 100 kopeks in a ruble and there are coins for 1, 5, 10, and 50 kopeks.

On August 17, 1998, a Russian government debt freeze and payments crisis sent the ruble into a tailspin. As a result, the ruble/dollar exchange rate went from about 6.5 rubles to the dollar in early August to around 17 rubles at month's end. It has since hovered between 16–20 rubles to the dollar. Needless to say, this has created economic chaos—imagine Americans waking up one morning to find their savings gone and a cash dollar now worth about 35 cents. Note that for purposes of conversion, most Russian values still compute around 6.5 rubles to the *dollar* for American and British visitors; monetary devaluation mostly applies to Russians and their own currency transactions.

Still, while some might say that this problem "affects only Russians," nothing could be further from the truth. The bank payments crisis which caused the ruble's devaluation has made it difficult at times for travelers to make payments with credit cards (except, of course, at larger, Western-managed hotels), to wire in and out money, and (for those doing business there) to receive payments from Russian companies. While traveling, particularly outside the two capitals, expect to have to make all payments in cash and be happily surprised if plastic is accepted.

This said, foreigners have been somewhat buffered from this economic crisis, as real dollar prices have stayed more or less the same. Because of this, this guidebook has opted to list prices in dollars since the ruble rate for Russians is still subject to wild fluctuations (and expected to remain so for some time). Keep in mind, however, that all cash transactions must be made in rubles.

Rubles cannot be obtained at banks outside Russia, but if you somehow obtain them (through friends or acquaintances) it is legal to import or export them, although you will need to declare them and you cannot bring out of Russia more money (however valuated) than you brought in. There is no limit, however, on the amount of foreign currency you may bring in with you. Most establishments these days (hotels, stores, and restaurants) accept payment in rubles and/or credit cards. Major credit cards (American Express, Diners Club, JCB, MasterCard, and Visa) are now widely accepted. Of course it is safest to carry your money in traveler's checks, but you will want to have at least $100 in cash (in 10s and 20s). If you don't mind the risk of theft or loss, bring more; you are bound to need it. Worn or torn foreign bills are often refused by Russian merchants, so make sure your bills are crisp and clean. On your way out of Russia you can change excess rubles back into dollars at any bank or at the airport. For this you will need your passport.

EXCHANGING MONEY

You can exchange foreign currency for rubles (and vice versa) at state-run exchange offices and at any of the numerous currency exchange booths (*obmen valyuty*). Traveler's checks can be cashed at the state-run offices, at private banks, and at most major hotels.

➤ EXCHANGE SERVICES: Chase *Currency To Go* (☎ 800/935–9935). **International Currency Express** (☎ 888/842–0880 on the East Coast, 888/278–6628 on the West Coast). **Thomas Cook Currency Services** (☎ 800/287–7362 for telephone orders and retail locations).

TRAVELER'S CHECKS

Do you need traveler's checks? It depends on where you're headed. If you're going to rural areas and small towns, go with cash; traveler's checks are best used in cities. Lost or stolen checks can usually be replaced within 24 hours. To ensure a speedy refund, buy your own traveler's checks—don't let someone else pay for them: Irregularities like this can cause delays. The person who bought the checks should make the call to request a refund.

PACKING

PACKING LIST

No matter what time of year you visit, **bring a sweater.** St. Petersburg

SMART TRAVEL TIPS

THE GOLD GUIDE / SMART TRAVEL TIPS

especially can be unexpectedly cold in summer. A raincoat and fold-up umbrella are also musts. Since you will probably be doing a lot of walking outdoors, bring warm, comfortable clothing, and be sure to **pack a pair of sturdy walking shoes.**

Russians favor fashion over variety in their wardrobes, and it is perfectly acceptable to wear the same outfit several days in a row. Be sure to **pack one outfit for dress-up occasions,** such as theater events. Coat-check attendants at theaters and restaurants will scold you if you do not have a loop sewn into the back of your coat for hanging. The layer system works well in the unpredictable weather of fall and spring; wear a light coat with a sweater that you can put on and take off as the weather changes. If you visit in winter you will of course need to prepare for the cold. Take heavy sweaters, warm boots, a wool hat, a scarf and mittens, and a heavy coat. Woolen tights or long underwear are essential during the coldest months. Russian central heating can be overly efficient, so you'll use the layer system again to avoid sweltering in an over-heated building or train.

To avoid running out of the essentials, **bring all your own toiletries and personal hygiene products with you.** Women should bring a supply of sanitary napkins or tampons. Of course you'll want to pack as light as possible, but consider whether you might want any of the difficult or impossible-to-find items: ballpoint pens, insect repellent (in summer and fall mosquitoes can be a serious problem), film, camera batteries, laxatives, antidiarrhea pills, travel-sickness medicine, aspirin, and any over-the-counter medicine or prescription drug you take regularly.

Toilet paper is plentiful in hotels but less so in public buildings, so **bring small packages of tissue paper** to carry around with you. If you're a stickler for cleanliness and you are staying in one of the old Intourist hotels, bring disinfectant spray for the bathroom. Premoistened cleansing tissues will also come in handy, especially if you are traveling by train. A small flashlight may also prove useful, since streets are often dimly lit at night. Laundry facilities in hotels are unpredictable, so you will probably end up washing some clothes by hand. Bring your own laundry detergent and a round sink stopper (not always provided in hotel rooms). If you're a coffee drinker, bring some instant coffee with you; when the restaurant runs out of coffee, you can ask for a cup of hot water and make your own.

If you meet any Russians socially, chances are they will give you something; Russians tend to give small gifts even on short acquaintance. You may want to be prepared to reciprocate with souvenirs from your home-town or state, such as postcards, pens, or decorative pins.

In your carry-on luggage **bring an extra pair of eyeglasses or contact lenses** and **enough of any medication you take** to last the entire trip. You may also want your doctor to write a spare prescription using the drug's generic name, since brand names may vary from country to country. **Never put prescription drugs or valuables in luggage to be checked.** To avoid customs delays, carry medications in their original packaging. And don't forget to copy down and carry addresses of offices that handle refunds of lost traveler's checks.

PASSPORTS & VISAS

When traveling internationally, **carry a passport even if you don't need one** (it's always the best form of I.D.), and make **two photocopies of the data page** (one for someone at home and another for you, carried separately from your passport). If you lose your passport, promptly call the nearest embassy or consulate and the local police.

AUSTRALIAN CITIZENS

Citizens of Australia need a valid passport to enter Russia. Requirements are very similar to those outlined for U.S. citizens (☞ *below*).

CANADIAN CITIZENS

You need a valid passport to enter Russia. Canadian citizens are required to obtain a visa to enter Russia. Requirements are very similar to

those outlined for U.S. citizens
(☞ *below*).

➤ VISAS: **Russian Consulate General**
(✉ 3655 Avenue du Musée, Montréal, Québec, H3G 2E1, ☎ 514/843–
5901).

U.K. CITIZENS

Citizens of the United Kingdom need
a valid passport to enter Russia.
Requirements are very similar to
those outlined for U.S. citizens
(☞ *below*).

➤ VISAS: **Russian Consulate General**
(✉ Kensington Palace Gardens 5,
London W8, ☎ 0171/229–3215).
The cost for a single-entry visa is £10.

U.S. CITIZENS

All U.S. citizens, even infants, need a
valid passport to enter Russia for
stays of any length. Your passport
must be valid for at least three
months beyond the date on which
your travel in Russia will end.

U.S. citizens traveling to Russia are
also required to obtain a visa. You
will need to submit the following
items to the Russian Consulate at
least 21 days before departure: a
completed application, a copy of the
signed page(s) of your passport, three
photos, reference numbers from the
hotels you'll be staying at (to prove
that you have confirmed reservations)
or a properly endorsed business
invitation from a host organization, a
self-addressed stamped envelope, and
a $65 application fee. The fee is
higher if you need a faster turnaround
time ($75 for seven days, $105 for
four business days, $145 for next-day
service). Requirements vary slightly if
you'll be staying as a guest in a private home or if you're traveling on
business.

➤ VISAS: **Russian Consulate General**
(✉ 11 E. 91st St., New York, NY
10128, ☎ 212/348–0926 or 800/
634–4296).

PASSPORT OFFICES

The best time to apply for a passport
or to renew is during the fall and
winter. Before any trip, be sure to
check your passport's expiration date
and, if necessary, renew it as soon as
possible. (Some countries won't allow

you to enter on a passport that's due
to expire in six months or less.)

➤ AUSTRALIAN CITIZENS: **Australian
Passport Office** (☎ 131–232).

➤ CANADIAN CITIZENS: **Passport
Office** (☎ 819/994–3500 or 800/
567–6868).

➤ NEW ZEALAND CITIZENS: **New
Zealand Passport Office** (☎ 04/494–
0700 for information on how to
apply, 0800/727–776 for information
on applications already submitted).

➤ U.K. CITIZENS: **London Passport
Office** (☎ 0990/21010), for fees and
documentation requirements and to
request an emergency passport.

➤ U.S. CITIZENS: **National Passport
Information Center** (☎ 900/225–
5674; calls are charged at 35¢ per
minute for automated service, $1.05
per minute for operator service).

SAFETY

Travel to Russia in this time of great
change is fraught with many unusual
challenges, plus the normal safety and
security issues you would associate
with travel to any large city. Here is a
list of hard-won tips for the first-time
traveler to Russia (reprinted with
permission from *Russian Life* magazine):

• Learn some key Russian phrases,
like "help" (*pomoshch*) and "fire"
(*pozhar*). Learn to use Russian
phones.

• Reduce your vulnerability by
lowering your visibility. Don't
stand about with cameras. Don't
talk loudly in public. Dress conser-
vatively.

• Pay attention. Street thieves in
Moscow, as anywhere, usually seek
distracted people, whether they are
making a purchase or enjoying the
sights. Most all crimes are oppor-
tunistic, not planned. Keep your
guard up in unfamiliar areas.

• Travel light. Carry just the money
you need. To deter a pickpocket,
keep your money in a front pants
pocket.

• Get to know Moscow and the
neighborhood you are living in.
Avoid remote newly built districts.

THE GOLD GUIDE / SMART TRAVEL TIPS

THE GOLD GUIDE / SMART TRAVEL TIPS

Maryino, Orekhovo-Borisovo, Belyaevo, and other remote areas are overcrowded with unemployed *limitchiks*—persons with limited residence permits, and other transient populations which have higher levels of crime incidence.

- Don't leave your purse, briefcase, or suitcase unattended. Ever.

- Always walk confidently and at a steady pace. Criminals tend to prey on those who seem to feel unsure of themselves.

- Be alert while crossing the street. Moscow's motorbikers have become particularly adept at robbing pedestrians of their handbags when crossing the street.

- Be wary of talking with strangers in the street. When approached by suspicious people, enter a public place (e.g., a restaurant or store).

- Fast-food restaurants in Moscow have proven to be dangerous places at times—when walking out of a McDonald's with hamburgers, don't be flashy with money.

- Crime in the subway has been on the rise. Gangs of gypsies have been especially active in this respect, using a razor blade to cut handbags while the children distract the victim and cling to him or her. Do not be soft on these kids. The best proven tactic is to be very loud. Do not let them grab you. Swing your arms and/or umbrella. Do not be passive.

- Also avoid isolated cars in the metro. Try to stand close to the exit in the car. Avoid standing at the far end of the platform while waiting for the train. Do not let anyone stand behind you in the metro or on the platform. If you feel uncomfortable, try to find a support. Lean against the marble wall.

- Do not stare at drunks. At best, a Moscow drunkard will try to open a protracted conversation with you and you risk missing your stop on the metro. At worst, he may react angrily, taking your glance as a provocation.

- Stick to taxis clearly marked as such (with the green light glowing in the windshield). Do not ever get in a car that already has a passenger. Avoid taxis which suddenly pull out from the curb or from around the corner when you stand down in the street. Do not ride with *chastniki* (private drivers).

- Don't be afraid to show your fear: Scream, whistle, or do anything to attract attention. Yet, if someone grabs your purse or bag, let him have it: Your purse can be replaced, your life cannot. Keep in mind the above suggestions are meant as precautions for general safety and do not in themselves guarantee a safe trip. Remember, common sense and street-smarts are the paramount qualities on the road for any traveler.

SENIOR-CITIZEN TRAVEL

Russia is often a difficult place to travel for persons of any age. For senior citizens who have any special medical needs, have reduced mobility, or are not able to handle the greater-than-average travel discomforts that still come with travel to Russia, this is not the ideal destination. Still, many senior citizens can and do travel to Russia and have enjoyable trips by and large.

To qualify for age-related discounts, **mention your senior-citizen status up front** when booking hotel reservations (not when checking out) and before you're seated in restaurants (not when paying the bill). Note that discounts may be limited to certain menus, days, or hours. When renting a car, **ask about promotional car-rental discounts,** which can be cheaper than senior-citizen rates.

➤ EDUCATIONAL PROGRAMS: **Elderhostel** (✉ 75 Federal St., 3rd floor, Boston, MA 02110, ☎ 617/426–8056).

STUDENT TRAVEL

TRAVEL AGENCIES

To save money, **look into deals available through student-oriented travel agencies.** To qualify you'll need a bona fide student I.D. card. Members of international student groups are also eligible.

➤ STUDENT I.D.s & SERVICES: **Council on International Educational Exchange** (CIEE, ✉ 205 E. 42nd St., 14th floor, New York, NY 10017, ☎ 212/822–2600 or 888/268–6245, FAX 212/822–2699), for mail orders only, in the United States. **Travel Cuts** (✉ 187 College St., Toronto, Ontario M5T 1P7, ☎ 416/979–2406 or 800/667–2887) in Canada.

➤ STUDENT TOURS: **Contiki Holidays** (✉ 300 Plaza Alicante, Suite 900, Garden Grove, CA 92840, ☎ 714/740–0808 or 800/266–8454, FAX 714/740–2034).

TAXES

Russia currently has a 20% value-added tax (VAT) charged on most everything and refundable on almost nothing (interestingly, the VAT law specifically says the VAT does not apply to exported goods, but there is simply no mechanism worked out for handling refunds at the airport; goods bought at duty-free shops in the airport are free of VAT). In addition, a 1% tax will be added on top of this to your Moscow hotel bill.

TELEPHONES

COUNTRY CODES

The country code for Russia is 7. The city code for Moscow is 095; for St. Petersburg, 812. When dialing a Russian number from abroad, drop the initial 0 from the local area code.

DIRECTORY & OPERATOR INFORMATION

There is a country-wide number (☎ 09). Since directory workers and operators are underpaid, overworked, and only speak Russian, foreigners will have a better chance of getting telephone information from their hotel concierge or a friendly assistant at a business center.

INTERNATIONAL CALLS

AT&T, MCI, and Sprint international access codes make calling the United States relatively convenient, but you may find the local access number blocked in many hotel rooms. First ask the hotel operator to connect you. If the hotel operator balks, ask for an international operator, or dial the international operator yourself. One way to improve your odds of getting connected to your long-distance carrier is to travel with more than one company's calling card (a hotel may block Sprint, for example, but not MCI). If all else fails, call from a pay phone in the hotel lobby.

Most hotels offer satellite telephone booths where, for several dollars a minute, you can make an international call in a matter of seconds. If you want to economize, you can visit the main post office and order a call for rubles (but you will still pay about a dollar or two a minute). From your hotel room or from a private residence, you can dial direct. To place your call, dial 8, wait for the dial tone, then dial 10, then the country code (for the United States, 1) followed by the number you are trying to reach. In the new joint-venture hotels, rooms are often equipped with international, direct-dial (via satellite) telephones, but beware that the rates are hefty.

If you want to save money, you can set up an international callback account in the United States before you go. These services can often save you as much as half off the rates of the big carriers. You simply dial a pre-established number in the United States from any phone in Moscow or St. Petersburg, let the call ring a few times, then hang up. In a few minutes, a computer calls you back and makes a connection, giving you a U.S. dial tone, from which you dial any number in the United States.

➤ ACCESS CODES: **AT&T Direct** (from Moscow to the U.S.: ☎ 8–755–5042 or 8–10800–497–7211; from St. Petersburg to the U.S.: ☎ 325–5042; ☎ 800/435–0812 for other areas). **MCI WorldPhone** (from Russia to the U.S.: ☎ 747–3320 or 747–3322; ☎ 800/444–4141 for other areas). **Sprint International Access** (from Russia to the U.S.: ☎ 8–108–001–102011; ☎ 800/877–4646 for other areas).

➤ CALLBACK COMPANIES: **Kallback** (☎ 800/959–5255). **Primecall** (☎ 800/698–1232).

PUBLIC PHONES

Most coin-operated telephones in Moscow and St. Petersburg now take the plastic subway tokens (*zhetony*), which you can purchase at all subway stations and at some kiosks for 1,500 rubles a piece (at press time; price increases are inevitable). There are also still very few phones around that take coins (*monety*), but these are gradually being replaced.

TIPPING

Tipping is now the accepted norm in Russia. Cloakroom attendants, waiters, porters, and taxi drivers will all expect a tip. Add an extra 10% to 15% to a restaurant bill or taxi fare. Some restaurants are now adding a service charge to the bill automatically, so double-check before you leave a big tip. If you're paying by credit card, leave the tip in cash—the waiter is less likely to see it if you add it to the credit-card charge.

TOUR OPERATORS

Buying a prepackaged tour or independent vacation can make your trip to Moscow and St. Petersburg less expensive and more hassle-free. Because everything is prearranged, you'll spend less time planning.

Operators that handle several hundred thousand travelers per year can use their purchasing power to give you a good price. Their high volume may also indicate financial stability. But some small companies provide more personalized service; because they tend to specialize, they may also be more knowledgeable about a given area.

BOOKING WITH AN AGENT

Travel agents are excellent resources. In fact, large operators accept bookings made only through travel agents. But it's a good idea to **collect brochures from several agencies,** because some agents' suggestions may be influenced by relationships with tour and package firms that reward them for volume sales. If you have a special interest, **find an agent with expertise in that area;** ASTA (☞ Travel Agencies, *below*) has a database of specialists worldwide.

Make sure your travel agent knows the accommodations and other services. Ask about the hotel's location, room size, beds, and whether it has a pool, room service, or programs for children, if you care about these. Has your agent been there in person or sent others you can contact?

Do some homework on your own, too: Local tourism boards can provide information about lesser-known and small-niche operators, some of which may sell only direct.

BUYER BEWARE

Each year consumers are stranded or lose their money when tour operators—even very large ones with excellent reputations—go out of business. So **check out the operator.** Find out how long the company has been in business, and ask several travel agents about its reputation. If the package or tour you are considering is priced lower than in your wildest dreams, **be skeptical.** Try to **book with a company that has a consumer-protection program.** If the operator has such a program, you'll find information about it in the company's brochure. If the operator you are considering does not offer some kind of consumer protection, then ask for references from satisfied customers.

➤ TOUR-OPERATOR RECOMMENDATIONS: **American Society of Travel Agents** (☞ Travel Agencies, *below*). **National Tour Association** (NTA, ✉ 546 E. Main St., Lexington, KY 40508, ☎ 606/226–4444 or 800/755–8687). **United States Tour Operators Association** (USTOA, ✉ 342 Madison Ave., Suite 1522, New York, NY 10173, ☎ 212/599–6599 or 800/468–7862, FAX 212/599–6744).

GROUP TOURS

Among companies that sell tours to Moscow and St. Petersburg, the following are nationally known, have a proven reputation, and offer plenty of options. The classifications used below represent different price categories, and you'll probably encounter these terms when talking to a travel agent or tour operator. The key difference is usually in accommodations, which run from budget to better, and better-yet to best.

➤ Super-Deluxe: **Abercrombie & Kent** (✉ 1520 Kensington Rd., Oak Brook, IL 60521-2141, ☎ 630/954–2944 or 800/323–7308, FAX 630/954–3324). **Travcoa** (✉ Box 2630, 2350 S.E. Bristol St., Newport Beach, CA 92660, ☎ 714/476–2800 or 800/992–2003, FAX 714/476–2538).

➤ Deluxe: **Globus** (✉ 5301 S. Federal Circle, Littleton, CO 80123-2980, ☎ 303/797–2800 or 800/221–0090, FAX 303/347–2080). **Maupintour** (✉ 1515 St. Andrews Dr., Lawrence, KS 66047, ☎ 785/843–1211 or 800/255–4266, FAX 785/843–8351). **Norvista** (228 East 45th St., N.Y., NY 10017, ☎ 212/818–1198 or 800/677–6454, FAX 212/818–0585.)

➤ First-Class: **Brendan Tours** (✉ 15137 Califa St., Van Nuys, CA 91411, ☎ 818/785–9696 or 800/421–8446, FAX 818/902–9876). **Caravan Tours** (✉ 401 N. Michigan Ave., Chicago, IL 60611, ☎ 312/321–9800 or 800/227–2826, FAX 312/321–9845). **Cedok Travel** (✉ 10 E. 40th St., Suite 3604, New York, NY 10016, ☎ 212/725–0948 or 800/800–8891). **Collette Tours** (✉ 162 Middle St., Pawtucket, RI 02860, ☎ 401/728–3805 or 800/340–5158, FAX 401/728–4745). **Delta Vacations** (☎ 800/872–7786). **General Tours** (✉ 53 Summer St., Keene, NH 03431, ☎ 603/357–5033 or 800/221–2216, FAX 603/357–4548). **Insight International Tours** (✉ 745 Atlantic Ave., Suite 720, Boston, MA 02111, ☎ 617/482–2000 or 800/582–8380, FAX 617/482–2884 or 800/622–5015). **Intourist** (✉ 12 S. Dixie Hwy., Suite 201, Lake Worth, FL 33460, ☎ 561/585–5305 or 800/556–5305, FAX 561/582–1353). **Isram World of Travel** (✉ 630 3rd Ave., New York, NY 10017, ☎ 212/661–1193 or 800/223–7460). **Mir Corporation** (✉ 85 S. Washington, Suite 210, Seattle, WA 98104, ☎ 206/624–7289 or 800/424–7289, FAX 206/624–7360). **Norvista** (228 East 45th St., N.Y., NY 10017, ☎ 212/818–1198 or 800/677–6454, FAX 212/818–0585). **Russian Travel Bureau** (✉ 225 E. 44th St., New York, NY 10017, ☎ 212/986–1500 or 800/847–1800, FAX 212/490–1650). **Trafalgar Tours** (✉ 11 E. 26th St., New York, NY 10010, ☎ 212/689–8977 or 800/854–0103, FAX 800/457–6644).

➤ Budget: **Cosmos** (☞ Globus, *above*).

PACKAGES

Like group tours, independent vacation packages are available from major tour operators and airlines. The companies listed below offer vacation packages in a broad price range.

➤ Air/Hotel: **Abercrombie & Kent** (☞ Group Tours, *above*). **Delta Vacations** (☞ Group Tours, *above*). **Five Star Touring** (✉ 60 E. 42nd St., New York, NY 10165, ☎ 212/818–9140 or 800/792–7827, FAX 212/818–9142). **General Tours** (☞ Group Tours, *above*). **ITS Tours & Travel** (✉ 1055 Texas Ave., Suite 104, College Station, TX 77840, ☎ 409/764–0518 or 800/533–8688, FAX 409/693–9673). **Mir Corporation** (☞ Group Tours, *above*). **Intourist** (☞ Group Tours, *above*). **Russian Travel Bureau** (☞ Group Tours, *above*). **Sun Valley Travel** (✉ Box 6600, 220 1st Ave., Suites C–D, Ketchum, ID 83340, ☎ 208/726–6006 or 800/231–4451, FAX 208/726–6002).

THEME TRIPS

➤ Art: **Esplanade Tours** (✉ 581 Boylston St., Boston, MA 02116, ☎ 617/266–7465 or 800/426–5492, FAX 617/262–9829). **Five Star Touring** (☞ Packages, *above*). **Mir Corporation** (☞ Group Tours, *above*). **Russian Travel Bureau** (☞ Group Tours, *above*).

➤ Home Stays: **American-International Homestays** (✉ Box 1754, Nederland, CO 80466, ☎ 303/642–3088 or 800/876–2048, FAX 303/642–3365). **Host Family Association** (☎ 202/333–9343, FAX 011/7/812/275–1992 in St. Petersburg, email alexei£hofak.hop.stu.neva.ru). **Mir Corporation** (☞ Group Tours, *above*).

➤ Learning: **Earthwatch** (✉ Box 9104, 680 Mount Auburn St., Watertown, MA 02272, ☎ 617/926–8200 or 800/776–0188, FAX 617/926–8532) for research expeditions.

Smithsonian Study Tours and Seminars (✉ 1100 Jefferson Dr. SW, Room 3045, MRC 702, Washington, DC, 20560, ☎ 202/357–4700, FAX 202/633–9250).

➤ MUSIC & LITERATURE: **Dailey-Thorp Travel** (✉ 330 W. 58th St., Suite 610, New York, NY 10019-1817, 212/307–1555 or 800/998–4677, FAX 212/974–1420). **Mir Corporation** (☞ Group Tours, *above*).

➤ RIVER CRUISES: **Cruise Marketing International** (✉ 200-A Industrial Rd., San Carlos, CA 94070, ☎ 800/578–7742 or 650/592–1397, FAX 650/591–4970). **EuroCruises** (✉ 303 W. 13th St., New York, NY 10014-1207, ☎ 800/688–3876, FAX 212/366–4747). **International Cruises and Tours** (✉ 2476 N. University Pkwy, Suite B1, Provo, UT 84058, ☎ 801/344–8747 or 888/827–8357, FAX 801/356–3150). **OdessAmerica** (✉ 170 Old Country Rd., Mineola, NY 11501, ☎ 800/221–3254 or 516/747–8880, FAX 516/747–8367). **Smithsonian Study Tours and Seminars** (☞ Learning, *above*). **Uniworld** (✉ 16000 Ventura Blvd., Suite 200, Encino, CA 91436, ☎ 818/382–7820 or 800/733–7820, FAX 818/382–7854).

TRAIN TRAVEL

In Russia, take the train for the most reliable and convenient transportation. Remarkably, most trains leave exactly on time; there is a broadcast warning five minutes before departure, but no whistle or "all aboard!" call, so be careful not to be left behind.

Trains are divided into four classes. The highest class, "deluxe," is usually only available on trains traveling international routes. The deluxe class offers two-berth compartments with soft seats and private washrooms; the other classes have washrooms at the end of the cars. The first-class service is called "soft-seat," with spring-cushioned berths; there are two berths in each compartment. There is no segregation of the sexes and no matter what class of service you choose, chances are good that you will find yourself sharing a compartment with someone of the opposite sex. The second, or "hard-seat," class has a cushion on wooden berths, with four berths to a compartment. The third class—wooden berths without compartments—is rarely sold to foreigners unless specifically requested. Most compartments have a small table, limited room for baggage (including under the seats) and a radio that can be turned down, but not off. In soft class there is also a table lamp. The price of the ticket may or may not include use of bedding; sometimes this fee (which increases daily with the inflation rate) is collected by the conductor.

All the cars are also equipped with samovars. Back in the days of Communism, the conductor would offer tea to passengers before bedtime. This was interrupted for a few years, but train service is definitely on the mend, and it is not uncommon in soft class to be offered tea in the evening and morning, plus have a small boxed meal as part of your fare. There are also vendors running up and down train cars at and between stops, offering drinks and sandwiches. The communal bathrooms located at both ends of each car are notoriously dirty, so bring premoistened cleansing tissues for washing up and water for brushing your teeth. Definitely pack toilet paper. Also be sure to pack a heavy sweater. The cars are often overheated and toasty warm, but sometimes they are not heated at all, so in winter it can get very cold.

There are numerous day and overnight trains between St. Petersburg and Moscow. The past few years have witnessed increased crime on the overnight trains; the safest option for travel between Moscow and St. Petersburg is the high-speed day-train Avrora, which makes the trip in just under six hours. If you are traveling alone on an overnight train, you should take extra security precautions. The doors to the compartments can be locked, but the locks can be picked, so you might consider bringing a bicycle chain or securing the door tightly shut with a strong leather belt. You may also want to buy out the entire compartment so as not to risk your luck with unknown compartment-mates. Conductors who find out you have done this will often insist this is not possible, and threaten to put a cabin mate in with you. Do not allow this.

Train travel in Russia offers an unrivaled opportunity to glimpse the quaint Russian countryside, which is dotted in places with colorful wooden cottages. If you are traveling by overnight train, be sure to set your alarm and get up an hour or so before arrival so that you can watch at close hand the workers going about their morning rounds in the rural areas just outside the cities.

Purchasing a domestic train ticket outside the CIS can be difficult, but tickets are easily purchased within the country. Tickets go on sale 10 days prior to departure. You must now show your passport when purchasing train tickets (this was introduced to limit scalping of tickets). A one-way ticket between Moscow and St. Petersburg on an overnight train now costs just under $50.

TRANSPORTATION

In general, the best, safest and most efficient way to get around Russia is by train. You can travel in relative comfort and there are plenty of overnight trains between Moscow and St. Petersburg. Travel by bus is quite a bit sketchier and not for the traveler uninitiated to travel in Russia and/or without basic facility in Russian. Travel by car can be convenient, but less safe, given the poor condition of the roads and the astronomical increase in the number of drivers on the road—particularly substandard drivers. Travel by plane within Russia is of course preferred for longer distances, but only if you can get on flights of the most reputable and safe carriers (Transaero and Aeroflot-Russian International Airlines, not the many minicarriers that still call themselves Aeroflot).

TRAVEL AGENCIES

A good travel agent puts your needs first. Look for an agency that has been in business at least five years, emphasizes customer service, and has someone on staff who specializes in your destination. In addition, **make**

sure the agency belongs to a professional trade organization, such as ASTA in the United States. If your travel agency is also acting as your tour operator, *see* Buyer Beware in Tour Operators, *above*).

➤ LOCAL AGENT REFERRALS: **American Society of Travel Agents** (ASTA, ☎ 800/965–2782 24-hr hot line, FAX 703/684–8319). **Association of Canadian Travel Agents** (✉ 1729 Bank St., Suite 201, Ottawa, Ontario K1V 7Z5, ☎ 613/521–0474, FAX 613/521–0805). **Association of British Travel Agents** (✉ 55–57 Newman St., London W1P 4AH, ☎ 0171/637–2444, FAX 0171/637–0713). **Australian Federation of Travel Agents** (☎ 02/9264–3299). **Travel Agents' Association of New Zealand** (☎ 04/499–0104).

U.S. GOVERNMENT

Government agencies can be an excellent source of inexpensive travel information. When planning your trip, **find out what government materials are available.**

➤ ADVISORIES: **U.S. Department of State** (Overseas Citizens Services Office, ✉ Room 4811, N.S., Washington, DC, 20520, ☎ 202/647–5225 or FAX 202/647–3000 for interactive hot line; ☎ 301/946–4400 for computer bulletin board); enclose a self-addressed, stamped, business-size envelope.

➤ PAMPHLETS: **Consumer Information Center** (✉ Consumer Information Catalogue, Pueblo, CO 81009, ☎ 719/948–3334 or 888/878–3256) for a free catalog that includes travel titles.

VISITOR INFORMATION

TOURIST INFORMATION

➤ CITY AND GOVERNMENT OFFICES: **Moscow City Tourist Office** (✉ 300 Lanidex Plaza, 3rd floor, Parsippany, NJ 07054 U.S., ☎ 973/428–4709, FAX 973/884–1711) can provide information about traveling to Moscow. The **Russian Consulate General** (✉ 11 E. 91st St., New York, NY 10128 U.S., ☎ 212/348–0926; in Canada, ✉ 3655 Ave. du Musée, Montréal, Québec H3G 2E1, ☎ 514/843–5901; in the U.K., ✉ 5 Kensing-

THE GOLD GUIDE / SMART TRAVEL TIPS

ton Palace Gardens, London W8, ☎ 0171/229–8027) can also provide some assistance with travel plans.

➤ RUSSIAN NATIONAL TOURIST OFFICE: In the U.S.: ⊠ 800 3rd Ave., Suite 3101, New York, NY 10022, ☎ 212/758–1162, FAX 212/758–0933. In Canada: ⊠ 1801 McGill Ave., Suite 930, Montréal, Québec H3A 2N4, ☎ 514/849–6394, FAX 514/849–6743. In the U.K.: ⊠ Kennedy House, 115 Hammersmith Rd., London W14 OQH, ☎ 0171/603–1000, FAX 0171/602–4000.

➤ WEB SITES: http://www.friends-partners.org/friends: Friends and Partners should be your first stop for any Russia-related information. Entirely database-driven, it pulls together tons of links and keeps them organized by area of interest.

http://www.rispubs.com. : this is the *Russian Life* magazine online base, which includes archives of articles from the magazine, links to other useful sites, and the Access Russia catalog for purchasing books in English about Russia.

http:/www.bucknell.edu/departments/russian.: this site includes a great chronology of Russian history as well as links to other sites about Russia.

http://www.russiatoday.com. Russia Today.: one of the best online sources for news about Russia, this site has late-breaking information on Russia, particularly politics.

http://www.rferl.org/newsline. Newsline.: online archive of a free daily email-news service ("Newsline") on Russia, this is searchable by topic, city, names, etc. You can also sign up for the email news wire from here.

http://www.pitt.edu/àcjp/rees.html. REESWEL Virtual Library: this offers incredibly extensive lists, by category, of other websites related to Russia.

http://www.sptimes.ru, http://www.moscowtimes.ru.: the home page for the English language *St. Petersburg Times* and *Moscow Times,* both published by Independent Media—the best starting points for information on either of the two cities, and you can even read a daily online-version of the papers here.

http://www.moscow-guide.ru.: the official guide put online by the Moscow City Tourist Office is also a good starting point for information on the city.

http://www.russia-rail.com.: an online travel service specializing in Russia's railways, this site can handle everything from rail reservations (train timetables are online) to visa invitations.

WHEN TO GO

The climate in Russia and the Ukraine changes dramatically with the seasons. Both Moscow and St. Petersburg are best visited in late spring or early autumn, just before and after the peak tourist season. The weather is always unpredictable, but you are most apt to encounter pleasantly warm and sunny days in late May and late August. In Moscow, summers tend to be hot, although thunderstorms and heavy rainfall are common in July and August. In St. Petersburg, on the other hand, it rarely gets very hot, even at the height of summer. If this maritime city is your only destination, try to visit St. Petersburg during the White Nights (mid-June to early July), when the northern day is virtually endless.

In winter months both cities are covered in an attractive blanket of snow, but only the hardiest tourists should visit between late November and early February, when the days are short and dark—extremely so in St. Petersburg—and the weather is often bitterly cold.

CLIMATE

Below are the average daily maximum and minimum temperatures for Moscow.

Jan.	16F	– 9C	May	67F	19C	Sept.	61F	16C
	4	–16		47	8		45	7
Feb.	22F	– 6C	June	70F	21C	Oct.	49F	9C
	7	–14		52	11		38	3
Mar.	32F	0C	July	74F	23C	Nov.	36F	2C
	18	– 8		56	13		27	– 3
Apr.	50F	10C	Aug.	72F	22C	Dec.	23F	– 5C
	34	1		54	12		14	–10

➤ FORECASTS: **Weather Channel Connection** (☎ 900/932–8437), 95¢ per minute from a Touch-Tone phone.

1 Destination: Moscow and St. Petersburg

THE RUSSIAN CONUNDRUM

By Paul E. Richardson

YOU CANNOT UNDERSTAND Russia with your mind. You can't measure it with universal dimensions. Russia has something special. In Russia you must simply believe." This simple stanza, written by the 19th-century Russian poet Fyodor Tyutchev, has calmed many a tortured Western soul seeking to comprehend Russia or Russians by "rational" criteria. Indeed, this vast country with its complex, ancient history seems inordinately difficult for an outsider to understand by any means, rational or otherwise.

How was it that one of the most isolated, illiterate societies in Europe produced, in the 19th century, so many giants of literature, science, music, and the arts? Why is it that such a conservative, deeply religious, and agrarian-feudalist society so eagerly embraced the revolutionary, atheistic, and industrial ideology of Communism—and then, 80 years later, with equal vigor, cast this ideology aside in favor of the previously despised "bourgeois capitalism"? Why has Russia so often embraced dictators and so readily destroyed its geniuses? How is it that Russians, who in friendship will bare their souls and willingly and warmly offer aid, are such masters of obfuscation and obduracy in public and official life?

There are no easy answers. And that is what fascinates so many people—often for a lifetime. For once you have visited Russia, have tasted its rich history and culture, there is no turning back. Russia will be with you forever, setting up its myriad paradoxes, posing unanswerable questions, and beckoning you to return.

The Russia of a decade ago, under Communism, offered the mystique and flavor of a Le Carré novel. Experiencing today's Russia is no less intoxicating, for the country is undergoing a host of concurrent social, political, and economic upheavals that would crush a less hardy society. In the past 10 years, Russia has cast off an ideology that permeated and dictated all aspects of everyday life; demolished a centrally planned economy built up over six decades; destroyed the world's largest and most oppressive internal, secret police organization, along with a massive system of internal labor camps; carried out the largest-ever sell-off of state assets in the history of the world; dismantled the last empire on earth; created from scratch free-market systems for banking, stock markets, international, and retail trade; developed, again from scratch (and certainly in need of improvement), democratic political structures and the laws necessary to support them. Needless to say, the remarkable extent of these changes is often overlooked by "observers" quick to point out how much further Russia still has to go.

Russia's course in the past decade can be likened to that of a rusted, sinking supertanker that is being turned around in a very narrow space, while at the same time—without aid of a dry dock—being completely overhauled as a modern cruise liner. Sure, there are plenty of leaks and systems that aren't yet working up to code, but one can't help but marvel at the speed and extent of the transformation so far.

This is evident everywhere. The crew-cut *biznesmen* in the sharkskin suit wielding a $400 digital cell phone, the audacious street-corner bookseller, the 19-year-old securities trader, the publisher of an independent political newsweekly, the teenager racing around a central square on in-line skates, the politician speaking out for restoration of the monarchy—all these "new" Russians, whose activities seem so normal to the Western eye, are engaged in things that a decade ago were illegal or impossible.

New freedoms and opportunities have set off an almost palpable exuberance and energy, particularly in Moscow and St. Petersburg. After a period of fascination with things Western, Russians are rebuilding, restoring, and reinvesting in their own culture and history with a renewed vigor. With the departure of the sickle, the scepter is making a comeback: Ancient Imperial monuments are being dusted off and repaired to reflect their former glory. The Russian Orthodox Church is slowly, discreetly regaining a modicum of its prerevolutionary power and moral influence. New office buildings, restaurants, and service establishments are brightening up previously unused corners of the cities, while old buildings are being given a fresh coat of paint or a restored facade.

Of course, not all is as yet as it should be. In the free-market Russia, new liberties have all too often been interpreted as unrestrained license. Pornography is rampant now that there is freedom to publish what you will; alcoholism is at an all-time high (and life expectancy at an all-time low) because the state no longer monopolizes vodka production; organized crime permeates the entertainment, advertising, sports, natural resource, and other lucrative sectors, because there is no money to enforce laws properly; common public-sector services such as education, health care, and prisons are seriously underfunded; military conscripts suffer through inhumane hazing and a lack of proper housing and clothing; the economy is unpredictable, largely "controlled" by about a half dozen powerful oligarchs.

While visitors marvel at the paradox of huge, superficial changes coupled with such ongoing problems, the Russian people must live in such a world. They must come to grips with a world turned upside-down in the space of half a generation. Not so long ago, the government guaranteed security of employment, education, and health and welfare from cradle to grave, at the cost of servility to warped political and economic theories. Now, the government guarantees essentially nothing—even pensions and student stipends do not offer sustainable incomes—and so, loyalty and civility are at all-time lows. When store shelves were nearly bare, the average Russian stood in line up to three hours a day to buy food and consumer goods. Now, anything can be bought in the shops, but prices are frequently beyond the average citizen's means. Before, Russians could draw comfort from the fact that, although things were bad, everyone (except the political elite) was equally straitened. Now, wealth seems to correlate with dishonesty and unscrupulous behavior, and there is a growing gap between rich and poor.

And yet, the indomitable Russian spirit marches on. The natives like to recall the old saying, "Russia is always defeated, but never beaten." The spirit that impassioned the Russian forces to beat back Napoleon and Hitler, each of whom conquered nearly every other nation he engaged in battle on the European continent . . . the spirit that asked the Russian people to endure over 30 years of international and civil war from 1914 to 1945, and seven decades of the *gulags* . . . the spirit that kept artistic creativity alive despite centuries of censorship, imprisonment, exile, servitude, and death—it is this spirit that is Russia's greatest hope and its deepest pride. If you are lucky, and travel through this country with an open mind, you will find a glimmer of this spirit in a conversation shared over vodka and pickles on a train; in a golden summer day spent at a *banya* (sauna) or *dacha* (country house); in a winter evening spent at the Bolshoi Opera; or an afternoon spent at the Tretyakov Gallery.

After Russian people themselves, the land of Russia will most amaze you. The "two capitals"—Moscow, a sprawling, teeming beehive of a metropolis, and St. Petersburg, an aristocratic, almost Scandinavian city—are both quite distinctive and worthy of several lengthy visits. The smaller towns of the Golden Ring, with their medieval monasteries and provincial, riverfront kremlins, preserved like chrysalises in amber, are in warm and welcome contrast to the capital cities. And yet, these locales are only a mere introduction, only a reflection of a country so vast that it spans 11 time zones and two continents. There is the endless expanse of Siberia—a name that evokes a hundred images. There are the slumbering volcanoes of Kamchatka, the barren eastern island of Sakhalin, the hidden realm of Tuva, the bottomless waters of Lake Baikal, the forbidding Arctic sea, and the broad, welcoming Volga. And, of course there is the Trans-Siberian Railroad, whose seven-day journey across the breadth of Russia offers perhaps the greatest illustration of the immensity of this 1,000-year-old land.

To connoisseurs, Russian food is one of the world's most unheralded, original, even great cuisines. Whereas just a few years ago traveling in Russia meant facing shamefully unappetizing hotel meals masquerading as authentic national fare, today the secrets of great Russian cuisine are being rediscovered. And what better introduction to Russian culture could there be than a steaming dish of beef *pelmeni* (dumplings) alongside a mound of black caviar? Or a piping-hot bowl of *borshch,* with onions glimmering in a deep purple broth? Or breaded *kotlety po-tsarsky* (cutlets à la tsar) lathered with a rich brown sauce? Or the fantastical "bird's milk" torte? Yes, Russian cuisine is built on starches and creams, but it is also, when prepared properly, replete with fresh vegetables, fresh fish, copious amounts of healthy herbs and garlic, and, possibly, some of the best mushrooms you may ever taste.

Many pleasant surprises—not the least of which is this new cuisine—await the visitor to Russia. There is the gawking astonishment as you climb the incline into Red Square and see for the first time the marvelous, multicolored onion domes of St. Basil's Cathedral and the imposing walls of the Kremlin. There is the colorful splendor of the golden fountains at Peterhof, or the reflection of the sky-blue facade of the Hermitage shimmering in puddles after a morning shower. There is the impressive strength and beauty of the Suzdal Kremlin holding forth above the Kamenka river. There is the gleaming stand of arrow-straight, white birch trees next to an endless expanse of tilled black earth. There is the smile of a train conductress as she offers you, unbidden, a cup of morning coffee. There is the invigorating plunge into a snowbank after a midwinter steam in a banya.

Every trip to Russia is full of such surprises. Without a doubt, you will meet some interesting people. If you are well prepared, you will visit some fascinating historical sites, attend fine cultural events, and savor one of the world's most overlooked cuisines. And, like many visitors to Russia, while you will leave Russia, Russia will never leave you. Long after your trip is over, your personal experience of Russia will continue to evoke an interest in things Russian, in the myriad riddles of Russia and its people. And while, à la Tyutchev, you may never be able to fully understand Russia, as any traveler knows, there is joy in the attempt.

WHAT'S WHERE

Moscow

The end of Communism has undoubtedly affected the ancient capital of Rus-

sia. The central streets have largely reverted to their old prerevolutionary names, and the number of places named after Lenin has been drastically reduced. The new advertising billboards, many in English as well as Russian, point to profound economic change. Western investment and cooperative agreements have led to a fever of new construction, notably of hotels and business complexes. And then there is the recent spate of additions to the Moscow skyline by the city's ambitious mayor Yuri Luzhkov, the most significant of which is surely the resurrected Christ the Savior Cathedral. But there are many others, like the grandiose monument to Peter the Great, the memorial complex at Poklonnaya Gora, and the underground complex at Manezh Square. Yet for all this, the face of Moscow appears curiously impervious to change. Its Stalinist physiognomy, born in the 1930s, continues to brazen it out; the Gothic heights of the old Ukraine Hotel and the Foreign Ministry look contemptuously down over modest Western-style shops below. Building after building, made redundant by the demise of Communism, have now been taken over by new organizations and refuse to budge. Although Moscow now has much in common with its great Western counterparts—Paris, London, New York—it still has a stubbornly Russian stamp.

St. Petersburg

Planned from the very first brick as a great capital city, St. Petersburg has not fallen short of Peter the Great's original vision. It has not served as the capital of Russia since the time of the Bolshevik Revolution, but it still carries itself as though it were. Indeed, the imposing grandeur of its most important landmarks—Palace Square and the Winter Palace—and the stylish sophistication of its residences make this 300-year-old city one of the great urban centers of the world. Czar Peter's intention was to reorient Russia to the West by making the city a "window looking into Europe," and indeed the geometric elegance of its layout and the perfect planning of its architecture owe more to the grand cities of Europe than to its own counterparts to the east. It has also been called the northern Venice, for it is a city built on more than a hundred islands cradled in the watery lap of the winding Neva and the intricate network of canals carved into the soft ground at the mouth of the Gulf of Finland.

Side Trips from Moscow

The so-called "Golden Ring" near Moscow (actually more of a parallelogram than a circle) consists of several medieval towns built up against the Volga, Klyazma, and Nerl rivers—strategic lines of defense against invasion and, later, important routes for trade. These towns—Rostov, Yaroslavl, Vladimir, Kostroma, and Pereslavl-Zalessky—were, in the 12th to 14th centuries, the most important centers in Russia. They owed their prominence to Prince Yuri Dolgoruky and his son, Andrei Bogolyubsky, who were instrumental in shifting the center of power in Rus' (as Russia was then known) from Kiev in the west to Suzdal and Vladimir in the east. Later, in the 14th and 15th centuries, as the shadow of the Mongol Yoke receded, Moscow usurped their prominence. This stopped construction and development in these towns, except for some mercantile building in the 18th century (notable in the town arcades); most of 19th- and 20th-century industrialization passed them by. As a result, a trip to these preserved-in-time towns can be a journey back to the late Middle Ages.

PLEASURES AND PASTIMES

Ballet

Over the last 150 years, few *corps de ballet* could match the Russian product. The Bolshoi and Kirov ballets have produced some of the world's greatest dancers; indeed, the names Pavlova, Nijinsky, Nureyev, Plisetskaya, Barishnikov, Massine, and Diaghilev, all homegrown talents, are synonymous with ballet brilliance. Faltering standards, due to chronic underfunding and the attraction of the West, has led to an unstoppable hemorrhaging of Russia's greatest dancers, beginning with the defection of Rudolf Nureyev in 1961. The demise of Communism has exposed decades of complacency and institutional rigidity, and has done little to stop the drain—Britain's Royal Ballet poached Russia's current great danseur, Irek Mukhamedov, in 1991. Despite such problems, an evening at the Kirov or the Bolshoi is a must for those wishing to take a peek at the heart of some of the world's most historic dance venues.

Bathhouses

A visit to the Russian *banya,* or bath, should not be missed. It has been part of the national culture for centuries; indeed, the bathhouses of Moscow and St. Petersburg were once the ultimate in luxury. Yegerov's in St. Petersburg, for example, had a tented disrobing room decked out in Moorish style with cushions and settees, and a swimming pool spanned by a grottolike bridge and rockery, Classical-style statues, and trailing greenery.

Bring your own towel, shampoo, and plastic shoes or sandals. You may be given a plastic bathing robe and offered a *venik,* the bundle of birch twigs without which no visit to the bath is complete. By brushing the soaked twigs lightly across the body, striking more boldly with each turn, it is said one stimulates the circulation of the blood and draws out toxins. Most Russians finish with a glass of tea or water or even a shot of vodka, but be careful not to overindulge: Sip, don't gulp, any liquids.

Dining

The dining scene in Russia has changed dramatically in the past few years. In terms of sheer numbers and types of restaurants, Moscow is far ahead of St. Petersburg, but in both cities you'll find a choice of cuisines and price ranges.

In Russia, breakfast is often a familiar omelet or fried eggs, but don't be surprised if the meal includes cabbage salad, fish, or hot dogs (served with cold peas), all standard breakfast fare. The main meal of the day is served in mid-afternoon and usually consists of a starter, soup, and a main course. Supper is traditionally a lighter meal, with just an appetizer and a main course. The main course will be either meat or fish; the fish you are most likely to be served are sturgeon, halibut, or herring. A favorite meat dish is beef Stroganov, beef stewed in sour cream and served with mushrooms and fried potatoes. The soup is likely to be borshch, a beet soup, or *shchi,* cabbage soup. Other national dishes include *pirozhki,* fried turnovers filled with cabbage or meat, and *blini,* small, light pancakes rolled and filled with caviar, fish, melted butter, fruit preserves, or sour cream.

Nature

If you ask Russians which characteristic they think most identifies them as Russian, do not be surprised if they say that it is their intimate association with nature. At the turn of the century, it was estimated that 90% of the population was rural, and while this figure has dropped over the course of the 20th century, the peoples' attachment to the natural world has remained binding. Every major city has at least one large park where citizens can spend entire days enjoying the greenery in the company of friends and family. On weekends, families stream out of the cities to their countryside dachas or to budget hotel complexes. There they can indulge in one of the greatest of Russian pastimes, *mushrooming*. From early June to mid-October, the countryside is awash with genuflecting men and women picking mushrooms, which are then eaten at a *shashlik,* or barbecue.

Vodka

The national drink is an inseparable part of Russian social life. Vodka is drunk literally everywhere, with the effect of breaking down inhibitions and producing a state of conviviality the Russians refer to as *dusha-dushe* (soul-to-soul). When a Russian taps his throat, beware: It's impossible to refuse this invitation to conviviality.

Vodka is often flavored and colored with herbs and spices. *Limonaya*, lemon-flavored vodka, is particularly popular with American tourists, as is *pertsovka,* pepper-flavored vodka. Other varieties include *starka* (a dark, smooth "old" vodka), *pshenichnaya* (made from wheat), *ryabinovka,* in which ashberries have been steeped, and *tminaya* (caraway-flavored vodka). Be wary of *krepkaya* vodka, which at 110 proof is the strongest variety.

Normally served from an ice bucket, vodka is drunk neat in a single gulp, then "chased" with a mouthful of food. It goes down particularly well with *zakuski* (hors d'oeuvres)—smoked salmon, salted herring, marinated mushrooms, salami, caviar, and such. To quell the fiery taste, some Russians advise exhaling before gulping, while others recommend deep inhalation. Many Russians swear by a shot of vodka with a dash of pepper as a cure for the common cold.

Winter Sports

Skiing packages to Moscow and St. Petersburg are available. Cross-country skiing is a particularly popular sport in Russia, and both cities have acres of wooded parkland perfect for it. Outdoor skating rinks also abound, and there are downhill-skiing facilities just outside of Moscow. Rentals of skis and skates are available only sporadically, so you should bring your own equipment or make prior arrangements.

NEW AND NOTEWORTHY

Post-Soviet Russia has, politically, been defined largely through the person and power of Boris Yeltsin, who rose to prominence in the late-Soviet period by virtue of being ousted from the Politburo. In the historic past, such exclusion normally signaled the end of a politician's career. But, in 1987, when so much else was being challenged, this was just the beginning for Boris Yeltsin. He was soon elected to the new Russian Federation Parliament (1989) and gained stature as its chairman, striding on to the newly created post of president and, in that capacity, helping bring down the Soviet Union on Christmas Eve 1991. But, just as Russia was embarking on its most ambitious reforms, Yeltsin's fame and favor went into decline with the war in Chechnya and the 1993 tank attack on rebels barricaded inside the Russian White House, the august building that remains the governmental seat in Moscow. Hanging on, Yeltsin eked out a surprise presidential re-election victory in 1996, but his second term was haunted by the unsettled war in Chechnya and financial scandals. The tense times running up to the election in 2000 (if Yeltsin's shaky health and status does not compel an earlier election) will prove decisive in Russia's political future. That election will represent the first time ever that Russia seeks to make a peaceful transition of elected executive power. One can expect the course of this campaign to be the focus of much political jockeying by Russia's different power elites.

But all this will only make for an exciting backdrop to travel in Russia. On that front there has been irreversible change, for the better. More and more hotels open up yearly (but with a decided lack of decent, mid-class hotels), and there is no longer any difficulty finding a bite to eat anywhere in the major cities, almost any time of the day or night. Nearly any travel need can be accommodated in Moscow or St. Petersburg with sufficient money and the assistance of a savvy travel agent or concierge.

Moscow

While, for the individual Muscovite, life goes on much as it always did, there is no denying that the face of Moscow has changed dramatically in recent years. The gilded domes of Christ the Savior Cathedral have risen again alongside the Moscow river, not far from a somewhat controversial sculpture honoring Peter the Great, which was unveiled in 1997 on the occasion of the 300th anniversary of the Russian Navy. Neighboring the Kremlin, the vast underground Manezh mall and restaurant complex has become a new magnet for downtown promenaders, where one can—a little sacrilegiously—enjoy a slice of pizza and a beer while looking out a window at the Eternal Flame. Russia's most Russian museum, the Tretyakov Gallery, has been totally renovated and made the centerpiece of a wonderful riverside park area. Together with all this municipal construction and renovation, banks and commercial buildings are sprouting up all over the city—thanks to the seemingly bottomless wells of capital among the nouveau riche (among which are the oft-bemoaned Russian "mafia"). The frenzy of construction activity is paralleled by an astronomical growth in street traffic that daily threatens to clog every city artery. A growing number of vehicles are foreign cars, and a decreasing number public transport buses, trams, and trolleys, with the expected effect on pollution levels.

St. Petersburg

In July 1998, Russia formally closed a sensitive chapter in its history when the remains of the murdered Romanov family were buried in Peter and Paul Cathedral, in St. Petersburg's fortress of the same name. It was a chance for the city to shine and while it continues to lag behind Moscow in terms of general prosperity, the positive growth resulting from the introduction of a market economy has had tangible effects. Like the capital, St. Petersburg is full of new projects for hotels and business centers, and it has been relatively successful in attracting foreign business. The Hermitage and Alexander Palace have both been beneficiaries of large grants to aid their restoration as historical monuments. And one should expect the pace of "sprucing up" and investment in other monuments to escalate as the city approaches its 300th anniversary, to be celebrated in 2003. Prices are lower in this genteel city, and the nouveau riche evident in Moscow seem to be absent here, even if the plague of organized crime is as widespread as—some say more so than—in Moscow.

Around Moscow

The advent of reforms has changed little in the towns around Moscow, except for a slight, general improvement to the tourist infrastructure on which they all rely. There is now a choice of accommodations options and attractive, private restaurants in the town centers, where previously the only option was graying Soviet Intourist "complexes." Crime is usually of little concern in these smaller towns, as they tend to be controlled by a single "band." Prices for food and lodging will also be lower here than in either Moscow or St. Petersburg.

FODOR'S CHOICE

No two people will agree on what makes a perfect vacation, but it's sometimes helpful to know what others think. We hope you'll have a chance to experience some of Fodor's Choices yourself while visiting Moscow, St. Petersburg, and their environs. For detailed information about each entry, refer to the appropriate chapters within this guidebook.

Churches and Monasteries

★ **Alexander Nevsky Lavra, St. Petersburg.** One of only four highest-ranking monasteries in Russia and the Ukraine, the burial place of St. Alexander Nevsky—and many other famous names—was built in 1710 by Peter the Great.

★ **Donskoy Monastery, Moscow.** The once secret archives at this 16th-century monastery are a fascinating memorial to Russian architecture and art.

★ **New Maiden's Convent and Cemetery, Moscow.** This immaculately preserved ensemble of 16th- and 17th-century architecture borders a fascinating cemetery where some of Russia's greatest literary, political, and military figures are buried.

★ **Smolny Convent and Cathedral, St. Petersburg.** This magnificent five-domed, blue-and-white masterpiece by Bartolomeo Rastrelli seems to have leapt off the pages of a fairy tale.

★ **St. Ipaty Monastery, Kostroma.** This monastery owes much of its fame to being the birthplace of the Romanov dynasty, but it has a wonderful cathedral and the neighboring Museum of Wooden Folk Architecture is the oldest of its kind in Russia.

★ **St. Yefimy Monastery, Suzdal.** This imposing fortress on the banks of the Kamenka river dates to 1350 and has served repeatedly as a cinematic stand-in for the Moscow Kremlin.

★ **Zagorsk (Sergeyev-Posad), Moscow.** Pilgrims have been worshipping at the monastery here, Russia's most important center of pilgrimage, for more than 500 years.

Historical Buildings and Sites

★ **Armory Palace, Moscow.** A broad selection of Imperial regalia and historical artifacts is stored in the vast galleries of the Kremlin's oldest and richest museum.

★ **Kremlin, Moscow.** There are few buildings in the world that can match the historical importance of the Kremlin, *the* symbol of Russia's mystery and power since the 15th century.

★ **Kremlin, Rostov.** Few places in Russia can match this pastoral medieval ensemble for beauty and a weighty sense of history. The bells are so glorious, their sound has attracted composers from all over the world.

★ **Pavlovsk, St. Petersburg.** High on a bluff overlooking the river and a 1,500-acre park, the Great Palace was built as a summer residence for Paul I.

★ **Petrodvorets, St. Petersburg.** This former Imperial palace on the shores of the Baltic sea, complete with lush parks, monumental cascades, and gilded fountains, will leave a lasting impression.

★ **Red Square, Moscow.** Surprisingly, the Bolshevik Revolution did not give this magnificent and beautiful square its name; the Russian word for "beautiful," strangely enough, comes from the word "red."

★ **Strelka, St. Petersburg.** The easternmost tip of Vasilievsky Island, lined with brightly colored houses, affords a dazzling view of the city and its glorious architecture.

★ **Winter Palace, St. Petersburg.** Created by Bartolomeo Rastrelli for the Empress Elizabeth I, the former Imperial residence has over 1,000 rooms replete with works of art and historical objects.

Hotels

★ **Grand Hotel Europe, St. Petersburg.** The service shines in the midst of pre-revolutionary splendor, making it the finest hotel in town. *$$$$*

★ **Metropole, Moscow.** One of the capital's most elegant hotels, it successfully combines the opulence of its 19th-century decor with the efficiency of its late 20th-century service and amenities. *$$$$*

Monuments

★ **Bronze Horseman, St. Petersburg.** This city landmark, depicting Peter the Great astride a rearing horse, is a symbol of Russia rising up to crush its enemies, shown here in the form of a serpent.

★ **Egyptian Sphinxes, St. Petersburg.** It may have taken the Russians more than a year to transport them from Thebes, but it was worth it, if only for the magnificent view of the old city from the supporting quay.

Museums

★ **Hermitage, St. Petersburg.** One of the world's richest repositories of art, the Hermitage attracts thousands of visitors every month. Great Rembrandts and Matisses are the lures, while the building itself—one of the most splendiferous palaces ever constructed—isn't bad either.

★ **Kolomenskoye Estate Museum, Moscow.** This estate, once a favorite summer residence of Moscow's grand dukes and czars, has been turned into an impressive open-air museum that includes a Siberian prison tower and Peter the Great's cottage.

★ **Pushkin Museum of Fine Arts, Moscow.** After St. Petersburg's Hermitage, this is the largest museum of fine art in Russia, with a veritable smorgasbord of world-class art.

★ **State Museum of Russian Art, St. Petersburg.** The scores of Russian masterpieces on display here have made this one of the country's most important art galleries.

★ **Tretyakov Art Gallery, Moscow.** Newly reconstructed, Russia's largest and most important repository of its national art is housed in a fanciful building designed in the Russian Art Nouveau style.

Parks and Gardens

★ **Gorky Park, Moscow.** The 110-acre park is Moscow's most popular, and in summer families throng to its many attractions, including a giant Ferris wheel.

★ **Kirovsky Park on Yelagin Island, St. Petersburg.** An open-air theater, boating stations, and a beach are among the attractions at this park, which covers an entire island.

★ **Manezh Square, Moscow.** This newly built above- and below-ground shopping and leisure complex is the capital's new magnet for summertime strolls.

★ **Summer Gardens, St. Petersburg.** Pavilions, ponds, and an intricate network of fountains, along with sculptures and statues from all over the world, make up this brainchild of Peter the Great, who wanted to create a Russian Versailles.

Restaurants

★ **Europe, St. Petersburg.** The opulent dinner served at this elegant restaurant is fit for a czar. $$$$

★ **Le Romanoff, Moscow.** The subdued atmosphere and exquisite cuisine at this upscale establishment are geared toward the city's foreign community. $$$$

★ **Savoy, Moscow.** This might be the only restaurant where you can truly eat like a czar: It features a re-creation of one of the menus served at the coronation of Czar Nicholas II in 1896. $$$$

Special Moments

★ **Red Square at night.** The best time to view the impressive square is when the red stars of the Kremlin towers light up the night and the entire area is floodlit.

★ **Your first glimpse of St. Basil's Cathedral.** The eight onion-shaped domes of this distinctive cathedral are one of the great architectural symbols of Russia and will not disappoint.

★ **An evening of classical music at the Tchaikovsky Conservatory.** Fine performances can be enjoyed at this auditorium named after one of Russia's greatest composers.

★ **A midnight cruise along the Neva River during the White Nights.** In June and July, when the northern day is virtually endless, the Imperial palaces sparkle along the embankments and the colorful facades of the riverside estates glow gently as you wind your way around this northern Venice.

FESTIVALS AND SEASONAL EVENTS

With the demise of the Soviet Union and the accompanying religious revival, church holy days are now more widely celebrated than traditional political holidays. These days, November 7, the anniversary of the Bolshevik Revolution, merits only a minor military parade in Moscow. In St. Petersburg, November 7 is now celebrated as the anniversary of the city's renaming from Leningrad back to St. Petersburg. Listed below are the current major holidays celebrated in Russia.

DEC.➤ **New Year's Eve** is a favorite holiday marked by merrymaking and family gatherings. Friends and family exchange small gifts, putting them under a New Year's tree, a tradition that began when Christmas and other religious holidays were not tolerated by the Soviet authorities. December Nights is a monthlong festival of music, dance, theater, and art held in Moscow.

DEC.–JAN.➤ **Christmas Musical Meetings in Northern Palmira,** offers a wide variety of winter music performances at the St. Petersburg Conservatory and concert halls.

JAN.➤ **New Year's Eve** is celebrated twice—first on December 31, with the rest of the world, and then again on January 13, "Old" New Year's Eve (according to the Julian calendar used in Russia until the revolution). **Russian Orthodox Christmas** has become an increasingly important holiday and is celebrated on January 7 with lights, *yolkas* (fir trees), and modest gifts under the tree.

FEB.➤ February 23, **Defenders of the Fatherland Day** (formerly Soviet Army and Navy Day), is somewhat similar to Father's Day in the United States. Since just about every male ends up in the army, the holiday traditionally honors all men, not just members of the military. In recent years the holiday has acquired political significance for Communists and nationalists who seek a revival of the Soviet Union. The day ends with fireworks in the evening.

FEB.–MAR.➤ **Maslenitsa** (Butter Week) is a subdued, Slavic version of Carnival which takes place the week before Lent. It is largely a celebration of the sun and spring, which explains the round, sun-shape *blini* (special Russian pancakes) which are consumed in massive amounts this week.

FEB.–MAR.➤ **St. Petersburg Tennis Cup,** Russia's second-largest tennis tournament, is held in the waning days of winter.

MAR.➤ March 8, **International Women's Day,** is a popular holiday similar to Mother's Day, but honoring all women, especially wives. Giving a gift of flowers or a torte to female friends is *de rigueur* for men.

MAR.–APR.➤ **Orthodox Easter** is a major national holiday in both Russia and the Ukraine. Visitors should attend the festive services, which begin at midnight and run through the night.

APR.➤ **Spring Jazz Festival,** St. Petersburg, features the finest jazz performers from across Russia.

MAY➤ May 1, formerly **International Labor Day,** has in recent years turned into a celebration of spring (in Russian, *Prazdnik Vesny*). May 9, **Victory Day,** is one of the country's most important holidays; World War II veterans appear on the streets decked out in their medals and are honored throughout the day at open-air festivals and parades. On Victory Day or during the first 10 days of May, Russia's annual **Soccer Championship Final** is held at Moscow's Luzhniki Stadium. **Moscow Stars,** a music and dance festival, is held in Moscow May 5 to 13. May 30, the

Day of Kostroma, celebrates the city's anniversary and usually stretches for three days. On May 31, Yaroslavl takes its turn with the **Day of Yaroslavl.**

SUMMER

JUNE➤ The first Sunday of June is the **Festival of Pushkin's Poetry,** celebrated in the poet's hometown of Pskov. In 1999 there will be an extra-large celebration in Pskov as well as throughout Russia, as it is the 300th anniversary of the poet's birth. June 12 is **Russian Independence Day. The International Moscow Film Festival** is held every other year (in odd-numbered years; the 21st annual festival will be held in

1999) and showcases both international and Russian film offerings. **Ivan Kupala Day** (June 24) is based on a pagan celebration of the Summer Solstice that has had Christian tones superimposed on it. In St. Petersburg, the **White Nights Music Festival** is held during the last two weeks of June. Finally, the **Tchaikovsky Music Competition** is held in June every fourth year—the next one will be in 2002.

JULY➤ The last Sunday in July is **Fleet Day** in St. Petersburg, which features wonderful naval parades and celebrations at the mouth of the Neva.

AUG.➤ In August, the **Spartak Cup,** held at Moscow's Luzhniki Stadium, features a play-off of Russian hockey stars playing in the NHL vs. domestic Russian hockey clubs.

AUTUMN

SEPT.➤ September 12, **Day of Alexander Nevsky, St. Petersburg,** is an annual festival with a typically Russian flavor, featuring brass bands and choruses and centered on St. Petersburg's Alexander Nevsky square.

OCT.➤ **The Kremlin Cup,** Russia's biggest tennis tournament, is held every October at Moscow's Olimpiysky Stadium.

NOV.➤ November 7, **Day of Accord and National Reconciliation,** formerly celebrated as the Anniversary of the Bolshevik Revolution, is mainly now an excuse for a day off, and for pro- and anti-Communist demonstrations.

2 MOSCOW

Prerevolutionary Moscow has finally awakened from a long sleep. In almost every district work is under way to restore the splendor of the city's ancient monasteries and palaces, statues have been toppled, street names have changed, and the city is a hive of new restaurants, advertising offices, dance clubs, and supermarkets. Capitalism has not come lightly here, or cheaply, but at last crowded streets and squares resound with the noise and activity of commerce.

By Lauri del
Commune

Updated by
Catherine
Belonogoff,
Paul E.
Richardson,
Kevin O'Flynn,
Julia Solovyova,
and Mary
MacVean

IT MAY BE DIFFICULT FOR WESTERNERS to appreciate what an important place Moscow holds in the Russian imagination as a symbol of spiritual and political power. Throughout much of its history the city was known as Holy Moscow, and was valued as a point of pilgrimage not unlike Jerusalem, Mecca, or Rome. Founded more than 850 years ago as the center of one of several competing minor principalities, Moscow eventually emerged as the center of a unified Russian state in the 15th century. One hundred years later it had grown into the capital of a strong and prosperous realm, one of the largest in the world. Although civil war and Polish invasion ravaged the city in the early 17th century, a new era of stability and development began with the establishment of the Romanov dynasty in 1613.

The true test for Moscow came under Peter the Great. Profoundly influenced by his exposure to the West, Peter deliberately turned his back on the old traditions and established his own capital—St. Petersburg—on the shores of the Baltic Sea. Yet Western-looking St. Petersburg never succeeded in replacing Moscow as the heart and soul of the Russian nation. Moscow continued to thrive as an economic and cultural center, despite its demotion. More than 200 years later, within a year of the Bolshevik Revolution in 1917, the young Soviet government restored Moscow's status as the nation's capital. In a move just as deliberate as Peter the Great's, the new Communist rulers transferred the seat of government back to the Russian heartland, away from the besieged frontier and Russia's imperial past.

Moscow thus became the political and ideological center of the vast Soviet empire. And even though that empire has now broken apart, the city retains its political, industrial, and cultural sway. With a population of more than 9 million, Moscow is Russia's largest city and is home to some of the country's most renowned cultural institutions, theaters, and film studios. It is the country's most important transportation hub (even today most flights to the former Soviet republics are routed through Moscow's airports). To salvage and propel its giant economy, the Russian government and business communities are actively pursuing outside investment, even turning to foreign governments for assistance and advice, and everywhere setting their own economic plans and agendas. For visitors this translates into increased availability of Western-style services and products, with Moscow increasingly becoming a hub of international business activity. Despite this sea change, the metropolis is determinedly holding onto its identity as the heart and soul of Russia.

As Russia moves toward the 21st century, development and reconstruction is at an all-time high and parts of the city, especially within the Boulevard Ring, are now sparkling clean and well kept. While the Russians are protecting their architectural heritage, they are also creating a new legacy in the form of skyscrapers, shopping malls, and churches. Most are designed to be harmonious with the ancient Russian style, but an occasional glass-and-steel office tower finds its way in, especially in central Moscow. The new century promises growth, excitement, and hurdles to overcome. Moscow is ready. It is a city very much on the move and aims to offer the visitor interesting views of both the past and present of its mysterious mother country.

Pleasures and Pastimes

The Arts

Gone are the days when the Bolshoi Theater and the Moscow Arts Theater ruled the cultural life of the Russian capital. Since the fall of Communism, Moscow's arts scene has taken a decidedly adventurous turn, with smaller, innovative theater companies and musical ensembles giving the old standbys a run for their money. Musicians, writers, and directors are now flexing their artistic muscles after years of bending to rigid, state-imposed guidelines. One feisty opera troupe, appropriately called the Novaya Opera (New Opera), is challenging the Bolshoi Opera's ascendancy by staging new productions of old warhorses, many from the Russian repertory. As is often the case with upstarts, the New Opera has no permanent home; it mounts productions at shifting venues throughout the city over the course of a season.

Churches and Monasteries

All over Moscow churches are being painted, refurbished, polished, resurfaced, and in some cases, rebuilt from the ground up. At almost every turn you'll run into a church surrounded by scaffolding on which diligent artisans are tending to the rebirth of Orthodoxy. Many of these restoration projects are already finished and one of the joys of meandering through the city is suddenly happening upon the gleaming cupolas and brightly painted facade of a church from the Moscow Baroque period. Brief services are conducted throughout the day in many of these churches, most of which are open to the public. Visitors to Moscow with an interest in Orthodoxy and architecture will also enjoy touring one or more of the area's splendid monastery complexes. A few are within the city limits; others, including the venerated Sergeyev-Posad (Zagorsk) are just a day trip away. Women are advised to wear knee-length or longer skirts when visiting churches and monasteries, and to carry head coverings.

Dining

The dining scene in the Russian capital changes almost convulsively. From the state-run restaurants, once the only choice available, to the collectively owned cooperatives that followed perestroika, to the private-enterprise restaurants now proliferating, the changes are nothing short of astonishing. Whereas only two years ago, one was hard pressed to find any decent—let alone outstanding—food, there is no such shortage now: You may pick and choose among all three types of establishments. The contrasts, however, may leave you a bit wobbly. At a small restaurant or *stolovaya* you can experience the discomforts of Soviet-management techniques, but right up the same street may be an establishment so elegant it could compete in Paris or New York.

Lodging

A number of world-class luxury hotels have opened their doors in Moscow in the last few years, and for the traveler who is able and willing to splurge, they offer a level of amenities and pampering unavailable to tourists just a few years ago. Gourmet restaurants, business centers, cafés and cocktail bars, health clubs, and attentive service are now the norm rather than the exception at the top hotels. (There is evidence that mid-level establishments are also getting the message to upgrade their facilities and level of service.) Leaders among deluxe properties today are the National, the Metropole, the Savoy, the Radisson Slavyanskaya, and the Baltschug Kempinski.

Nightlife

Moscow's after-hours scene has virtually created itself in the past few years. It may still have a long way to go, but there are already a fair number of choices despite the predictable lapses in good taste (some clubs and bars feature erotic floor shows that rival those of the recent Times Square in New York City). Casinos, with their special brand of tackiness, also abound, but those interested in less flashy entertainment may take heart: As incomes rise and exposure to new types of leisure activity spreads, a wider range of nightspots is appearing. Nowadays you'll find clubs that specialize in particular kinds of music—jazz, country, blues, rock. And there are now a few gay and lesbian venues to choose from. No matter your taste or inclination, you'll find something to keep you out late, and in Moscow, late is very late: Most clubs and bars are open until dawn.

When to Tour Moscow

Spring and fall, when temperatures are moderate, remain the optimal times for a visit. Unless you feel you must have a picture of the Kremlin under freshly fallen snow, it's best to stay away during November, December, and January. Although the winter air in Moscow is dry and crisp, these months are by and large fairly miserable. On the other hand, the dead of summer can be stiflingly hot. Of course, the obvious advantage of visiting in July and August is that on the weekends the streets are relatively uncrowded, and there will generally be no problem gaining access to museums and sights since most Muscovites abandon the city from Friday to Monday.

EXPLORING MOSCOW

Though the layout of the city may seem confusing when you first look at a map, you'll soon see it has a logic of its own: Moscow is a series of concentric circles radiating outward from the Kremlin at the center. The main streets of downtown Moscow start at the Kremlin and extend spokelike, their course intersecting the so-called Boulevard Ring and then the Garden Ring. Moscow's downtown proper, and most of the city's famous sights, are located within the Garden Ring. You can walk most of the areas below on foot, but to be efficient in your tour of the city, especially if you have only a few days, you will need to familiarize yourself with the subway system (☞ Moscow A to Z, *below*).

Great Itineraries

To see all of the main sights of Moscow and its environs you need at least two weeks. Add another week to that if you want to do a thorough job of exploring the city's many museums along the way. Short-term visitors will have to be very selective in planning excursions.

IF YOU HAVE 3 DAYS
Start with a stroll across **Red Square,** a tour of **St. Basil's Cathedral,** the shopping arcades of **GUM,** and, if you're a devoted student of Soviet history and/or embalming techniques, the **Lenin Mausoleum.** Then walk through **Aleksandrovsky Sad** (the Alexander Gardens) to reach the tourist entrance to the **Kremlin.** Plan on spending the better part of your first day exploring the churches, monuments, and exhibits within the grounds of this most famous of Russian fortresses. The must-see sights on a brief visit to the Kremlin include the **Arkhangelsky Sobor** (Cathedral of Archangel Michael), the **Uspensky Sobor** (Cathedral of the Assumption), the **Blagoveshchensky Sobor** (Cathedral of the Annunciation), the **Almazny Fond** (Diamond Fund), and, of course, the world's largest cannon (the Czar Cannon) and the world's largest bell (the Czar Bell). On the second day, spend the morning sightseeing and shopping on **Tverskaya ulitsa** and the afternoon exploring **Kitai Gorod** and the churches and historical buildings on **Varvarka ulitsa,** which

extends from the eastern edge of Red Square, just behind St. Basil's. Try also, toward the end of the day, to squeeze in a stroll across **Teatralnaya Ploshchad** to see the **Bolshoi** and **Maly** theaters. Devote the third morning to the **Tretyakov Gallery,** which has the finest collection of Russian art in the country, and in the afternoon stroll down the **Arbat,** where you'll find plenty of options for haggling over Russian souvenirs.

IF YOU HAVE 7 DAYS

Follow the three-day itinerary above, then take our tour of the **Old Moscow of Bolshaya Nikitskaya ulitsa** on day four. Devote day five to the **Pushkin Museum of Fine Arts** and an exploration of some of the streets in the surrounding **Kropotkinsky District.** Come back the next day and walk **from the Russian State Library to the Kropotkinsky District,** being sure to include the **Pushkin Memorial Museum** and a walk along the **Kremlyovskaya naberezhnaya** (the embankment of the Moscow River) in the late afternoon for the spectacular views of the cupolas and towers of the Kremlin. On the final day, depending on whether your interests tend toward the religious or the secular, spend the morning visiting either the **Novodevichy Convent and Cemetery** or complete the rest of our tour of the **Gorky Park Area,** which includes the Tretyakovskaya Gallery and the **Tolstoy House Estate Museum.**

IF YOU HAVE 10 DAYS

In this amount of time it is possible to see most of the seven-day itinerary above, then travel farther afield on day trips to visit the cathedrals and museums of **Kolomenskoye, Zagorsk (Sergyev-Posad),** the **Arkhangelskoye Estate Museum,** and the **New Jerusalem Monastery.** Depending on your interests, you could also use this extra time to visit some of the smaller museums devoted to the lives and accomplishments of prominent Russians; these include the **Pushkin Apartment Museum** and the **Chaliapin House Museum,** as well as museums devoted to the writers **Chekhov, Dostoyevsky, Lermontov, Mayakovsky,** and **Tsvetayeva;** the composers **Tchaikovsky, Glinka,** and **Scriabin;** and the artists **Viktor Vaznetsov** and **Vasily Tropinin.**

Heart of Russia: The Kremlin and Red Square

❶ Few buildings in the world possess the historical resonance of the Kremlin. The first wooden structure was erected on this site sometime in the 12th century. As Moscow grew, it followed the traditional pattern of Russian cities, developing in concentric circles around the elevated fortress at its center (the Russian word *kreml* means citadel or fortress). After Moscow emerged as the center of a vast empire in the late 15th century, the Kremlin came to symbolize the mystery and power of Russia, as it has ever since. In the 20th century the Kremlin became synonymous with the Soviet government, and "Kremlinologists," Western specialists who studied the movements of the politicians in and around the fortress, made careers out of trying to decipher Soviet Russian policies. Much has changed in the last decade, as the former Soviet Union has unraveled. But despite the dramatic changes, the Kremlin itself remains mysteriously alluring. You'll find many signs of the old—and new—Russian enigma as you tour the ancient Kremlin grounds, where, before the black-suited men of the Bolshevik Revolution took over, czars were ceremoniously crowned and buried.

You can buy tickets (with rubles) for the Kremlin grounds and cathedrals at the kiosk in the Aleksandrovsky Sad (Alexander Garden) outside the Kremlin walls. There is a two-tiered price system for admission to the cathedrals and museums; foreigners pay significantly more than Russians. There are separate fees for seeing the Kremlin, each of its churches, the Armory Museum and the Diamond Fund. Although you can purchase the Armory and Diamond Fund tickets inside as well, tickets to the cathedrals are sold only here, so be sure to get all the tickets you need now and save yourself the trip back. If you've decided that you want to visit all the sights, tell the clerk that you want "fsye bil-YE-ti" (all tickets). Also, for entrance to the Armory and Diamond Fund, foreigners must pay in hard currency, a rule that is strictly enforced. Beware of scalpers offering tickets to the Armory at reduced prices; they are usually invalid for foreigners. Admission to the Diamond Fund is by its own separate ticket; at $20, the highest priced of all of them, it is available at the entrance to the vaulted chambers or at one of two kiosks on either side of the Kutafya watchtower. A complete ticket to the territory of the Kremlin—the Uspensky Sobor, the Blagoveshchensky Sobor, the Arkhangelsky Sobor, the Sobor Dvenadtsati Apostolov, and the Tserkov Rizopolozheniya—costs $25. A ticket good for just the Uspensky Sobor, the Blagoveshchensky Sobor, and the Arkhangelsky Sobor costs 100 rubles. Alternately, you can buy tickets inside the Kremlin for each of the churches, including the Sobor Dvenadtsati Apostolov, for 40 rubles each. Tickets to special temporary exhibitions in the Ivan the Great Bell Tower cost $5 and can be bought at the kiosks outside the Kutafya Tower. Keep in mind that you need to buy a $1 ticket if you wish to take pictures with your non-professional camera, and that video cameras are not allowed. You can check your video camera and any large baggage in the *kamera hranenye,* which is located in Alexandrovsky Sad to the right and down the stairs from the ticket kiosks.

Numbers in the text correspond to numbers in the margin and on the Moscow and Kremlin maps.

A Good Walk

The oldest part of the city, the **Kremlin** ① is situated at the very center of Moscow, atop Borovitsky (Pine Grove) Hill. Start at the **Aleksandrovsky Sad** (Alexander Garden) subway stop, or from **Teatralnaya** station, both outside the fortress walls, in order to visit a few sights on your way to the Kremlin gates. To the right as you emerge from the **Teatralnaya** stop are the Kremlin's battlement walls. In some places 65 ft high and 10 to 20 ft thick, they have stood practically unchanged since the end of the 15th century. At the northernmost point of the battlements is the so-called **Sobakina (Arsenal) Tower** ②. Adjacent to the tower is the monumental wrought-iron gate that marks the entrance to the **Aleksandrovsky Sad.** Just beyond the garden entrance, to your left against the Kremlin wall, is the **Tomb of the Unknown Soldier** ③. To your right is the underground **Okhotny Ryad** shopping mall and plaza. Looking up from the garden to the Kremlin walls, you will see a large yellow building, the **Arsenal.**

Continuing along the garden's path, you reach a double bastion lined by a stone bridge on nine pillars. The outer tower is the **Kutafya** ④, the massive tower at the far side is the **Troitskaya Bashnya** ⑤. Up to the right is the exit for the Alexandrovsky Sad subway stop, and farther up, as you ascend around to the right going toward the tower, you will find the kiosk where you purchase tickets to the Kremlin grounds and cathedrals. Enter the Kremlin through the white Kutafya Tower. Cross the bridge to pass through the Troitskaya Bashnya. The big gray building to your right as you enter is the **Dvorets Syezdov** ⑯. The yellow building to your left is the **Arsenal.** Continue straight ahead, the **Czar Cannon** sits in front of the **Sobor Dvenadtsati Apostolov** ⑮. Continue on to the **Czar Bell,** which is mounted on a large pedestal. The bell sits in front of the Ivan the Great Bell Tower. It will be to your right.

18

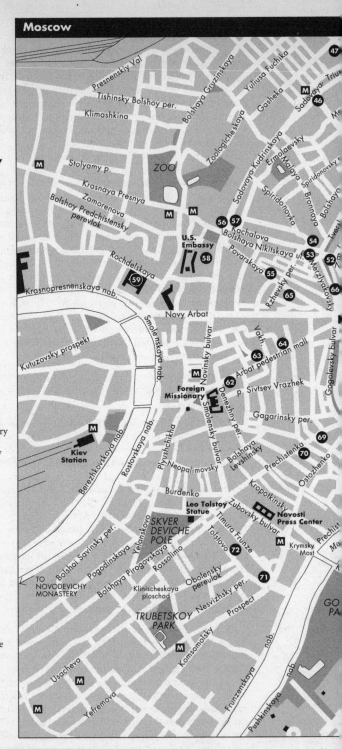

Moscow

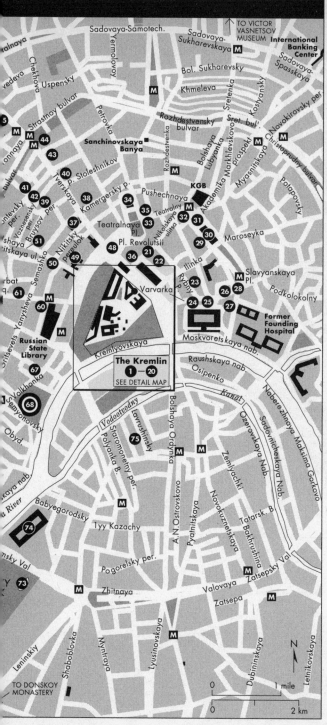

Dvorets = palace
Ploshchad = square
Sobor = cathedral

The Kremlin

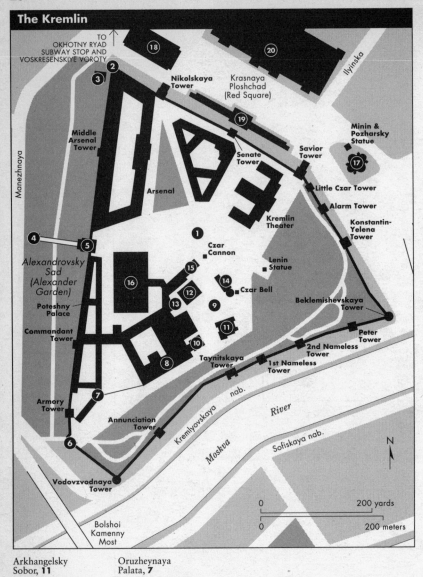

TO
OKHOTNY RYAD
SUBWAY STOP AND
VOSKRESENSKIYE VOROTY

Nikolskaya Tower

Krasnaya Ploshchad (Red Square)

Ilvinska

Middle Arsenal Tower

Minin & Pozharsky Statue

Senate Tower

Savior Tower

Little Czar Tower

Arsenal

Alarm Tower

Konstantin-Yelena Tower

Manezhnaya

Kremlin Theater

Czar Cannon

Lenin Statue

Alexandrovsky Sad (Alexander Garden)

Czar Bell

Beklemishevskaya Tower

Poteshny Palace

Peter Tower

Commandant Tower

2nd Nameless Tower

Taynitskaya Tower

1st Nameless Tower

Armory Tower

Moskva River

Kremlyovskaya nab.

Annunciation Tower

Sofiskaya nab.

Vodovzvodnaya Tower

N

Bolshoi Kamenny Most

0   200 yards

0   200 meters

Arkhangelsky Sobor, **11**

Blagoveshchensky Sobor, **10**

Bolshoi Kremlyovsky Dvorets, **8**

Borovitskaya Tower, **6**

Cathedral Square, **9**

Dvorets Syezdov, **16**

GUM, **20**

Istorichesky Muzey, **18**

Kremlin, **1**

Kolokolnya Ivan Veliky, **14**

Kutafya Tower, **4**

Mavzolei Lenina, **19**

Oruzheynaya Palata, **7**

Sobakina (Arsenal) Tower, **2**

Sobor Dvenadtsati Apostolov, **15**

St. Basil's Cathedral, **17**

Tomb of the Unknown Soldier, **3**

Troitskaya Bashnya, **5**

Tserkov Rizopolozheniya, **13**

Uspensky Sobor, **12**

Take a left at the bell and enter the historical heart of the Kremlin, **Cathedral Square** ⑨. To your immediate left as you enter the square is the massive bell tower, the **Kolokolnya Ivan Veliky** ⑭. Continuing around the square in a counterclockwise manner, the dominating structure is the massive **Uspensky Sobor** ⑫ bordering the north side of the square. To the left of Uspensky Sobor is the smaller, single-domed **Tserkov Rizopolozheniya** ⑬. As you exit the Uspensky Sobor you will face the **Arkhangelsky Sobor** ⑪. To the right and set back from the Arkhangelsky Sobor is the **Blagoveshchensky Sobor** ⑩. All three cathedrals here are open to the public as museums. Exit Cathedral Square by the Blagoveshchensky Sobor.

You will come out to the road where vehicular traffic passes; across the road are the working buildings of the Russian government. They are off-limits to the public, and uniformed policemen blow whistles at trespassers. Walk down the hill to the **Bolshoi Kremlyovsky Dvorets** ⑧, a cluster of buildings that includes the Terem and the 15th-century Granovitaya Palata (Palace of Facets). Although most of the buildings are closed to the public, a portion of the Granovitaya Palata's facade is visible from the Square of Cathedrals. The yellow building to your right houses the **Oruzheynaya Palata** ⑦, the oldest and richest museum in the Kremlin. In the same building is the **Almazny Fond.** To exit the Kremlin retrace your steps to the Kutafya Tower.

Turn right after exiting through the Kutafya Tower and walk back down to the Alexander Garden. Retrace your steps through the garden past the Tomb of the Unknown Soldier. Turn right once again, following the wall of the Kremlin. Walk through the ornate wrought-iron gates topped with gold past the rear of the redbrick **Istorichesky Muzey** ⑱. After passing by the statue of General Zhukov astride a horse take a right to reach the awesome multicolored **Voskresenskiye Voroti,** which houses a small chapel. The bronze plaque in the ground in front of the chapel marks kilometer zero for the Russian highway system. Pass through the gates to reach **Krasnaya Ploshchad**—in English, Red Square.

As you enter the square, the stunning sight of the multicolored onion domes of **St. Basil's Cathedral** ⑰ slowly comes into view. Outside the cathedral doors are the **Lobnoye Mesto** and the **Minin and Pozharsky statue;** to the left is the **Spassky Tower.** Opposite St. Basil's, at the north end of Red Square, stands the redbrick Istorichesky Muzey. On the west side of the square, running along the Kremlin wall, is the **Mavzolei Lenina** ⑲, the world-famous and much-visited resting place of Communism's greatest icon. Bordering the east side is the long facade of the **GUM** ⑳ department store.

TIMING

There are four daily tours of the Oruzhenaya Palata (Armory Palace): at 10, noon, 2:30, and 4. The tour lasts about two hours. Join the line that forms outside the Armory entrance about 15 minutes before the tour. If you don't want to tackle all of this solo, you should consider a tour of the Kremlin grounds that includes the Armory, available from virtually any tour service of your choice in Moscow. The Kremlin grounds and cathedrals are open 10–5 every day except Thursday. The Armory and Diamond Fund are also closed on Thursdays. Beware that the Kremlin occasionally closes on other days due to official functions. Check with your hotel concierge. Again, joining a tour is recommended, not least because there are no signs, in any language, explaining the displays. If you wish to see Red Square in all its splendor, come back in the evening, when the square and its surrounding buildings are beautifully illuminated. Plan to spend at least half a day touring the Kremlin.

Sights to See

Aleksandrovsky Sad (Aleksander Garden). Laid out in the 19th century by the Russian architect Osip Bove and named after Alexander I, the garden stretches along the northwest wall of the Kremlin, where the Neglinnaya River once flowed. The river now runs beneath the garden, through an underground pipe. The Classical columns topped with an arc of chipped bricks was added by Bove. In the 19th century such "romantic" imitation ruins were popular additions to gardens. Today this mock-ruin is blocked by a gate, but in eras past it was a famous place for sledding in winter. ⊠ *Manezhnaya ul. Metro: Aleksandrovsky Sad.*

★ **Almazny Fond** (Diamond Fund). This amazing collection of diamonds, jewelry, and precious minerals was established in 1922 by the young Soviet government. The items on display date from the 18th century to the present. Highlights of the collection are the Orlov Diamond, a present from Count Orlov to his mistress, Catherine the Great; and the Shah Diamond, which was given to Czar Nicholas I by the Shah of Persia as a gesture of condolence after the assassination in 1829 of Alexander Griboyedov, the Russian ambassador to Persia and a well-known poet. ⊠ *Kremlin. Metro: Aleksandrovsky Sad*

⓫ **Arkhangelsky Sobor** (Cathedral of the Archangel). This five-domed cathedral was commissioned by Ivan III (also known as Ivan the Great), whose reign witnessed much new construction in Moscow and in the Kremlin in particular. The cathedral was built in 1505–09 to replace an earlier church of the same name. The architect was the Italian Aleviso Novi, who came to Moscow at the invitation of the czar. You will notice distinct elements of the Italian Renaissance in the cathedral's ornate decoration, particularly in the scallop-shape gables on its facade. Until 1712, when the Russian capital was moved to St. Petersburg, the cathedral was the burial place of Russian princes and czars. Inside you will find 46 tombs, including that of Ivan Kalita (Ivan "Moneybags"), who was buried in the earlier cathedral in 1340. Ivan Moneybags, who earned his nickname because he was so good at collecting tribute, was the first Russian ruler to claim the title of grand prince. The tomb of Ivan the Terrible is hidden behind the altar; that of his young son Dmitry is under the stone canopy to your right as you enter the cathedral. Dmitry's death at the age of seven is one of the many unsolved mysteries in Russian history. He was the last descendant of Ivan the Terrible, and many believe he was murdered, since he posed a threat to the ill-fated Boris Godunov (who at the time ruled as regent). A government commission set up to investigate Dmitry's death concluded that he was playing with a knife and "accidentally" slit his own throat. The only czar to be buried here after 1712 was Peter II (Peter the Great's grandson), who died of smallpox while visiting Moscow in 1730.

The walls and pillars of the cathedral are covered in frescoes that tell the story of ancient Russian history. The original frescoes, painted right after the church was built, were repainted in the 17th century by a team of more than 50 leading artists from several Russian towns. Restoration work in the 1950s uncovered some of the original medieval frescoes, fragments of which can be seen in the altar area. The pillars are decorated with figures of warriors; Byzantine emperors; the early princes of Kievan Rus', Vladimir, and Novgorod; as well as the princes of Moscow, including Vasily III, the son of Ivan the Great. The frescoes on the walls depict religious scenes, including the deeds of Archangel Michael. The carved Baroque iconostasis is 43 ft high and dates from the 19th century. The icons themselves are mostly 17th century, although the revered icon of Archangel Michael is believed to date back to the 14th century. ⊠ *Kremlin.*

Arsenal. Begun in 1701 by Peter the Great, it was finished only at the end of the 18th century; its present form dates from the early 19th century, when it was reconstructed by Bove (the same architect who designed the Alexander Garden), after it was partially destroyed in the 1812 fire. The simple yet impressive two-story building was originally commissioned by Peter the Great as a weapons arsenal; today it houses government offices. ⊠ *Kremlin.*

⑩ **Blagoveshchensky Sobor** (Annunciation Cathedral). This remarkable monument of Russian architecture, linking three centuries of art and religion, was the private chapel of the royal family. Its foundations were laid in the 14th century, and in the 15th century a triangular brick church in the early Moscow style was erected on the site. Partially destroyed by fire, it was rebuilt during the reign of Ivan the Terrible, when six gilded cupolas were added. Czar Ivan would enter the church by the southeast-side porch entrance, built especially for him. He was married three times too many (for a total of six wives) and was therefore, under the bylaws of the Orthodox religion, not allowed to enter the church through its main entrance. The interior is decorated by brilliant frescoes painted in 1508 by the Russian artist Feodosy. The polished tiles of agate jasper covering the floor were a gift from the Shah of Persia. Most striking of all is the chapel's iconostasis. The fine icons of the second and third tiers were painted by some of Russia's greatest masters—Andrei Rublyov, Theophanes the Greek, and Prokhor of Gorodets. ⊠ *Kremlin.*

⑧ **Bolshoi Kremlyovsky Dvorets** (Great Kremlin Palace). The palace actually consists of a group of buildings. The main section is the newest, built between 1838 and 1849. Its 375-ft-long facade faces south, overlooking the Moskva River. This was for centuries the site of the palace of the grand dukes and czars, but the immediate predecessor of the present building was badly damaged in the 1812 conflagration. For a few years it was the seat of the Russian parliament, which has now changed locations. It is not currently open to the general public.

The other buildings of the Great Kremlin Palace include the **Terem,** one of the oldest parts of the Kremlin, where the czarina received visitors, and the 15th-century **Granovitaya Palata** (Palace of Facets). Both of these buildings are also closed to the public. ⊠ *Kremlin.*

⑥ **Borovitskaya Tower.** This pyramid-shaped tower, the main entrance to the Kremlin, rises to more than 150 ft. At its foot a gate pierces its thick walls, and you can still see the slits for the chains of the former drawbridge. Black Volgas carrying government employees to work go whizzing through the vehicular entrance. Uniformed security guards stand at the separate pedestrian entrance, which is where group tours enter. ⊠ *Kremlin. Manezhnaya ul. Metro: Borovitskaya.*

⑨ **Cathedral Square.** The paved square, the ancient center of the Kremlin complex, is framed by three large cathedrals in the old Russian style, the imposing Ivan the Great Bell Tower (☞ Kolokolnya Ivan Veliky, *below*), and the Granovitaya Palata (☞ Bolshoi Kremlyovsky Dvorets, *above*). ⊠ *Kremlin.*

Czar Bell. The world's largest bell is also the world's most silent: It has never rung once. Commissioned in the 1730s, the bell was damaged when it was still in its cast. It weighs more than 200 tons and is 20 ft high. The bas-reliefs on the outside show Czar Alexei Mikhailovich and Czarina Anna Ivanovna. ⊠ *Kremlin.*

Czar Cannon. This huge piece of artillery has the largest caliber of any gun in the world, but like the Czar Bell that was never rung, it has never fired a single shot. Cast in bronze in 1586 by Andrei Chokhov, it weighs 40 tons and is 17½ ft long. Its present carriage was cast in 1835, purely for display purposes. ⊠ *Kremlin.*

⑯ Dvorets Syezdov (State Kremlin Palace). This rectangular structure of glass and aluminum was built in 1961 to accommodate meetings of Communist Party delegates from across the Soviet Union. Today it is affiliated with the Bolshoi Theater and is used exclusively for concerts and ballets. A sizable portion of the palace is underground: The architect designed it this way so that it wouldn't be higher than any of the other Kremlin buildings. ⊠ *Kremlin.*

⑳ GUM. Pronounced "goom," the initials are short for *Gosudarstvenny Universalny Magazin* or State Department Store. Formerly called the Upper Trading Rows, this staggeringly enormous emporium was built in 1889–93 and has long been one of the more famous sights of Moscow. Three long passages with three stories of shops run the length of the building. Each passage is covered with a glass roof, and there are balconies and bridges on the second and third tiers. Another series of passages runs perpendicular to the three main lines, creating a maze-like mall. In feel, it resembles a cavernous turn-of-the-century European train station. There are shops aplenty here now, Western and Russian, and you may enjoy a saunter down at least one of its halls. ⊠ *3 Red Sq.* ☉ *Mon.–Sat. 8–8, Sun. 10–6. Metro: Pl. Revolutsii.*

⑱ Istorichesky Muzey (Historical Museum). This redbrick museum was built in 1874–83 in the pseudo-Russian style, which combined a variety of architectural styles. You may remember the building's twin towers from watching Soviet military parades on television. Against the backdrop of the towers' pointed spires, the tanks and missiles rolling through Red Square seemed to acquire even more potency. The museum was closed in 1986 for restoration, and finally reopened in 1997. Its extensive archaeological and historical materials outline the development of Russia as well as that of the peoples of the former Soviet Union. The museum also contains a rich collection of Russian arms and weaponry. ⊠ *1/2 Red Sq.,* ☏ *095/228–8452.* 🎟 *$5.* ☉ *Wed.–Mon. 11–7. Closed 1st Mon. of month. Metro: Pl. Revolutsii.*

⑭ Kolokolnya Ivan Veliky (Ivan the Great Bell Tower). This is the tallest building in the Kremlin. The octagonal main tower is 263 ft high—3 ft higher than the Hotel Rossiya (on the opposite side of Red Square), in accordance with the tradition established by Boris Godunov that the bell tower remain the tallest building in Moscow. The first bell tower was erected on this site in 1329. It was replaced in the early 16th century, during the reign of Ivan the Great (hence the bell tower's name). But it was during the reign of Boris Godunov that the tower received its present appearance. In 1600, the main tower was rebuilt, crowned by an onion-shape dome, and covered with gilded copper. For many years it served as a watchtower; Moscow and its environs could be observed for a radius of 32 km (20 mi). Altogether, the towers have 52 bells, the largest weighing 70 tons. The annex of the bell tower is used for temporary exhibits of items from the Kremlin collection, tickets for which may be purchased at the entrance. ⊠ *Kremlin.*

★ Krasnaya Ploshchad (Red Square). World famous for the grand military parades staged here during the Soviet era, it was originally called the Torg, the Slavonic word for marketplace. You may think that the name "Red Square" has something to do with Communism or the Bolshevik Revolution. In fact, however, the name dates back to the 17th century. The adjective *krasny* originally meant "beautiful," but over the centuries the meaning of the word changed to "red," hence the square's present name. The square is most beautiful at night. It is both romantic and impressive when entirely illuminated by floodlights, its ruby-red stars atop the Kremlin towers glowing against the dark sky. There are five stars in all, one for each of the tallest towers. They made their appearance in 1937 to replace the double-headed eagle, a czarist symbol that is again finding favor as an emblem of Russia. The glass stars, which are lighted from inside and designed to turn with the wind, are far from dainty: The smallest weighs a ton. *Metro: Pl. Revolutsii.*

④ Kutafya. This white bastion once defended the approach to the drawbridge that linked Aleksandrovsky Sad (☞ *above*) to the Kremlin. In Old Slavonic *kutafya* means "clumsy" or "confused"; this adjective was applied to the tower because it differs so in shape and size from the other towers of the Kremlin. This tower marks the main public entrance to the Kremlin, which opens promptly at 10 AM every day except Thursday. The guards may ask where you are from and check inside your bags; there is a small security checkpoint to walk through, similar to those at airports. ⊠ *Manezhnaya ul. Metro: Aleksandrovsky Sad.*

Lobnoye Mesto. The name of the strange, round, white-stone platform in front of St. Basil's Cathedral (☞ *below*) literally means "place of the forehead," but it has come to mean "execution site," for it was right next to the platform where public executions were carried out. The platform was built in 1534 and was used by the czars as a podium for public speeches. Imperial *ukazy* (decrees) were proclaimed from here, and when the heir apparent reached the age of 16, he was presented to the people from this platform. ⊠ *Red Sq. Metro: Pl. Revolutsii.*

⑲ Mavzolei Lenina (Lenin Mausoleum). Except for a brief interval during World War II, when his body was evacuated to the Urals, Lenin has lain in state here since his death in 1924. Whether it is really Lenin or a wax look-alike is probably one of those Russian mysteries that will go down in history unanswered. From 1924 to 1930 there was a temporary wooden mausoleum, replaced by the pyramid-shape mausoleum you see now. It is made of red, black, and gray granite, with a strip of black granite near the top level symbolizing a band of mourning. It was from the balcony of the mausoleum that Soviet leaders watched parades.

In the past, there were notoriously endless lines of people waiting to go in, but this is no longer the case. A visit to the mausoleum, however, is still treated as a serious affair. The surrounding area is cordoned off during visiting hours, and all those entering are observed by uniformed policemen. It is forbidden to carry a camera or any large bag. Inside it is cold and dark. It's considered disrespectful to put your hands inside your pockets (the same applies when you visit an Orthodox church), and the guards have been known to reprimand people for unbuttoned collars or sweaters. If you are inclined to linger at all, they will gently but firmly move you along. Before you know it you are ushered out of the mausoleum to the special burial grounds outside the mausoleum. When Stalin died in 1953, he was placed inside the mausoleum alongside Lenin, but in the early 1960s, during Khrushchev's tenure, the body was removed and buried here, some say encased in heavy concrete. Also here are such Communist leaders as Zhdanov, Dzerzhinsky, Brezhnev, Chernenko, and Andropov, now mostly discredited. The American journalist John Reed is buried alongside the Kremlin wall. Urns set inside the wall contain ashes of the Soviet writer Maxim Gorky; Lenin's wife and collaborator, Nadezhda Krupskaya; Sergei Kirov, the Leningrad Party leader whose assassination in 1934 (believed to have been arranged by

Stalin), was followed by enormous purges; the first Soviet cosmonaut, Yuri Gagarin; and other Soviet eminences.

The hourly changing of the guard outside Lenin's tomb, once a staggeringly formal event, has been eliminated. Local policemen, much more jocular in demeanor, have replaced the ramrod-stiff soldiers who once guarded the way into the tomb. ✉ *Red Sq.* ☉ *Tues.–Thurs. and Sat. 10–1, Sun. 10–2. Metro: Pl. Revolutsii.*

Minin and Pozharsky Statue. Built in 1818 by sculptor Ivan Martos, the statue honors Kozma Minin and Prince Pozharsky, who drove Polish invaders out of Moscow in 1612. The statue originally stood in the center of the square, but was later moved to its present spot in front of St. Basil's. The inscription on the pedestal reads, "To citizen Minin and prince Pozharsky from a thankful Russia 1818." Incidentally, this statue was the first monument of patriotism funded by the public. ✉ *Red Sq.. Metro: Pl. Revolutsii.*

★ ❼ **Oruzheynaya Palata** (Armory Palace). The Armory Palace is the oldest and richest museum in the Kremlin. It was originally founded in 1806 as the Imperial Court Museum, which was created out of three royal treasuries: the Court Treasury, where the regalia of the czars and ambassadorial gifts were kept; the Stable Treasury, which contained the royal harnesses and carriages used by the czars during state ceremonies; and the Armory, a collection of arms, armor, and other valuable objects gathered from the country's chief armories and storehouses. The Imperial Court Museum was moved to the present building in 1851. It was further enhanced and expanded after the Bolshevik Revolution with valuables confiscated and nationalized from wealthy noble families as well as from the Patriarchal Sacristy of the Moscow Kremlin. It now contains some 4,000 exhibits dating from the 12th century to 1917, including a rare collection of 17th-century silver. The museum tour begins on the second floor, which may cause some confusion if you visit the Armory on your own. Halls VI–IX are on the first floor, Halls I–V on the second.

Hall I displays works of goldsmiths and silversmiths of the 12th through 19th centuries, and **Hall II** contains a collection of 18th- to 20th-century jewelry. One of the most astounding exhibits is the collection of Fabergé eggs on display in Hall II (case 23). Among them is a silver egg whose surface is engraved with a map of the Trans-Siberian Railroad. The "surprise" inside the egg, which is also on display, was a golden clockwork model of a train with a platinum engine, windows of crystal, and a headlight made of a tiny ruby.

Hall III contains Oriental and Western European arms and armor, including heavy Western European suits of armor from the 15th to 17th centuries, pistols, and firearms.

Hall IV has a large collection of Russian arms and armor from the 12th to early 19th centuries, with a striking display of helmets. The earliest helmet here dates from the 13th century and is ascribed to Prince Yaroslav, father of Alexander Nevsky. Here, too, you will find the helmet of Prince Ivan, the son of Ivan the Terrible. The prince was killed by his father at the age of 28, an accidental victim of the czar's unpredictable rage. The tragic event has been memorialized in a famous painting by Ilya Repin (now in the Tretyakov Gallery; ☞ Gorky Park to the Tretyakov Gallery, *below*) showing the frightened czar holding his mortally wounded son. Russian chain mail, battle-axes, maces, harquebuses, ceremonial armor, and Russian and Oriental sabers are also in this hall. A highlight of the collection is the large Greek quiver belonging to Czar Alexei, his Oriental saber, and a heavy golden mace presented to him by the Persian Shah Abbas. Among the sabers on display here are those of Kuzma Minin and Dmitry Pozharsky, the national heroes who led the battle to oust the Polish forces from Moscow during the Time of Troubles in the early 17th century. Later you will see their statue on Red Square.

Hall V is filled with foreign gold and silver objects, mostly ambassadorial presents to the czars. History buffs will be interested in the "Olympic Service" of china presented to Alexander I by Napoléon after the signing of the Treaty of Tilsit in 1807.

Hall VI has vestments of silk, velvet, and brocade, embroidered with gold and encrusted with jewels and pearls. They were once worn by the czars, patriarchs, and metropolitans.

Hall VII contains the regalia and the Imperial thrones. The oldest throne, veneered with carved ivory, belonged to Ivan the Terrible. The throne of the first years of Peter the Great's reign, when he shared power with his older brother Ivan, has two seats in front and one hidden in the back. The boys' older sister Sophia, who ruled as regent from 1682 to 1689, sat in the back, prompting the young rulers to give the right answers to the queries of ambassadors and others. Another throne, covered with thin plates of gold and studded with more than 2,000 precious stones and pearls, was presented to Czar Boris Godunov by Shah Abbas of Persia. The throne of Czar Alexei, also from Persia, is decorated with 876 diamonds and 1,223 other stones. Among the crowns, the oldest is the sable-trimmed Cap of Monomakh, which dates to the 13th century. Ukraine is now asking for it back, since it originally belonged to the Kievan prince Vladimir Monomakh. It was a gift to the prince from his grandfather, the Byzantine emperor, and is revered as a symbol of the transfer of religious power from Byzantium to Russia. Also on display in this section are several coronation dresses, including the one Catherine the Great wore in 1762.

Hall VIII contains dress harnesses of the 16th through 18th centuries. On display are Russian saddles, including one used by Ivan the Terrible, and other items once belonging to the Moscow Kremlin Equestrian Department.

Hall IX has a marvelous collection of court carriages. The oldest one came from England and is believed to have been presented to Czar Boris Godunov by King James I. Here you will find the Winter Coach that carried Elizabeth Petrovna (daughter of Peter the Great and someone who clearly liked her carriages) from St. Petersburg to Moscow for her coronation. Catherine the Great's French carriage, painted by François Boucher, is arguably the most attractive of the collection. ⊠ *Kremlin.*

Patriarch's Palace (Patriarshiy Palaty). Adjoining the Sobor Dvenadtsati Apostolov the Patriarch's Palace has housed the **Museum of 17th Century Applied Art** since 1963. The exhibits here were taken from the surplus of the State Armory Museum and include books, tableware, clothing, and household linen. A taped explanation is available. ⊠ *Kremlin.*

Poteshny Dvorets (Amusement Palace). Behind the State Kremlin Palace stands the amusement palace—so called because it was used by *boyar* (nobleman) Alexei in the 17th century as a venue for theatrical productions. Later, both Stalin and Trotsky had apartments here. ⊠ *Kremlin.*

② **Sobakina (Arsenal) Tower.** More than 180 ft high, the Sobakina Tower at the northernmost part of the thick battlements that encircle the Kremlin, was an important part of the Kremlin's defenses. Its thick walls concealed a secret well, which was of vital importance during times of siege. ⊠ *Manezhnaya ul., Kremlin Metro: Pl. Revolutsii.*

⑮ Sobor Dvenadtsati Apostolov (Cathedral of the Twelve Apostles). Built in 1655–56 by Patriarch Nikon, this was used as his private church. The Cathedral has an exhibition featuring icons removed from other Kremlin churches destroyed by the Soviets. The silver containers and stoves were used to make holy oil. Next door to the church is the **Patriarshiy Dvorets** (Patriarch's Residence), which is also open to the public. ✉ *Kremlin.*

Spassky Tower (Tower of the Savior). Until Boris Yeltsin's presidency this tower served as the main entrance to the Kremlin. Indeed, in the centuries before Communist power, all who passed through it were required to doff their hats and bow before the icon of the Savior that hung on the front of the tower. The icon was removed, but you can see the outline of where it was. The embellished roof, as well as the first clock, was added in 1625. ✉ *Red Sq., Kremlin. Metro: Pl. Revolutsii.*

★ **⑰ St. Basil's Cathedral.** Although it is popularly known as St. Basil's Cathedral, the proper name of this whimsical structure is Pokrovsky Sobor (Church of the Intercession). It was commissioned by Ivan the Terrible to celebrate his conquest of the Tatar city of Kazan on October 1, 1552, the day of the feast of the Intercession. The central chapel, which rises 107 ft, is surrounded by eight towerlike chapels linked by an elevated gallery. Each chapel is topped by an onion dome carved with its own distinct pattern and dedicated to a saint on whose day the Russian army won battles against the Tatars. The cathedral was built between 1555 and 1560 on the site of an earlier Trinity Church where the Holy Fool Vasily (Basil) had been buried in 1552. Basil was an adversary of the czar, publicly reprimanding Ivan the Terrible for his cruel and bloodthirsty ways. He was protected from the czar by his status as a Holy Fool, for he was considered by the Church to be an emissary of God. Ironically, Ivan the Terrible's greatest creation has come to be known by the name of his greatest adversary. In 1558 an additional chapel was built in the northeast corner over Basil's remains, and from that time on the cathedral has been called St. Basil's.

Very little is known about the architect who built the cathedral. It may have been the work of two men—Barma and Postnik—but now it seems more likely that there was just one architect, Postnik Yakovlyev, who went by the nickname Barma. Legend has it that upon completion of the cathedral, the mad czar had the architect blinded to ensure he would never create such a masterpiece again.

After the Bolshevik Revolution, the cathedral was closed and in 1929 turned into a museum dedicated to the Russian conquest of Kazan. Although services are occasionally held here on church holidays, the museum is still open. The antechamber contains displays outlining the various stages of the Russian conquest of Kazan as well as examples of 16th-century Russian and Tatar weaponry. Another section details the history of the cathedral's construction, with displays of the building materials used. After viewing the museum exhibits, you are free to wander through the cathedral. Compared to the exotic exterior, the dark and simple interiors are a disappointment. The brick walls are decorated with faded flower frescoes. The most interesting chapel is the main chapel, which contains a 19th-century Baroque iconostasis. The **statue of Minin and Pozharsky** just outside St. Basil's originally stood in the center of the square. It depicts Kuzma Minin, a Nizhni-Novgorod butcher, and Prince Dmitry Pozharsky, who liberated Moscow in October 1612 from Polish-Lithuanian occupation. The work of Ivan Martos, it was erected in 1818, paid for by public subscription. ✉ *Red Sq.,* ☎ *095/298–3304.* ▨ *$5.* ☉ *Wed.–Mon. 10–4:30. Closed 1st Mon. of month. Metro: Pl. Revolutsii.*

③ Tomb of the Unknown Soldier. Dedicated on May 9, 1967, the 22nd anniversary of the Russian victory over Germany, this red granite monument contains the body of an unidentified Soviet soldier, one of those who, in the autumn of 1941, stopped the German attack at the village of Kryukovo, just outside Moscow. To the right of the grave there are six urns holding soil from the six "heroic cities" that so stubbornly resisted the German onslaught: Odessa, Sevastopol, Volgograd (Stalingrad), Kiev, Brest, and Leningrad (St. Petersburg). Very likely, no matter what time of year you are visiting, you'll see at least one wedding party. The young couple in full wedding regalia, along with friends and family, customarily stops here after getting married, leaving behind flowers and snapping photographs along the way. The gray obelisk just beyond the Tomb of the Unknown Soldier was erected in 1918 to commemorate the Marxist theoreticians who contributed to the Bolshevik Revolution. It was created out of an obelisk put up three years earlier, in honor of the 300th anniversary of the Romanov Dynasty. The arched "ruins" along the Kremlin wall, opposite the Obelisk, were designed by Osip Bove when he created the park. In the 19th century it was fashionable to include authentic-looking ruins in a landscaped park. ⊠ *Manezhnaya ul., Aleksandrovsky Sad. Metro: Pl. Revolutsii.*

⑤ Troitskaya Bashnya (Trinity Tower). Rising 240 ft above the garden, this is the tallest *bashnya* (tower) in the Kremlin wall. This tower is linked to the Kutafya Tower by a bridge which once spanned a moat. This is the tower you will pass through to reach the Kremlin territory. Its deep, subterranean chambers were once used as prison cells. It is said that Napoléon lost his hat when he entered the Kremlin through this gate in 1812. ⊠ *Aleksandrovsky Sad, Kremlin. Metro: Aleksandrovsky Sad.*

⑬ Tserkov Rizopolozheniya (Church of the Deposition of the Virgin's Robe). This single-domed church was built in 1484–86 by masters from Pskov. Once the private church of the Moscow patriarch, it was rebuilt several times and restored to its 15th-century appearance by Soviet experts in the 1950s. The building boasts brilliant frescoes dating from the mid-17th century covering all of its walls, pillars, and vaults. Its most precious treasure is the iconostasis by Nazary Istomin. On display inside the church is an exhibit of ancient Russian wooden sculpture from the Kremlin collection. ⊠ *Kremlin.*

⑫ Uspensky Sobor (Assumption Cathedral). The dominating structure of Cathedral Square is one of the oldest edifices of the Kremlin. Designed after the Uspensky Sobor of Vladimir, it was built in 1475–79 by the Italian architect Aristotle Fiorovanti, who had spent many years in Russia studying traditional Russian architecture. Topped by five gilded domes, it is both austere and solemn. The ceremonial entrance faces Cathedral Square; the visitor's entrance is on the west side (to the left). After visiting the Archangel and Annunciation cathedrals (☞ Arkhangelsky Sabor and Blagoveshchensky Sobor, *above*), you will be struck by the spacious interior here, unusual for a medieval church. Light pours in through two rows of narrow windows. The cathedral contains rare ancient paintings, including the icon of the Virgin of Vladimir (the work of an 11th-century Byzantine artist), the 12th-century icon of St. George, and the 14th-century Trinity. The carved throne in the right-hand corner belonged to Ivan the Terrible, and the gilt wood throne to the far left was the seat of the czarina. Between the two is the patriarch's throne. Until the 1917 Revolution, Uspensky Sobor was Russia's principal church. This is where the crowning ceremonies of the czars took place, a tradition that continued even after the capital was transferred to St. Petersburg. Patriarchs and metropolitans were enthroned and buried here. After the Revolution the church was turned into a museum, but in 1989 religious services were resumed here on major church holidays. ✉ *Kremlin.*

Voskresenskiye Voroti (Resurrection Gates). The gates, which formed part of the Kitai Gorod defensive wall (☞ Kitai Gorod, *below*), were named for the icon of the Resurrection of Christ which hangs above them. However, the gates are truly "resurrection" gates since they have been resurrected many times since they were built in 1534. In 1680 the gates were rebuilt and a chapel honoring the Iberian Virgin Mary was added. In 1931 they were destroyed by the Soviets. They were only rebuilt in 1994–95. Today the redbrick gates with the bright green and blue chapel to the Iberian Virgin are truly a magnificent sight and a fitting entrance to Red Square. The Chapel of the Iberian Virgin Mary is open from 8 AM to 10 PM. The bronze compass inlaid in the ground in front of the chapel marks kilometer zero in the Russian highway system. ✉ *Red Sq. Metro: Pl. Revolutsii.*

Kitai Gorod: From Moscow's Wall Street to the Bolshoi Theater

This tour explores the twisting and winding streets of Kitai Gorod, the oldest section of Moscow outside the Kremlin. The literal translation of Kitai Gorod is Chinatown, but there has never been a Chinese settlement here. The origin of the word *kitai* is disputed; it may come from the Tatar word for fortress, but most likely it derives from the Russian word *kita,* in reference to the bundles of twigs that were used to reinforce the earthen wall that once surrounded the area.

Kitai Gorod begins where Red Square ends. Settlement of this area began in the 12th century, around the time that the fortified city of Moscow was founded on Borovitsky Hill (the site of the present-day Kremlin). By the 14th century Kitai Gorod was a thriving trade district, full of shops and markets. At that time it was surrounded by earthen ramparts, which were replaced in the 16th century by a fortified wall. Remnants of that wall remain, and you will pass them later. As Moscow grew, so did Kitai Gorod. At the time of the Bolshevik Revolution it was the city's most important financial and commercial district, with major banks, warehouses, and trading companies concentrated here. These days, with the multitude of shops and new banks springing up throughout it, the area is reestablishing itself as a commercial center.

A Good Walk

A good starting point for your tour is Nikolskaya ulitsa, which begins at the corner opposite the Historical Museum and runs along the north side of GUM. If you are coming from St. Basil's, walk away from St. Basil's towards the Historical Museum alongside GUM. If you are coming from outside of Red Square, get to Nikolskaya by way of Teatralnaya square. If you are standing with your back to the Bolshoi, walk straight ahead, cross the street and enter through the narrow passageway to the right of the Ploshchad Revolutsii metro station (as you are facing it). It is crowded, easily spotted, and is lined with small shops and kiosks. Taking a right out of the passageway, you find yourself on Nikolskaya ulitsa. Go a short way farther to the right, to the cobblestone edge of Red Square, to begin your walk.

Named after the Kremlin's Nikolskaya Gate Tower, Nikolskaya ulitsa is one of the oldest streets in Moscow. At the corner with Red Square is the **Kazansky Sobor.** Leaving the church, take a left to make your way through the teeming crowds of shoppers on Nikolskaya ulitsa to No. 7, the **Zaikonospassky Monastery** ㉑, the former Slavonic-Greco-Latin Academy. Farther down the street, also on the left-hand side, is a once brightly painted white-and-aqua building with an elaborate facade (No. 15). The building was erected in 1810–14 on the site of the 16th-century Pechatny Dvor (Printing Yard), where Russia's first printed book was assembled in 1553. Today the building is home to the Moscow Institute of Historical Records. Cross the street to go down Bogoyavlensky pereulok. Halfway down the block, opposite the entrance to the Ploshchad Revolutsii subway, is the **Bogoyavlensky Sobor** ㉒. Continue down the street to where it intersects with Ilinka ulitsa. Before the 1917 revolution, this was Moscow's Wall Street. It is lined with the impressive facades of former banks. On the left-hand corner is the former **Ryabushinsky Bank.** As you cross the street, look to your right; Ilinka ulitsa leads directly to the Kremlin's Savior Gate Tower. At No. 3 stands the **Tserkov Sv. Ilii** from which the street is named. The church, which dates to 1520, is in disrepair except for its facade. Continue down Ilinka to Khrustalny pereulok, one of the border streets of the **Gostinny Dvor** ㉓ merchant's arcade. Turn left and walk the length of Khrustalny pereulok to reach one of the oldest streets in Moscow, Varvarka ulitsa (Barbara Street). The opposite side of the street is lined with quaint old churches and buildings, but the first thing you notice behind the small **Tserkov Velikomuchenitsy Varvary** is the gray bulk of the massive **Rossiya Hotel.**

At the farthest corner of the street, to your right, is the **Tserkov Velikomuchenitsy Varvary** ㉔. Adjacent is the **Old English Court.** Next comes the white-stone **Tserkov Maksima Blazhennovo.** The pointed bell tower situated just before the semicircle sidewalk leading to the upper-level entrance to the Rossiya Hotel was once attached to the redbrick **Znamensky Sobor** ㉕ on the other side of the sidewalk; with its foundation on the slope below, it is set back from the street. At No. 10 is the **Palaty Romanovych v Zaryadye** ㉖, the Romanov Palace Chambers, considered the birthplace of Czar Mikhail Romanov. Before leaving this street of museums and churches, take note of the last one, the blue **Tserkov Georgiya na Pskovskoy Gorke** ㉗ at No. 12. If you stand to the left of the church (on the walkway leading to the Rossiya Hotel) you can glimpse a remnant of the 16th-century brick fortification wall. It is to your left, opposite the hotel's eastern facade. Return now to Varvarka ulitsa and cross to the other side, going a short hop past the final church. Take a right and climb up the narrow Ipatevsky pereulok, which will lead up to a number of governmental and administrative buildings. At the top of the incline to the right, you will find one of Moscow's best-preserved 17th-century churches, the **Tserkov Troitsy v Nikitnikach** ㉘.

Continue down the lane to the right of the church to reach **Novaya Ploshchad,** or New Square, which is more like a boulevard than a square. To your right, at the far bottom of the hill, **Slavyanskaya Ploshchad** (Slavic Square) opens up. At the bottom of the hill is the redbrick **Church of All-Saints in Kulishki.** From Novaya Ploshchad, stroll for a long block or two past the governmental buildings, where the Central Committee of the Communist Party once sat. Now they house the Duma of the Moscow Region. Soon you will come to the beginning of a busy intersection. To your right, in the median strip that divides Novaya Ploshchad, is a park that holds the Plevna Memorial, an octagonal, towerlike monument commemorating the Russian soldiers who fell in the Battle of Plevna in the Russo-Turkish War (1878). Keep walking up the street on the left side to go to the **Museum of the History of Moscow** ㉙.

Before you reach it, you will notice a building on the opposite side of the street that takes up the entire block. This is the **Polytechnical Museum** ㉚. Directly north of the museum is the **Mayakovsky Library and Museum** ㉛, which includes a re-creation of the study of the great revolutionary poet. A short distance from the library, Novaya Ploshchad intersects with the circular **Lubyanskaya Ploshchad** ㉜, where you can behold the Lubyanka Prison and the former KGB headquarters which now house the FSB—the new Russia's federal security service. The store on the west side of the square is **Detsky Mir** (Children's World), a large department store that used to specialize in toys.

Still bearing left, walk past Lubyanka Square to the west side, down to where it converges with the broad street of **Teatralny proyezd.** In a side street to your right stands the ornate and luxurious Savoy Hotel (⊠ 3 Rozhdestvenka ul.), which, like the Metropol Hotel, was built in connection with the celebrations honoring 300 years of the Romanov Dynasty. On the left-hand side of the street you will pass a statue of Ivan Fyodorov, the printer who produced Russia's first book at the Old Printing House you passed earlier on Nikolskaya ulitsa. The arched gateway just beyond the statue links Teatralny proyezd with Nikolskaya ulitsa in Kitai Gorod, the street on which you started the tour. Theater Passage leads into Theater Square, where three of Moscow's most important theaters are located.

The first building you will encounter, taking up the block on the southeast corner, to your left as you approach Theater Square, is the **Metropol Hotel** ㉝. Reaching the square, you will see at the center a large monument to Karl Marx, carved on the spot from a 200-ton block of granite and unveiled in 1961. Across the boulevard stands the **Bolshoi Theater** ㉞, flanked on the left, on the corner farthest away from you, by the Central Children's Theater, and, to the right, by the **Maly Theater** ㉟. Turn left at the corner of the Metropol Hotel, walk by the park and the hotel's main entrance. The fragmented brick wall ahead is the other surviving remnant of the 16th-century fortification wall that once surrounded Kitai Gorod. Refurbishments to the wall will be finished sometime in 1999. When you reach the Ploshchad Revolutsii metro station, you may want to take a moment to admire the exterior of the massive redbrick building on the corner—the **Tsentralny Muzey V. I. Lenina** ㊱ (Lenin Museum, now closed). If you still have some time but not much energy, consider hopping on Trolleybus 2 which can be caught at the bus stop opposite the Bolshoi Theatre. The trolleybus ride takes about 45 minutes and makes a loop passing by Lubyanskaya square, Kitai Gorod, Ploshchad Pobedi, the Borodino Battle Panorama and World War II monument, Kievsky vokzal, the Novy Arbat (☞ The Arbat, Old and New, *below*), Alexandrovsky Sad (☞ The Kremlin and Red Square, *above*) and returns to Teatralnaya square. You can purchase a ticket for 50 cents from the driver. Try to have exact change. Make sure to punch the ticket on board the bus.

TIMING
Taken at a leisurely pace, with stops to at least glance at the interiors of the many churches along the route, this walk should take about five hours. If you intend to have at least a quick look at the exhibits in the museums along the way, you'll need an entire day. Both the English Court and the Museum of the History of Moscow are worth coming back to for a more leisurely look at their holdings.

Sights to See

㉒ **Bogoyavlensky Sobor** (Cathedral of the Epiphany). This church is all that remains of the monastery that was founded on this site in the 13th century by Prince Daniil of Moscow. A good example of the Moscow Baroque style, the cathedral is now undergoing a long overdue renovation, and, unfortunately for tourists, some of the structure will remain hidden by scaffolds for at least another year. It is, however, open for services (Sun. at 7 and 9:30 AM) and there's a shop in the foyer that sells icon cards, religious objects, and books about the Russian Orthodox faith (entry is from the courtyard around back). ✉ *Bogoyavlensky per. Metro: Pl. Revolutsii.*

★ ☾ ㉞ **Bolshoi Theater.** Formerly known as the Great Imperial Theater, Moscow's "big" (*bolshoi* means "big") and oldest theater was completely rebuilt after a fire in 1854. Today, it's being rebuilt once again: During the summer of 1998 a hurricane blew through Moscow and did extensive damage to the Bolshoi's roof. Check with your concierge to find out if the theater is back open, because you won't want to miss the resident opera and ballet troupes—two of the most famous performing-arts companies in the world. The building itself is remarkable: Its monumental colonnade is topped by a quadriga of bronze horses pulling the chariot of Apollo, patron of music. Its crimson-and-gold interior is similarly grand. If you have the pleasure of seeing a performance at the Bolshoi—be sure to book one of its 2,155 seats as far as possible in advance, as performances can sell out quickly—don't leave before the stage curtain is lowered at the end of the performance. It falls resplendent, in a thick weave of hammers and sickles. An interesting footnote in the theater's and the Soviet Union's history: Lenin made his last public speech here, in 1922. To the left of the Bolshoi is the **Central Children's Theater,** which puts on traditional performances for a younger audience. This is also where you'll find the Bolshoi's main ticket office. The plaza with fountains and fine wooden benches is a nice spot for a relaxing look at the theater. ✉ *Teatralnaya Pl.,* ☎ *095/ 292–0050. Metro: Teatralnaya.*

Detsky Mir (Children's World). This large store used to specialize exclusively in toys and clothing for children, but these days you'll find just about anything in its crowded aisles, including a Syrian grocery store. ✉ *2 Teatralny proyezd. Metro: Lubyanka.*

NEED A
BREAK?

The small café-bar at the **Savoy Hotel** (✉ 3 Rozhdestvenka ul.) is a sophisticated spot for a drink and anything from soup to cake. It's quite expensive, but the calming effect of the indoor fountain and the gilt interior create a small oasis in this busy part of town. The hotel also has a famous—and very expensive—restaurant. The bar menu, although by no means cheap, is more reasonably priced than the one you'll find in the hotel's restaurant. If you'd rather have a full meal for less money, Moscow's best Mexican restaurant **Hola Mexico!** (✉ 7/5 Pushechnaya ul.) is just across the street. It is a favorite spot with Moscow's foreign community and for good reason: The portions are huge and the prices reasonable.

English Court. Built in the mid-16th century, this white-stone building with a steep shingled roof and narrow windows became known as the English Court because Ivan the Terrible—wanting to encourage foreign trade—presented it to English merchants trading in Moscow. Reopened as a branch of the Museum of the City of Moscow in late 1995, its displays about Russian-British trade relations over the centuries may be particularly interesting to visitors from the United Kingdom. The museum hosts music evenings at 4:30 PM on the last Saturday of every month. ✉ *4 Varvarka ul.,* ☎ *095/298–3952 or 095/298–3961.* ▦ *$1.50.* ☺ *Tues., Thurs., and weekends 10–6; Wed. and Fri. 11–7. Metro: Pl. Revolutsii or Kitai-Gorod.*

㉓ **Gostinny Dvor** (Merchants' Arcade). This market, which takes up an entire block between ulitsa Ilinka and Varvarka ulitsa, just east of Red Square, is made up of two imposing buildings: Running the length of Khrustalny pereulok is the Old Merchant Arcade, erected by the Italian architect Quarenghi in 1791–1805; on the other side of the block, bordering Rybny pereulok, is the New Merchant Arcade, built in 1838–40 on the site of the old fish market. The entire complex has been renovated and is filled with all manner of shops. ⊠ *ul. Ilinka. Metro: Pl. Revolutsii or Kitai-Gorod.*

Ivanovsky Monastery (St. John's Convent). Built in the 16th century and restored in the 19th, this monastery was used as a prison in the Stalinist era and was in shambles for many years after that. Fortunately, it is once again being refurbished, but, with much restoration work to be done, the reopening is some time off. Among the noblewomen who were forced to take the veil here were Empress Elizabeth's illegitimate daughter, Princess Tarankova, and the mad serf owner Dariya Saltykova, who was imprisoned here after she murdered 138 of her serfs, most of them young women. ⊠ *Zabelina ul. and Maly Ivanovsky per. Metro: Kitai-Gorod.*

Kazansky Sobor (Cathedral of Our Lady of Kazan). Built in 1633–36 to commemorate Russia's liberation from Polish occupation during the Time of Troubles, this church was purposely blown up in 1936, and not rebuilt and fully restored until 1993. Its salmon-and-cream painted brick and gleaming gold cupolas are now a colorful magnet at the northeast corner of Red Square, between the Historical Museum and GUM. Inside and outside hang icons of Our Lady of Kazan; the small chapel affords an excellent look at the traditional iconostasis and interior design of Russian churches. In the front vestibule, you can buy candles to light a prayer; you'll also find other religious articles for sale. Many of the faithful visit throughout the day. ⊠ *Nikolskaya ul., at Red Sq.* ☉ *Daily 8–7, except Mon., when it closes at the end of the 5 PM vespers service. Sun. services at 7 and 10 AM. Metro: Pl. Revolutsii.*

㉜ **Lubyanskaya Ploshchad.** This circular "square" was recently returned to its prerevolutionary name. In 1926 it had been renamed Dzerzhinsky Square, in honor of Felix Dzerzhinsky, a Soviet revolutionary and founder of the infamous CHEKA, the forerunner to the KGB. His statue once stood in the center of the square, but was toppled in August 1991, along with the old regime. A huge round flower bed has replaced it. The large yellow building facing the square, with bars on the ground-floor windows, was once the notorious Lubyanka Prison and KGB headquarters. Be careful walking around this area at night. Pensioners have been known to come here to sell their prescription medication. The mayor made an effort to clean up the area and pensioners rarely sell here anymore, but kids still hang about. *Metro: Lubyanka.*

㉟ **Maly Theater.** Opened in 1824 and formerly known as the Little Imperial Theater (*maly* means "little"), this house is famous for its productions of Russian classics. Maxim Gorky once called the Maly "the Russian people's university." Out front stands a statue of a beloved and prolific playwright whose works are often performed here, the 19th-century satirist Alexander Ostrovsky. ⊠ *1/6 Teatralnaya Pl.,* ☎ *095/923–2621. Metro: Teatralnaya.*

㉛ **Mayakovsky Library and Museum.** This museum of Russia's great revolutionary poet (1919–30) is in his former home. The collection comprises archival documents, photos, manuscripts, paintings, and posters. ⊠ *3/6 Proeyzd Serova,* ☎ *095/255–0186 or 095/928–6092.* ▤ *$1.50.* ☉ *Tues., Fri.–Sun. 10–5; Thurs. 1–8. Metro: Lubyanka.*

㉝ **Metropol Hotel.** Built in the early 20th century in preparation for the anniversary celebrations commemorating 300 years of the Romanov dynasty, the Metropol was reconstructed in the late 1980s, and its brilliant Art Nouveau facade has been restored to its original colorful appearance. The ceramic mosaics are especially arresting as the sun bounces off the tiles. Look for the Princess "Greza" panel made by M. Vrubeley, which was inspired by the plays of Edmond Rostand. On the main facade of the building is the mosaic picturing the four seasons. The venue of many a historical speech, including a few by Lenin, the hotel was the focus of heavy fighting during the revolution, and for some time the Central Committee of the Russian Soviet Federal Republic met here under its first chairman, Yakov Sverdlov. Until 1994, Theater Square, the wide-open space across from the hotel, facing the Bolshoi Theater, was named Sverdlov Square, in his honor. (☞ Lodging, *below,* for more information.)

Monetny Dvor (The Mint). Next door to the Kazansky Sobor, the former mint built in 1697 is an excellent example of old Baroque architecture. Find its facade in the courtyard of the 18th-century building immediately next to the Kazansky Sobor. ⊠ *Nikolskaya ul., at Red Sq. Metro: Pl. Revolutsii.*

㉙ Museum of the History of Moscow. Housed in the former **Church of St. John the Baptist** (1825), this museum presents Moscow's architectural history using paintings and artifacts. It's a small, manageable museum, and it's worth stopping in for a brief visit to get a fuller view of the Moscow you've been getting only glimpses of while exploring the city's older districts. ⊠ *12 Novaya Pl.,* ☎ *095/924–8490.* ▣ *1.50.* ☉ *Tues., Thurs., weekends 10–6; Wed., Fri. 11–7. Closed last day of month. Metro: Lubyanka.*

㉖ Palaty Romanovych v Zaryadye (Romanov Palace Chambers in Zaryadye). It is believed that Mikhail Romanov was born in this house. Today the mansion houses a lovely museum devoted to the boyar lifestyle of the 16th and 17th centuries. The rooms are furnished to show how the boyars lived, with period clothing, furniture, and household items on display. During the week, the museum is generally open only to groups with advance reservations, but if you ask, you may be allowed to join a group. On Sundays the museum is open to the general public. Once again, tourists can visit only in groups, but after a short wait, enough people will gather to form a tour. You'll find the entrance downstairs, opposite the lower doorway of the hotel. ⊠ *10 Varvarka ul.,* ☎ *095/298–3706.* ▣ *4.50.* ☉ *Mon., Thurs.–Sun. 10–6; Wed. 11–5. Metro: Kitai-Gorod.*

㉚ Polytechnical Museum. This museum, which takes up the entire block and was opened in 1872 (it was originally called the Museum of Applied Knowledge), today houses exhibits devoted to achievements in science and technology, including an awesome collection of old Russian cars. ⊠ *3/4 Novaya Pl.,* ☎ *095/923–0756.* ▣ *$1..* ☉ *Tues.–Sun. 10–6. Closed last Thurs. of month. Metro: Lubyanka.*

Rossiya Hotel. With accommodation for 6,000, the Rossiya is one of Europe's largest hotels. Russians often joke that the Soviets chose this site for the hotel because foreign tourists wouldn't ever have to leave their room: Varvarka ulitsa, with its rich mixture of architecture, was all they would ever need to see. (☞ Lodging, *below,* for more information.) ⊠ *6 Varvarka ul. Metro: Kitai-Gorod.*

Ryabushinsky Bank. This Art Nouveau masterpiece was designed by Fyodor Shekhtel at the turn of the century for the rich merchant Ryabushinsky. The pale-orange building on the opposite side of the street is the former Birzha (Stock Exchange). Built in the Classical style at the end of the 19th century, it now houses Russia's Chamber of Commerce and Industry. ⊠ *Birzhevaya Pl. at Ilinka ul. Metro: Pl. Revolutsii.*

Sandunovskaya Banya. The Sandunovsky sauna has been popular ever since it was built in the late 19th century. If you plan to use the baths here, beware of a few ground rules. Men and women are strictly separated. Soap is not acceptable as the steam will eventually clean you. Beating yourself with birch twigs or *veniki* is encouraged since it increases circulation. Remember to keep yourself hydrated and if you take it slow, the experience will be all the more relaxing. Manicures, pedicures, and massages are also available. ⊠ *14 Neglinniy pereulok.,* ☎ *095/925–4631 or 095/928–4633.* ☎ *$6–12.* ☉ *Wed.–Mon. 8– 10. Metro: Teatralnaya.*

㊱ **Tsentralny Muzey V. I. Lenina.** The Lenin Museum, in Soviet Russia a solemn and sacred place, is now closed, but the magnificent redbrick exterior is well worth a look.

㉗ **Tserkov Georgiya na Pskovskoy Gorke** (Church of St. George on Pskov Hill). The graceful five-domed church with blue cupolas studded by gold stars, built in 1657 by merchants from Pskov, stands right next to the Romanov Mansion, in front of the Rossiya Hotel. The bell tower was an addition from the 19th century. Unfortunately, the interior of the church is completely bare and is not open to the public. ⊠ *12 Varvarka ul. Metro: Kitai-Gorod.*

Tserkov Maksima Blazhennovo (Church of St. Maxim the Blessed). Built in 1698 on the site where the Holy Fool Maxim was buried is the white-stone church between St. Barbara's and the Znamensky Sobor (in front of the northern side of the Rossiya Hotel). The church is closed to the public. ⊠ *6 Varvarka ul. Metro: Kitai-Gorod.*

㉘ **Tserkov Troitsy v Nikitnikach** (Church of the Trinity in Nikitniki). This lovely redbrick creation—one of the most striking churches in the city—mixes Baroque decoration with the principles of ancient Russian church architecture. Painted with white trim and topped by five green cupolas, the church was built in 1635–53 for the merchant Grigory Nikitnikov. The private chapel on the south side was the family vault. The murals and iconostasis were the work of Simon Ushakov, a famous icon painter whose workshop was located nearby, in the brick building across the courtyard. Unfortunately the structure is now closed for restoration, but it's still worth seeking out for a look at its exterior. ⊠ *3 Nikitnikov per.,* ☎ *095/298–5018. Metro: Kitai-Gorod.*

㉔ **Tserkov Velikomuchenitsy Varvary** (St. Barbara's Church). This peach-and-white church, built in the Classical style at the end of the 18th century, lends its name to the street. It is now once again an active church, with daily services. Its gift shop sells religious items as well as souvenirs. ⊠ *Varvarka ul. off of Red Sq. Metro: Pl. Revolutsii.*

Tserkov Vsekh Svyatykh na Kulishkakh (Church of All-Saints in Kulishki). This graceful church, a fine example of 17th-century religious architecture, is one of the few survivors of the Soviet reconstruction of the area. It was recently returned to the Orthodox Church and is now open for services (Sun. at 10 AM and 5:30 PM). ⊠ *Pl. Varvarskych Vorot. Metro: Kitai-Gorod.*

㉑ **Zaikonospassky Monastery** (Monastery of the Savior Behind the Icons). Russia's first institution of higher learning, the Slavonic-Greco-Latin Academy, was opened in this building in 1687. The monastery itself was founded at the beginning of the 17th century by Boris Godunov. Many an illustrious student studied here including Lomonosov from 1731 to 1735. Hidden inside the courtyard is the monastery's cathedral, **Spassky Sobor,** built in 1600–61 in the style of Moscow Baroque. It is currently under renovation but a Sunday service is still held here, and on other days you can usually gain access. ⊠ *7 Nikolskaya ul. Metro: Pl. Revolutsii.*

㉕ **Znamensky Sobor** (Cathedral of the Sign). This was part of the monastery of the same name, built on the estate of the Romanovs in the 16th century, right after the establishment of the Romanov dynasty. After the death of the last heir to Ivan the Terrible, a dark period set in, marked by internal strife and foreign intervention. That period, commonly known as the Time of Troubles, ended in 1613, when the Boyar Council elected the young Mikhail Romanov czar. ⊠ *8a Varvarka ul. Metro: Kitai-Gorod.*

Tverskaya Ulitsa: Moscow's Fifth Avenue

Tverskaya ulitsa is Moscow's main shopping artery, attracting shoppers hungry for the latest trend, as well as the foreign investor looking for a lucrative place to set up shop. The street is lined with massive apartment buildings whose ground floors house some of the city's best and biggest stores. A stroll up Tverskaya promises window shopping of a very fancy order and a look at some of Moscow's attractive buildings, several graced by a fine Art Nouveau style. It is a lovely, wide boulevard lined with perfumeries, banks and exchanges, eateries, and bookshops. On a sunny day, it is an especially pleasant walk. Keep an eye out for plaques etched in stone on building walls. These will tell you about the famous people, usually artists, politicians, or academicians, who lived or worked there.

Tverskaya ulitsa was given its present form in the mid '30s, during the first plan of reconstruction, though it had been an important route for centuries—the line of the road that led from the Kremlin to the ancient town of Tver. Later that road was extended all the way to the new capital on the Baltic Sea, St. Petersburg. From 1932 to 1990 Tverskaya was known as Gorky Street, in honor of the writer Maxim Gorky, the father of Soviet socialist realism. In 1990, the first section of the street, leading from the heart of town to Triumfalnaya Square, was given back its prerevolutionary name. The renaming was completed a year later, when the second section, ending at the Belorussian Railway Station, was also returned to its old name—Tverskaya Yamskaya. Until the rebuilding in the 1930s, Tverskaya ulitsa was narrow and twisting, lined in places with wooden houses. Today it is a broad, busy avenue, a tribute to the grandiose reconstruction projects of the Stalinist era.

A Good Walk

Walking up the left-hand side of the street, you pass, at No. *5*, the **Yermolova Theater.** One short block farther, on the same side of the street, you come to the **Central Telegraph Office** �37. On the opposite side of the avenue, Kamergersky pereulok leads off to the right. The small green building on the left-hand side of this street houses the **Moscow Art Theater** �38. If you're interested in antiquarian bookshops, you'll find some here.

Returning to Tverskaya, continue on along the left-hand side of the street. If you want to take a break from the hustle and bustle of Tverskaya, wander down ulitsa Nezhdanovoi, a side street to the left. You enter the street through the arched passageway of No. 11, which is the **Russian Federation of Science and Technology.** This street has long been home to many of Moscow's successful artists. At the end of the block, you come upon the pretty **Tserkov Voskreseniya** �39. Go back to Tverskaya ulitsa. The handsome red building just ahead with impressive iron gates to its adjacent side street is the **Moscow City Council** (Mossoviet). Across the street, another short stretch brings you to the small square **Tverskaya Ploshchad** ⓐ. Farther up the street, again on the left-hand side, you pass ulitsa Leontevsky. Wander down this street to No. 7 to reach the **Russian Folk Art Museum** ㊶. Along the way, you'll pass by the **Stanislavsky House Museum** ㊷ at No. 6 as well as many graceful 18th- and 19th-century buildings housing embassies. Retrace your steps to Tverskaya. At No. 14 you find **Yeliseyevsky's** ㊸, the most dazzling of all of Moscow's stores. Head farther up the street, toward **Pushkinskaya Ploshchad** ㊹, named after the revered poet and writer. Bordering the west side of the square is the **Pushkinskaya Cinema.**

Bordering the square to the right and left of the park are the offices of some of Russia's largest and most influential newspapers. Easily spotted is *Izvestia* (*News*), once the mouthpiece of the Soviet government and now considered a liberal newspaper. Between 18 and 20 Tverskaya, if you look down the alley, you'll see the striking facade of *Trud* (*Labor*), the official newspaper of the trade unions and of late a conservative voice. Looking back to the far corner that you came from, you'll see the building of *Moskovskie novosti* (*Moscow News*), the newspaper that helped give *glasnost* true meaning back in the early years of *perestroika*. Its brave editor allowed articles on topics then considered extremely controversial, from Stalinist collectivization to the ethnic strife in Armenia and Azerbaijan.

Continuing along Tverskaya ulitsa, you reach the attractive railings of the former **English Club** ㊺, now the Museum of the Revolution. As you continue in the same direction, you'll pass the Moscow Art Theater, which bears the name of Stanislavsky. The next major intersection is **Triumfalnaya Ploshchad** ㊻. On the north side of Triumfalnaya Ploshchad, Tverskaya ulitsa becomes **Tverskaya-Yamskaya ulitsa.** Continue on by walking on the left-hand side of Triumfalnaya Ploshchad on Bolshaya Sadovaya ulitsa. Take a left on Malaya Bronnaya ulitsa. **Patriarshy Prud** is just a few steps away on your right.

TIMING

Allow at least three hours for this tour, five or six if you plan to visit the museums along the route.

Sights to See

㊲ **Central Telegraph Office.** The striking semicircular entrance is adorned with a large, illuminated, and constantly revolving globe and a huge digital clock. Inside, you can buy stamps, send a fax home, or make a phone call abroad. You will find currency-exchange counters in the lobby and the main post office as well. ✉ *7 Tverskaya ul.,* ☎ *095/924–9004.* ☺ *Daily, 24 hrs. Metro: Okhotny Ryad.*

Dostoyevsky Memorial Apartment. This museum devoted to the great Russian novelist is located on the grounds of the hospital where he was born and where his father worked as a doctor. Dostoyevsky lived here from 1823 to 1837. ✉ *2 ul. Dostoevskovo,* ☎ *095/281–1085 or 095/284–3148.* ☜ *$1.* ☺ *Thurs., weekends 11–6; Wed., Fri. 2–6:30. Closed last day of month. Metro: Novoslobodskaya.*

㊺ **English Club.** The onetime social center of the Moscow aristocracy has an entrance flanked by two smirking lions. Built by Giliardi in 1787, the mansion was rebuilt in the Classical style after the Moscow Fire of 1812. Since 1926, it has housed the **Museum of the Revolution.** Although it retains many of its former exhibits—heavily imbued with Soviet propaganda—the museum has been updated to reflect the changing political situation in Russia. The permanent exhibit, located on the second floor, begins with a review of the first workers' organizations in the 19th century. The exhibits outlining the 1905 and 1917 revolutions include the horse-drawn machine-gun cart of the First Cavalry Army, the texts of the first decrees of the Soviet government on peace and land, dioramas and paintings portraying revolutionary battles, and thousands of other relics. The next rooms outline the history of Soviet rule, with extensive material devoted to Stalin's rise to power. The final exhibit is dedicated to the August 1991 coup. It features a reconstructed version of the barricades set up outside the Russian Parliamentary Building, where Yeltsin made his famous appeals to the Russian people. Explanations of the exhibits are only in Russian, but you can arrange for a guided tour in English by calling ahead. The entrance fee is low, even though foreigners pay more than Russians. You will also find interesting temporary exhibits on the first floor of the museum. Snoop through their gift shop, which features standard Russian souvenirs (including some beautiful amber) and great vintage items like flags and political-rally posters. ✉ *21 Tverskaya ul.,* ☎ *095/299–6724.* 🎫 *$1.50.* ☼ *Tues.– Sat. 10–5:30; Sun. 10–4:30. Closed last Fri. of month. Metro: Tverskaya.*

47 **Glinka Museum.** This museum is devoted to the history of music, with a special emphasis on Glinka and other Russian composers of the 19th century. There is a fine collection of musical instruments, including a Stradivarius violin. Concerts and lectures are also held here; check the schedule at the door. Excursions and tours to other musical sites, sometimes given in English, are available, but these always need to be booked in advance. ✉ *4 ul. Fadeyeva,* ☎ *095/972–3237 or 095/251– 1066.* 🎫 *$1.* ☼ *Tues.–Sun. 11–7. Closed last day of month. Metro: Mayakovskaya.*

38 **Moscow Art Theater (MKhAT).** One of Moscow's most historically important theaters, it is renowned for its productions of the Russian classics, especially those of Chekhov. Founded in 1898 by the celebrated actor and director Konstantin Stanislavsky (1863–1938) and Vladimir Nemirovich-Danchenko (1858–1943), the theater staged the first productions of Chekhov's and Gorky's plays. It was here that Stanislavsky developed the "Stanislavsky Method," based on the realistic traditions of the Russian theater. Visit the Stanislavsky House museum (☞ *below*) if you want to see where he spent the last 17 years of his life. After the successful production of Chekhov's *Seagull* (the first staging in St. Petersburg had bombed), the bird was chosen as the theater's emblem. An affiliated, more modern theater, with a seating capacity of 2,000, also confusingly called the Moscow Art Theater, was opened in 1972 on Tverskaya ulitsa, near Stanislavsky's home. The mural opposite the theater depicts Anton Chekhov. ✉ *3 Kamergersky per.,* ☎ *095/299– 8760 or 095/290–5128. Metro: Okhotny Ryad.*

Moscow City Council (Mossoviet). This impressive structure was built at the end of the 18th century by Matvey Kazakov for the Moscow governor-general. During the reconstruction of Tverskaya ulitsa in the 1930s, the building was moved back about 45 ft in order to widen the street. The top two stories—a mirror image of the mansion's original two stories—were added at that time. ✉ *22 Tverskaya ul. Metro: Tverskaya.*

Moscow Wax Museum. A Russian Madame Tussaud's, this place has figures of important leaders, all the way up to Yeltsin. Renovations of the museum begun in 1998 should be finished by the end of 1999. ✉ *14 Tverkaya ul.,* ☎ *095/229–8552.* ☼ *Tues.–Sun. 11–7. Metro: Tverskaya.*

Patriarshy Prud (Patriarch's Pond). The beginning of Russian satirist and novelist Mikhail Bulgakov's (1891–1940) novel *Master and Margarita* is set in this small park. Bulgakov is most famous for this novel and his hilarious play *Heart of a Dog.* The park and pond were named after the Patriarch of the Orthodox Church, who once owned the area. Shaded by trees and with plenty of benches, it's a nice spot for a break. In winter the pond is used as a skating rink. Café Margarita sits at 28 Malaya Bronnaya and is worth a look especially if you've read any Bulgakov. ⊠ *Malaya Bronnaya ul. at Yermoleyevsky per. Metro: Mayakovskaya.*

④④ Pushkinskaya Ploshchad (Pushkin Square). The city's first McDonald's is at this site, where Moscow's first outer ring, the bulvar (boulevard), crosses Tverskaya ulitsa. If you're longing for that familiar burger, stop for lunch. There are rarely lines anymore (branches have opened throughout the city), but you'll quickly see how popular it remains. The counters are always crowded, with disorganized but swiftly moving lines. The menu hews to the original, and prices are cheaper than in the States. Russians come by the score but don't dawdle—they take the term "fast food" literally! The park on the right-hand side of the street is a popular meeting place for Muscovites. A fountain stands in the center of a terraced park, which is lined with benches. A bronze statue of Pushkin stands at the top of the park. It is the work of Alexander Opekushin and was erected by public subscription in 1880. Summer and winter, fresh flowers on the pedestal prove that the poet's admirers are still ardent and numerous. *Metro: Pushkinskaya.*

Pushkinskaya Cinema. Built in 1961, the theater stands on the site of the former Strastnoi Monastery (Convent of the Lord's Passion), whose history dated back to the mid-17th century; it was destroyed in 1937. All that remains of the ancient monastery is the white-stone Church of the Nativity near the corner with ulitsa Chekhova (to the far left as you face the theater). This theater hosts the Moscow International Film Festival every two years. Today the cinema shows major Hollywood movies, but you might be able to catch a Russian movie from time to time. ⊠ *Pushkinskaya Pl.,* ☎ *095/229–2111. Metro: Pushkinskaya.*

④① Russian Folk Art Museum. Founded by a wealthy merchant and patron of the arts, Savva Morozov, the museum displays a rich collection of Russian folk art dating from the 17th century to the present, including antique and modern pottery, ceramics, glassware, metalwork, wood, bone, embroideries, lace, and popular prints. Theater director Konstantin Stanislavsky, founder of the Moscow Art Theater, lived for a time in the building at No. 6. ⊠ *7 Stanislavskovo ul.,* ☎ *095/291–8718.* ▣ *$1.50* ⊙ *Daily, 11–5:30. Metro: Tverskaya.*

④② Stanislavsky House Museum. Konstantin Stanislavsky (1863–1938) was a Russian actor, director, and producer who is famed as the founder of method acting. He also was one of the founders of the Moscow Art Theater (☞ *above*). Stanislavsky lived and worked in this house during the last 17 years of his life. The house has been kept as it was while he lived there and showcases photos and theater memorabilia. ⊠ *6 Leontivsky per.,* ☎ *095/229–2442 or 095/229–2855.* ⊙ *Wed. and Fri. 2–8; Thurs. and weekends 11–6.* ▣ *$1.50. Closed last Thurs. of month. Metro: Pushkinskaya.*

④⑥ Triumfalnaya Ploshchad. This major intersection is where the grand boulevard of Moscow, the Sadovaya (Garden) Ring, crosses Tverskaya ulitsa. Traffic here also passes through a tunnel running below Tverskaya ulitsa, and there is an underpass for pedestrians. A statue of the revolutionary poet Vladimir Mayakovsky (☞ Kitai Gorod, *above*) stands in the center of the square. It is generally believed that Mayakovsky committed suicide in 1930 out of disillusionment with the revolution he had so passionately supported. *Metro: Mayakovskaya.*

Triumfalnaya Ploshchad is a center of Moscow's cultural life. The **Tchaikovsky Concert Hall** stands on the corner nearest you. It was opened in 1940 and seats 1,600. The **Satire Theater** is right next door, on the Sadovaya Ring. On the far side of the square stands the **Moskva Cinema;** the popular **Mossoviet Theater** is also located nearby, at 16 Bolshaya Sadovaya. To your far left you see the multitiered tower of the imposing **Peking Hotel,** opened in 1956 as a mark of Sino-Soviet friendship. Looking to your right, you'll see the **American Bar and Grill,** popular with Russians as well as the foreign community.

While you're here, it's worth riding the escalator down for a peek at the spectacular interior of the **Mayakovskaya subway station.** Its ceiling is decorated with colorful, pastel mosaics depicting Soviet achievements in outer space. Like many of the early subway stations, it is deep underground (it doubled as a bomb shelter during World War II). Stalin made a famous speech here on the 24th anniversary of the Bolshevik Revolution, at the height of the Siege of Moscow.

㊴ Tserkov Voskreseniya (Church of the Resurrection). Built in 1629, this is one of the few lucky churches to have stayed open throughout the years of Soviet rule. As a survivor, the church was the recipient of many priceless icons from less fortunate churches destroyed or closed by the Soviets. Services are still held here daily. Be sure to look at the beautiful ceilings in the chapels on either side of you as enter. Two famous icons, depicting the Coronation of the Virgin Mary and the Assumption of the Blessed Virgin Mary, hang in the vaults on either side of the vestibule. ✉ *2 Yeliseyevsky per.,* ☎ *095/229–6616. Metro: Tverskaya.*

㊵ Tverskaya Ploshchad. In the small park to your right stands a statue of Prince Yuri Dolgoruky, the founder of Moscow in 1147. The equestrian statue was erected in 1954, shortly after the celebrations marking Moscow's 800th anniversary. The square, which dates back to 1792, gets its name from the street, but in 1918 it was renamed Sovetskaya ploshchad. In 1994 its historical name, Tverskaya, was reinstated. *Metro: Tverskaya.*

Tverskaya-Yamskaya ulitsa. This last section of Tverskaya ulitsa has been the object of serious reconstruction in the past few years, and there is little of historical interest along this stretch. The street ends at the Belorussky Vokzal (Belorussian Railway Station), which has two interconnecting subway stations. A statue of Maxim Gorky, erected in the 1950s, stands in a small park outside the station. It is located near the site of the former Triumphal Gates, built in the 19th century by the architect Osip Bove to commemorate the Russian victory in the war with Napoléon. The gates were demolished in a typical fit of destruction in the 1930s. Fragments can be found on the grounds of the Donskoy Monastery (☞ Donskoy and Novodevichy Monasteries, *below*). A replica of the original gates was erected in 1968 near Poklonnaya Hill, at the end of Kutuzovsky Prospekt. *Metro: Mayakovskaya.*

NEED A BREAK?

Regardless of whether it's Friday or not, **T.G.I. Friday's** (✉ 18 Tverskaya ul., ☎ 095/209-3601) is always ready and waiting to serve you in their typical happy manner. So when you've had enough jostling out on the streets, pop in here to join another world. Friday's in Moscow serves American dishes and has been a hit since it opened. This is the perfect place for a quick snack and a well-earned break from Russian reality.

Victor Vasnetsov Museum. This house-museum was the home of the Russian artist Victor Vasnetsov from 1894 to 1926. Built by the artist himself, it is a charming example of the "fairy-tale" architectural style that was popular at the end of the 19th century. Inside the house, Vasnetsov's paintings of Russian fairy tales are on display. ✉ *13 per. Vasnetsova,* ☎ *095/281–1329.* ▦ *$1.50.* ◷ *Wed.–Sun. 10–4:30. Closed last Thurs. of month. Metro: Sukharevskaya.*

㊸ **Yeliseyevsky's.** Of all the stores and boutiques on Tverskaya ulitsa, you'll find the most dazzling interior in the grocery store at No. 14, just beyond Stanislavskovo but on the right-hand side of the street. Under Communist administration, the store had the official, generic title Gastronome No. 1, but it once again carries the name that most people continued to call it even then—Yeliseyevsky's, after the rich merchant from St. Petersburg who owned the store before the Revolution. The interior sparkles with chandeliers, stained glass, and gilt wall decorations. Products abound. It's here that you'll find loads of good cognac and Georgian wine (including Stalin's favorite Khvanchkava—still much touted even with its unsavory stamp of approval). They also have coffee beans, and in the back room are Russian chocolate and candy of all sorts. ✉ *14 Tverskaya ul.,* ☎ *095/209–0760* ⏲ *Mon.–Sat. 8 AM–9 PM, Sun. 10 AM–7 PM. Metro: Tverskaya.*

Yermolova Theater. The theater housed in this short building with an arched entrance was founded in 1937 and named after the famous Russian actress, Maria Yermolova. ✉ *5 Tverskaya ul.,* ☎ *095/203–7952 or 095/203–7628. Metro: Okhotny Ryad.*

The Old Moscow of Bolshaya Nikitskaya Ulitsa

Bolshaya Nikitskaya ulitsa (formerly ulitsa Gertsena, or "Herzen Street") is one of the many old streets radiating from the Kremlin, running more or less parallel with Tverskaya ulitsa to the northeast and Novy Arbat to the southwest. The street was laid out along the former road to Novgorod, an ancient town northwest of Moscow, and is divided into two sections. The first part is lined with 18th- and 19th-century mansions and begins at Manezh Square, across from the fortification walls of the Kremlin. The second section, notable for its enchanting Art Nouveau mansions, starts at Nikitskiye Vorota (Nikolai Gates) Square, where Bolshaya Nikitskaya Street intersects with the Boulevard Ring. Like most Moscow streets, Bolshaya Nikitskaya has been through a few name changes. Before the 1917 revolution, it was named Bolshaya Nikitskaya (the name most of the street signs still carry), after the Nikitsky Convent, which was founded in the 16th century. In 1920 it was renamed ulitsa Gertsena in honor of the 19th-century philosopher Alexander Herzen (☞ Arbat, Old and New, *below*). Although Herzen spent much of his life in self-imposed exile in London and Paris, he exerted a tremendous influence on Russian sociopolitical thought in the mid-19th century as a progressive writer and fierce advocate of liberal reform.

A Good Walk

The walk begins at **Manezhnaya Ploshchad** ㊽ (Manezh Square), which you can reach by subway, getting off at the Okhotny Ryad stop. Take the exit to the Okhotny Ryad shopping mall. Wander through the shopping mall at your leisure and leave the building through any exit to your left. This will lead you to lower Manezh Square where the Russian sculptor Zurab Tseretelli's bronze statues of Russian fairy-tale characters stand in a long fountain (the fountain is supposed to represent the Neglinnaya River, which once ran here, but has since been relegated underground). Make your way up the stairs on either side of the fountain to reach Manezh Square. Walk across the square away from the Kremlin and cross the street. You will come to the old campus of **Moscow State University** ㊾. Passing the university, you come to Bolshaya Nikitskaya ulitsa. Turn right, and one block up, at the corner of ulitsa Belinskovo, you reach the city's **Zoological Museum** ㊿. Farther up, on the left-hand side of the street at No. 13, is the **Tchaikovsky Conservatory** (51). Take a quick diversion off Bolshaya Nikitskaya ulitsa now, turning right onto ulitsa Voznesensky, which begins just past the conservatory, to Moscow's **Episcopal Church,** at No. 8. Continuing now up Bolshaya Nikitskaya ulitsa, you pass, on the left-hand side, the **Mayakovsky Drama Theater** ⑤. One more block brings you to the square named **Nikitskyie Vorota,** home to the TASS offices.

The busy road in front of you, intersecting Bolshaya Nikitskaya ulitsa, is the Boulevard Ring, which forms a semicircle around the city center. On the other side of the boulevard, facing the square, is the Classical **Tserkov Bolshovo Vozneseniya** ⑤. Bolshaya Nikitskaya ulitsa veers sharply to the left here, so that if you continue straight ahead, keeping to the right of the square, you'll end up on ulitsa Kachalova. About half a block down, near the corner, is a marvelous example of Moscow Art Nouveau, the **Ryabushinsky Mansion** ⑤. Follow the road behind the Church of the Ascension and continue straight onto Paliashvili ulitsa (which leads to the left off Bolshaya Nikitskaya ulitsa). As you walk down Paliashvili you pass several side streets with names like Stolovy (Dining Room), Skatertny (Tablecloth), and Khlebny (Bread). The streets are named after the servants of the czar (the waiters, the linen makers, the baker) who lived in this area. Today the district houses many foreign embassies. Walk down Paliashvili ulitsa until you reach the busy intersection with **Povarskaya ulitsa,** where you should turn right. The mansion at No. 25 (on the left-hand side of the street) houses the **Gorky Literary Museum** ⑤. Near the end of Povarskaya ulitsa, you pass the **Central House for Writers.** Povarskaya ulitsa comes out onto Novinsky bulvar; to the right is **Ploshchad Kudrinskaya** ⑤. If you head northeast the literary theme continues at the **Chekhov Museum** ⑤. Moving south, you can visit the **Chaliapin House Museum** ⑤, while to the the far left, you can see the U.S. Embassy and the **White House** ⑤.

TIMING
Because this walk covers quite a bit of territory and includes a number of detours down crooked streets in picturesque neighborhoods, it's best to allow a day to see everything at a leisurely pace. The tour runs from the Okhotny Ryad metro station to the Barrikadnaya station—roughly a 3 km (1½ mi) in a straight line—and there are no stations in between, so it's best to save this walk for a day when you're well rested.

Sights to See

⑤ **Bely Dom (White House).** Perched along the riverbank, the large, white modern building is across the river from the Hotel Ukraina, yet another one of the seven Stalin Gothic buildings. Before the August 1991 coup it was the headquarters of the Russian Republic of the USSR. Your first images of the building are probably from television coverage of its being shelled in October 1993. Today the building no longer houses the Russian Parliament and the President's offices, and is officially called the Council of Ministers and houses governmental offices. ⊠ *16 Vozdvizhenka ul.,* ☎ *095/290–1232. Metro: Arbatskaya.*

Central House for Writers. The CDL (Centralny Dom Literaterov) functions as an exclusive club for members of the Writers' Union. Its dining room is now one of the city's very best restaurants, open to the public (☞ Dining, *below*). Next door (No. 52) is a large mansion, enclosed by a courtyard, that houses the administrative offices of the Writers' Union. It is commonly believed that Leo Tolstoy used this mansion as a model for his description of the Rostov home in *War and Peace.* A statue of Tolstoy stands in the courtyard. ⊠ *50 Povarskaya ul.,* ☎ *095/291–1515. Metro: Barrikadnaya.*

⑤ **Chaliapin House Museum.** Theodore Chaliapin, one of the world's greatest opera singers, lived in this beautifully restored manor house from 1910 to 1922. Chaliapin was stripped of his Soviet citizenship while on tour in France in 1922; he never returned to Russia again. The Soviets turned his home into an apartment building, and until restorations in the 1980s, the building contained 60 communal apartments. With help from Chaliapin's family in France, the rooms have again been arranged and furnished as they were when Chaliapin lived here. The walls are covered with works of art given to Chaliapin by talented friends (such as the artists Mikhail Vrubel and Isaac Levitan). Also on display are Chaliapin's colorful costumes, which were donated to the museum by his son. When you reach the piano room, you are treated to original recordings of Chaliapin singing his favorite roles. Entrance is from inside the courtyard. English-language tours are available. ⊠ *25–27 Novinsky bulvar,* ☎ *095/252–2530.* ▦ *$1.* ☉ *Tues., weekends 10–6; Wed., Thurs. 11:30–6:30. Closed last day of month. Metro: Barrikadnaya.*

❺❼ Chekhov Museum. The museum is located in the home where Chekhov lived from 1886 to 1890. The rooms are arranged as they were when he lived here, with his personal effects on display. Also on exhibit are manuscripts, letters, and photographs. Chekhov was a doctor as well as a writer and the sign DR. CHEKHOV still hangs from the door. Typed pages explaining the rooms are available in English. Keep in mind that the cashier closes one hour before the museum itself. ⊠ *6 Sadovaya-Kudrinskaya ul.,* ☎ *095/291–6154 or 095/291–3837.* ▦ *$1.* ☉ *Tues., Thurs., weekends 11–3; Wed., Fri. 2–5. Closed last day of month. Metro: Barrikadnaya.*

Episcopal Church. The attractive red sandstone building was Moscow's only Episcopal church. After the Revolution it was closed and turned into a recording studio, but the English have taken it back. ⊠ *8 Voznesensky per. Metro: Okhotny Ryad.*

❺❺ Gorky Literary Museum. For Gorky buffs only, the museum is packed with the letters, manuscripts, and pictures of the great proletarian writer. There are also, rather remarkably, portraits of him by Nesterov and Serov. Americans may be particularly riveted to read the first page (in English) of *City of the Yellow Devil,* his book about visiting New York in 1906; its opening chapter is entitled "City of Mammon." There is even a red wooden replica of his childhood home, complete with village yard and outbuildings. You won't get to leave without signing the book of the kindly but fierce matrons who protect this place. ⊠ *25 Povarskaya ul.,* ☎ *095/290–5130.* ▦ *$1.* ☉ *Mon., Tues., Thurs. 10–5; Wed., Fri. noon–7. Closed 1st Thurs. of month. Metro: Barrikadnaya.*

❹❽ Manezhnaya Ploshchad (Manezh Square). Bordering one side of the square is the **Moskva Hotel.** Opened in 1935, it was one of the first buildings erected as part of Stalin's reconstruction plan for Moscow. If you look carefully at the facade, you'll notice that the design on the west side doesn't match the design on the east side. Legend has it that Stalin was given a preliminary draft that showed two possible versions for the hotel. He was supposed to sign under the one he liked best, but instead he signed his name right across the middle. The story goes that the architects, too timid to go back to Stalin a second time, went ahead and built the hotel with its asymmetrical facade.

The building next to the National Hotel houses the offices of **Intourist,** the travel agency that once held a monopoly over the entire tourist industry of the former Soviet Union. Until 1950 the building housed the U.S. Embassy. Older city residents still fondly recall how the Americans posted here joined in the spontaneous celebrations that erupted all over the city when the end of World War II was announced. They'll tell you how the Americans kept the party going, rolling beer kegs out these doors and onto Red Square across the way.

When the Soviets razed Manezh Square in 1938, many of the area's old buildings were lost. The plan was to build a superhighway through the area. Luckily the plan did not succeed. In 1967 the square was renamed "50th Anniversary of the October Revolution Square." In the 1990s its original name was returned and construction of an underground shopping mall was begun. Construction was halted in 1993 in order to let archaeologists excavate the area. The team found a plethora of construction and items dating from as far back as the 13th century. In 1997 the shopping mall (☞ *below*) was finally opened, to the chagrin of most Muscovites. The present (and prerevolutionary) name comes from the Imperial Riding School, or **Manezh** (Manezh—a Russian transliteration of the French word Manège, ☞ *below*) situated on the opposite side of the square from the Moskva Hotel.

Manezh. Built in 1817, the Manezh, once the Imperial Riding School, is now an exhibition hall. The building has an interesting design: There are no internal columns supporting its huge roof—just the four walls. After the revolution the building was used as the Kremlin garage and then, in the late '50s, was revamped into the present Central Exhibition Hall, which is used primarily for temporary art exhibitions and car shows. Admission charges vary depending on the show on view. ✉ *1 Manezhnaya Pl.*, ☎ *095/202–8252.* ▢ *Free–$1.50.* ◔ *Daily 11–6. Metro: Okhotny Ryad.*

㊷ Mayakovsky Drama Theater. This three-story brick house, with the word TEATP (theater) printed in black on a sign hanging down the side, was for a time known as the Theater of Revolutionary Satire. ✉ *19 Bolshaya Nikitskaya ul.*, ☎ *095/290–2752/6241 Metro: Okhotny Ryad.*

㊹ Moscow State University. Russia's oldest university was founded in 1755 by the father of Russian science, Mikhail Lomonosov. The Neoclassical buildings here were originally designed by Matvei Kazakov, in 1786–93. They were rebuilt and embellished in the mid-19th century, after the 1812 fire. The university's new campus is situated on Sparrow Hills (formerly Lenin Hills) in the largest of the so-called Stalin Gothic skyscrapers, though some of the law and journalism schools are still housed in the old halls. ✉ *Mokhovaya ul. Metro: Okhotny Ryad.*

National Hotel. Built in 1903, the ornate building that is the National Hotel is an excellent example of Art Nouveau. Beautiful mosaics adorn the hotel facade and inside are rooms and restaurants in line with total luxury. (☞ Lodging, *below*). Note the restaurant entrance is at 14/1 Mokhovaya ul. ✉ *14/1 Okhotny Ryad. Metro: Okhotny Ryad.*

Nikitskiye Vorota. This square was named after the gates (*vorota*) of the white-stone fortification walls that once stood here. To your right is a modern building with square windows; this is home to TASS, once the official news agency of the Soviet Union and the mouthpiece of the Kremlin. In the park in the center of the square stands a monument to Kliment Timiryazev, a famous botanist.

The busy road in front of you, intersecting Bolshaya Nikitskaya ulitsa, is the **Boulevard Ring**, which forms a semicircle around the city center. It begins at the banks of the Moskva River, just south of the Kremlin, running in a northeastern direction. It curves eastward, and then south, finally reaching the riverbank again after several miles, near the mouth of the Yauza River, northeast of the Kremlin. Its path follows the lines of the 16th-century white-stone fortification wall that gave Moscow the name "White City." The privilege of living within its walls was reserved for the court nobility and craftsmen serving the czar. The wall was torn down in 1775, on orders from Catherine the Great, and was replaced by the present Boulevard Ring. It is divided into 10 sections, each with a different name. Running along its center is a broad strip of trees and flowers, dotted with playgrounds and benches. You may want to take a break and rest on its benches. *Metro: Arbatskaya.*

Oriental Art Museum. The museum has a large collection of art from the Central Asian republics, China, Japan, and Korea. The special temporary exhibits usually have annotations in English while the rest of the museum is strictly in Russian. The museum's permanent collection is a treasure trove of glass cases filled to capacity with artwork and clothing. It's a cool and calm place to take a leisurely look at their magnificent holdings. ⊠ *12A Nikitsky bulvar,* ☎ *095/202–4555.* ✉ *$5.* ☉ *Tues.–Sun. 11–8. Metro: Arbatskaya.*

56 **Ploshchad Kudrinskaya** (Kudrinsky Square). To the far left of the square cars race in front of you along the busy Sadovoye Koltso (Garden Ring), the major circular road surrounding Moscow. If you approach the ring from Bolshaya Nikitskaya ulitsa or Povarskaya ulitsa, the first thing to catch your eye will be the 22-story skyscraper directly across Novinsky bulvar. One of the seven Stalin Gothics, this one is 525 ft high. The ground floor is taken up by shops and a movie theater, and the rest of the building contains residential apartments. This area saw heavy fighting during the uprisings of 1905 and 1917 (until recently the plaza was named Ploshchad Vosstaniya, or Insurrection Square). The Barrikadnaya (Barricade) subway station is very close by. Cross the street and bear right, through the park and down the hill; you'll see people streaming into the station to your right. *Metro: Barrikadnaya.*

Povarskaya ulitsa (Cook Street). This is where the czar's cooks lived. After the Revolution the street was renamed Vorovskovo, in honor of a Soviet diplomat who was assassinated by a Russian, but has returned to its prerevolutionary name. Povarskaya ulitsa is an important center of the Moscow artistic community, with the film actors' studio, the Russian Academy of Music (the Gnesin Institute), and the Central House of Writers all located here. Many of the old mansions have been preserved, and the street retains its prerevolutionary tranquillity and charm. In the first flush days of summer, your walk is likely to be accompanied by a rousing drum set or tinkling piano sonata issuing from the open windows of the music school. *Metro: Arbatskaya.*

54 **Ryabushinsky Mansion.** This marvelous example of Moscow Art Nouveau was built in 1901 for a wealthy banker and designed by the architect Fyodor Shektel. (If you arrived in Moscow by train, you probably noticed the fanciful Yaroslavl Railway Station, another of his masterpieces, just opposite the Leningrad Railway Station.) The museum has been wonderfully preserved. This was thanks in part to the fact that Maxim Gorky, the father of Soviet socialist realism, lived here from 1931 until his death in 1936. Although Gorky was a champion of the proletariat, his home was rather lavish. Gorky himself apparently hated the *style moderne,* as Art Nouveau was termed back then. Those who don't, however, will be charmed by this building of ecru brick and stone painted pink and mauve atop gray foundations. Step back and look up at the beautiful mosaic of irises that forms a border around the top of most of the house, and see how the strangely fanciful yet utilitarian iron fence matches the unusual design of the window frames. The spectacular interior is replete with a twisting marble staircase that looks like a wave of gushing water, and a stained-glass roof. Excursions in English available. If you want to take a self-guided tour you can read the typed pages available in each room in English. ⊠ *6/2 Malaya Nikit-*

skaya ul., ☎ *095/290–0535.* ☑ *Free.* ☉ *Thurs. and weekends 10–5, Wed., Fri. 12–7. Closed last Thurs. of month. Metro: Arbatskaya.*

㉛ Tchaikovsky Conservatory. You may have seen its magnificent concert hall on television; this is where the famous Tchaikovsky Piano Competition takes place. The conservatory was founded in 1866 and moved to its present location in 1870. Rachmaninoff, Scriabin, and Tchaikovsky are among the famous composers who worked here. There is a statue of Tchaikovsky in the semicircular park outside the main entrance. It was designed by Vera Mukhina, a famous Soviet sculptor. You can buy tickets (at very reasonable prices) to excellent concerts of classical music in the lobby ticket office in the main building. ✉ *13 Bolshaya Nikitskaya ul.,* ☎ *095/229–2183. Metro: Arbatskaya.*

㉝ Tserkov Bolshovo Vozneseniya (Church of the Great Ascension). Like Moscow University, this Classical church was designed by Matvei Kazakov and built in the 1820s. For years it stood empty and abandoned, but it has been under major repair, and though the work is not yet complete, religious services have already been resumed here. The church is most famous as the site where the Russian poet Alexander Pushkin married the younger and far less intelligent Natalya Goncharova (Pushkin died outside St. Petersburg six years after their wedding, in a duel defending her honor). History has judged Natalya harshly; she was probably not guilty of adultery, although she did enjoy flirting. The statue in the park to the left of the church as you face it is of Alexey Tolstoy, a relative of Leo's and a well-known Soviet writer of historical novels. A house museum dedicated to him is next to the Ryabushinsky Mansion. ✉ *36 Malaya Nikitskaya ul. Metro: Arbatskaya.*

☺ Zoo. Another of Zurab Tsaretelli's—Moscow's most ubiquitous sculptor—creations, the Moscow's small zoo has an impressive facade and whimsical design. ✉ *1 Bolshaya Gruzinskaya ul.,* ☎ *095/255–5375.* ☑ *$2.50.* ☉ *Apr.–Sept., daily 9–8; Oct.–Mar., daily 9–5. Metro: Barrikadnaya.*

☺ ㊿ Zoological Museum. This museum, founded in 1902, is always swarming with schoolchildren, who take a special delight in its huge collection of mammals, birds, amphibians, and reptiles. The museum also has a collection of more than 1 million insects, and another collection of more than 100,000 butterflies donated by a Moscow resident. ✉ *6 Bolshaya Nikitskaya ul.,* ☎ *095/203–3569.* ☑ *$1.* ☉ *Tues.–Sun. 10–5. Closed last Tues. of month. Metro: Okhotny Ryad.*

The Arbat, Old and New

Two of downtown Moscow's most interesting and important avenues are the Arbat and Novy Arbat (New Arbat), which run parallel to each other. Arbat Street is revered among Muscovites, who usually refer to it simply as "the Arbat." One of the oldest sections of Moscow, it dates from the 16th century, when it was the beginning of the road that led from the Kremlin to the city of Smolensk. At that time it was also the quarter where court artisans lived, and several of the surrounding streets still recall this in their names—from Plotnikov (Carpenter) to Serebryany (Silversmith) to Kalashny (Pastry Cook). Early in the 19th century it became a favorite district of the aristocracy, while a century later it became a favorite shopping street, a role it has recently reclaimed. Now under a preservation order, the area has been transformed into an attractive, cobbled pedestrian precinct with many gift shops, cafés in restored buildings, and kiosks selling all manner of souvenirs. Closed to all traffic, the Arbat has a carnival feel and attracts portrait artists, poets, and musicians as well as enthusiastic admirers of their work.

Novy Arbat has both a different history and spirit. For almost 30 years it was named Kalinin Prospekt, in honor of Mikhail Kalinin, an old Bolshevik whose prestige plummeted after 1991. The stretch from the Kremlin to Arbat Square has been given back its prerevolutionary name of ulitsa Vozdvizhenka. The second section—which begins where Vozdvizhenka ends and runs west for about a mile to the Moscow River—is now called Novy Arbat. In contrast to ulitsa Vozdvizhenka, which has retained some of its prerevolutionary charm, and the Arbat, which is actively re-creating the look of its past, New Arbat is a modern thoroughfare. Once a maze of narrow streets and alleys, the avenue was widened and modernized in the 1960s, with the goal of making it the showcase of the Soviet capital. In typical Soviet fashion concrete and glass skyscrapers were erected. Now these eyesores house apartments and department stores. There is little of historical interest here.

A Good Walk

Take the subway to either the Arbatskaya station on the dark-blue line or to Biblioteka Imeni Lenina (Lenin Library) on the red line. (To confuse matters, there is also an Arbatskaya station on the light-blue line, but that would leave you at the wrong end of Arbat Square.) When you come out of the station, bear left, walking away from the Kremlin. The large gray building on the corner of ulitsa Vozdvizhenka and ulitsa Mokhovaya is the **Biblioteka Imeni Lenina,** Moscow's main library. The square in front of the library is a favorite meeting place. **Ulitsa Vozdvizhenka** is lined with plenty of prerevolutionary buildings, most of which were renovated during the mid-1990s. The drawings and photographs at the **Shchusev Architecture Museum** ⑥⓪, however, can give you an idea of what the area used to look like. The entrance to this museum is just a few steps down **Staravagankovsky pereulok,** the first side street to your left. Return to ulitsa Vozdvizhenka and continue west, away from the Kremlin. Using the underpass, cross to the right-hand side of the street to get a closer look at the curious **Friendship House** ⑥①. Just beyond this eccentric mansion (continuing west) is the busy intersection of **Arbatskaya Ploshchad.** To your left as you emerge from the crowded underpass is the **Arbat;** to your right, **Novy Arbat.** In the distance to your far left stands a statue erected in the 1950s of the 19th-century Russian writer Nikolai Gogol. Go left to start your stroll down the Arbat, where you could easily spend a whole day browsing through the stores and stopping for a break in any of its numerous cafés.

The end of the Arbat is marked by one of the Gothic-style "Seven Sisters" skyscrapers that Stalin ordered built; this one is the Ministry of Foreign Affairs. Continuing down the Arbat, almost to the end, you'll come to the **Pushkin Apartment Museum** ⑥② and the **Bely Apartment Museum,** both on the left-hand side of the street. Once you've toured the museums and/or browsed in the gift shop (at the front), continue down the street towards McDonald's and take a left at Plotnikov pereulok, then a left onto Krivoarbatsky pereulok to take a look at the constructivist-style **Melnikov House,** which will be on the left-hand side at No. 10. Continue on Krivoarbatsky pereulok to reach the Arbat once again. You will now be standing in front of an impressive building with columns at No. 26. This is the **Vakhtangov Theater** ⑥④. Once you've surveyed the facade of the Vakhtangov and checked out its offerings for the season, turn off of Arbat onto Kaloshin pereulok then take a right on Sivtsev Vrazhek ulitsa to reach the **Herzen Museum.** Retrace your steps to the Vakhtangov and take a right onto narrow Bolshoi Nikolopeskovsky pereulok. Continue along the left-hand side of the street until you reach No. 7. Walk through the archway and head straight back to see **Spasso House,** the residence of the American Ambassador, and, to the garden's left, the lovely **Church of the Transfiguration on the Sands.**

The garden here has plenty of benches and is surrounded by tall trees making it a pleasant spot for a break. Retrace your path back to Bolshoi Nikolopeskovksky pereulok and turn left to continue. A few doors up, on the left-hand side of the street, you come to the **Alexander Scriabin Museum** ⑬. Continue up the street past the Scriabin Museum for approximately one block, then take the stairs in the narrow passageway between the two skyscrapers to reach the busy and noisy Novy Arbat.

To have a look at the street's full offerings, turn right as you come out onto Novy Arbat, and make your way back toward Arbat Square, where the walk began. As you elbow your way through the crowds of shoppers and vendors, you may want to keep your eye out in particular for the country's largest bookstore, **Dom Knigi,** on the left-hand side near the street's end. Past Dom Knigi, at the corner of Povarskaya ulitsa, on a tiny grassy knoll, stands a charming 17th-century church, the **Tserkov Simeona Stolpnika** ⑥⑤. To get to the **Lermontov Museum,** take a left on Povarskaya ulitsa then another left on Bolshaya Molchanovka ulitsa. The street will turn into Malaya Molchanovka and on the right-hand side is the museum. After a quick tour of the museum, continue down Malaya Molchanovka and take a right on Borisoglebsky pereulok to No. 6 where the **Tsvetaeva Museum** sits. After a look at the museum, take a left onto Borisoglebsky pereulok, which will deposit you back onto the Novy Arbat. Then continue walking towards Arbat Square. When you reach Arbat Square, turn left up Nikitsky bulvar. Inside the first courtyard to your left is a **Gogol statue** ⑥⑥ worth seeing.

TIMING

Without stops at any of the museums, this tour should only take about two hours to complete. If you're interested in doing some souvenir shopping, however, you'll want to allot an additional few hours to browse the numerous shops and street kiosks you'll see along the way. If you want to avoid crowds, do this tour on a weekday; the pedestrian zone on the Old Arbat, in particular, draws big crowds on the weekends. The museums included on this tour are all fairly small; you'll need no more than an hour in each of them.

Sights to See

⑬ **Alexander Scriabin Museum.** This charming, dusty house-museum is housed in the composer's last apartment, where he died of blood poisoning in 1915. Visitors here are rare, as Muscovites long ago apparently tired of their own museums, and foreign tourist groups are not usually brought here. The rooms are arranged and furnished just as they were when Scriabin lived here. Downstairs there is a concert hall where accomplished young musicians perform his music. If you want to hear a concert, you should call ahead to find out the current schedule; they are usually held on Wednesday and Friday evenings. ⊠ *11 Bolshoi Nikolopeskovsky per.,* ☎ *095/241–1901.* ⊡ *$1.* ☉ *Thurs., weekends 10–5; Wed., Fri. noon–7. Closed last Fri. of month. Metro: Arbatskaya.*

Andrei Bely Memorial Apartment. Right next door to the Pushkin Apartment Museum, this museum (now, unfortunately, undergoing major renovations and closed indefinitely) features artifacts from the life of the writer Andrei Bely (1889–1934), considered to be one of the great Russian Symbolists and most famous for his novel *Petersburg.* The keepers of the museum offer exhaustive tours of the apartment in Russian. If you only want to stop in for a short visit make sure to study the "Lines of Life" drawing on the wall of the first room, which shows the "energy" of Bely's life (the blue line in the middle) marked by dates and names of people he knew during specific times. The general entrance to the museum is through the souvenir shop. ⊠ *55 Arbat,* ☎ *095/241–7702. Metro: Smolenskaya.*

Arbatskaya Ploshchad (Arbat Square). This busy intersection is where ulitsa Vozdvizhenka crosses the Boulevard Ring. To reach the other side of the square, take the pedestrian underpass, which has become a bustling marketplace (before you head underground take a look behind you at the Khudozhesvenny Kino, which was opened in 1912— it's one of Russia's oldest movie theaters). The stairs are lined with women selling tiny kittens and puppies; their furry heads stick out from a bag or from underneath a coat, and they are nearly irresistible, so it's best not to stop and look. In the underpass itself, artists set up their easels, trying to entice passersby into having their portraits painted. And in spring and summer you'll find lots of impromptu flower vendors with the season's latest blooms (usually homegrown) for sale. When you emerge from the dizzying minimarket of the underpass, you will be in front of the Praga restaurant, a three-story Neoclassical building whose history dates back to before the Revolution. *Metro: Arbatskaya.*

Dom Knigi (House of Books). The country's largest bookstore has an English-language section, but you'll probably find a bigger selection at the individual vendors' stalls outside the store. Keep in mind that this bookstore still subscribes to the cashier system. To actually purchase a book or map involves some patience. First find what you want, then determine the price. Look above the counter where you found the book to see at which kassa you must pay, then wait in line at the cashier, tell her the price of your book and the number of the counter. She will issue a receipt upon payment, then you must return to the counter. Give the salesperson the receipt, which will allow you to receive your book. Whew! ⊠ *26 Novy Arbat,* ☎ *095/290–4507.* ☼ *Mon.–Fri. 10–7:30, Sat. 10–6. Closed Sun. Metro: Arbatskaya.*

NEED A
BREAK?

There are a plethora of cafés along the **Arbat** where you can take a break and have a drink. One particularly cheap and good one is **Délifrance** (⊠ 16 Arbat), a fast-food chain selling croissants with sweet and savory fillings as well as soups and sandwiches. The café sits next to the brightly tiled **Stena Mira** (Peace Wall). Incidentally the Peace Wall was made by a Berkeley, California artist in the 1980s. There is a similar wall in Berkeley, which the artist also made.

---

61 **Friendship House** (Dom Druzhby). One of Moscow's most interesting buildings—it looks like a Moorish castle—was built in the late 19th century by the architect V. A. Mazyrin for the wealthy (and eccentric) industrialist Morozov (Tolstoy mentions this home in his novel *Resurrection*). The interior is a veritable anthology of decorative styles, ranging from imitation Tudor to Classical Greek and Baroque. The building's name is a holdover from the Soviet days when Russians and foreigners were supposed to meet only in officially sanctioned places. Today its more popular name is Dom Evropy since the Federation Internationale Maisons de l'Europe is headquartered here. Unfortunately, the building is not open to the public. ⊠ *16 Vozdvizhenka ul. Metro: Arbatskaya.*

66 **Gogol statue.** This statue of a melancholy Gogol originally stood at the start of Gogol Boulevard but was moved to this courtyard and replaced by a more "upbeat" Gogol. The statue stands inside the first courtyard to your left, near the apartment building where the writer spent the last months of his life. The statue actually captures Gogol's sad disposition perfectly. He gazes downward, with his long, flowing cape draped over his shoulder, protecting him from the world. Gogol is probably best known in the West for his satirical drama *Revizor* (*The Inspector General*), about the unannounced visit of a government official to a provincial town. Characters from this and other Gogol works are engraved on the pedestal. ⊠ *7 Nikitsky bulvar. Metro: Arbatskaya.*

Herzen Museum. Ring the bell to be allowed to enter. Learn not only about the writer, philosopher, and revolutionary Alexander Herzen (1812–70), but also about life in the 1840s in Russia and the Decembrists who rebelled against czarist rule in 1825. Explanations in English are available. Don't forget to put on the slippers which the matrons of the museum will lend you. Herzen may be most famous for his novel *Who Is to Blame?* as well as his short stories *Magpie the Thief* and *Dr. Krupov.* ✉ *27 ul. Sivtsev Vrazhek,* ☎ *095/241–5859.* 🎫 *$1.* ⏲ *Tues., Thurs., and weekends 11–6; Wed. and Fri. 1–6. Closed Mon. and the last day of month. Metro: Arbatskaya.*

Khram Spasa Preobrazheniya na Peskhakh (Church of the Transfiguration on the Sands). Built in the 17th century, this elegant church was closed after the 1917 Revolution and turned into a cartoon-production studio. Like many churches throughout Russia, it has been returned to its original purpose and is being restored. The church is depicted in Vasily Polenov's well-known canvas *Moskovsky Dvornik* (*Moscow Courtyard*), which now hangs in the Tretyakov Gallery (☞ Gorky Park to the Tretyakov Gallery, *below*). ✉ *4 Spasapeskovsky per.,* ☎ *095/241–6203. Metro: Smolenskaya.*

Lermontov Museum. The museum is devoted to the Romantic poet and novelist Mikhail Lermontov (1814–41) and is located in the house where he lived with his grandparents from 1830 to 1832. The first room is where his grandmother slept. The second room is a small salon where Lermontov wrote poetry and drew pictures of his love interest. You can see these artifacts on the writing desk here. The third room is the big salon where the family entertained guests. Four small friezes depicting the War of 1812, as well as family portraits, hang on the walls. The fourth room contains remarkably good pen-and-ink drawings by Lermontov. The last room, which is reached by a steep staircase, is Lermontov's room complete with guitar on the bed, a sketch on an easel, and portraits of Pushkin and others he admired. ✉ *2 Malaya Molchanovka ul.,* ☎ *095/291–5298.* 🎫 *$1.* ⏲ *Thurs., weekends 11–6; Wed., Fri. 2–4. Metro: Arbatskaya.*

Melnikov House. This cylindrical concrete building was designed by the famous Constructivist architect Konstantin Melnikov in the late 1920s. The house is as remarkable outside with its wall-length windows as it is inside with its spiral staircases linking the three floors. Plans to open it as a museum are underway, but his son and daughter are the current occupants. ✉ *10 Krivoarbatsky per. Metro: Smolenskaya.*

(62) **Pushkin Apartment Museum.** The poet Alexander Pushkin lived here with his bride, Natalya Goncharova, for several months in 1831, right after they were married. The museum is currently closed for renovations for an undetermined amount of time, but it's worth stopping by to check if it's open since experts have recreated the original layout of the rooms and interior decoration. ✉ *53 Arbat,* ☎ *095/241–2674. Metro: Smolenskaya.*

(60) **Shchusev Architecture Museum.** This gallery has unofficially taken the place of the museum housed in an 18th-century Neoclassical mansion around the corner at 5 ul. Vozdvizhenka (now closed for renovation). The gallery features temporary exhibits covering contemporary and ancient Moscow architecture. Reach the gallery via Starovagankovsky pereulok (formerly Marx and Engels Street), the first side street to your left as you approach from the Kremlin. When you enter this narrow street, the first building on the right is an old, white-brick, two-story one that was the court apothecary in the 17th century. Turn right into its courtyard; the entrance to the museum is to your immediate left.

✉ *25 ul. Starovagonskaya,* ☎ *095/290–4855.* 🎫 *$1.* ☉ *Tues.–Fri. 10–6, weekends 10–4. Metro: Biblioteka Imeni Lenina.*

Spasso House. The yellow mansion behind the iron gate is the residence of the American ambassador. This Neoclassical mansion was built in the early 20th century for a wealthy merchant. What you first see is actually the back side of the building; it is much more impressive from the front. To get there, bear right at the small park, which is usually filled with neighborhood kids and their grandmothers. It's a pleasant place to take a break. *Spasopeskovskaya pl. Metro: Smolenskaya.*

65 **Tserkov Simeona Stolpnika** (Church of St. Simon the Stylite). The 17th-century church stands out above in stark contrast to the modern architecture dominating the area. During the reconstruction of New Arbat in the 1960s many old churches and buildings were destroyed, but this one was purposely left standing, as a "souvenir" of the past. For years it housed a conservation museum, but now it has been returned to the Orthodox Church and is active. Nothing remains, however, of the original interiors. ✉ *4 ul. Novy Arbat. Metro: Arbatskaya.*

Tsvetaeva Museum. Marina Tsvetaeva (1892–1941), the renowned poet, lived in an apartment on the second floor of this building from 1914 until 1922. Currently the building houses not only a museum dedicated to her but also a cultural center which arranges international literary evenings and annual conferences covering the Silver Age and Tsvetaeva. You must ring the bell to enter the building. The museum is on the second floor consists of six rooms spread over three floors. Guided tours in English are sometimes available. Although the rooms are decorated in the style of the early 1900s, they are not as they were when Tsvetaeva lived there. The poetry written on the wall in her bedroom has been re-created. The children's room features some stuffed animals which are to remind visitors of the real animals—a dog, a squirrel, and a turtle to name a few—Tsvetaeva kept in her home. This place is well worth a visit even if you're not familiar with Tsvetaeva's work as the staff is enthusiastic and the apartment is well representative of the period. ✉ *6 per. Borisoglebski,* ☎ *095/202–3543.* 🎫 *Free.* ☉ *Daily noon–5. Metro: Arbatskaya.*

64 **Vakhtangov Theater.** Named after Stanislavsky's pupil Evgeny Vakhtangov (1883–1922), this impressive structure is home to an excellent traditional theater. The gold statue of Princess Turandot and stone fountain to the right of the theater were created in honor of the 850th Anniversary of Moscow in 1997. ✉ *26 Arbat,* ☎ *095/241–1679,* 🖷 *095/241–2625. Metro: Arbatskaya.*

Moscow of the Nobles: From the Russian State Library to the Kropotkinsky District

This tour takes you through a picturesque old neighborhood still commonly known as the Kropotkinsky District. It takes its name from its main street, which was called Kropotkinskaya ulitsa under the Soviets but has now been returned to its 16th-century name: ulitsa Prechistenka. It is yet another ancient section of Moscow whose history dates back nearly to the foundation of the city itself. Almost none of its earliest architecture has survived, but this time the Soviets are not entirely to blame. The area suffered badly during the 1812 conflagration of Moscow, so most of its present buildings date to the postwar period of reconstruction, when Neoclassicism and the so-called Moscow Empire style were in vogue. Before the Revolution, the Kropotkinsky District was the favored residence of Moscow's old nobility, and it is along its thoroughfares that you'll find many of their mansions and homes, often called "nests of the gentry." It was also the heart of the literary and artistic community, and there were several famous literary salons here. Prince Kropotkin, for whom the street was named, compared it with the Saint-Germain quarter of Paris.

A Good Walk

Start at the **Russian State Library** at the bottom of ulitsa Vozdvizhenka, at the corner of Mokhovaya ulitsa (Moss Street, where moss used for wall caulking was once sold). To reach it, take the subway to the station called Biblioteki Imeni Lenina, which is directly beneath the Lenin Library. Walk south from the library along broad Mokhovaya ulitsa to reach **Borovitskaya Ploshchad** (Borovitsky Square), where several old streets converge. To your left, ulitsa Znamenka descends toward the **Borovitsky Gate** of the Kremlin and then continues across the Great Stone Bridge of the Moskva River; to your right it leads up a steep incline in the direction of the Arbat. Ulitsa Volkhonka lies straight ahead, leading into the Kropotkinsky district. On the hillock to your right, facing the Kremlin gates, is one of Moscow's most beautiful old mansions, the **Pashkov House.** Cross the square and continue straight onto **ulitsa Volkhonka,** which was first laid out sometime in the late 12th or early 13th century. It received its present name in the mid-18th century, in honor of Prince Volkhonsky, who lived in the mansion at No. 8. After a block you reach Moscow's museum of foreign paintings, the **Pushkin Museum of Fine Arts** ⑥⑦, in the middle of a small park to your right.

Just past the Pushkin Museum lies an entire block between Volkhonka and the quay of the Moskva River where the gigantic new **Cathedral of Christ Our Savior** ⑥⑧ stands. Just beyond the cathedral, ulitsa Volkhonka intersects with the Boulevard Ring. To your right, across the street, is the entrance to the Kropotkinskaya subway station. At this point ulitsa Volkhonka ends, splitting into ulitsa Prechistenka (to the right) and ulitsa Ostozhenka (to the left). A small park between the two streets holds a statue of Friedrich Engels and, behind it, a restored 17th-century boyars' chamber. Cross the square and walk up ulitsa Prechistenka. At the corner with Prechistensky pereulok stands the **Pushkin Memorial Museum** ⑥⑨. Not far from the Pushkin Museum, on the opposite side of the street, is the **Tolstoy Memorial Museum** ⑦⓪.

If you are feeling energetic and want to see more of the area's mansions, you can continue walking straight along ulitsa Prechistenka. Number 17, on the left-hand side, belonged to the poet Denis Davidov; and a bit farther, at No. 19, you find the former mansion of Prince Dolgoruky. Number 21 now houses the Russian Academy of Arts. The mansion originally belonged to Count Potemkin and then later to the wealthy merchant Savva Morozov, whose private art collection was one of the largest in Moscow (you can see it in the Pushkin Fine Arts Museum).

To make your way back toward the Kropotkinskaya subway station, turn left after you exit the Tolstoy museum onto Lopukhinsky pereulok, and walk one block to ulitsa Ostozhenka, which runs roughly parallel to ulitsa Prechistenka. Across the street and down to the right, you can see the remnants of the **Zachatievsky Monastery,** which is worth a closer look. Returning to ulitsa Ostozhenka, turn right, walk two blocks back in the direction of the new cathedral, and then turn right onto Vtoroi (2nd) Obydensky pereulok. Soon you come to the pretty St. Prophet Elijah Church, built in one day in 1702. Continue past the church and turn left onto Kursovoy pereulok. At the bottom of the street, to the right on Soymonovsky proyezd, is the steep-roofed Art Nouveau **Pertsov House.** From here continue around the Pertsov House by taking a left and then crossing the street to reach the **Cathedral of Christ Our Savior.** After touring the church walk toward the embankment of the Moskva River. The views from the Prechistenskaya naberezhnaya and its extension, the Kremlyovskaya naberezhnaya, are spectacular. This river walk takes you along the southern wall of the Kremlin to the Moskvoretsky Bridge. Walk out onto the bridge for one of the best views of St. Basil's Cathedral and Red Square. From here you could either walk back to Red Square (the nearest subway stop here is Ploshchad Revolutsii), or, if this walk has worn you out, continue across the bridge and settle into the comfy Café Kranzler at the Baltschug Kempinski Hotel for some coffee and incredibly rich pastry, or beer and sandwiches.

If, on the other hand, you decide you want to linger in the Kropotkinsky district, there are several interesting houses along ulitsa Ostozhenka that are worth seeing. The anarchist Bakunin was raised at No. 49. Number 38 was a governor's home in the 1700s; later it became a school, where one of its students was Ivan Goncharov, author of *Oblomov*; today it is the Institute of Foreign Languages. Next, No. 37 is a small rustic house where one of Russia's greatest writers, Ivan Turgenev, lived and worked. He set his famous story *Mu Mu* at this location. The private home of the Art Nouveau architect Kekushev, who was a contemporary of Shekhtel, stands at No. 21.

Leaving from the upper end of ulitsa Ostozhenka, you come out at the Park Kultury subway station. At the other end (back at Soymonovsky proyezd), is the Kropotkinskaya station.

TIMING

Taken at a leisurely pace, this walk could easily take three to four hours; add an extra half hour if you plan on taking the walk along the riverbank at the end. With stops at any of the various museums along this route, though, your exploration could easily expand to two days (the Pushkin Museum alone is worth a day). If you are definitely interested in visiting some of the museums in this district, do *not* do this tour on a Monday, as most of the museums are closed that day.

Sights to See

68 **Cathedral of Christ Our Savior.** This cathedral carries an amazing tale of destruction and reconstruction. Built between 1839 and 1883 as a memorial to the Russian troops who fell in the War of 1812 with Napoléon, the cathedral was the largest single structure in Moscow and dominated the city's skyline. It had taken almost 50 years to build what only a few hours would destroy. On December 5, 1931, the cathedral was blown up. Under Stalin, the site had been designated for a mammoth new "Palace of Soviets," intended to replace the Kremlin as the seat of the Soviet government. Plans called for topping the 1,378-ft structure with a 300-ft statue of Lenin, who—had the plans ever materialized—would have spent more time above the clouds than in plain view. World War II delayed construction, and the entire project was scrapped when it was discovered that the land along the embankment was too damp to support such a heavy structure.

The site lay empty and abandoned until 1958, when the **Moscow Pool,** one of the world's largest outdoor swimming pools, was built. Divided into several sections, for training, competition, diving, and public swimming, it was heated and kept open all year long, even in the coldest days of winter. The pool was connected to the locker rooms by covered tunnels, and you could reach it by swimming through them. The pool was dismantled in 1994. Then—in perhaps one of architectural history's stranger twists—the cathedral was resurrected in 1997 from the ruins at a cost of more than $150 million. Today the giant cathedral is complete, but interior construction will take a few more years. As this church proves, everything has come full circle in the post-perestroika and -glasnost years. ✉ *ul. Volkhonka. Metro: Kropotkinskaya.*

Pashkov House. Designed by Vasily Bazhenov, one of Russia's greatest architects, the mansion was erected in 1784–86 for the wealthy Pashkov family. The central building is topped by a round belvedere and flanked by two service wings. In the 19th century it housed the Rumyantsev collection of art and rare manuscripts. Following the 1917 revolution, this museum was closed, the art collection was transferred to the Hermitage and Pushkin museums of fine art, and the manuscripts were donated to the Lenin Library. The building now belongs to the Russian State Library and is off-limits to the general public. ✉ *Mokhovaya ul. and ul. Znamenka. Metro: Borovitskaya.*

Pertsov House. One of the finest examples of Moscow Art Nouveau was built in 1905–07 by the architects Schnaubert and Zhukov. The facade of the steep-roofed and angled building is covered in colorful mosaics. Walk all the way to its end, coming out at the river, and straight across you'll see a large, redbrick compound. This is the **Red October candy factory.** Look to your left, where the buildings of the Kremlin line the distance, the golden cupolas of its churches all agleam. Look to the right and see the behemoth Peter the Great statue (☞ Gorky Park to the Tretyakov Gallery, *below*). ✉ *Soymonovsky per. and Kropotkinskaya nab. Metro: Kropotkinskaya.*

69 **Pushkin Memorial Museum.** Pushkin never lived here and probably never even visited this fine yellow mansion, built in the 19th century by the architect Afansey Grigoriev, so it is a rather dry museum, full of manuscripts and letters. The museum is currently closed for renovations for the near future. The museum is closed for renovations for the immediate future. ✉ *12 ul. Prechistenka,* ☎ *095/202–7998.*

★ **67** **Pushkin Museum of Fine Arts.** Famous for its Gauguin, Cézanne, and Picasso paintings, this museum was founded by Ivan Vladimirovich Tsvetayev (1847–1913) of Moscow University, father of poet Marina Tsvetaeva (☞ Arbat, Old and New, *above*). The museum was originally established as a teaching aid for art students, which explains why a large sector of its collection is made up of copies. The present building dates from 1895 to 1912 and was first known as the Alexander III Museum. It was renamed the Pushkin Museum in 1937, on the centennial of the Russian poet's death.

The first-floor exhibit halls contain a fine collection of ancient Egyptian art (Hall 1); Greece and Rome are well represented, though mostly by copies (Room 7). The Italian school from the 15th century (Room 5) is represented by Botticelli's *The Annunciation,* Tomaso's *The Assassination of Caesar,* Guardi's *Alexander the Great at the Body of the Persian King Darius,* and Sano di Pietro's *The Beheading of John the Baptist,* among others. When you reach the Dutch School of the 17th Century (Hall 10), look for Rembrandt's *Portrait of an Old Woman,* whose subject may have been the artist's sister-in-law. Flemish and Spanish art from the 17th century are also well represented, with paintings by Murillo, Rubens, and Van Dyck (Hall 11).

On the museum's second floor you are treated to a stunning collection of Impressionist, Postimpressionist, and Modern art. There are many fine canvases by Picasso (Hall 17), including several from his "blue" period. The same hall contains fascinating works by Henri Rousseau, including *Jaguar Attacking a Horse.* French Postimpressionism is represented by Cézanne, Gauguin, and Matisse. There are a total of 10 works by Gauguin, mainly in Hall 18, where you also find Cézanne's

Pierrot and *Harlequin*. The museum owns several works by Matisse (Hall 21), although often they are not all on display. In the same hall you find the poignant *Landscape at Auvers After the Rain* by Vincent van Gogh. The collection ends at Hall 23, where you find works by Degas, Renoir, and Monet, including Monet's *Rouen Cathedral at Sunset*. ✉ *12 ul. Volkhonka,* ☎ *095/203–7998 or 095/203–9578.* 🎟 *$6.* ⊘ *Tues.–Sun. 10–7. Metro: Kropotinskaya.*

Russian State Library. Still called Biblioteka Imeni Lenina, or the Lenin Library, it is Russia's largest, with more than 30 million books and manuscripts. The main facade is adorned with bronze busts of famous writers and scientists. The portico, supported by square black pillars, is approached by a wide ceremonial staircase. The modern building was built between 1928 and 1940. A 12-ft (3.7-meter) statue of the great Russian novelist Dostoyevsky, author of such literary classics as *Crime and Punishment* and *The Brothers Karamazov,* was erected in front of the library in 1997 in honor of the 850th anniversary of Moscow. Dostoyevsky, sculpted by Alexander Rukavishnikov, sits where the Soviets once considered erecting a giant Lenin head. ✉ *3 ul. Vozdvizhenka,* ☎ *095/202–5790.* ⊘ *Mon.–Sat. 9–9. Metro: Biblioteki Imeni Lenina.*

⓻ Tolstoy Memorial Museum. Yet another creation by architect Afanasey Grigoriev (housing yet another literary museum), this museum opened in 1920. The mansion, a fine example of the Moscow Empire style, belonged to the minor poet Lopukhin, a distant relative of Tolstoy's. The exhibit halls contain a rich collection of manuscripts and photographs of Tolstoy and his family, as well as pictures and paintings of Tolstoy's Moscow. Even if you don't speak Russian, you can read the writer's life story through the photographs, and in each room there is a typed handout in English to help explain its holdings. If you decide to visit, look for the picture of 19th-century Moscow in the second hall (on the left-hand wall). The huge cathedral taking up more than half the photograph is the Cathedral of Christ Our Savior—the one once replaced by the Moskva swimming pool. ✉ *11 ul. Prechistenka,* ☎ *095/201–3811.* 🎟 *$2.* ⊘ *Tues.–Sun. 11–5:30. Closed last Fri. of month. Metro: Kropotkinskaya.*

Zachatievsky Monastery (Convent of the Conception). Founded in the 16th century, this is the oldest structure in the district, although nothing remains of the original buildings. Only the 17th-century redbrick Gate Church survives, and even that is in catastrophic condition. It was built by the last surviving son of Ivan the Terrible, in what amounted to a plea to God for an heir (hence the monastery's name). He and his wife failed to have a son, however, and Boris Godunov became the next Russian leader. ✉ *Zachatievsky per. Metro: Kropotkinskaya.*

Gorky Park to the Tretyakov Gallery

Gorky Park, popularized by Martin Cruz Smith's cold war novel of the same name, is situated along the right bank of the Moskva River, just beyond Krymsky Most (Crimea Bridge). The highlights of this area are Moscow's famous Russian Art Museum, the Tretyakov Gallery, Bolshaya Ordinka ulitsa lined with Russian Orthodox churches, and the park itself and its various surrounding sites of interest.

A Good Walk

Gorky Park is between two major subway stops—the Oktyabrskaya station on the orange and circle lines and the Park Kultury station on the red and circle lines. The walk begins at the Park Kultury stop, but if your only destination is Gorky Park, the Oktyabrskaya station is closer.

Leave the Park Kultury subway station, turn right (as you face the bridge ahead) and walk along Komsomolsky Prospekt one long block. When you reach the corner with ulitsa Lva Tolstovo (Leo Tolstoy Street) you will see the striking church **Tserkov Nikoly v Khamovnikakh** ⑦; turn right here to go around to the church's entrance, which is on the side. The next stop is the **Tolstoy House Estate Museum** ⑫, the novelist's winter home. As you start your walk up the street named in his honor, look for an old white-stone building with a wood-shingled roof, on your right. Tolstoy's estate is a bit farther up the street, on the left-hand side, behind a long, red-wood fence.

Retracing your steps to the Park Kultury subway stop, go right when you reach the corner with busy Zubovsky bulvar, over the Krymsky most. The bridge spans the Moskva River, and in nice weather it offers a fine vantage point. Visitors no doubt will feel a surge of excitement looking at the flashing signs of Gorky Park and its attractions beckoning from below. If you want to save on walking, you can take either trolleybus 10 or B (both stop on Zubovsky bulvar, right in front of the subway entrance); they will drop you off directly in front of the main entrance to **Gorky Park** ⑬. Directly across the street is the **House of Artists** ⑭, with three floors of exhibit halls and a sculpture garden. After looking at the House of Artists, walk away from the bridge on Krymsky Val ulitsa to Kaluzhskaya Ploshchad, which features a giant Lenin statue. Bear left of the statue and continue walking on Zhitnaya ulitsa. After a block you will come to a pedestrian underpass. Descend into the underpass and bear left and then take the first left. Ascend the stairs and you will be on Bolshaya Ordinka ulitsa. The first stop is **Tserkov Ekaterini,** which sits on the corner of Bolshaya Ordinka and Pogorelsky pereulok. After a quick look, continue on Pogorelsky pereulok and take a right on Shchetininksky pereulok. At No. 10 is the **Tropinin Museum** with a great collection of serf art. Continue on Shchetininksky pereulok and take a right on pearvy (1st) Kazachy pereulok, then a right back onto Bolshaya Ordinka ulitsa. Continue up the street to No. 24, the **Marfo-Mariinskaya Obitel.** Unfortunately, you can only peek through the gates to get a glimpse of the church. Cross the street at the next crosswalk to No. 27 to see **Tserkov Nikoly v Pyzhakh.** Continue up Bolshaya Ordinka ulitsa and take a right on Klimentovsky pereulok. Push your way through the throngs exiting the metro to the middle of the small alleyway to view the now dilapidated but still impressive Baroque **Tservkov Klimenta.** Retrace your steps to Bolshaya Ordinka ulitsa and cross the street and take a right. A few steps away is the yellow **Tserkov Bogomateri Vsekh Skorbyashchikh Radosti.** From the courtyard of the church take a left onto Bolshaya Ordinka ulitsa. St. Basil's (☞ Kremlin and Red Square, *above*) floats on the horizon as you walk up the street. From here you will walk up Bolshaya Ordnika to the river where you should take a right. Continue along the riverbank until Lavrushky pereulok, where you will take a left. At No. 12 on this pedestrian alleyway is the famous Russian art museum, the **Tretyakov Art Gallery** ⑮. You can see the spires of the Moscow Baroque **Tserkov Voskreseniya v Kadashakh** to your left as you head to the gallery. From the Tretyakov gallery retrace your steps to the river and cross the pedestrian bridge. From here you can see the behemoth **Peter the Great statue.** The gardens on the other side of the bridge are a perfect spot for a well-deserved break. The statue in the park is a Soviet-era sculpture of the famous Russian painter Ilya Repin, whose paintings hang in the Tretyakov Art Gallery. To get back to the center you can continue walking to the left of the statue through the garden. Crossing the street to your right you will see a bridge that stretches to the Kremlin. Great views can be had from here. The Cathedral of Christ Our Savior (☞ Noble Moscow: From the Russian State Library to the Kropotkinsky District, *above*) is to the left and the Kremlin is to the right.

TIMING

This tour covers a fair amount of territory, and if you do it all on foot, it could easily take four to five hours just to see the sights. If you plan on touring the Tolstoy House Museum, add another two hours. If you want to tour the Tretyakov Gallery, it's probably best to plan that visit separately. A full exploration of Gorky Park could also easily take an afternoon. Note that both the Tolstoy House Museum and the Tretyakov are closed on Mondays.

Sights to See

🖐 ⑦ **Gorky Park.** Muscovites usually refer to it as Park Kultury (Park of Culture); its official title is actually the Central Park of Culture and Leisure. The park was laid out in 1928 and covers an area of 275 acres. It is definitely the city's most popular all-around recreation center, and in summer, especially on weekends, it is crowded with children and adults enjoying its many attractions. The park's green expanse is dominated by a giant Ferris wheel; if you're brave enough to ride it, you'll be rewarded with great views of the city; for the even braver, there is also a roller coaster. Stretching along the riverside, the park includes the Neskuchny Sad (Happy Garden) and the Zelyony Theater (Green Theater), an open-air theater with seating for 10,000. The park has a boating pond, a fairground, sports grounds, a rock club, and numerous stand-up cafés. In summer, boats leave from the pier for excursions along the Moskva River, and in winter the ponds are transformed into skating rinks. ⊠ *9 Krymsky Val.* ▨ *$1.50.* ⊙ *Apr.–Sept., daily 9–midnight; Oct.–Mar., daily 10–10. Metro: Oktyabrskaya.*

⑦ **House of Artists.** This is a huge, modern building that also houses a branch of the Tretyakov Gallery. The entrance facing the street leads to the exhibit halls of the Artists' Union, where union members display their work, so this is a spot where you can browse for a sketch or watercolor to take home with you. The extensive exhibit halls are spread out on three floors. Next door to the House of Artists is the **Art Park** where contemporary sculpture and old statues of Soviet dignitaries stand side by side. It's a pleasant place for a stroll. ⊠ *10 Krymsky Val,* ☎ *095/238–9843.* ▨ *Free.* ⊙ *Tues.–Sun. 11–7. Metro: Park Kultury.*

Marfo-Mariinskaya Obitel (Martha and Mary Convent). The Martha and Mary Convent was opened in 1909 and is most noted for its white Church of the Intercession of the Virgin Mary—open for services on Sunday at 8:30 AM, but most days only visible when glimpsed through an arch in the convent's white-stone wall. The religious order of the convent was relocated across the street in 1992. ⊠ *24 Bolshaya Ordinka ul. Metro: Dobrininskaya.*

New Tretyakov Gallery. If you're looking for the branch of the Tretyakov Art Gallery familiarly known as the "New Branch," go around to the side entrance (☞ Tretyakov Art Gallery, *below*). This annex came into being when the original Tretyakov Gallery had to be closed for restoration work (from 1986 to 1995). From this time on, it has also been the location where the museum displays its collection of art created since the 1920s, encompassing pieces, some previously outlawed, from the Socialist Realist, Modern, and Postmodern periods. ⊠ *10 Krymsky Val (side entrance, on the right),* ☎ *095/230–1116 or 095/230–7788.* ▨ *$6.* ⊙ *Tues.–Sun. 10–7. Metro: Park Kultury.*

Peter the Great Statue. The enormous statue of the czar stands atop a base made in the form of a miniature ship. He is holding the steering wheel of a ship, symbolizing his role as the founder of the Russian naval force in the 1700s. The statue, measuring 90 ft. high, has been a source of controversy since construction started on it in 1996. Most Muscovites agree that the statue is not only an eyesore, but has no place in Moscow since Peter the Great was the one who moved the capital of Russia from Moscow to St. Petersburg. After citizens complained, a board of art experts was formed to decide if the statue would stay. They decided to keep it. The decision was made mostly in light of the fact that erecting the statue cost $20 million and dismantling it would cost half that amount. There is now a city ordinance that statues and public monuments must be approved by a board of experts before construction starts. When you finally set on eyes on it you will probably understand why common nicknames for it are Cyclops and Gulliver. The colossal statue is so tall that a red light had to be put on its head to warn planes. ⊠ *Krymskaya nab. Metro: Park Kultury.*

72 **Tolstoy House Estate Museum.** Tolstoy bought the house in 1882, at the age of 54, and spent nine winters here with his family, until 1901. In summer he preferred his country estate in Yasnaya Polyana. The years here were not particularly happy ones. By this time Tolstoy had already experienced his "religious conversion," which prompted him to disown his earlier great novels, including *War and Peace* and *Anna Karenina*. His conversion sparked a feud among his own family members, which manifested itself even at the dining table: Tolstoy's wife, Sofia Andreevna, would sit at one end with the sons, while the writer would sit with his daughters at the opposite end.

The ground floor has several of the children's bedrooms and the nursery where Tolstoy's seven-year-old son died of scarlet fever in 1895, a tragedy that haunted the writer for the rest of his life. Also here are the dining rooms and kitchen, as well as the Tolstoys' bedroom, in which you can see the small desk used by his wife to meticulously copy all of her husband's manuscripts by hand.

Upstairs, you will find the Tolstoys' receiving room, where they held small parties and entertained guests, who included most of the leading figures of their day. The grand piano in the corner was played by such greats as Rachmaninoff and Rimsky-Korsakov. When in this room, you should ask the attendant to play the enchanting recording of Tolstoy greeting a group of schoolchildren, followed by a piano composition written and played by him. Also on this floor is an Oriental den and the writer's study, where he wrote his last novel, *Resurrection.*

Although electric lighting and running water were available at the time to the lesser nobility, Tolstoy chose to forgo both, believing it better to live simply. The museum honors his desire and shows the house as it was when he lived there. Tickets to the museum are sold in the administrative building to the far back left. Inside the museum, each room has signs in English explaining its significance and contents, but you might want to consider a guided tour (which must be booked in advance). ⊠ *9 ul. Lva Tolstovo,* ☎ *095/246–9444.* ⊠ *$3.50.* ☉ *Apr.–Sept., Tues.–Sun. 10–6; Oct.–Mar., 10–4. Closed last Fri. of month. Metro: Park Kultury.*

NEED A BREAK? Delicious Georgian delights are waiting for you at **Guriya** (⊠ 7/3 Komsomolsky Prospekt, side entrance, on the right), ☎ 095/246–0738), a longtime favorite of expats and locals alike for its cheap prices, down-home style, and authentic food. Be ready to wait up to an hour if you visit during peak meal times.

★ **75** **Tretyakov Art Gallery.** The Tretyakov Gallery—now often called the "Old Tretyakov" in light of the annex, the "New Tretyakov" (☞

above)— is the repository of some of the world's greatest masterpieces of Russian art. Officially opened in 1892 as a public state museum, its origins predate that by more than 35 years, thanks to its remarkable philanthropic and altruistic genesis. In the mid-1800s, a successful young Moscow industrialist, Pavel Mikhailovich Tretyakov, was determined to amass a collection of national art that would be worthy of a museum of fine arts for the entire country. In pursuit of this high-minded goal, he began to purchase paintings, drawings, and sculpture, adjudged both on high artistic merit and on their place within the various important canons of their time. For the most part undeterred by critics' disapproval and arbiters of popular taste, he became one of the—if not *the*—era's most valued patrons of the arts, with honor and gratitude conferred upon him yet to this day.

Up until six years before his death, Tretyakov maintained his enormous collection as a private one, but allowed virtually unlimited free access to the public. In 1892, he donated it all to the Moscow city government, along with a small inheritance of other fine works collected by his brother Sergei. The holdings have been continuously increased by subsequent state acquisitions, including the nationalization of privately owned pieces after the Communist Revolution.

A visitor to the museum today will find works spanning the 11th to the 20th century, from sacred icons to stunning portrait and landscape art to the famous Russian Realists' paintings that culminated in the Wanderers' Group to the splendid creations of Russian Symbolism, Impressionism, and Art Nouveau, virtually all of them known far less intimately outside of Russia than should be the case for a collection of such critical importance.

Among the many delights to be found are icons painted by the master Andrei Rublyev, including his celebrated *The Trinity*; also featured are icons of his disciples, Daniel Chorny among them, as well as some of the earliest icons to reach ancient Kievan Rus', such as *The Virgin of Vladimir,* brought from Byzantium. The first floor, which houses the icon collection, is also where drawings and watercolors from the 18th to the 20th centuries are hung.

The second floor holds 18th-, 19th-, and 20th-century painting and sculpture and is where indefatigable Russian art lovers will find their aesthetic longings satisfied several times over. A series of halls of 18th-century portraits, including particularly fine works by Dmitri Levitsky, act as a time machine into the country's noble past, followed by rooms filled with the historical painting of the next century, embodying the burgeoning movements of romanticism and naturalism in such gems of landscape painting as Silvester Shchedrin's *Aqueduct at Tivoli* and Mikhail Lebedev's *Path in Albano* and *In the Park.* Other favorite pieces to look for are Bryullov's *The Last Day of Pompeii,* Ivanov's *Appearance of Christ to the People,* and Orest Kiprensky's well-known *Portrait of the Poet Alexander Pushkin.*

It may be the rich array of works completed after 1850, however, that will please museum goers the most, for it comprises a selection of pieces from each of the Russian masters, sometimes of their best works. Hanging in the gallery are paintings by Nikolai Ge (*Peter the Great Interrogating the Tsarevich Alexei*), Vasily Perov (*Portrait of Fyodor Dostoyevsky*), Vasily Polenov (*Grandmother's Garden*), Viktor Vasnetsov (*After Prince Igor's Battle with the Polovtsy*), and many others. Several canvases of the beloved Ivan Shishkin, with their depictions of Russian fields and forests, including *Morning in the Pine Forest,* of three bear cubs cavorting, fill one room, and of course a number by the equally popular Ilya Repin, whose most famous painting, *The Volga Boatmen,* also bedecks the walls. Later works, done near the century's end, range from an entire room devoted to the Symbolist Mikhail Vrubel (*The Princess Bride, Demon Seated*) to Nestorov's glowing *Vision of the Youth Bartholomew,* the boy who would become St. Sergius, founder of the monastery Sergeyev-Posad, to the magical pieces by Valentin Serov (*Girl with Peaches, Girl in Sunlight*). Before you leave, look for the compositions, of which there are a handful, done just before the revolution by Chagall, Kandinsky, and Malevich, and the stunning *Red Horse Swimming 1912* by Kuzma Petrov-Vodkin.

When you leave the gallery, pause a moment to look back on the building itself, which is quite compelling. Tretyakov's original home, where the first collection was kept, still forms a part of the gallery. As the demands of a growing collection required additional space, the house was continuously enlarged, with finally an entire annex built to function as the gallery. In 1900, when there was no longer a family living in the house, the artist Viktor Vasnetsov undertook to create the wonderful facade the gallery now carries, and more space was later added. Closed entirely in the years 1986 to 1995 for badly needed restoration (mostly inside), new wings and full reconstruction of the main one have given the museum a fresh loveliness meant to carry it well into the next century. Keep in mind that the ticket office closes at 6:30 PM. ⊠ *12 Lavrushinsky per.,* ☎ *095/ 230–7788 or 095/231–1362.* 🎟 *$7.* ☉ *Tues.–Sun. 10–8.*

Tropinin Museum. Vasily Tropinin was a serf artist in the late 18th century and early 19th century. The museum collection is home to miniatures and portraits by Tropinin and his contemporaries. The pretty period rooms and permanent painting collection offer a very interesting peek into a Moscow now long gone. ⊠ *10 Shchetininksky per.,* ☎ *095/957– 7857.* 🎟 *$1.25.* ☉ *Mon., Tues., and Thurs. 12–6:30; weekends 10– 6:30. Closed last day of month. Metro: Dobrininskaya.*

Tserkov Bogomateri Vsekh Skorbyashchikh Radosti (Church of the Virgin of All Sorrows). Designed by Osip Bove and built in 1828–35, this yellow Neoclassical-era church is an excellent example of the Empire style popular in the early 19th century. The original church, which burnt down in the fire of 1812, was built in 1783–91. The interior, filled with icons and gold, is nothing earth-shattering, but is good for getting the feel of a typical working church. Sunday services are at 10 AM, but the church is usually open. ⊠ *20 Bolshaya Ordinka ul. Metro: Tretyakovskaya.*

Tserkov Ekaterini (St. Catherine's Church). The white Classical-style church which stands here today was designed by Karl Blank and commissioned by Catherine the Great in 1763. The church was completed in 1767. The interior is in a bad state, but you can still make out some frescoes. St. Catherine's is a working church—Sunday service is at 10 AM, but the church is usually open to considerate wanderers. ⊠ *60 Bolshaya Ordinka ul. Metro: Dobrininskaya.*

Tservkov Klimenta (St. Clement's Church). Begun in 1743 and designed by Pietro Antonio Trezzini, the construction of this church took three decades to complete. Today it sits, in moldering glory, completely abandoned and derelict; however, its star-studded cupolas and redbrick Baroque building are still impressive. ⊠ *26 Klimentovsky per. Metro: Tretyakovskaya.*

❼ **Tserkov Nikoly v Khamovnikakh** (Church of St. Nicholas of the Weavers). The church, which remained open throughout the years of Communist government, is wonderfully preserved. Its elegant bell tower is particularly impressive. Built in 1679–82 and topped by five gilded domes, the saucy colorfulness of its orange and green trim against its perfectly white facade makes it look like a frosted ginger-bread house. In fact, the design was actually meant to suggest a festive piece of woven cloth, for it was the weavers who settled in considerable numbers in this quarter in the 17th century who commissioned the building of this church. Morning and evening services are held daily, and the church, with its wealth of icons, is as handsome inside as out. ⊠ *Komsomolsky Prospekt and ul. Lva Tolstovo. Metro: Park Kultury.*

Tserkov Nikoly v Pyzhakh (Church of St. Nicholas in Pyzhi). Currently undergoing reconstruction, St. Nicholas' Church is an ornate, bright white building with five gold cupolas, dating from 1670. ⊠ *10 Shchetininksky per.,* ☎ *095/231–3742.* ☉ *Mon., Tues., and Thurs. 12–6:30; weekends 10–6:30. Metro: Dobrininskaya.*

Tserkov Voskreseniya v Kadashakh (Church of the Resurrection in Kadosh). It's best to view this colorful church from far away as a high fence surrounds it. The church, which is currently undergoing a very slow renovation process, is an excellent example of the Moscow Baroque style and was built in 1687. ⊠ *7 Vtoroi Kadshovksy per. Metro: Tretyakovskaya.*

Donskoy and Novodevichy Monasteries

Novodevichy Monastyr (New Maiden's Convent) is one of Moscow's finest and best-preserved ensembles of 16th- and 17th-century Russian architecture. There is much to see here. The monastery is interesting not only for its impressive cathedral and charming churches but also for the dramatic chapters of Russian history that have been played out within its walls. It stands in a wooded section bordering a small pond, making this a particularly pleasant place for an afternoon stroll. Although it is no longer a functioning convent, one of its churches is open for services. After the Bolshevik Revolution, the convent was made part of the History Museum. Its exhibits boast rare and ancient Russian paintings, both ecclesiastical and secular, woodwork and ceramics, and fabrics and embroidery. There is also a large collection of illuminated and illustrated books, decorated with gold, silver, and jewels. Attached to the monastery is a fascinating cemetery where some of Russia's greatest literary, military, and political figures are buried. A few Metro stops away is another fabled religious institution, the Donskoy Monastery, founded in the 16th century by Boris Godunov, with a cathedral commissioned a century later by the Regent Sophia, Peter the Great's sister.

A Good Walk

To reach the **Novodevichy Monastyr,** take the subway to the Sportivnaya station. Leave the subway via the stadium exit, and then follow ulitsa Frunzensky Val to your right. It will lead you through a small park and eventually to the southeast corner of the monastery. When you come out onto Luzhnetsky proyezd, you will see the monastery's whitewashed walls to your right. Turning right, walk up the street; the main entrance is at the other end, off Bolshaya Pirogovskaya ulitsa.

Leaving the monastery, retrace your steps, walking back down Luzhnetsky proyezd to the right. The entrance to the **cemetery** is marked by a pair of green gates. Unless you have relatives buried here, you have to buy tickets to enter; tickets are sold in the small wooden kiosk directly across the street. You can also request a tour in English from the cemetery's excursion bureau, which we highly recommend. After touring the monastery and cemetery, retrace your steps to the Sportivnaya metro station, ride up two stops to Park Kultury station, switch to the

Ring line (your only choice for a transfer), ride one stop to Oktyabrskaya station, then go south on one stop to Shabolovskaya to the
Donskoy Monastyr.

TIMING
Reserve an entire day to explore Novodevichy Convent and Donskoy
Monastery. In fact, there is so much to see at these beautiful and historic sites, two full days might be warranted. Note that it will take you
about 45 minutes travel time each way from downtown Moscow.

Sights to See

Donskoy Monastyr. The 16th-century Donskoy Monastery is a fascinating memorial to Russian architecture and art. From 1934 to 1992,
a branch of the Shchusev Architecture Museum, keeping architectural
details of churches, monasteries, and public buildings destroyed under
the Soviets, was located—more or less secretly—inside its walls. Today
the monastery is once again functioning as a religious institution, and
the museum is slowly removing its exhibits from inside the churches.
But the bits and pieces of demolished churches and monuments remain,
forming a graveyard of destroyed architecture from Russia's past. ⊠
*1 Donskaya pl., ☎ 095/952–1646. ▣ $3. ☉ Daily 7–7. Metro:
Shabolovskaya.*

The monastery is situated in a secluded, wooded area in the southwest
section of Moscow. You can reach it by taking the subway to the
Shabolovskaya station. When you exit the subway, turn right and walk
one block to Donskaya ulitsa. Turn right again and follow the street
until you see the copper-topped domes of the monastery's churches above
the trees to your left. Follow the path along the redbrick fortification
wall until you reach the main entrance on the other side.

The monastery grounds are surrounded by a high defensive wall with
12 towers. Founded in the late 16th century, it was the last of the defense fortifications to be built around Moscow. It is situated on the site
where, in 1591, the Russian army stood waiting for an impending attack from Tatar troops grouped on the opposite side of the river. According to legend, the Russians awoke one morning to find the Tatars
gone. Their sudden retreat was considered a miracle, and regent Boris
Godunov ordered a monastery built to commemorate the miraculous
victory. Of course, it didn't happen quite like that, but historians confirm that the Tatars did retreat after only minor skirmishes, which is
difficult to explain. Never again would they come so close to Moscow.
The victory was attributed to the icon of the Virgin of the Don that
Prince Dimitry Donskoy had supposedly carried previously, during his
campaign in 1380 (in which the Russians won their first decisive victory against the Tatars). The monastery was named in honor of the
wonder-working icon.

When you enter through the western gates, an icon of the Mother of
the Don looks down on you from above the entrance to the imposing
New Cathedral. The brick cathedral was built in the late 17th century
by Peter the Great's sister, Sophia. It has been under restoration for
decades; services are held in the gallery surrounding the church, where
the architectural exhibits were once housed. The smaller, **Old Cathedral** stands to the right of the New Cathedral. The attractive red
church with white trim was built in 1591–93, during the reign of Boris
Godunov. It is open for services.

One of the most fascinating sections of the monastery is its graveyard,
where you will find many fine examples of memorial art. After the plaque
swept through Moscow in 1771, Catherine the Great forbade any
more burials in the city center. The Donskoy Monastery, at that time

on the city's outskirts, became a fashionable burial place for the well-to-do. The small **Church of the Archangel** built against the fortification wall on the far right was the private chapel and crypt of the prominent Golitsyn family (original owners of the Arkangelskoye estate). Many leading intellectuals, politicians, and aristocrats were buried here in the 18th, 19th, and 20th centuries.

Novodevichy Kladbishche (Cemetery). The Novodevichy contains a fascinating collection of memorial art, but it is difficult for non-Russian speakers to identify the graves. You may wonder how a cemetery could be controversial, but this one was. For more than a generation, the Novodevichy Cemetery was closed to the general public, in large part because the controversial Nikita Khrushchev is buried here, rather than on Red Square, like other Soviet leaders. Thanks to glasnost, the cemetery was reopened in 1987, and now anyone is welcome to visit its grounds, which are not unlike those of Père Lachaise in Paris in the scope of national luminaries from all walks of life for whom it is a final resting place.

Khrushchev's grave is near the rear of the cemetery, at the end of a long tree-lined walkway. If you can't find it, any of the *babushki* (a colloquial term used throughout Russia to refer to museum caretakers, often hearty grandmothers who wear babushki head coverings) will point out the way. They will usually reflect their opinion of him in the way they gesture, for they almost certainly will not speak English. The memorial consists of a stark black-and-white slab, with a curvilinear border marking the separation. The contrast of black and white symbolizes the contradictions of his reign. It caused a great furor of objection among the Soviet hierarchy when it was unveiled. The memorial was designed by the artist Ernest Neizvestny, himself a controversial figure. In the 1960s Khrushchev visited an exhibit of contemporary art that included some of Neizvestny's works. Khrushchev dismissed Neizvestny's contributions as "filth," and asked the name of their artist. When Neizvestny (which means "Unknown") answered, Khrushchev scornfully said that the USSR had no need for artists with such names. To this the artist replied, "In front of my work, I am the Premier." Considering the times, it was a brave thing to say to the leader of the Soviet Union. Neizvestny eventually joined the ranks of the emigré artists; he now lives in the United States.

Many of those buried in the cemetery were war casualties in 1941 and 1942. The memorials often include a lifelike portrait or a photograph of the person being remembered, or convey a scene from that person's life. Flowers and photographs of the dead are at almost all the graves. Among the memorials you might want to look for are those to the composers Prokofiev and Scriabin and the writers Chekhov, Gogol, Bulgakov, and Mayakovsky. Chekhov's grave is decorated with the trademark seagull of the Moscow Art Theater, the first to successfully produce his plays. Along the right-hand wall (the southwest wall of the monastery) you will find a memorial of a crash of a huge Soviet aircraft where all the crew members are interred. The grave of Stalin's wife, Nadezhda Aliluyeva, is marked by a simple tombstone with a bust of this poor woman. She supposedly committed suicide, and many hold Stalin responsible for her death. Theodore Chaliapin, the opera singer who was stripped of his Soviet citizenship while on tour in France in the 1920s, is also buried here. His remains were transferred here in 1984. His grave is marked by a marvelous lifelike representation of him that conveys the fervor and passion that characterized his singing. ✉ *Luzhnetsky proyezd,* ☎ *095/246–6614.* 🎫 *$1.50.* ⊙ *Daily 10–5. Metro: Sportivnaya.*

★ **Novodevichy Monastyr.** Enclosed by a crenellated wall with 12 colorful battle towers, the monastery comprises several groups of buildings.
Until the middle of the 20th century, when Moscow's population expanded rapidly, it effectively marked the city's southern edge. It was
founded in 1524 by Czar Vasily III to commemorate Moscow's cap-
ture of Smolensk from Lithuania and was intended to serve not only
as a religious institution but also as a defense fortification. Its location
was strategically significant, as it stands on the road to Smolensk and
Lithuania. Having been founded by the czar, it enjoyed an elevated position among the many monasteries and convents of Moscow and became a convent primarily for ladies of noble birth. Little remains of
the original structure. The monastery suffered severely during the Time
of Troubles, a period of internal strife and foreign intervention that
began in approximately 1598 and lasted until 1613, when the first Romanov was elected to the throne. Its present appearance dates largely
from the 17th century, when the monastery was significantly rebuilt
and enhanced. ⊠ *1 Novodevichy proyezd,* ☎ *095/246–8526 or 095/
245–3168.* ▦ *$3.* ⊘ *Wed.–Sat. and Mon. 10–5. Closed last Mon. of
month. Metro: Sportivnaya.*

Among the first of the famous women to take the veil here was Irina,
wife of the feebleminded Czar Fyodor and the sister of Boris Godunov.
Opera fans may remember the story of Boris Godunov, the subject of
a well-known work by Mussorgsky. Godunov was a powerful nobleman who exerted much influence over the czar. When Fyodor died, Godunov was the logical successor to the throne, but rather than proclaim
himself czar, he followed his sister to Novodevichy. Biding his time, Godunov waited until the clergy and townspeople begged him to become
czar. His election took place at the convent, inside the Cathedral of
Smolensk. But his rule was ill-fated, touching off the Time of Troubles.

In the next century, Novodevichy became the residence of yet another
royal: Sophia, the half-sister of Peter the Great, who ruled as his regent from 1682 through 1689, while he was still a boy. During this
time there was much new construction at the monastery. The power-
hungry Sophia, who did not wish to give up her position when the time
came for Peter's rule, had to be deposed by him. He then kept her prisoner inside Novodevichy. Even that was not enough to restrain the ambitious sister, and from her cell at the convent she organized a revolt
of the *streltsy* (Russian militia). The revolt was summarily put down,
and to punish Sophia, Peter had the bodies of the dead *streltsy* hung
up along the walls of the convent and outside Sophia's window. Despite his greatness, Peter had a weakness for the grotesque, especially
when it came to punishing his enemies. He left the decaying bodies hanging for more than a year. Yet another of the convent's later "inmates"
was Yevdokiya, Peter's first wife. Peter considered her a pest and rid
himself of her by sending her to a convent in faraway Suzdal. She out-
lived him, though, and eventually returned to Moscow. She spent her
final years at Novodevichy, where she is buried.

You enter the convent through the arched passageway topped by the
Preobrazhensky Tserkov (Gate Church of the Transfiguration), widely
considered one of the best examples of Moscow Baroque. To your left
as you enter is the ticket booth, where tickets are sold to the various
exhibits housed in the monastery. The building to your right is the Lo-
phukin House, where Yevdokiya lived from 1727 to 1731. Sophia's
prison, now a guardhouse, is situated to your far right, in a corner of
the northern wall.

The predominant structure inside the monastery is the huge five-domed
Sobor Smolenskoy Bogomateri (Cathedral of the Virgin of Smolensk),

dedicated in 1525 and built by Alexei Fryazin. It may remind you of the Kremlin's Assumption Cathedral, after which it was closely modeled. Inside, there is a spectacular iconostasis with 84 wooden columns and icons dating from the 16th and 17th centuries. Also here are the tombs of Sofia and Yevdokiya. Simon Ushakov, a leader in 17th-century icon art, was among the outstanding Moscow artists who participated in the creation of the icons. Yet another historical tale connected to the monastery tells how the cathedral was slated for destruction during the War of 1812. Napoléon had ordered the cathedral dynamited, but a brave nun managed to extinguish the fuse just in time, and the cathedral was spared.

To the right of the cathedral is the **Uspensky Tserkov** (Church of the Assumption) and **Refectory,** originally built in 1687 and then rebuilt after a fire in 1796. It was here that the blue-blooded nuns had their meals.

If a monastery can have a symbol other than an icon, then Novodevichy's would be the ornate belfry towering above its eastern wall. It rises 236 ft and consists of six ornately decorated tiers. The structure is topped by a gilded dome that can be seen from miles away.

NEED A   **U Pirosmani** (✉ 4 Novodevichy proyezd, ☎ 095/247–1926 or 095/
BREAK?   246–1638), a well-known restaurant specializing in the spicy cuisine of
             Georgia, is situated across the pond from the monastery. On weekdays,
             it is almost always possible to get a table without a reservation. If you
             are visiting on a weekend, you may want to book ahead.

The Monasteries of Southeast Moscow

This excursion will take you to three ancient monasteries located along the banks of the Moskva River, in the southeast section of Moscow. Their history dates back to Moscow's earliest days, when it was the center of a fledgling principality and constantly under threat of enemy attack. A series of monasteries was built across the river from the Kremlin to form a ring of defense fortifications. Two of the monasteries on this tour were once part of that fortification ring. This former suburban area did not fare well as the city grew. Beginning in the 19th century, factories were built along the banks of the river, including the famous Hammer and Sickle metallurgical plant. Today this is one of Moscow's bleaker sections, marked by busy highways, monolithic residential high rises, and factories. But in their midst you find the quaint monasteries of Moscow's past, not always in the best condition but nevertheless lasting reminders of Moscow's origins.

A Good Walk

The tour begins at **Novospassky Monastery,** which you can reach by taking the subway to the Proletarskaya station. Take only lefts to get out of the subway, and you will emerge on Sarinsky proyezd. Standing with your back to the metro, the busy street a short distance ahead is Trety (3rd) Krutitsky pereulok. This is also in the direction of the Moskva River, and as you head to where the streets intersect, the yellow belfry of the monastery gate church will appear in the distance to your right (southwest). When you reach the intersection, use the underground passageways to cross to the other side. From here it is just a short walk up a slight incline to the monastery's entrance.

Leaving the monastery, turn right to go back to the busy Sarinsky proyezd. To do this, you will have to pick your way across the tram and trolley lines. Once on the other side, before again reaching the Trety Krutitsky pereulok, you will see on your right an older, tree-lined street leading up an incline. This is the Chetvyorty (4th) Krutitsky pereulok. Climbing to the top of the hill, where you take a quick right, you will find the **Krutitskoye Podvorye,** site of the five-domed Uspensky Cathedral.

The next monastery on the tour is best reached by subway. Return to the Proletarskaya station and take the subway one stop to the Taganskaya station. Before exiting, transfer to the connecting station on the circle line; you will come out onto Taganskaya Square. Several streets intersect at this busy square. Go left as you come out of the station and cross the short street to be on the same corner as the **Taganka Drama and Comedy Theatre,** one of Moscow's most famous theaters and quite slyly subversive when founded in 1964. From here, you should cross the whole left flank of the square in order to reach ulitsa **Bolshaya Kommunisticheskaya** (Big Communist Street), which is the third street radiating out from your left as you exit the subway. This is an old residential area; the shady street is lined with tall birch trees and two-story apartment buildings. Various commercial enterprises (including Moscow's exclusive Commercial Club, for its business elite) have moved into its renovated residences. It's left to wonder when the street may be renamed, given the contradictions to it that it now displays. One block down, at No. 15, is the lovely **Church of St. Martin the Confessor.** Continue down this long street until you reach the bulging Andronevskaya Ploshchad. Carefully make your way to the opposite side of the square and turn left onto Andronevsky pereulok. On the left-hand side of the street there is a small park; you will pass through the middle of it to reach the entrance to the **Andronikov Monastery,** the last stop on this walk. The whitewashed walls of the monastery's fortification will be visible through the trees. Leave the monastery through the main gate and return to Andronevskaya Ploshchad. The nearest subway station is Ploshchad Ilyicha. To reach it, turn left from the square onto ulitsa Sergiya Radonezhskovo; the subway is just one long block away. If you want to return to the Taganskaya subway station, you can take Bus 53, which stops at the corner of Tukhinskaya and will let you off where you began on ulitsa Bolshaya Kommunisticheskaya.

TIMING

This is a fairly strenuous tour, with lots of walking, so be sure to have stored up your energy and put on your athletic shoes. (You should also wear appropriate dress for visiting churches.) It is not recommended to bring younger-than-teenage children, since the street crossings are complicated and, to Westerners unskilled in Muscovite ways, slightly treacherous. Always look for the pedestrian underpasses and crossing signs as you decide your best route to get to the other side.

Sights to See

Andrei Rublyov Museum of Ancient Russian Culture and Art. Located in the Andronikov Monastery, the museum is named after the monastery's most celebrated monk, the icon painter Andrei Rublyov, who is believed to be buried here. Rublyov lived in the early 15th century, a time of much bloodshed and violence. Russia was slowly loosening the Mongol-Tatar yoke, and people lived in constant fear as the divided Russian principalities fought among themselves and against the Mongol-Tatar invaders. Rublyov's icons seem even more remarkable when viewed against the backdrop of his turbulent era. His works are amazing creations of flowing pastels conveying peace and tranquillity. His most famous work, *The Holy Trinity,* is now housed in the Tretyakov Gallery (☞ Gorky Park to the Tretyakov Gallery, *above*). The museum in the Andronikov Monastery, strangely enough, does not contain a single Rublyov work. Its collection of ancient religious art is nevertheless a fine one and well worth a visit. Tickets to the exhibits are sold in the office located around the corner to the right as you enter the monastery grounds. The museum is divided into three sections, and you must purchase a ticket for each part that you want to see. ✉ *Andronevskaya Pl. 10,* ☎ *095/278–1429.* ✍ *$3.* ☉ *Thurs.–Tues. 11– 6. Closed last Fri. of month. Metro: Pl. Ilicha.*

Andronikov Monastery. The monastery underwent extensive reconstruction in the 1950s and was refurbished again in the late 1980s. It is in much better condition than the Novospassky Monastery or Krutitskoye Podvorye. A stroll inside its heavy stone fortifications is an excursion into Moscow's past. The rumble of the city is drowned out by the loud crowing of birds overhead. Even the air seems more pure here, perhaps because of the old birch trees growing on the monastery grounds and just outside its walls. The Andronikov Monastery was founded in 1360 by the metropolitan Alexei and named in honor of its first abbot, St. Andronik. The site was chosen not only for its strategic importance—on the steep banks of the Moskva River—but also because, according to legend, it was from this hill that the metropolitan Alexei got his first glimpse of the Kremlin.

The dominating structure on the monastery grounds is the **Spassky Sobor** (Cathedral of the Savior), Moscow's oldest stone structure. Erected in 1420–27 on the site of an earlier, wooden church, it rests on the mass grave of Russian soldiers who fought in the Battle of Kulikovo (1380), the decisive Russian victory that eventually led to the end of Mongol rule in Russia. Unfortunately, the original interiors, which were painted by Andrei Rublyov and another famous icon painter, Danil Chorny, were lost in a fire in 1812. Fragments of their frescoes have been restored, however. The cathedral is open for services at 5:30 PM on Saturday and 9 AM on Sunday.

The building to your immediate left as you enter the monastery is the former abbot's residence. It now houses a permanent exhibit entitled "Masterpieces of Ancient Russian Art" from the 13th through 16th centuries. The exhibit includes icons from the Novgorod, Tver, Rostov, and Moscow schools. A highlight of the collection is the early-16th-century *St. George Smiting the Dragon,* from the Novgorod School.

The next building, to the left and across the pathway from the Cathedral of the Savior, is the **Refectory.** Like the Novospassky Monastery, it was built during the reign of Ivan the Great, in 1504–06. Today it houses the museum's exhibit of new acquisitions, which consists primarily of icons from the 19th and 20th centuries. Attached to the Refectory is the Church of St. Michael the Archangel, another example of the style known as Moscow Baroque. It was commissioned by the Lopukhin family—relatives of Yevdokiya Lopukhina, the first, unloved wife of Peter the Great—as the family crypt in 1694. But there are no Lophukins buried here, as Peter had Yevdokiya banished to a monastery in faraway Suzdal before the church was even finished, and her family was exiled to Siberia.

The museum's last exhibit is located in the former monks' residence, the redbrick building just beyond the Church of St. Michael. The exhibit is devoted to Nikolai the Miracle Worker and contains icons depicting his life and work. ✉ *10 Andronevskaya pl.,* ☎ *095/276–9526.* ✍ *Free.* ☉ *Daily, 8–8. Metro: Ploschad Ilicha.*

Church of St. Martin the Confessor. This lovely church dates from the late 18th century and is in need of full restoration; its cupola is rusted and little trees are growing on its roof, but it remains a working church. Farther down the street, at No. 29, you will find another building of historical importance, the apartment house where the theater director Stanislavsky was born in 1863. ✉ *15 Bolshaya Kommunisticheskaya ul. Metro: Proletarskaya.*

Krutitskoye Podvorye (Krutitskoye Ecclesiastical Residence). This historical architectural complex is even older than the Novospassky Monastery; the first cathedral on this site was erected sometime in the 13th century. Its name comes from the word *kruta,* meaning "hill." This was originally a small monastery, a site of defense in the 14th century against the Tatar-Mongol invaders, whose prestige became further enhanced when it became the suburban residence of the Moscow metropolitan at the end of the 16th century. The church and grounds were completely rebuilt, and the present structures date from this period. As monasteries go, its period of flowering was short-lived; it was closed in 1788 on orders from Catherine the Great, who secularized many church buildings. In the 19th century it was used as an army barracks, and it is said that the Russians accused of setting the Moscow fire of 1812 were tortured here by Napoléon's forces. In the 20th century, the Soviets turned the barracks into a military prison. Although the buildings have now been returned to the Orthodox Church, the prison remains on the monastery grounds. There is also a police station right outside the main gate, so do not be alarmed if you are greeted by a small band of uniformed policemen as you enter.

To your left as you enter the monastery grounds is the five-domed, red-brick **Uspensky Sobor** (Assumption Cathedral), erected at the end of the 16th century on the site of several previous churches. Stylistically medieval, more than anything else, it is a working church, undergoing restoration like many of its counterparts throughout the city. Still very attractive inside, it has an assemblage of icons, lovely frescoes that have been half restored, and an impressive all-white altar and iconostasis. The cathedral is attached to a gallery leading to the **Teremok** (Gate Tower), a splendid example of Moscow Baroque. It was built in 1688–94, and its exterior decoration is the work of Osip Startsev. Except for the carved, once-white columns, the walls are completely covered with colorful mosaics. The red, green, and white tiles—all of different sizes and shapes—framed in the red brick of the adjoining buildings, give, despite the verging frenzy of the decoration, an overall effect of a compositional whole. The gallery and Teremok served as the passageway for the metropolitan as he walked from his residence (to the right of the Teremok) to the cathedral. Passing through the gate tower, you will see the military prison, replete with lookout towers, located on the opposite side of the Teremok gates.

You should go through, in order to have a full walk around the tranquil grounds. From this side, you can enter the bell tower, which dates from 1680. Taking the stairs inside, through the door off its first level, you'll have access to the gallery itself and can walk along the walls. As you go around the complex, you will encounter young artists who seem to have chosen this quiet place to make sketches for their school assignments. ✉ *Pevaya Kruititsky per.* ☎ *095/276–9256 for information about excursions.* ☉ *Wed.–Mon. 9–6, except first Mon. of month. Metro: Proletarskaya.*

NEED A BREAK?	The **Horse and Hound** (✉ 16 Malay Kommunisticheskaya ul., ☎ 095/912–6963) pub serves fish-and-chips as well as other traditional British pub grub in a warm and friendly atmosphere.

Novospassky (New Savior) Monastery. The monastery was built in 1462, but its history dates back to the 13th century. It was originally located inside the Kremlin, and it is called the "New" Monastery because its new site on the banks of the Moskva River was a transfer ordered by Ivan III, who wanted to free up space in the Kremlin for other construction. Often called Ivan the Great, Ivan III was the first Russian leader to categorically (and successfully) renounce Russia's allegiance to the khan of the Golden Horde. It was during his reign that a unified Russian state was formed under Moscow's rule. The Novospassky Monastery was just one of the numerous churches and monasteries built during the prosperous time of Ivan's reign. In uglier modern history, a site just outside the monastery's walls was one of the mass graves for those executed during Stalin's purges.

You enter the monastery at the near entrance to the left of the **Bell Tower Gate,** which was erected in 1786. It is now closed from the outside, though once inside the complex you can walk beneath its archway. The entire monastery is, sadly, in a state of semi-disrepair. Reconstruction *is* being done, but slowly; it has already taken more than 30 years. Since the early 1990s, however, when it was returned to the Orthodox Church, the pace has picked up. Still, except on Sunday and church holidays, the monastery grounds are often virtually deserted. A stroll among its decaying buildings will therefore feel like a very private, if not rather eerie, experience.

The first thing you see as you enter the monastery grounds is the massive white **Sobor Spasa Preobrazheniya** (Transfiguration Cathedral). You may notice a resemblance, particularly in its domes, to the Kremlin's Assumption Cathedral, which served as its model. The Transfiguration Cathedral was built in 1642–49 by the Romanov family, commissioned by the czar as the Romanov family crypt. The gallery leading to the central nave is decorated with beautiful frescoes depicting the history of Christianity in Rus'. It is worth timing your visit with a church service (daily at 5 PM) to see the interior. Even if the church is closed, the doors may be unlocked. No one will stop you from taking a quick look at the gallery walls.

In front of the cathedral, on the right-hand side, is the small red **Nadmogilnaya Chasovnya** (Memorial Chapel), marking the grave of Princess Alekseyevna Tarankova, the illegitimate daughter of Empress Elizabeth and Count Razumovsky. She lived most of her life as a nun in Moscow's St. John's Convent, forced to take the veil by Catherine the Great. During her lifetime her identity was concealed, and she was known only as Sister Dofiya. The chapel over her grave was added in 1900, almost a century after her death. Sister Dofiya's imposter played a more prominent role in Russian history than the real Princess Tarankova. A mysterious character of European origin, the imposter never revealed her true identity. She was imprisoned by Catherine the Great in St. Petersburg's Peter and Paul Fortress, where she died of consumption in 1775. Her death in her flooded, rat-infested cell was depicted in a famous painting by Konstantin Flavitsky in 1864.

None of the monastery's original 15th-century structures has survived. The present fortification wall and most of the churches and residential buildings on the grounds date from the 17th century. To the right as you face the cathedral stands the tiny **Pokrovsky Tserkov** (Church of the Intercession). Directly behind the cathedral is the **Tserkov Znamenia** (Church of the Sign). Painted in the dark yellow popular in its time, with a four-column facade, it was built in 1791–1808 by the wealthy Sheremetyev family and contains the Sheremetyev crypt. In the rear right-hand corner, running along the fortification walls, are the former monks' residences. ✉ *Bolshie Kamenshchiki at Novospassky per. Metro: Proletarskaya.*

DINING

Not so long ago the Moscow dining scene was as rosy as a flute of Crimean pink champagne. Today, with the government playing Russian roulette with the economy, Moscow's restaurant miniboom may be just that. Who knows? Next year, the town's new breed of ambitious chefs might be packing for the culinary equivalent of Siberia. However, if the new millennium starts off strong, the vast and recent improvements on the dining scene should continue to garnish the often delicious experience of eating out in Moscow. The city is no New York or Paris, but more than a few of its leading dining rooms now offer world-class cuisine. In the last few years, the sheer number of restaurants has mushroomed—Ivan Q. Public doesn't complain anymore of having nowhere to go. Of course, all of this culinary maturation has come at a price. If you have the cash, there are designer plates galore. Don't expect any bargains, as prices are still much higher than you'd expect to pay in the West (keep in mind that almost all the expensive hotel restaurants offer a New Orleans Jazz Brunch on Sunday, when you can enjoy their haute cuisine and decor at greatly reduced prices). Happily, however, the last year has seen a growth in medium and budget dining options, and it is possible to dine at a reasonable price with a bit of care. A stormy economic picture may even help increase this pattern. In addition, there's also a new breed of Russian restaurants, as the fad for Western food loses some, but by no means all, of its glamour. New ethnic restaurants have arrived as well and you can sample Tibetan, Indian, Chinese, Latin American, or Turkish any night of the week. Be warned, though, that chef turnover is high in Moscow and a restaurant can swiftly go downhill or uphill. So, expect to be surprised and realize that there will probably be a series of new, exciting restaurants waiting to be discovered once you arrive.

Reserve plenty of time for your meal. In Russia dining out is an occasion, and Russians often make an evening (or an afternoon) out of going out to eat, especially at those Moscow showplaces replete with gilded cornices, hard-carved oak, and tinkling crystal. At these spots, prepare to linger, as unhurried splendor is definitely the order of the day.

CATEGORY	COST*
$$$$	over $70
$$$	$40–$70
$$	$20–$40
$	under $20

per person for a three-course dinner, excluding drinks and service

WHAT TO WEAR

Dress at the restaurants reviewed below is casual, unless noted otherwise.

AMERICAN

$$$ ✕ **Le Gastronome.** This gorgeous place looks like a palazzo: marble columns, luxurious stained glass, mosaics, and immaculate, crisp tablecloths. Amazingly, it used to be nothing but a Stalin-era food store, a *gastronom,* whose shelves were empty most of the time. Today, Le Gastronome's tall ceilings and spaciousness add a certain grandeur to your dining experience. As expected from the name, the place has a certain French flavor but the chef is American and the mostly continental menu features giant T-bone steaks and other items of American cuisine, served on large, beautifully arranged plates. There are even live lobsters swarming in a large aquarium ready to be sacrificed for you. Do try the exceptional foie gras with papaya and raspberry or one of

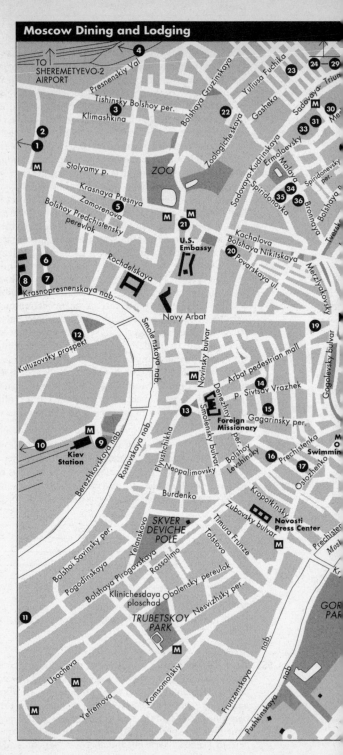

Moscow Dining and Lodging

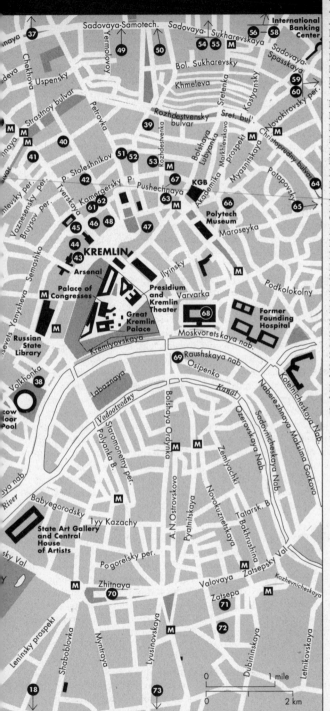

the fresh green salads. Live classical piano music fits in with the setting. ⊠ *1 Kudrinskaya Ploshchad,* ☎ *095/255–4433. DC, MC, V. Metro: Krasnopresnenskaya.*

$$$ ✕ **Uncle Guilly's.** Favored by many Americans because of its juicy selection of steaks, Uncle Guilly's is a warren of rooms in a vaulted cellar dating back nearly 300 years. Previously a brothel, a printing house, and home to one of Napoléon's bureaucrats during the 1812 invasion, the cellar was one of Moscow's first private restaurants. In 1993, it was nicknamed after Vladimir Gilyarovsky, a famous Moscow historian, and began specializing in American cuisine (with a dash of Russian thrown in). If you're in carnivore mode, you'll love the T-bone, buffalo wings, or New York sirloin. Or just settle for pelmeni or beef in a pot, Russian-style. For dessert, the all-time favorite is Bailey's cheesecake. If you pay 10% extra, you can dine in a private room decorated with original 19th-century prints. ⊠ *6 Stoleshnikov per.,* ☎ *095/229– 2050. AE, MC, V. Metro: Okhotny Ryad, Teatralnaya.*

$$ ✕ **Planet Hollywood.** You can't miss it. It's the only place for miles attracting attention to itself with neon, palm trees, and a barrage of blinking lights. Step inside and it's exactly like any other Planet Hollywood in any other world capital, so it's not the place to go if you're in the mood for balalaikas and blini, but it may be just the thing if you're feeling a little homesick. There is a crushed-glass bar top just made for drinkers and snug areas for the eaters. The menu—in Russian and in English—offers the standard Planet Hollywood fare, everything from *krylyshki "Buffalo"* (Buffalo wings) to *ryobryshki* (baby-back ribs) to thin-crust Tex-Mex pizza. The food and drinks are all very well prepared, and the service is friendly and efficient. ⊠ *23B Krasnaya Presnya,* ☎ *095/255–9191. AE, MC, V. Metro: 1905 Goda.*

$$ ✕ **Starlite Diners.** Open round-the-clock, these two diners are identical to those back in the United States—same bright-lit 1950's design, large portions, and great value for the price. In Moscow, these spots are popular options for late workers, exhausted early-morning party goers, and old friends getting together for a weekend brunch. It's always full of boisterous first-timers to Russia and expats looking for a taste of home. The Mayakovskaya locale is busier because of its center-city location and because of its summertime patio. Waiters are young and friendly, speak English, and serve fast. ⊠ *16 Bolshaya Sadovaya, in the garden by the Mossoviet theater/9Korovy Val,* ☎ *095/290–9638 or 095/959– 8919. AE, MC, V. Metro: Mayakovskaya/Oktyabrskaya.*

ASIAN

$$$$ ✕ **Tokio.** The ambience may be the best imitation of a Japanese dining salon in Moscow, but you might feel it still has the sterile feel of a corporate boardroom with its yellow walls, bright lighting, and modern design. Tables wrapped around the stoves allow you to watch the chef cook but you also have to deal with the wafting smells from the other diners' selections. Luckily, there are a few more intimate tables. The chef is Japanese and the menu is in English; unfortunately, the service is not very helpful and somewhat rude. ⊠ *6 ul. Varvarka, in the West block of the Rossiya hotel,* ☎ *095/298–5707 or 095/298–5374. Jacket and tie. Reservations essential. AE, DC, MC, V. Metro: Kitai-Gorod.*

$$$ ✕ **Bangkok.** Imported Thai chefs bring an authentic feel to this restaurant long popular with politicians and expats. The place may be a bit gloomy and the service not always up to scratch but the food is excellent; keep in mind there are four levels of hot spiciness—four-alarmer to mild—and the coconut soup is a must. The prices are high but the huge portions are big enough for two or three people. ⊠ *10 Bolshoi Strochyonovsky per.,* ☎ *095/237–3074. AE, DC, MC, V. Metro: Serpukhovskaya.*

$$$ ✕ **Beloye Solntse Pustyni.** Named after a legendary Soviet film, Beloye Solntse Pustyni (the White Sun of the Desert) is a theme restaurant which specializes in delicious Uzbek food. The restaurant's sun-bleached walls instantly sweep you down to Central Asia. Inside the illusion continues: a diorama with a ship marooned in the desert, Uzbek maidens as waitresses, intricately carved wooden doors. Make sure you try the salad bar, a mouthwatering array of vegetables. The Dastarkhan, a set meal, overwhelms you with food—unlimited access to the salad bar, numerous desserts, a *plov* (a Central Asian rice pilaf), and a main course. If you want to understand all the White Sun references, head for the foyer where you can buy the film. ✉ *29/14 Neglinnaya ul.,* ☎ *095/209–7525. Reservations essential. AE, MC, V. Metro: Kuznetsky Most.*

$$$ ✕ **Tamerlaine.** For a marauding tyrant, Tamerlaine has remarkably good taste in food and decor. This superb Mongolian-style restaurant is a tranquilly lit, elegant place just made for a business lunch. Two Kazakh chefs wield enormous chopsticks as they man the giant circular hot plate. You choose the ingredients—laid out before you—and the chefs stir-fry them in a couple of minutes. Set menus are provided to help you choose from the huge choice of meats, fresh vegetables, and spices, or you can create your own potpourri. The eat-as-much-as-you-like deal also includes a delicate pickled salad, homemade bread, and cheese. The business lunch deal between 12 and 2 PM is a good bargain. ✉ *30 Prechistenka,* ☎ *095/202–5649. DC, MC, V. Metro: Kropotkinskaya/Park Cultury.*

$$ ✕ **Five Spices.** The interior of Five Spices may look like an Oriental house of ill-repute but the food is as classy as you can get. If you get bored with the Chinese dishes you can always try the Indian selections, as Five Spices has a good number of Tandoori dishes. For starters try the crispy lamb or the honey-glazed pork and then move onto any of the many prawn dishes. It's one of the few places where you can get tofu and a good range of vegetarian dishes.✉ *3/18 Sivtsav Vrazhek,* ☎ *095/924–2931. Reservations essential. AE, DC, MC, V. Metro: Kropotkinskaya.*

$$ ✕ **Kohinoor.** It may a bit out of the center and the interior may be rather plain but Kohinoor is still the best Indian spot in town. Huge portions, excellent Mughlai and South Indian cuisine, and charming service makes the journey all worthwhile. The samosas are a treat as are the chicken dishes and the mammoth kebabs. It's all remarkably cheap as well and the business lunch deal can't be beat. ✉ *101 Prospekt Mira,* ☎ *095/287–8127. AE, DC, MC, V. Metro: Alekseevskaya.*

$$ ✕ **Tibet Kitchen.** The name may be slightly more prosaic than its competitor Tibet Himalaya but this restaurant follows Himalaya's lead with an exceedingly high standard of reasonably priced food. A huge picture of the Dalai Lama's former palace in Lhasa commands the room and dolls dressed in costumes made by Tibetan monks sit serenely in little cubbyholes. Located a few minutes from the Kremlin, Tibet Kitchen offers spiced-up Tibetan cuisine. If you want to try something more traditional order the Tsam-Thuk, a thick soup made from barley and speckled with slivers of meat and mushrooms. The restaurant is particularly appealing to vegetarians and offers a large number of cheap dishes like the Soen Labuk salad, shredded dyed pink radish with a touch of vinegar. ✉ *5/6 Kamergersky per.,* ☎ *095/923–2422 or 095/ 923–5649. Metro: Okhotny Ryad.*

FAST FOOD

$ ✕ **Coffee Bean.** Seattle-style coffee heaven has finally arrived in Moscow with the opening of Coffee Bean. Giant cappuccinos, service with a smile, and the best coffee in Moscow is on offer in both stores. The Kuznetsky Most place is a bit poky but the Pokrovka site positively blossoms in its huge space and corner site, ideal for watching the Pokrovkans walk by.✉ *18 Pokrovka/in arch beside Kuznetsky Most metro,* ☎ *095/ 923–9793 or 095/923–0219. No credit cards. Metro: Chistiye Prudy/Kuznetsky Most.*

$ ✕ **Delifrance.** Closeted inside the Tchaikovsky Concert Hall, Delifrance is a perfect pre- or post-concert place for a lemon tart and a coffee. There's always a decent selection of sandwiches, the pastries are freshly made, and you can get your croissants and baguettes there as well. Ingredients are brought in from France as is, seemingly, the convivial atmosphere. A newly opened café on Stary Arbat has an outdoor area in summer. ✉ *4/31 Triumfalnaya square in the Tchaikovsky Concert Hall,* ☎ *095/927–6040. No credit cards. Metro: Mayakovskaya.*

$ ✕ **Donna Klara.** A few minutes away from Patriarshy Prudy, Donna Klara's comfy window seats, laid-back staff, and selection of sticky cakes make this a cozy place to linger over a bottle of wine. The wine list may not be very big, and the reheated lasagna isn't a delight but the friendliness makes it all seem like a family place in which to relax the afternoon away. ✉ *21/13 Malaya Bronnaya. No credit cards. Metro: Mayakovskaya.*

FRENCH

$$$$ ✕ **Actor.** Russia's film industry may not be as healthy as it once was but the only restaurant to be located in Russia's Hollywood goes from strength to strength. Ranked by some as the best French restaurant in town, it flies in all its ingredients. ✉ *1 Mosfilmovskaya,* ☎ *095/143– 9400. Reservations essential. Jacket and tie. AE, DC, MC, V. Metro: Kievskaya and then trolleybus 34 or 17.*

$$$$ ✕ **Bely Lebed.** Just a few yards from the picturesque pond of Chistiye Prudy, Bely Lebed can be a bit imposing. The metal detector at the door gives off the wrong signals but the interior—a soothing display of peach and pastel—is from a different, kinder world. The food goes down easy, too. Black or red caviar served chilled with blini is a delight here as is the crayfish bisque. Service is unobtrusive and excellent. Make sure you sit by the window for a view down the bulvar. ✉ *12 Chistoprudny bulvar,* ☎ *095/924–1172. AE, DC, MC, V. Metro: Chisty Prudy.*

$$$$ ✕ **Club T.** This phenomenally expensive French restaurant is part eatery, part antiques showroom. Small and intimate, the restaurant attracts a number of New Russians splurging on the food and the goods. The menu is typically French and showcases dishes with delicious sauces. ✉ *21 Krasina ul.,* ☎ *095/232–2778. Reservations essential. Jacket and tie. AE, MC, V. Metro: Mayakovskaya, Belorusskaya.*

$$$ ✕ **Maxim's.** Located in the Hotel National, opposite the Kremlin, Maxim's captures the feel of the famous French restaurant Maxim's de Paris. The frosted glass and cozy surroundings create a snug setting, while the dance floor and soft cabaret music bring to mind a turn-of-the-century Parisian dance hall. The French-Russian cuisine is always reliable if at times uninspired. Dessert, though, can be a surefire winner, such as the almond blancmange with raspberry sauce or the cherry tart. Although Maxim's recently slashed its prices, it's still not a cheap option, but the service is always gracious and the interior splendid.✉ *15/1 Mokhovaya ul. in the National hotel,* ☎ *095/258–7000. Reservations essential. AE, DC, V. Metro: Okhotny Ryad.*

GEORGIAN RUSSIAN

$$ ✕ **Mama Zoya.** Along with Guriya, another place owned by the same Georgian family, Mama Zoya is a legendary bastion of good and cheap Georgian food. There is one big room as well as several private rooms, which don't provide much defense against the incredibly loud accordion players. The restaurant recently moved to a different location, but its design remained the same with an eclectic and often kitschy

decor replete with plastic flowers and ceiling fans that look like helicopter propellers. Exotic setting or a trip back in time to Soviet days? No matter, thanks to the hearty food served here. Vegetable dishes are especially impressive, including red lobio, a garlicky bean dish, and *abzhapsandal,* a plate of braised vegetables. The *khachapuri,* a traditional pancake filled with cheese, is always delicious. The Mama Zoya special is made up of chicken giblets, a fried egg, and a delectable eggplant-tomato-mayonnaise construction. Many authentic Georgian wines can be found and the service is speedy and good-humored. Lines on the weekends can be annoying so reserve ahead, or head instead to Guriya at 7/3 Komsomolsky Prospekt. ⊠ *12 ul. Ostozhenka,* ☎ *095/ 202–0445. No credit cards. Metro: Kropotkinskaya.*

$$ ✕ **U Pirosmani.** Named after the Georgian artist Niko Pirosmani, this popular restaurant is located near the Novodevichy Monastery and was once visited by President Bill Clinton. Its rustic interior, with whitewashed walls and wood-paneled ceilings, recreates the atmosphere of an artist's studio. Copies of Pirosmani's naive art decorate the walls. Make sure you get to sit by the window in the main hall so you can enjoy beautiful views of the 16th-century monastery across the pond from the restaurant. The menu reads like a Georgian cookbook. The speciality of the local Georgian chef is *shashlyk po-Mirzaansky,* or shish kebab with mushrooms, and *adzhakhuri,* cutlet with pomegranate seeds. The kitchen also serves delightful *khinkali,* Georgian meat dumplings. Order a bottle of Georgian wine to accompany your meal. Although the restaurant is very popular and often crowded, service is very good. ⊠ *4 Novodevichiy proyezd,* ☎ *095/247–1926. V. Metro: Sportivnaya.*

ITALIAN

$$$$ ✕ **Mario's.** Mario's has always ranked as one of the top Italian restaurants in Moscow but today some foodies say the two resident Italian
★ chefs have turned it into the best restaurant in town. Using ingredients flown in twice a week from Italy they create consistently wonderful pasta dishes. The carpaccio never fails and whereas other Italian restaurants fall down on meat or fish dishes, Mario's is excellent whatever you choose. ⊠ *17 Klimashkina ul.,* ☎ *095/253–6505. Reservations essential. Jacket and tie. DC, MC, V. Metro: 1905 Goda.*

$$$$ ✕ **Rossini.** Opened up by the pair who created the successful Teatro restaurant, Rossini has a lot to offer the well-heeled. Set in the sleek Ducat Plaza II, the restaurant is beautiful and has a bright airy atmosphere that makes you feel like you're in New York rather than Moscow. The decor is impressive—huge bouquets of flowers on old Singer sewing tables, Oriental rugs, white tablecloths, bright red chairs. Rossini's menu is a Mediterranean mix, but you can still find a real four-course Italian meal—antipasto, pasta, entrée, plus dessert—here. That special menu may be a bit much, but who can resist the desserts here? Try the apple pancakes with Calvados and vanilla ice cream—a savory flambé, or the cream custard with wild berries in balsamic vinegar. Rossini's only problems are the expense and the snail-like service. ⊠ *7 ul. Gasheka, Ducat Plaza II,* ☎ *095/785–0260. AE, DC, MC, V. Metro: Mayakovskaya.*

$$$$ ✕ **Teatro.** There are actually two restaurants at this location on the lower level at the rear of the Metropol Hotel, the side opposite the Bolshoi Theater. Once you've descended the opulent marble staircase you'll be confronted with the choice of turning left to enter the Lobster Grill, which prides itself on its fresh oysters, lobster, scampi, and prawns, or turning right into the much livelier, and more popular, Teatro proper, which specializes in the foods of the Mediterranean. With its whimsical murals, bright colors, potted palms, mirrors, and salsa band, this dining room almost feels like Los Angeles (which might help explain why it's so popular with Moscow's American expat community). ⊠ *1/4 Teatralny proyezd, in the Metropol Hotel,* ☎ *095/927–6678. Reservations essential. AE, MC, V. Metro: Teatralnaya.*

$$$ ✕ **Artistico.** Just off Tverskaya ulitsa and opposite the MKhAT Theater, Artistico is the perfect spot for a pre- or post-theater dinner. Waitresses wearing flowing velvet dresses perfectly fit the vintage dining room, with its Art Deco trim—a setting that is both elegant and cozy. Autographs of celebrities who have dined here—including Robert de Niro and Rod Stewart—welcome you to the new banquet room upstairs. The Italian menu continues the show-business theme with dishes like "Romeo and Juliet" and "Gone With the Wind." Artistico's range of business lunch deals is one of the best in the city center. ⊠ *5/6 Kamergersky per.,* ☎ *095/292–4042 or 095/292–6915. AE, DC, MC, V. Metro: Okhotny Ryad.*

$$$ ✕ **La Cipolla d'Oro.** This modern and bright Italian eatery is definitely above the pizza level, as you'll see if you order their fine homemade pastas or opt for seafood selections (many flown in from France and Tunisia). The menu changes completely every three months but you can always count on a large number of imaginative and exotic seafood dishes such as swordfish carpaccio. The portions are, unfortunately, not as big as they could be. The restaurant has an impressive wine list; wines come direct from Italy and the price reflects the quality. This is definitely a spot for a great family get-together. ⊠ *39 ul. Gilyarovskogo,* ☎ *095/281–9498 or 095/281–1339. AE, DC, MC, V. Metro: Prospekt Mira.*

$$$ ✕ **Spago.** No, this isn't related to the famed Los Angeles outlet, but is a sturdily good Italian eatery, located a few minutes away from Lubyanka. Everything is imported direct from Italy, including the chef—and it looks as if he's brought grandma's tiramisu with him. Otherwise the seafood garners the top marks; opt for the grilled sea bass with aromatic herbs and balsamic or the swordfish. The yellow walls and blue ceiling make for an especially relaxing setting. ⊠ *1 Bolshaya Zlatoustinsky per.,* ☎ *095/921–3797. AE, DC, V. Metro: Lubyanka.*

$$ ✕ **Patio Pizza.** An airy place to find pizza bliss, this cheerful restaurant has a huge back room with glass ceiling and walls, so the sun pours in all day. The original is a stone's throw from the Pushkin Fine Arts Museum; a newer branch is located in the front section of the Intourist Hotel at the tip of Tverskaya ulitsa. Another branch sits opposite the statue of Mayakovsky on Triumfalnaya Ploshchad and more are popping up all over town. The menu runs the gamut of pizzas, with a real salad bar and Italian entrées. The pizza has a thin and dusty crust; daily specials include such dishes as lasagna and cannelloni. Tables are comfortably spaced, topped with checkerboard tablecloths. Pop music plays softly, and the rooms are always filled with a pleasantly bustling crowd. ⊠ *30 ul. Volkhonka,* ☎ *095/201–0050. AE, DC, MC, V. Metro: Kropotkinskaya.*

MEXICAN

$$$ ✕ **Hola Mexico.** If you're in the mood for margaritas, big fajitas, and a loud mariachi band who mix Andean ditties with American pop hits, this is the place for you. You wouldn't want to go here when you are tired, but for high-energy party goers on their way to the nearby Hungry Duck, this is one of the best Tex-Mex eateries in town. Large portions of nachos, a hill of beans and chips smothered with cheeses and tomatoes, might make it difficult to finish the meal you came for. There's plenty of dancing and a crowded bar of tequila-drinking clientele. A few tables are set aside in a quieter, dimly lit dining room for those looking to escape the spectacle. ⊠ *7/5 Pushechnaya ul.,* ☎ *095/ 928–8251. AE, DC, MC, V. Metro: Kuznetsky Most.*

$$ ✕ **Azteca.** One of Moscow's most popular places, this noisy watering hole offers a satisfying Mexican menu of traditional favorites for Southwestern palates. Among the nachos, guacamole, and fajitas are several chicken dishes and a few exotic ones, such as roasted duck tacos. Pretty much any drink is served from the well-stocked bar, which makes a potent margarita. For a final flourish, flag down the roving *compadre* whose holster packs tequila bottles instead of six-shooters. The walls are covered in a bright Aztec motif, and the staff's mood matches the festive costumes. They have been known to break out in spontaneous dance while taking your order, inspired no doubt by the ensemble of guitar, drum, and pipe players who cheerfully rally the dinner crowd with Latin melodies all night long. Another location is at the top of the Intourist hotel—it's little more than a couple of small rooms, but the food is decent and there is a great panoramic view over the Kremlin. ✉ *11 Novoslobodskaya, str. 1,* ☎ *095/956–8467 or 095/972–0511. MC, V. Metro: Okhotny Ryad/Novoslobodskaya.*

RUSSIAN

$$$$ ✕ **CDL.** You'll find one of the city's most beautiful dining rooms—and one of the best places to sample authentic Russian cuisine—located in this elegant mansion. In the 19th century the house served as the headquarters for Moscow's Freemasons; more recently it was a meeting place for members of the Soviet Writers' Union. The name is the Russian abbreviation for "Central House of Writers." Now entirely reconstructed and renovated, with its crystal chandeliers, rich wood paneling, fireplaces, and antique balustrades, CDL is one of the warmest and most sumptuous eateries in the city. Everything here is extremely well prepared, but it's best to stick to the Russian items on the menu: try the borshch or *pelmeni* (tender meat dumplings)–or both!—for starters, and then move on to the rabbit Stroganoff. If you're feeling very adventurous, cleanse your palate between courses with a glass of Russian *kvas* (bread-beer). ✉ *50 Povarskaya ul.,* ☎ *095/291–1515. AE, DC, MC, V, or rubles at restaurant exchange rate.* Metro: Barrikadnaya.

$$$$ ✕ **Grand Imperial.** This truly old-style restaurant serves superbly prepared and often Croesus-rich dishes, such as roast veal à la Romanoff. The succulent food is well matched by the surroundings—double-headed Imperial eagles, gilded Empire-style chairs worthy of a czar, original art, crystal chandeliers, bouquets of flowers, even the antique silver service personally collected by the owners. The dining room is relatively small, made more intimate by a fountain and an old grand piano, where a pianist plays daily, joined by a guitarist singing Old Russia tunes in the evening. The restaurant boasts what is probably the most expensive starter in town—whole goose liver for $125. The Grand Imperial's secretive banquet hall is a favorite dining place for Russia's oligarchs who cherish the grandeur and privacy it offers—Prime Minister Viktor Chernomyrdin, Vladimir Zhirinovsky, and President Yeltsin's daughter Tatyana Danchenko have all feasted here. ✉ *9/5 Gagarinsky per.,* ☎ *095/291–6063. Reservations essential. Jacket and tie. AE, DC, MC, V. Metro: Kropotkinskaya.*

$$$$ ✕ **Grand Opera.** Walk into Grand Opera and you find yourself in a splendid auditorium straight out of Odessa in the 1920s. Diners sit at tables in ornate boxes surrounded by plush burgundy velvet and gold decorations, listening to a straw-hatted big band and watching actors sing and dancers can-can the evening away. The restaurant, full of wealthy foreigners and high-ranking *chinovniks* (bureaucrats) is one of the only cabaret-type venues in Moscow. The menu is an odd mix of Russian/Ukrainian, French, and Jewish dishes that echoes the cuisine of old Odessa, but the food is, unfortunately, not as delicious as the surroundings, which fairly buzz with excitement. The nightly festivities carry a cover charge of $10 per person or $15 if you're in a box. Remember: The show begins at 8 PM. ✉ *2/18 Petrovskiye Linii, near Hotel Budapest,* ☎ *095/923–9966 or 095/921–4044. AE, MC, V. Metro: Kuznetsky Most.*

$$$$ ✕ **Le Romanoff.** How do you say champagne in Russian? This is one of Moscow's finest culinary delights and its imposing oval room, featuring views of the Kremlin over the Moskva River, is a perfect spot for a grand-occasion dinner. Located on the second floor of the Baltschug Hotel, it is exquisitely managed and offers Russian/French cuisine that pleases both the eye and the palate. The German chef specializes in delicate sauces. Try his *loup de mer,* cooked right at your table and served with Mediterranean-style steamed vegetables. For dessert, raspberries Romanoff, mixed with vanilla ice cream and Grand Marnier, is a must. The wine list is superb, with a wide variety of ports as well. ✉ *1 ul. Balchug,* ☎ *095/230–6500. Reservations essential. Jacket and tie. AE, DC, MC, V. Metro: Kitai-Gorod or Novokuznetskaya.*

$$$$ ✕ **Metropol.** Recalling the splendor of prerevolutionary Russia, the renovated interiors of the Metropol Hotel's grand dining hall are a stunning memorial to Russian Art Nouveau. The nearly three-story-high dining room is replete with stained-glass windows, marble pillars, and leaded-glass roof, and the beautifully laid tables and formally dressed waiters add to the elegance. In terms of its opulent atmosphere, visitors will be pleased, but they might find themselves disappointed when it comes to the service. The kitchen offers a selection of French and Russian delicacies for connoisseurs—fried duck with wild cherry sauce and baked apple is a favorite—and there is also a special chef's menu with a different theme each month. Many diners order cheese and wine to cap the meal—the Metropol has an impressive cellar. Live classical music starts at 7 PM on Mondays or Tuesdays; on other nights you'll be listening to loud Russian pop. A grand breakfast is also offered here. ✉ *1/4 Teatralny proyezd,* ☎ *095/927–6061. Reservations essential. Jacket and tie. AE, DC, MC, V. Metro: Pl. Revolutsii.*

$$$$ ✕ **Praga.** Centrally located on Arbat Square, in a handsome prerevolutionary building, this restaurant once played host to Leo Tolstoy and Ilya Repin. During the Soviet era it was the most prestigious restaurant in town before slipping into near terminal decline. Now, after major renovation in 1997 it offers no fewer than nine restaurants to choose from—six Russian, Brazilian, an Italian, and an Asian. All in all, it's a vast, brash, extravagant, often tasteless, yet appealing place. You could spend days wandering about the luxurious interior; gold and marble abound (even the metal detector is covered in marble) and there's a garish nightclub on the top floor. If you want to rise above the masses, get treated like an emperor in the Czar's Hall. For $600, excluding drinks, you become the czar, served by bewigged waiters in the manner of Peter the Great. Other restaurants have gentler price tags; the Brazilian buffet is the best all-round bargain. ✉ *2 Stary Arbat,* ☎ *095/290–6171. Reservations essential. AE, DC, MC, V. Metro: Arbatskaya.*

$$$$ ✕ **Savoy.** Located in the Savoy Hotel, this restaurant's fancy interior ★ and elegant menu are likely to please Russophiles and gourmands alike. The food—a mixture of Russian and French—is excellent. Ingredients are trucked in from Finland, and the Russian chef has won several international awards for his imperial creations. The restaurant features a special Czar's Menu, a re-creation of one of the 12 menus served at the coronation of Czar Nicholas II in 1896. Food aside, the real reason to come here is to see the interiors. With its delicate, gilt wall coverings, long mirrors, and gilt-framed ceiling paintings, it echoes the opulence of St. Petersburg's Imperial palaces. Dinner can be extremely expensive; you may prefer the more reasonable prix-fixe lunch. ✉ *3 Rozhdestvenka ul.,* ☎ *095/929–8600. Reservations essential. Jacket* *and tie. AE, DC, MC, V. Traveler's checks accepted. Metro: Kuznetsky Most.*

$$$$ ✕ **The Tsar's Hunt.** Even though it's a long way from the city center, this spot is fashionable enough to have attracted such luminates as Boris Yeltsin and Jacques Chirac. Housed in a traditional log house, it is designed in Russian Country: Carved wood decorations, bear and wolf skins on the floors and chairs, moose horns on the walls, and an antique Russian stove instill an atmosphere so warm it feels as if you've just returned from an ermine-covered troika ride. Perhaps remembering that Peter the Great once adored peasant dishes, diners flock for simple and good food, like the rosemary ribs with hot sauce and the *okroshka,* a delicious cold summer soup. No matter what you order, you must start out with the Russian *zakuski* (Russian appetizers, traditionally enjoyed with vodka), displayed on a cart like a salad bar. ✉ *186a Rublevo-Uspenskoye Shosse, Zhukovka village,* ☎ *095/418–7983. Reservations essential. AE, MC, V. By car or train from Belorusskaya railroad station.*

$$$ ✕ **Rytzarsky Klub.** Located under the ski jump at the Sparrow Hills, the restaurant has one of the best views in the city, since it overlooks most of Moscow from its highest geographical point. In summer, your best choice is to sit at the nice bare wood balcony (even though you may not be able to see some Moscow landmarks because of intruding tall trees). Rytzarsky Klub, which means the Knight Club, was designed to imitate the style of the Middle Ages, with knight paraphernalia on show throughout the rooms. The Georgian owner is even a member of the St. Constantin Order for his support of the arts, and he's made the restaurant's White Room into an elegant art gallery promoting young artists. The Knight Room is a vision out of the Middle Ages, complete with fireplace and heavy oak chairs. The place's elite clientele includes diplomats and show-business stars (including Mick Jagger), who may appreciate the live music often on tap. As for the hearty Georgian food, start with the eggplant stuffed with walnuts. For the main course, try the *kuchmachi,* a dish made from tongue, heart, and liver. None of the staff speak English. ✉ *28 ul. Kosygina,* ☎ *095/930–0726. V. Metro: Leninsky Prospekt or Universitet.*

$$$ ✕ **Shinok.** Have you ever dined while a horse stared at you as you eat your meal? This place, located next door to Bochka (☞ *below*), offers a unique dining experience: Half Disneyland, half collective, its dining room is a faux-Ukrainian farmyard complete with goats, hens, cockerels, and a knitting granny (and said horse). Luckily the enclosure is completely sound- and smell-proof and the animals don't really impinge on the meal. Ukrainian food doesn't differ that much from Russian. Many of the dishes are the same, such as borshch, *vareniki* (pelmeni stuffed with cottage cheese, Ukrainian-style) and *solyanka* (meat and vegetable soup). The helpful staff are adept at giving advice, although not all speak English. Try *salo,* thin slices of fat, for an unusual taste of the Ukraine. Go on an empty stomach as the food can be very filling, stodgy if you're unlucky. Note that this place is open 24 hours daily. ✉ *2 ul. 1905 Goda,* ☎ *095/255–0204. AE, V. Metro: 1905 Goda.*

$$ ✕ **Bochka.** Popular among the after-rave set, Bochka is another of Moscow's numerous open-round-the-clock restaurants and is always a dependable place for good Russian food. Opposite the Mezhdunarodnaya Hotel, it attracts its fair share of New Russians and businessmen. If you're brave, turn up on Fridays, when a giant spit is set up for the roasting of wild game, including bulls and goats. If that doesn't appeal, the salads are all well worth a try, although we're not too sure about the *kholodets,* a portion of meat served wobbling in its own jelly. This spot is open 24 hours daily. ✉ *2 ul. 1905 Goda,* ☎ *095/252–3041. AE, V. Metro: 1905 Goda.*

$$ ✕ **Mesto Vstrechi.** A few minutes away from Pushkin Square, Mesto Vstrechi is a cool place for a relaxing, inexpensive meal before hitting the town. Located in a cellar, it attracts a young crowd, partly because bands accompany diner most nights (there are, however, plenty of nooks to hide in if you want to have some peace and quiet). Although never amazing, the mix of European and Russian food is always well-crafted and satisfying. Mesto Vstrechi, which means "meeting place," also has an unusually good choice of beers and can even pack a picnic for you if you're heading into the countryside to cook up traditional Russian kebabs. ⊠ *9 Gnezdnikovsky per.,* ☎ *095/229–2373. AE, DC, MC, V. Metro: Pushkinskaya.*

$$ ✕ **Uncle Vanya's.** Even though it is located on one of Moscow's finest opera and ballet addresses and its name is the title of one of Anton Chekhov's most famous plays, Uncle Vanya's owners insist that their restaurant has nothing to do with the theater world. But step inside, and you feel swept back in time to a 19th-century country home right out of a Chekhov novel. Dark wooden paneling, old gramophones, books by classic Russian writers, and tea served in glasses with traditional silver glass holders all enhance the illusion. The menu is good, wholesome Russian home cooking. Beside the usual fare of borshch and pirogi, you can also find dumplings with fresh cherries, buckwheat with mushrooms and onions, and chicken giblets baked in a pot. Live jazz and blues is played every night and the place attracts an artistic crowd. One of the cheapest in the city center, the restaurant has a menu in English but its friendly staff speaks only Russian. This popular place is open 24 hours daily. ⊠ *17 Bolshaya Dmitrovka,* ☎ *095/232–1448. AE, MC, V. Metro: Chekhovskaya.*

SCANDINAVIAN

$$$$ ✕ **Scandinavia.** Whereas many restaurants in Moscow seem to have gone for glitz, the owners of Scandinavia have opted for cozy and comforting. This is one of the most serene dining rooms in the city: Burnt-orange walls with blue-green trim, comfortable wooden chairs and upholstered benches, candles in wine bottles on red-and-white tablecloths, and arrangements of dried flowers on deep window ledges all combine to make you feel as if you're in a Swedish country manor. Three Swedish chefs are in charge of the menu, resulting in a mixture of Scandinavian, modern European, and American cuisines. The proof is in the pudding or, rather, the chèvre cheesecake with cloudberry compote—a nouvelle delight that combines French goat cheese with Swedish sauce in an American dish. If you're out for a purely Scandinavian selection, try the marinated herring with a drop of aquavit, a traditional herbal spirit. Despite being just a few yards away from the bustle of Tverskaya ulitsa, Scandinavia's balcony—which overlooks the avenue's beer garden—is one of the most tranquil places to eat outside in the summer. ⊠ *7 Maly Palashevsky per.,* ☎ *095/200–4986. Reservations essential. AE, DC, MC, V. Metro: Pushkinskaya.*

SEAFOOD

$$$$ ✕ **Crab House.** Just a few minutes stroll from the Kremlin, this relatively new seafood restaurant is more upbeat and expensive than its American cousins. The spacious, three-deck dining area has a feel of a stylish ocean liner with its relaxing modern mix of wood and steel, blue marine walls, and exotic fish in aquariums. The wait staff, clad in sailors' uniforms, is friendly and always at hand. The restaurant boasts the largest oysters in town, specially flown in twice a week from the United States, along with all the other seafood. The menu's showpiece is the positively decadent Imperial Platter, a mixture of stuffed lobster, baked oysters with black caviar, mussels, and scallops with ham and grilled vegetables. ⊠ *6 Tverskaya,* ☎ *095/292–5360 or 095/292–5359. AE, DC, MC, V or rubles. Metro: Okhotny Ryad.*

$$$$ ✕ **Sirena.** There are probably as many live fish as dead denizens of the deep at this seafood showplace, a longtime favorite of the famous, including Sting and Liza Minnelli. One room has a glass floor beneath which huge sturgeon squirm; in another, aquariums surround you, with numerous fish watching you eat their brethren. Hey, doesn't anybody know that fish have feelings too? The entrance is shaped like the stern of a ship, the waiters are dressed like sailors, the wide array of fish main courses, like the mixed seafood in parchment, rarely disappoints (unlike the appetizers), but Sirena is still far too expensive. ⊠ *15 Bolshaya Spasskaya,* ☎ *095/208–1412. AE, DC, MC, V or rubles. Metro: Sukharevskaya.*

TURKISH

$$ ✕ **Amalteya.** Moscow's top Turkish restaurant, near the Plekhanov Economic Academy, is renowned for its friendly service, succulent kebabs, and huge choice of starters. The small, tasteful interior is dominated by a pale blue pillar and fishpond straight out of a Turkish fable. Live music usually includes a magical collection of Middle Eastern melodies, Western pop also gets a look in, and the belly dancers shimmy up to your table in search of tips. The Turkish manager is ever ready to give advice on the myriad varieties of kebabs, and the portions are big enough to warrant a doggy bag every time. ⊠ *28/1 Stremyanny per.,* ☎ *095/ 236–0256. AE, DC, MC, V, or rubles according to restaurant exchange rate. Metro: Serpukhovskaya.*

LODGING

You might think that a world capital with a population of more than 9 million would have a large number of hotels, but this is not the case in Moscow—at least not yet. As Russia comes in from the cold, the city's hotel scene is expanding slowly, often painfully (five top players in the field have been assassinated in recent years), and always with eyes on the Kapitalist prize. Some hotels have dropped prices a bit in the last few years, but the best hotels can—and do—charge astronomical rates that mostly get charged to expense accounts (one benefit: these hotels often offer steeply discounted weekend rates). Today, for the traveler who is able and willing to splurge, Moscow's top hotels offer a level of amenities and pampering that were unavailable just a few years ago. Gourmet restaurants, business centers, cafés and cocktail bars, health clubs, and attentive service are now the norm at hotels that are oriented toward the business traveler. Mid-level establishments seem to be getting the message, and there's evidence that they, too, are improving their facilities and service. For example, most now have card key locks and it's rare to find rooms that are not clean, even if they're a bit tattered.

That noted, the city suffers from a dearth of decent mid-range hotels, and hangovers are still evident at the old Intourist standbys. Some of the latter have improved their service and refurnished their rooms, and will be a pleasant surprise. But too often, the Soviet decor—mouse-brown and tarnished gold-patterned polyester on plywood—remains. Competition is growing, however slowly, but for now foreign tourists should not be surprised by a lower level of service than they know at home. When reserving, it really pays to ask for a room that has been renovated; the cost usually is the same and the difference can be startling, particularly in the lower-priced hotels. If it matters, you should also ask whether your double room has twin beds or one large one; either is possible.

All prices are quoted in U.S. dollars.

CATEGORY	COST*
$$$$	over $350
$$$	$250–$350
$$	$125–$250
$	$60–$125
¢	under $60

All prices are for a standard double room, excluding taxes and service charge.

$$$$ ⊞ **Baltschug Kempinski.** Situated on the banks of the Moskva River, opposite the Kremlin and Red Square, this five-star Swiss-managed hotel boasts extraordinary views—and prices, too. Long in a state of disrepair, its 19th-century building, once an aristocratic apartment house, has been completely reconstructed. The modern interiors sparkle, but they lack the prerevolutionary character of the Metropol or Savoy hotels. Even so, the spacious, stately rooms are equipped with all amenities, down to bedroom slippers. For a real blast of luxury, head to the Library, a formal, eighth-floor room that can be rented for parties or meetings and has a balcony with a glorious, panoramic view. Since the hotel's location is central but not particularly convenient—it's a 15-minute walk from the nearest metro station, and the city's main attractions are on the other side of the river—you're best off having a car and driver if you stay here. Make sure you specify that you want a room with a view, which costs more; otherwise you could end up staring at the factory bordering the hotel's eastern side. ✉ *1 Balchug ul., 113035,* ☎ *095/230–6500,* FAX *095/230–6502; from outside Russia,* ☎ *7501/230–6500,* FAX *7501/230–6502. 204 rooms with bath, 30 suites. 3 restaurants, bar, café, minibar, no-smoking floor, 24-hr room service, indoor pool, sauna, exercise room, business center, meeting rooms, bank. AE, DC, MC, V. Traveler's checks accepted. Metro: Tretyakovskaya or Pl. Revolutsii.*

$$$$ ⊞ **Metropol.** Originally built in 1899–1903, this lavish, first-class
★ hotel has been the setting for some fabled events: Lenin spoke frequently in the assembly hall of the building, in 1918–19 the Central Committee of the Russian Republic met here under its first chairman, Yakov Sverdlov (for whom the square outside the hotel was named until 1991), and, finally, David Lean filmed part of *Dr. Zhivago* in the restaurant. Today, this hotel—a member of the Inter-Continental Hotel group—remains one of Moscow's most elegant, with outstanding service and amenities. The lobby, restaurants, and other common areas will transport you back a century, while guest rooms feature hardwood floors, Oriental rugs, large closets, and modern furnishings. Antiques grace all the suites, and the two presidential suites come with private saunas. The location, opposite the Bolshoi Theater and a five-minute walk from the Kremlin, is top-rate. ✉ *1/4 Teatralny proyezd, 103012,* ☎ *095/927–6000,* FAX *095/927–6010; from outside Russia,* ☎ *7501/ 927–6000,* FAX *7501/927–6010. 292 rooms with bath, 76 suites. 3 restaurants, 3 bars, café, no-smoking rooms, 24-hr room service, sauna, exercise room, casino, business services, meeting rooms, travel services. AE, DC, MC, V. Traveler's checks accepted. Metro: Teatralnaya, Okhotny Ryad.*

$$$$ ⊞ **National.** If price is no object—but luxury, quiet, and elite service
★ are—this is the place to stay. When built in 1903, the National was one of Moscow's premier hotels. Reopened in 1995 after years of renovation, it is once again the city's most elegant accommodation, with a superb location across a plaza from Red Square and at the foot of the increasingly chic Tverskaya ulitsa. In the stunning landmark building, you'll find the grandeur of the original Art Nouveau style and the

serenity of a bygone era. A great marble staircase spirals upward with a winding railing of pewter vine; the elevators, topped by silvered twists of ivy, echo the design. Behind the stairs, through lavender and light green stained glass, you can glimpse the atrium and Viennese-style café below. There are four styles of suites (including ultradeluxe corner ones with balconies), two styles of doubles, and two of singles. All rooms, except for a few doubles done in a more modern style, are plush with polished oak furniture upholstered in silk. The white-tiled Italianate bathrooms are sparkling and modern, if a bit small. The views can be superb, but you pay extra for them. You might ask for No. 107, a two-room suite (for $800 a night) where Lenin lived for a time in 1918. Literally topping all of it is the pool in the top-floor fitness center, where swimmers look out, eye level, at the crenellated top of the Kremlin and the cupolas and domes of its cathedrals—a magnificent sight, particularly at night. ⊠ *14/1 Okhotny Ryad, 103012,* ☎ *095/258–7000,* ℻ *095/258–7100. 195 rooms with bath, 36 suites. 2 restaurants, 2 bars, café, minibars, 24-hr room service, indoor pool, beauty salon, massage, sauna, exercise room, business services, currency exchange, meeting rooms. AE, DC, MC, V. Metro: Okhotny Ryad.*

$$$ 🏨 **Aerostar.** The Aerostar, not to be confused with the rundown
★ Aeroflot Hotel next door, is a Canadian-Russian joint venture that opened in 1992. The Canadian team transformed an austere Soviet design into a Western-style hotel, with a cheery lobby and rooms with European furnishings and redwood paneling. Rooms on the northeast look out onto Petrovsky Palace, the striking, crenelated brick stopover for the czars journeying between St. Petersburg and Moscow. Business travelers find the location—on the way from the city center to Sheremetyevo International Airport—convenient, but tourists may find it too far from the city's major attractions. Café Taiga has fresh lobster, flown in from Nova Scotia, Friday and Saturday nights and a lavish Sunday champagne brunch. ⊠ *37 Leningradsky Prospekt, 125167,* ☎ *095/213–9000,* ℻ *095/213–9001; from outside Russia,* ☎ *7502/231–9000,* ℻ *7502/213–9001. 386 rooms with bath, 31 suites. 2 restaurants, 2 bars, no-smoking rooms, 24-hr room service, massage, sauna, exercise room, concierge, business services, 24-hr currency exchange, meeting rooms. AE, DC, MC, V. Metro: Dinamo or Aeroport.*

$$$ 🏨 **Art Hotel.** Fine-art lovers take note: The German owner of this hotel, which opened in November 1996, owns a gallery in Berlin, and he has covered the hotel walls with the works of contemporary Russian artists—all of them for sale. When you get tired of the paintings, you can also take in the interesting views out the windows: Rooms look out either onto Central Army Sports Stadium, where you can watch soccer games, or onto the park and the hotel beer garden, which has live music and weekend brunch. Indeed, at the edge of a park and away from the urban crush, this hotel can make you feel as if you are in the country. There are two tennis courts for guests. Guest rooms are clean and basic, while breakfast is included in the room price. Twenty minutes by car from Red Square, the hotel is far from public transport: 20 minutes of walking and riding a trolleybus after the Metro. Art Hotel is popular with European businesspeople. ⊠ *2 Third Peschannaya ul., 125252,* ☎ *095/955–2300,* ℻ *095/955–2310. 81 rooms with bath, 2 suites. Restaurant, beer garden, no-smoking rooms, 24-hr room service, massage, sauna, exercise room, 2 meeting rooms. AE, DC, MC, V. Metro: Sokol.*

$$$ 🏨 **Hotel Tverskaya.** Designed by a Russian architect in the Art Nouveau style, this American-managed hotel opened in 1995, just a 20-
★ minute walk up Tverskaya ulitsa from Red Square and five minutes from the metro. A four-story atrium and a small, peaceful lobby give the hotel a cozy, warm atmosphere that extends to the Italian restau-

rant, Gratzi, whose alcove booths overlook the lobby. Of the eight floors, one is non-smoking. The rooms are understated—ivory, rose, and olive comprise the palette, with darker notes provided by wood furniture. A sunny guests-only lounge offers coffee and tea in the mornings, drinks at the end of the day. On some floors, old black-and-white prints of Moscow scenes line the walls. At press time, a small addition was under construction. ✉ *34 Pervaya Tverskaya-Yamskaya ul., 125047,* ☎ *095/258–3000,* FAX *095/258–3099; from outside Russia,* ☎ *7501/258–3000,* FAX *7501/258–3099. 115 rooms with bath, 7 suites. Restaurant, bar, 24-hr room service, sauna, exercise room, business services, 24-hr currency exchange, meeting rooms. AE, DC, MC, V. Metro: Belorusskaya.*

$$$ 🏨 **Marco Polo Presnya.** Opened in 1904 as a residential hotel for English teachers and later the exclusive domain of the Communist Party, this small hotel is an intriguing choice for those interested in the Soviet era. For instance, an auditorium now used for meetings was once the movie house where party insiders came to see Western films unavailable to most Muscovites. Most rooms have been renovated, and are functional if not luxurious. The hotel is located in a prestigious residential neighborhood not far from Patriarch's Pond, and many rooms have balconies furnished with chairs from which to survey the scene. Service is friendly and efficient, the atmosphere quiet and composed. In warm months, the inner courtyard is an attractive place to sit for snacks or meals. ✉ *9 Spiridonevsky per., 103104,* ☎ *095/244–3631,* FAX *095/926–5404. 48 rooms with bath, 20 suites. Restaurant, lobby lounge, outdoor café (in summer), minibars, no-smoking rooms, 24-hr room service, sauna, exercise room, business services, meeting rooms, 24-hr currency exchange. AE, DC, MC, V. Metro: Pushkinskaya or Mayakovskaya.*

$$$ 🏨 **Mezhdunarodnaya.** With a name that means "international," this big gray hotel has been nicknamed "the Mezh" by foreign residents. Built with financial backing from the American financier Armand Hammer in 1980, this huge complex, called the World Trade Center, includes the hotel and shopping center and two buildings for offices and apartments. Although it has lost some of its original prestige, it's a frequent site for conferences and near the city exposition center. The rooms are big, and renovations are under way, but in the older rooms, the Italian furnishings have seen better days. Bathrooms are clean and modern. The hotel is located within sight of the city center but far from the subway, and only one city bus stops near the hotel. ✉ *12 Krasnopresnenskaya nab., 123610,* ☎ *095/258–1212,* FAX *095/253–2051. 544 rooms with bath, 33 suites. 5 restaurants, 3 bars, minibars, room service, pool, beauty salon, sauna, exercise room, shops, business services, 24-hr currency exchange, meeting rooms, travel services. AE, DC, MC, V. Metro: ul. 1905 Goda.*

$$$ 🏨 **Moscow Marriott Grand Hotel.** Once you step inside past the renovated turn-of-the-century Art Nouveau facade, you'll feel very much at home—if home is the United States. You'll even find eggs Benedict on the breakfast buffet. Marriott opened its nine-story hotel amid the bustle of Tverskaya ulitsa in 1997, just in time to celebrate Moscow's 850th anniversary. The Western-furnished rooms are spacious, with some looking out to a peaceful courtyard. The lobby has a central round staircase under a sunny atrium. Service is pleasant and efficient. Red Square is 1 km (½ mi) away. ✉ *26 Tverskaya ul., 103050,* ☎ *095/935–8500,* FAX *095/935–8501; from outside Russia,* ☎ *7502/935–8500. 377 rooms with bath, 13 suites. 3 restaurants, 2 bars, minibars, no-smoking floors, 24-hr room service, indoor pool, beauty salon, massage, sauna, exercise room, concierge, business services, meeting rooms, bank. AE, DC, MC, V. Metro: Mayakovskaya.*

$$$ ⚏ **Radisson Slavyanskaya.** Designed for business travelers, the hotel of-
★ fers every modern American-style amenity: no-nonsense comfort in an
efficient atmosphere. Its huge, two-story lobby—great for people-
watching—is lined with restaurants, luxury shops, a popular English-
language theater with first-run movies, and other businesses. It also has
one of the city's best health clubs. The second-floor business center is
frequently busy (in part because the open space includes several large
tables for guests to use for meetings—no advance booking required, but
people often get there early to reserve the space they want). The hotel's
location is not quite central, but alongside the Kiev railway station, with
its transients and homeless population. Of course, there are security guards
at the hotel entrance, and some businesspeople rarely leave the hotel dur-
ing their stays. This is a good choice for visitors who favor comfort and
service over character. ⊠ *2 Berezhkovskaya nab., 121059, ☎ 095/941–
8020, ℻ 095/941–8000; from outside Russia, ℻ 7502/224–1225.
Reservations may be made through Radisson Hotels in U.S., ☎ 800/333–
3333. 407 rooms with bath, 24 suites. 3 restaurants (including a sushi
bar), café, lobby lounge, refrigerators, 24-hr room service, indoor lap
pool, massage, sauna, health club, business services, 24-hr currency ex-
change, meeting rooms, travel services. AE, DC, MC, V. Metro: Kievskaya.*

$$$ ⚏ **Savoy.** The Savoy opened in 1913 in connection with celebrations
commemorating the 300th anniversary of the Romanov dynasty. Most
of its working life, however, it was an Intourist hotel called the Berlin.
After the demise of the Soviets, it was Moscow's first joint-venture hotel
to be completely renovated. Its interiors, replete with gilded chandeliers, ceiling paintings, and polished paneling, invoke the spirit of prerevolutionary Russia. And the dining room, where breakfast—included
in room price—is served, is a knockout: romantic and ornate, with a
pianist, fountain, and painted cherubs floating across clouds. The
rooms are somewhat small, but the Oriental rugs, parquet floors, and
ivory wallpaper make them cozy. The views are mostly negligible,
owing to the hotel's side-street location, but this gives the advantage
of quiet. You can stay in the gilt suite where Luciano Pavarotti stayed
while performing at the Bolshoi Theater; the piano bought for him now
is in the restaurant. Popular with businesspeople, the Savoy is centrally
located, just off Theater Square and within walking distance of the Kremlin. The staff is cheerful and helpful. At press time, the bar was under
reconstruction due to a fire next door. ⊠ *3 Rozhdestvenka ul., 103012,
☎ 095/929–8500, ℻ 095/230–2186. 85 rooms with bath, 17 suites.
Restaurant, 2 bars, minibars, 24-hr room service, business services, travel
services. AE, DC, MC, V. Metro: Kuznetsky Most.*

$$$ ⚏ **Sheraton Palace Hotel Moscow.** While the Fortune 500 crowd seems
to prefer the Slavyanskaya, the European business community loves
this place, thanks to its amenities, which include a chauffeur-driven fleet
of cars, among them a stretch Lincoln—a rarity in Moscow. With a
certain crowd in mind, the hotel is heavy on double rooms for the sin-
gle traveler; you'll find these offer all you need, though they are a bit
crowded with furniture. The real winners are those who can afford the
duplexes, which have two upstairs bedrooms (each with full, separate
bath), a dining room, and a living room below, decorated in rose-and-
mint furnishings with tasteful paintings and sculpture throughout.
The hotel's location, at the far upper end of Tverskaya ulitsa, is ex-
cellent, but this main road isn't always easy to navigate by car. ⊠ *19
Pervaya Tverskaya-Yamskaya ul., 125047, ☎ 095/931–9700, ℻ 095/
931–9708; from outside Russia, ☎ 7502/256–3000, ℻ 7502/256–
3008. 221 rooms with bath, 18 suites. 3 restaurants, 2 bars, café, mini-
bars, no-smoking rooms, 24-hr room service, massage, health club,
concierge, business services, meeting rooms, currency exchange. AE,
DC, MC, V. Metro: Belorusskaya.*

$$$ 🖭 **Sofitel Iris.** Under French management, this hotel opened in 1991 in a bleak residential district on the northwestern outskirts of town, adjacent to the world-famous Fyodorov Eye Institute and about halfway between the city center and the airport. Its distant location is unfortunate, because this is a fine foreign-run hotel with spacious, cheery rooms that have lots of closet space, large bathrooms, and balconies. The views are quite dismal, though. There are few shops or restaurants of interest to the tourist in the area. However, complimentary shuttle buses run hourly until 11 PM to two central stops. The hotel also offers guests free bus tours of the city and excursions to the popular weekend crafts market in Izmailovsky Park. ✉ *10 Korovinskoye Shosse, 103051,* ☎ *095/488–8000,* 𝖥𝖠𝖷 *095/488–8888; from outside Russia,* 𝖥𝖠𝖷 *7502/220–8888. 155 rooms with bath, 40 suites. 2 restaurants, bar, minibars, no-smoking floor, 24-hr room service, indoor pool, sauna, exercise room, business services, meeting rooms. AE, DC, MC, V.*

$$ 🖭 **Holiday Inn Moscow-Vinogradovo.** At press time, the Holiday Inn chain's first hotel in Russia was still a few months from opening. Its rural location north of Moscow is 8 km (5 mi) from Sheremetyevo II airport, and the hotel hopes to attract airline crews as well as conferences and families. There's a garden outside where families can play and walk, two ponds nearby, and complimentary shuttle buses planned to the airport and city center. ✉ *171 Dmitrovskoye Shosse, 127204,* ☎ *095/937–0670,* 𝖥𝖠𝖷 *095/937–0671; from outside Russia,* ☎ *7502/ 937–0670,* 𝖥𝖠𝖷 *7502/937–0671. 146 rooms with bath, 8 suites. Restaurant, bar, breakfast room, café, minibars, no-smoking rooms, 24-hr room service, indoor pool, beauty salon, sauna, exercise room, video games, business services, meeting rooms. AE, DC, MC, V.*

$$ 🖭 **Hotel Budapest.** Opened in 1876 as a club for noblemen, this hotel later became a hostel in Soviet days for people in Moscow for official business. Now, it's a comfortable hotel in a busy city-center location, with a homey old style: high ceilings, Oriental rugs, leather chairs, and small touches such as the wrought-iron mailbox in the lobby. While the hotel has no restaurant, it serves breakfast in guest rooms. A luxury restaurant is next door, and there's a popular, inexpensive café called Shury Mury just up the block. ✉ *2/18 Petrovsky Line, 103051,* ☎ *095/ 923–2356,* 𝖥𝖠𝖷 *095/921–1266; from outside Russia,* 𝖥𝖠𝖷 *7502/221–1665. 90 rooms with bath, 30 suites. Pub, minibars, no-smoking rooms, business services, meeting rooms. AE, DC, MC, V. Metro: Kuznetsky Most.*

$$ 🖭 **Hotel Danilovsky.** Located within the walls of the Orthodox St. Daniel Monastery—the official residence of Patriach Alexy II of Moscow and All Russia—this hotel is just a five-minute walk from a metro station and is close to one of the city's better farmers' markets. The site is serene and lovely, with fountains, flowers, and, of course, the domed monastery buildings. Throughout the hotel, there are religious-themed paintings and photographs. The church holds conferences here, and also sponsors concerts and exhibitions. The rooms (breakfast is included) are basic but clean and spacious. Standard double rooms have two twin beds; only suites have double beds. Some rooms have showers, no tubs (and the scratchy toilet paper will remind you of Soviet times). The Russian menu in the restaurant is well priced, but the green decor feels slightly institutional. ✉ *5 Bolshoi Starodanilovsky per., 113191* ☎ *095/954– 0503,* 𝖥𝖠𝖷 *095/954–0750. 93 rooms with bath, 23 suites. 2 restaurants, bar, refrigerators, 24-hr room service, indoor pool, massage, sauna, business services, 24-hr currency exchange, meeting rooms. AE, DC, MC, V. Metro: Tulskaya.*

$$ 🖭 **Intourist.** Centrally located at the bottom of Tverskaya ulitsa, at the back of the National Hotel, this aging skyscraper is a popular holding spot for tourist groups. There's a good pizza restaurant (Patio Pizza) outside the hotel entrance, but there is also a seedy-looking presence outside the front doors that can often make coming and going, particularly at night, rather unpleasant. Its smoke-filled lobby features the usual oversize and drab decor—although the souvenir shops are better stocked than most—and the staff is helpful. The interior has changed little since the hotel opened in 1970, so the rooms are a bit shabby. Although they all come with refrigerators, telephones, and televisions, you also get stained furnishings, worn carpeting, and monotone polyester curtains. Despite the drawbacks, the rates remain relatively high—mostly due to the hotel's prime location. ⊠ *3/5 Tverskaya ul., 103009,* ☎ *095/956–8400 or 095/956–8426,* FAX *095/956–8360. 369 rooms with bath, 89 suites. 3 restaurants, 6 bars, beauty salon, travel services. AE, DC, MC, V. Metro: Okhotny Ryad.*

$$ 🏨 **Novotel.** If you need a room near Sheremetyevo II Airport, this is the place to stay. Professional European soccer teams patronize Novotel because of its few distractions. The rooms and beds are comfortable, the halls quiet. In addition, the staff is eager to please, and the modern facilities are well maintained. There is a 24-hr shuttle bus to the airport, which is just a quarter mile away, and a complimentary bus to the city center as well. Clients are, predictably, primarily businesspeople and airline personnel. The hotel also offers day rates of less than half the normal rates. ⊠ *Sheremetyevo II Airport, 103339,* ☎ *095/926–5900,* FAX *095/926–5903/5904; from outside Russia, 7502/220–6604. 466 rooms with bath, 22 suites. 2 restaurants, lobby lounge, indoor pool, sauna, exercise rooms, 24-hr currency exchange, meeting rooms. AE, DC, MC, V.*

$$ 🏨 **Renaissance Moscow.** Opened in 1991 as one of Moscow's first joint-venture hotels, this hotel is a busy place for conferences and meetings, and has an English-language movie theater. Rooms are large and fully equipped with every amenity. The fitness center is one of the best in town, and if you endure the red tape, it is possible to swim in the Olympic pool in the sports complex across the street. An executive floor has a lounge for breakfast and relaxing, butler service, and a separate reception area. The hotel is far from the city center, but it's a good value and convenient to all major arterial roads, and the Prospekt Mira subway stop is a 15-minute walk away. Athletes competing or musicians performing in the Olympic Sports Stadium—used for volleyball, tennis, swimming, and other sporting events as well as for large-scale concerts—often stay here. The café has its own bakery, which turns out delicious pastries—none too common in Moscow. ⊠ *18/1 Olympisky Prospekt, 129110,* ☎ *095/931–9000,* FAX *095/931–9076. 475 rooms with bath, 13 suites. 4 restaurants, bar, café, minibars, no-smoking floor, 24-hr room service, indoor pool, sauna, exercise room, business services, 24-hr currency exchange, meeting rooms. AE, DC, MC, V. Metro: Prospekt Mira.*

$$ 🏨 **Ukraina.** One of the seven Stalin Gothics, this imposing skyscraper
★ is a familiar landmark on the banks of the Moskva River. The red carpeting and high ceilings are trademarks of the Stalinist era. The rooms are worn but clean. Redwood and oak furnishings and fancy chandeliers create an atmosphere of faded elegance. The old tradition of floor attendants, or *dezhurnayas*, has been retained here, so you'll find a hotel staff member on every floor. The hotel is situated across the river from the Russian White House, where the president works. Rooms on the higher floors—it's 30 stories tall—on this side have great views. This is an almost-central location, where Kutuzovsky Prospekt, which is becoming a chic place to shop, meets up with the Novy Arbat. Metro riders, however, will find their station is a good 10-minute trek away. ⊠ *2/1 Kutuzovsky Prospekt, 121249,* ☎ *095/243–2596; 095/243–3030 reservations;* FAX *095/956–2078. 934 rooms with bath, 83 suites. 3 restaurants, 9 bars, café, refrigerators, 24-hr room service, massage, sauna, casino, business services, 24-hr currency exchange. AE, DC, MC, V. Metro: Kievskaya.*

$ ⊞ **Belgrad.** Built in 1975 as one of two twin towers (the other is now the Zolotoye Koltso), this former Intourist-run hotel is a typical Brezhnev-era high-rise. The hotel's main advantage is its central location, near the subway and the Arbat. The interior decor is unimaginative, and the hotel has the same institutional feeling as the Intourist. The rooms could use some sprucing up, and renovations are under way, if slow-going, to replace the somewhat shabby furniture and worn industrial carpeting. The hotel sometimes loses hot water for a couple of weeks in summer for maintenance work. ⊠ *8 Smolenskaya ul., 121099,* ☎ *095/248–2841 or 095/248–1676,* FAX *095/230–2129. 400 rooms with bath, 26 suites. 2 restaurants, 2 bars, 2 snack bars, currency exchange. DC, MC, V. Metro: Smolenskaya.*

$ ⊞ **Hotel Moskva.** This is another oversized Russian hotel, but it has a lopsided facade with an interesting if unconfirmed tale behind it. The story is told that Stalin was presented with two designs. When he signed his approval across the middle of the two, everyone was afraid to ask him which one he meant and the hotel was built using both designs. It was used for government congresses, film festivals, and other official events. Today, it's a slightly battered place, with a first floor that is too big to feel very welcoming. But the location is superb, the staff is friendly, and the rooms satisfactory, especially those that have been renovated. Request a room looking onto Red Square. ⊠ *2 Okotny Ryad, 103159,* ☎ *095/292–2040,* FAX *095/928–5938. 987 rooms with bath. 3 restaurants, 2 bars, refrigerators, room service, sauna, currency exchange, meeting rooms. AE, DC, MC, V. Metro: Okhotny Ryad.*

$ ⊞ **Kosmos.** This huge, 26-story hotel was built by the French for the
★ 1980 Olympics. It is French-equipped and furnished, and years of heavy tourist traffic have dulled its shine, but the rooms are adequate and clean. Accommodations here are superior to those at the Intourist Hotel, another popular destination with tourist groups. Decor? Well, its spacious, two-story lobby is decorated with a sculpture strongly reminiscent of the molecule models in your sixth-grade science class. The hotel is across the street from the All-Russia Exhibition Center, a part of town that has interesting sights, but is far from downtown (though the metro is right across the street). ⊠ *150 Prospekt Mira, 129366,* ☎ *095/217–0785, 095/217–0786, 095/215–6791, or 095/215–7880;* FAX *095/215–8880. 1,777 rooms with bath. 4 restaurants, 8 bars, beauty salon, sauna, bowling, casino. AE, DC, MC, V. Metro: VDNKh.*

$ ⊞ **Leningradskaya.** This Soviet fortress is another of Moscow's seven Stalin Gothic skyscrapers. Its awe-inspiring, monumental interior features high ceilings, red carpets, and heavy bronze chandeliers. A faded gem of the Communist era, its sumptuous decor was at one time labeled decadent by party hard-liners. Upstairs, guest rooms are modestly furnished but clean and well-maintained. Ask for a room high up—the views from the lower floors are strictly industrial. The location is relatively central but not exactly calm: The hotel stands at a busy intersection, right across from the Leningrad, Kazan, and Yaroslav railway stations—architectural gems themselves. To reach the metro, you have to dash across the highway and then make your way through the unsavory crowds that live at the train station. Nevertheless, the reasonable rates here make this an okay choice for budget-minded travelers (though not recommended for women traveling alone). Maintain your patience; the hotel staff can seem weary of their jobs. ⊠ *21/40 Kalanchevskaya ul., 107245,* ☎ *095/975–3032,* FAX *095/975–1802. 346 rooms with bath. Restaurant, 2 cafés, lobby lounge, minibars, room service, casino, currency exchange. AE, DC, MC, V. Metro: Komsomolskaya.*

$ ⊞ **Rossiya.** Pack your compass and map if you're staying here, because negotiating the seemingly endless corridors of this huge hotel will require them. The mammoth building is one of Europe's largest hotels, able to accommodate up to 6,000 guests. Opened in 1967, it once numbered among the Soviet Union's finest hotels, but it suffered two fires and service and accommodations rapidly sped downhill; it had a bad reputation for cockroaches and other vermin. However, a new director who began work in early 1998 seems to have brought improvements in services and cleanliness. The furnishings are very basic. As with the Intourist, the main reason to stay here is the location: just off the edge of Red Square, with stupendous views of it and the Kremlin, if you have a room on the west side. This is one of the cheapest choices in central Moscow. ✉ *6 Varvarka ul., 103495,* ☎ *095/232–5000,* 𝖥𝖠𝖷 *095/232–6248. 3,126 rooms with bath. 9 restaurants, 2 bars, 20 cafés, sauna, nightclub, currency exchange, meeting rooms. AE, MC, V. Metro: Kitai-Gorod.*

$ 🏨 **Soyuz.** Yugoslav-built in 1980, this hotel on the northwestern outskirts of town has an interesting avant-garde design. Its distant location keeps its rates in the inexpensive category, though the service and atmosphere here are good. The rooms come with modern furnishings and cheery, flowery wallpaper; the bathrooms are tiled in a startling red. Some of them have views of the Moskva River, where in summer Muscovites come in droves to swim and sunbathe. The location is a serious drawback. The surrounding area is likely to have a dispiriting effect on first-time visitors, and the hotel is convenient only to the Sheremetyevo Airport (15 minutes away). The closest subway stop—Rechnoy Vokzal, the last stop on the green line—is a 20-minute bus ride away, and it can take more than an hour to reach the city center by car. ✉ *12 Levoberezhnaya ul., 125475,* ☎ *095/457–2088,* 𝖥𝖠𝖷 *095/457–2096. 158 rooms with bath. Restaurant, 2 bars, currency exchange. AE, DC, MC, V. Metro: Rechnoy Vokzal.*

¢ 🏨 **Hotel Izmailova.** Until recently, this hotel included five buildings that made it Europe's largest, with thousands of rooms. Now it's four hotels, and this one—two buildings big—is most commonly used by foreigners. Situated a two-minute walk from Moscow's lively and terrific weekend crafts and flea market, this is a convenient place for the serious souvenir shopper. It's also adjacent to a metro station, and across from a large park where Peter the Great learned to sail, but it's otherwise a trek from tourist sites. The rooms are basic. ✉ *71 Izmailovskoye Shosse, 105187,* ☎ *095/166–4490,* 𝖥𝖠𝖷 *095/166–7486. 2,000 rooms with bath. 4 restaurants, 3 bars, room service, sauna, currency exchange, meeting rooms. AE, DC, V. Metro: Izmailovsky Park.*

¢ 🏨 **Molodyozhnaya.** Its name means "youth," and the hotel traditionally catered to groups of young people traveling under the auspices of Sputnik (the former Soviet youth tourist agency). It was built for the 1980 Olympics and features the typical drab decor of a Brezhnev-era high-rise, except for its bright blue exterior. The rock-bottom prices may make you indifferent to its cement-and-steel lobby decorated with a mosaic depicting happy proletariat youth. The rooms are standard size, adequate if slightly institutional, and clean. Some rooms have showers but no tubs. The hotel is popular with groups of schoolchildren and young travelers. The three- and five-person "suites" are good for friends traveling together. The hotel is on the outskirts of town, far from the city's tourist attractions, but there's a subway stop within walking distance. ✉ *27 Dmitrovskoye Shosse, 127550,* ☎ *095/977–3155,* 𝖥𝖠𝖷 *095/956–1078. 600 rooms with bath. Restaurant, 4 bars, refrigerators, dance club, currency exchange, meeting rooms. MC, V. Metro: Timiryazevskaya.*

¢ 🏨 **Travelers Guest House Moscow.** For those on a severe budget, this is the place. It's clean and friendly, with several blocks of rooms that each include a five-person room, a double, and a single. There are no phones in the rooms and no televisions. Guests can use the kitchen two floors down to cook their own meals, but there are few dishes and not much equipment. The guest house also will do laundry for a fee. As in most Russian apartments, the hot water is turned off for a month in the summer for system maintenance. More than half the guests here are young Americans, and the staff speaks English. While this is not unlike a youth hostel, the guest house is not affiliated with a hostel association, and you need not be a member to stay here. ✉ *50 Bolshaya Pereyaslavskaya, 10th floor, 129041,* ☎ *095/971–4059,* ℻ *095/280– 7686. 33 rooms, 14 with bath. MC, V. Metro: Prospekt Mira.*

NIGHTLIFE AND THE ARTS

The Arts

Moscow is famed for its rich cultural life. The city boasts more than 60 officially registered theaters, with new ones opening all the time. At most theaters tickets can be obtained for rubles at the theaters themselves or at theater box offices (*teatralnaya kassa*) scattered throughout the city. If you're intimidated by the language barrier, avail yourself of the **EPS Theater Box Office** in the main lobby of the Metropol Hotel (☎ 095/927–6982 or 095/927–6983) or the service bureau in your hotel. The prices are inflated, but they can often get tickets to sold-out performances. Another alternative is to purchase a ticket from a scalper immediately prior to the performance, but there is no guarantee that you'll get a good seat.

Every Friday the English-language newspaper *Moscow Times* publishes a schedule of cultural events for the coming week.

Art Galleries

Numerous private galleries have sprung up in the past few years. If you want to buy Russian art, head for galleries like M'ARS and Moscow Fine Art. Otherwise go direct to the artists who sell their works in front of the Central House of Artists and at Izmailovsky Outdoor Market. If you're interested in conceptual and performance art your best bet is either the Guelman gallery or XL-Gallery.

The Friday edition of the *Moscow Times* carries a review of current exhibits. Check out the latest opening and watch out for the one-man Coat Gallery (a.k.a. Alexander Petrelli) who has paintings hidden within his overcoat. Just go up to him and ask and he'll open up and show you his wares. For opening hours, check with the galleries themselves; some are open only by appointment, and most are closed on Sunday and Monday.

A-3 Gallery (✉ 39 Starokonyushenny per., ☎ 095/291–8484, Metro: Arbatskaya). This gallery enjoys links with the Goethe Institute which provide a steady stream of exhibitions by contemporary German artists, plus regular shows of modern Russian art.

Aidan Gallery (✉ 23/7 Novopeschanaya Pl., ☎ 095/943–5348, Metro: Sokol). Owned by Aidan Salakhova, this gallery specializes in young, little-known artists who experiment with new technologies, such as c omputer-generated art.

Central House of Artists, or TsDKh (✉ 10 Krymsky Val., ☎ 095/238– 1245, Metro: Park Kultury). This vast exhibition center represents many different galleries. If you wander long enough you're sure to find something to fit your tastes, from traditional landscapes to the latest avant-garde outrage. In front of TsDKh, a huge painting market snakes its way along the river. Among the piles of kitsch and boring landscapes you can find some real gems. Be prepared to bargain.

In case you want to see the world.

At American Express, we're here to make your journey a smooth one. So we have over 1,700 travel service locations in over 120 countries ready to help. What else would you expect from the world's largest travel agency?

do more.

http://www.americanexpress.com/travel

Travel

In case you want to be welcomed there.

We're here to see that you're always welcomed at establishments everywhere. That's why millions of people carry the American Express® Card – for peace of mind, confidence, and security, around the world or just around the corner.

do more

Cards

In case you're running low.

We're here to help with more than 118,000 Express Cash locations around the world. In order to enroll, just call American Express before you start your vacation.

do more

Express Cash

And just in case.

We're here with American Express® Travelers Cheques and Cheques *for Two*® They're the safest way to carry money on your vacation and the surest way to get a refund, practically anywhere, anytime.

Another way we help you...

do more ®

Travelers
Cheques

Dar Gallery (⊠ 7, building 5 Malaya Polyanka, ☏ 095/238–6554, Metro: Polyanka). Naive and primitive art are the specialties here.

Dom Nashchokina Gallery (⊠ 12 Vorotnikovsky per., ☏ 095/299–1178, Metro: Mayakovskaya). This is a well respected gallery focusing on famous emigré Russian artists of the older generation, like Ernest Neizvestny and Mikhail Shemyakin.

Guelman Gallery (⊠ 7/7, building 5 Malaya Polyanka, ☏ 095/238–8492, Metro: Polyanka).The most famous and controversial independent gallery in Moscow, this is run by Marat Guelman, an influential figure in and outside the art world. This gallery is always at the cutting edge of what's hip in the modern art world in Russia and it's certainly the best place to see provocative performance art.

L-Gallery (⊠ 26 Oktyabrskaya, ☏ 095/289–2491, Metro: Rizhskaya, take tram 5 to Oktyabrskaya ulitsa). This hip gallery provides an outlet for young artists, emigré and foreign, and also hosts a broad range of contemporary art shows.

NB Gallery (⊠ 6/2 Sivtsev Vrazhek, ☏ 095/203–4006, Metro: Kropotkinskaya). An always interesting gallery, this is run by Natalya Bykova, a friendly English-speaking art lover who's happy to offer advice on other top art venues in Moscow.

Spider and Mouse Gallery (⊠ 59 Leningradsky Prospekt, ☏ 095/287–1360, Metro: Aeroport). Returning from New York, Nikolai Palashchenko started up this gallery. The American influence is evident in the energetic exhibits he puts together featuring modern art by Russian and foreign artists.

TV Gallery (⊠ 6 Bolshaya Yakimanka, ☏ 095/238–0269, Metro: Oktyabrskaya). This features Russian and foreign video art.

XL-Gallery (⊠ 6 Bolshaya Sadovaya, ☏ 095/299–3724, Metro: Mayakovskaya). This intimate gallery specializes in small-scale conceptual art. Drawings, photographs, installations and occasional performance art are also on tap.

And the best galleries to buy more traditional art:

M'ARS gallery (⊠ 32 Malaya Filyovskaya, ☏ 095/146–2029, Metro: Pionerskaya); **Moscow Fine Art** (⊠ 3/10 Bolshaya Sadovaya, ☏ 095/251–7649, Metro: Polyanka); **New Collection gallery** (⊠ 16 Bolshaya Polyanka, ☏ 095/959–0141, Metro: Polyanka), by appointment only; **Phoenix Cultural Center** (⊠ 3 Kutuzovsky Prospect, ☏ 095/243–4958, Metro: Kievskaya).

Drama

Even if you do not speak Russian, you might want to explore the intense world of Russian dramatic theater. The partial listings below cover Moscow's major drama theaters. Take heed that evening performances here begin at 7 PM *sharp*.

Chekhov Moscow Art Theater, or MKhAT (⊠ 3 Kamergersky per., ☏ 095/229–8760 or 095/229–5370, Metro: Okhotny Ryad). Founded in 1898 by the celebrated actors and directors Konstantin Stanislavsky and Vladimir Nemirovich-Danchenko, this theater is famous for its productions of the Russian classics, especially those of Chekhov. Keep an eye out for the The American Studio at the Chekhov Art Theater, which presents performances, typically Russian classics, in English a few times a year on the theater's new stage.

LenKom Theater (✉ 6 Malaya Dmitrovka ul., ☎ 095/299–9668 or 095/299–0708, Metro: Pushkinskaya). Routinely good theater with often flashy productions, this troupe is somewhat tired these days.

Maly Theater (✉ 1/6 Teatralnaya Pl., ☎ 095/925–9868, Metro: Teatralnaya). Moscow's first dramatic theater is famous for its staging of Russian classics, especially those of Ostrovsky.

Mossoviet Theater (✉ 16 Bolshaya Sadovaya ul., ☎ 095/299–2035 or 095/200–5943, Metro: Mayakovskaya). This spot is good for contemporary drama, comedies, and musicals.

Sovremenik Theater (✉ 19A Chistoprudny bulvar, ☎ 095/921–6629 or 095/921–6473, Metro: Chistiye Prudy). Not as influential as it once was, this troupe still presents plays of high quality.

Taganka Theater (✉ Taganskaya Pl., ☎ 095/915–1217, Metro: Taganskaya). Run by the legendary Yuri Lyubimov, the Taganka theater is one of world's most famous theaters. Most famous is their dramatization of Mikhil Bulgakov's *The Master and the Margarita*. Be warned: Performances sell out far in advance.

The following troupes offer a wider repertory of presentations:

Estrada Theater (✉ 20/2 Bersenyovskaya nab., ☎ 095/230–0444, Metro: Biblioteka Imeni Lenina). With humorist Gennady Khazanov as an artistic director, all the best Russian stand-up comics perform here along with a number of variety shows.

Operetta Theater (✉ 6 Pushkinskaya ul., ☎ 095/292–2345, Metro: Biblioteka Imeni Lenina). Lighthearted Old World versions of American musicals are on offer by composers such as Strauss and Offenbach.

Tereza Durova Clowning Theater (✉ 6 ul. Pavlovskaya, inside the DK Zavoda Ilyicha, ☎ 095/237–1689, Metro: Serpukhovskaya). The attraction here are shows based on Commedia dell'Arte for children and adults, with music, dance, and acrobatics.

Movies

Russians have always been big devotees of motion pictures. The Russian film industry enjoyed its zenith from the 1940s through the 1960s in the Soviet era. Since then, it has seen its quality nosedive and its popularity plummet. Now, after a total eclipse of interest, the boom has been reborn thanks to a newly resurgent industry and six new Western-style, high-tech movie theaters built in Moscow over the last few years. Celluoid connoisseurs still gather at the Cinema Museum, which shows films for all tastes ranging from all-time classics to quirky experimental videos.

American House of Cinema (✉ 2 Berezhkovskaya nab., at the Radisson Slavjanskaya Hotel, ☎ 095/941–8747, Metro: Kievskaya). This one-screen cinema only shows English movies.

Cinema Center (✉ 15 Druzhinnikovskaya ul., ☎ 095/205–7306, Metro: Krasnopresnenskaya). This arthouse cinema shows a mixture of blockbusters and European favorites.

Cinema Museum (✉ 15 Druzhinnikovskaya ul., ☎ 095/255–9057, Metro: Krasnopresnenskaya). Specializing in the classic repertory, this is a second home for Moscow movie buffs.

Dome Cinema (✉ Renaissance Moscow Hotel, 18/1 Olimpisky Prospekt, ☎ 095/931–9873, Metro: Prospekt Mira). This is another hotel movie house catering to the expatriate community.

Kodak Cinema World (✉ 2 Nastasinsky per., ☎ 095/209–4359, Metro: Prospekt Mira). The trendiest and the most popular cinema in Russia. Book ahead for a ticket—but make sure the film is in English and not a dubbed disaster.

Strela (✉ 23/25 Smolenskaya-Sennaya Pl., ☎ 095/244–0553, Metro: Smolenskaya). Moscow's latest, this is also the capital's most exquisitely designed Western movie house.

Music

Moscow's musical life has always been particularly rich; the city has a number of symphony orchestras as well as song-and-dance ensembles. Moiseyev's Folk Dance Ensemble is well known in Europe and America, but the troupe is on tour so much of the year that when it performs in Moscow, tickets are very difficult to obtain. Other renowned companies include the State Symphony Orchestra and the Armed Forces Song and Dance Ensemble. Except for tickets for special performances, tickets usually are easily available and inexpensive.

Glinka Music Museum Hall (✉ 4 Fadeyeva ul., ☎ 095/972–3237, Metro: Mayakovskaya). This is one of many small concert halls scattered throughout the city.

Russian Army Theater (✉ 2 Suvorovskaya Pl., ☎ 095/281–5120, Metro: Novoslobodskaya). This theater is home to the Armed Forces Song and Dance Ensemble.

Scriabin Museum Hall (✉ 11 Bolshoi Nikolopeskovsky per., ☎ 095/299–1192, Metro: Smolenskaya). Performances are held in a small concert hall located in the apartment building where the composer Alexander Scriabin lived.

Tchaikovsky Concert Hall (✉ 4/31 Triumfalnaya Pl., ☎ 095/299–0378, Metro: Mayakovskaya). This huge concert hall with seating for more than 1,600 is home to the State Symphony Orchestra.

Tchaikovsky Conservatory (✉ 13 Bolshaya Nikitskaya ul., ☎ 095/229–8183 or 095/229–0658, Metro: Okhotny Ryad). The acoustics of the magnificent Great Hall are superb, and portraits of the world's great composers hang above the high balcony. Rachmaninoff, Scriabin, and Tchaikovsky are among the famous composers who have worked here. The adjacent Small Hall is usually reserved for chamber-music concerts.

Opera and Ballet

Bolshoi Opera and Ballet Theater (✉ 1 Teatralnaya Pl., ☎ 095/292–9986, Metro: Teatralnaya). Visitors always get a thrill out of a visit to this world-renowned theater. The current quality of its productions is erratic, however, due to management changes and the loss of many of its best performers. The gilt, 19th-century auditorium is itself a sight to behold, as is the Russian flair for set and costume design, which alone is enough to keep an audience enthralled.

Kremlin Palace of Congresses (✉ 1 ul. Vozdvizhenka, in the Kremlin, ☎ 095/929–7901 or 095/929–7971, Metro: Biblioteka Imeni Lenina). This modern concert hall, where Soviet Communist Party congresses were held, now has regular performances by opera and ballet troupes, including those from the Bolshoi. Of late it also has become the venue for international megastars such as Elton John, Diana Ross, Julio Iglesias, and Tina Turner. Entrance is through the whitewashed Kutafya Gate, near the Manezh.

Pokrovsky Chamber Musical Theater (✉ 71 Leningradsky Prospekt, ☎ 095/151–4747, Metro: Belorusskaya). This experimental theater stages interesting productions of Russian classics.

Stanislavsky and Nemirovich-Danchenko Musical Theater (✉ 17 Bolshaya Dmitrovka ul., ☎ 095/229–8388, Metro: Teatralnaya). This offers classical and modern operas, ballets, and operettas. It may be less well known than the Bolshoi but it's also less expensive and often far superior.

Nightlife

Before you go out, remember that as a foreigner, you should take special precautions at night. Exaggerated press reports have made Moscow out to be the crime capital of the world. While the city can be dangerous, it's no more so than London and probably less so than New York. Just keep in mind that foreign tourists are easy crime targets, so use common sense and make arrangements for the trip home before you leave for a night out. Remember: The more vodkas you drink, the more vulnerable you can become. Do not drive under any circumstances if you drink; laws here are harsher than at home, and traffic police are entitled to stop cars at will—and they do.

Bars

All the major hotels have their own bars and nightclubs. The lobby bars in the National, Savoy, and Metropol hotels feature glitzy, pre-revolutionary decor and a soothing atmosphere. The Palace and the Slavyanskaya have more energized lobby bars, filled with businesspeople and *novy russky* types. The top-floor bar of the Baltschug Hotel offers magical views of the Kremlin. At the other end of the spectrum are the bars of the old Intourist hotels (Belgrade, Kosmos, Intourist), where the atmosphere ranges from sleazy to scary. Be forewarned that hard-currency prostitution is a thriving business in most hotels. Actually, there's no reason for any traveler to get stuck in a hotel—Moscow has an enormous variety of bars to choose from.

Armadillo Tex-Mex Bar (✉ 1 Khrustalny per., ☎ 095/298–5091). Name notwithstanding, this is a longtime favorite Moscow hangout for drinks.

John Bull Pub (✉ 4 Kutuzovsky Prospekt, ☎ 095/243–5688). This English-style pub almost captures that London atmosphere. There's a good selection of beers and a cheap Chinese take-away next door for a post-pub snack.

Mesto Vstrechi (✉ 9/8 Maly Gnezdnikovsky per., ☎ 095/229–2373). A pleasant brick-cellar bar, this offers an escape from the bustle of nearby Tverskaya ulitsa.

Rosie O'Grady's (✉ 9 ul. Znamenka, ☎ 095/203–9087). This is another popular spot where the natives like to relax and have fun.

Sally O'Brien's (✉ 4 Kutuzovsky Prospekt, ☎ 095/243–5688). This is probably the best of the numerous Irish pubs in town, with a friendly staff and a happy crowd of regulars to make you feel at home.

Sixteen Tons (✉ 6 Presnensky Val, ☎ 095/208–4637). A popular pub, with a club upstairs, this spot serves its own home-brewed beer.

Casinos

Moscow has a serious case of casino fever. The number of casinos, both upscale and back-alley, that have opened in the past few years, at last unofficial count, equaled the number in Las Vegas. If you feel like trying your luck, here are some of the better-known places. Don't feel so lucky that you forget where you are, though; flashing your cash is a *bad* idea. Most casinos will provide complimentary car service to and from big hotels; check with your hotel bureau. Casinos usually open late (11 or 12) and stay open until morning.

Alexander Blok (☎ 095/255–9323). This is a floating casino on a ship moored permanently near the Mezhdunarodnaya Hotel.

Casino Royal (✉ Begovaya ul. 22, ☎ 095/945–1410). The gem of the Moscow casinos, this is located in the elegant Hippodrome, built for Nicholas I in 1834.

The **Savoy, Metropol, Mezhdunarodnaya, Leningradskaya,** and **Ukraina** hotels all have their own casinos.

Other casinos in Moscow include **Horseshoe Casino** (✉ 71 ul. Prof-soyuznaya, ☎ 095/333–6210); **Karo** (✉ 2 Pushkinskaya Pl., ☎ 095/229–0003); and **Metelitsa Cherry Casino** (✉ 21 Novy Arbat, ☎ 095/291–1170).

Clubs

The Moscow club world, like many ways of life in Russia, is going through tough times, but there's still an array of choices for clubbers whether they want techno, Russian pop, or blues. Prices are easing down to London and New York levels, but whether inflationary prices will return is unknown. Whatever the tariff, clubs are generally still staying open as late as ever. Big rock concerts are usually held in the city's sports stadiums and Western stars generally perform at the Kremlin Palace. For listings of upcoming concerts, check the Friday edition of the *Moscow Times*. Happily, many Moscow clubs present a band at least a couple of nights a week.

Bedniye Lyudi (✉ 11/6 Bolshaya Ordynka ul., ☎ 095/951–3342). Regular host to local rock bands, and the odder selection as well, Bedniye Lyudi, or Poor People, is also a relaxing bar in its quieter moments.

Hungry Duck (✉ 9/6 Pushechnaya ul., ☎ 095/923–6158). With a carousing clientele often dancing atop its bar, the Hungry Duck is now known as one of the craziest places in Moscow. Fueled by cheap drinking sessions and impromptu strip shows—by customers as well as professional performers—this is on its way to becoming the most talked-about bar in Europe.

Krizis Zhanra (✉ 22/4 Prechistensky per., ☎ 095/241–2940). This very popular student hangout often packs a band into its cramped underground bar.

Night Flight (✉ 17 Tverskaya ul., ☎ 095/229–4165). This Swedish-Russian joint venture was Moscow's first authentic disco, and it always attracts a lusty crowd of businessmen.

Papa John's (✉ 22 Myasnitskaya ul, ☎ 095/755–9554). A tamer version of the Hungry Duck, Papa John's is packed most nights with wet T-shirt contests, strip egg and spoon races, and any number of other silly games the management can think of.

Propaganda (✉ 22/7 Bolshoi Zlatoustinsky per., ☎ 095/924–5732). Great DJs pump the music up here for a crowd that is trendy but never too trendy.

Territoria (✉ 5/6 Tverskaya ul., ☎ 095/737–8865). An intimate club with comfy lounges during the day, Territoriya becomes a super trendy rave club at night.

Titanic (✉ Young Pioneer's Stadium, 31 Leningradsky Prospekt, ☎ 095/213–6095). A hard-core techno place, this is populated by the rich and beautiful of the Moscow clubbing scene.

Trety Put (✉ 4 Pyatnitskaya ul., ☎ 095/924–5732). This Bohemian hangout opens on weekends in an artist's flat. Drink at the cheap bar, play chess, watch the band, or look at the pictures in the gallery in the back room.

Vermel (⌂ 4/5 Raushskaya nab., ☎ 095/924–5732). Firmly placed on the circuit for Moscow bands, Vermel is also worth visiting just for a drink and its splendid view of St. Basil's—never more remarkable than when you emerge here at five in the morning.

Moscow has a growing gay scene and a number of openly gay clubs.

Central Station (⌂ 16/2 Bolshaya Tatarskaya ul., ☎ 095/208–6343). A more democratic alternative to Chance, this place has two dance floors, go-go dancers, and a dark room for the more adventurous.

Chameleon (⌂ 14 Presnensky Val, ☎ 095/959–6343). This now ranks with Chance as the best gay joint in Moscow. Its large dance floor and summer garden make it a friendly place for gays and straights.

Chance (⌂ 11/15 ul. Volocharskovo, ☎ 095/956–7102). Moscow's biggest gay club is famous for its large dance floor, and late-night nude erotic synchronized swimming show (in a giant aquarium that forms the wall of one of the main rooms).

Dyke (⌂ 4 Trubnaya Pl., ☎ 095/163–8002). Saturdays from 4 to 11 PM, it's ladies only.

Jazz, Blues, and Beyond
Jazz has long been a favorite with the Russians and in Moscow you can hear it live at the **Blue Bird Jazz Café** (⌂ 11 23/15 Malaya Dmitrovka ul., ☎ 095/299–2225); **Krasnaya Ploshchad** (⌂ 1 Krasnaya Pl., inside the Historical museum, ☎ 095/925–3600); or **Birdland** (⌂ 16 ul. Shchipok ☎ 095/236–3363).

Funky blues is played at the **BB King Blues Club** (⌂ 4/2 ul. Sadovaya-Samotyochnaya, ☎ 095/299–8206), a venue whose premiere opening featured the man himself. Visiting Western stars often end up jamming here after their concerts. Otherwise try the **Arbat Blues Club** for regular concerts (⌂ 11 Filippovsky per., ☎ 095/291–1546).

For karaoke fun, try **Yanpen Karaoke lounge** (⌂ Under the Novoye Vremya office, Pushkinkaya Pl., ☎ 095/229–6637), where you can sing along in Russian, English, and Korean.

OUTDOOR ACTIVITIES AND SPORTS

Participant Sports

Access to Moscow's municipal athletic facilities is usually restricted to those holding a season pass or to club members. In addition, most facilities—particularly when it comes to pools—require a doctor's certificate attesting to one's good health. In principle, it is possible to obtain such a certificate by visiting a Russian clinic, but this can be time-consuming. Temporary certificates often are available for a fee at the facility. The listings here are therefore limited to those places that are open to short-term visitors and where it is not necessary to obtain a doctor's certificate. If you call, be prepared for people who speak only Russian at many of these facilities.

All of this doesn't mean you must be sedentary in Moscow. Muscovites have taken up rollerblading with a passion. While rare in the city center, joggers are common in parks; they are replaced in winter by cross-country skiers of all ages. Indeed, the harsh winter rarely keeps anyone indoors. If you prefer field hockey, juggling, or even parasailing, check the listings in the *Moscow Times* for meetings and games.

Or just stroll through the larger parks, and you're likely to come upon a match. If you've forgotten your spandex tights, sporting goods stores have opened all over the city. You can find Nike, Reebok, Puma, and other Western brand names as easily as, if more expensively than, at home.

The **Luzhniki Sports Palace** (with Lenin Stadium) is a sports complex located on the banks of the Moskva River at the foot of Sparrow Hills (✉ 24 Luzhnetskaya nab., ☎ 095/201–1806; 095/201–1851 for tennis; 095/201–0764 for the pool, Metro: Sportivnaya). It is the equal of many top Western facilities. The **Olympisky Sports** compound (✉ 16 Olympisky per., ☎ 095/288–2018, Metro: Prospekt Mira) opened for the 1980 Olympics and has gyms, courts, pools, and tracks. You should check which ones are available for use during your stay.

Bowling

The bowling alley at the **Kosmos Hotel** (✉ 150 Prospekt Mira, near the VDNKh subway station, ☎ 095/234–1116) is open daily 2 PM–10:30 PM, with the last reservation an hour earlier. For tickets, inquire at the service bureau off the first-floor lobby.

Cycling

There is a cycle racetrack in the **Krylatskoye Sports Complex** (✉ 2 Krylatskaya ul., ☎ 095/140–0347 or 095/141–2224, Metro: Krylatskoye). They also have a rowing canal.

Fitness Centers

Unfortunately, virtually all of Moscow's **gyms** are expensive and for members only. Some offer short-term memberships, so if you are in town for a while, you can explore that option. Most good hotels have their own fitness centers, but use is often restricted to guests. You can pay a fee for single visits to the gym and pool at the **Radisson Slavyanskaya** (✉ 2 Berezhkovskaya nab., ☎ 095/941–8020, Metro: Kievskaya). The **Palace Hotel** (✉ 19 Pervaya Tverskaya-Yamskaya, ☎ 095/931–9700, Metro: Belorusskaya) has a weight-machine room, Jacuzzi, and sauna but no pool. The **Presnya Hotel** (✉ 9 Spiridonevsky per., ☎ 095/244–3631, Metro: Pushkinskaya or Mayakovskaya) has a tiny gym, massage room, and sauna.

Golf

One of just two golf clubs in Russia, the **Moscow City Golf Club** (✉ 1 Donvzhenko ul., ☎ 095/147–2079 or 147–8330, FAX 095/147–6252) will open its nine-hole course to visitors, provided they fax a request in advance. Weekends and holidays are reserved for members. The joint Russian-Swedish club rents equipment and has a pro shop, sauna, and restaurant. In winter, there's a driving range.

Horseback Riding

At the **Bitsa Riding Grounds** (✉ 33 Balaklavsky Prospekt, ☎ 095/318–5744, Metro: Chertanovskaya or Kaluzhskaya) you can rent horses or get indoor lessons or a guided ride in the forest of southern Moscow. There also are ponies for children. Reservations are advised.

Running

The best spots for **jogging** are along Luzhniki's riverside or on the trails through Izmailovsky, Filyovsky, or Sokolniki parks. You will definitely want to avoid Moscow's heavy traffic and accompanying noxious fumes. If you like running in a group, the Hash House Harriers, a "drinking group with a running problem," meets weekly and often is listed in the *Moscow Times* community bulletin board. Like any city unaccustomed to many joggers, it can be difficult to find a comfortable running route and you probably will be in a conspicuous minority.

Skating

If you've packed your skates, head straight for **Gorky Park** (⊠ 9 Krymsky Val, Metro: Oktyabrskaya), where in winter months the park's lanes are flooded to create ad hoc skating rinks. The park also has two large rinks where you can skate to piped-in Russian pop music. Be prepared for some cultural differences, however. Russians do not skate in orderly circles or clean snow off the ice regularly, and rental skates can be rather shabby. The park is open 10–10; the closest subway station is the Oktyabrskaya on the orange and circle lines. You can rent skates at **Sokolniki Park** (⊠ 16 Sokolnichesky Val, ☎ 095/268–8277, Metro: Sokolniki). Hours are daily 10–7. Luzhniki's popular **Northern Lights** rink (⊠ Luzhnetskaya nab., ☎ 095/201–1655, Metro: Sportivnaya) is open to all skaters over the age of seven. There is a fee for entry and skate rental; the hours vary, so call first. You also may see one of the many neighborhood rinks flooded each winter.

Skiing/Sledding

On a crisp, clear winter day in Moscow, cross-country skiers can be found in the wooded parks that dot the city. Try Filyovsky, Ismailovsky, or Bitsevsky parks, or near Novedevichy convent. You'll be in the good company of skiers of all abilities, from toddlers to grandparents. Moscow also has a few small downhill slopes. The one at **Sparrow Hills** (Metro: Universitet) has ski jumping. At the **Krylatskoye Ski Center,** there is a 950-meter slope, equipment rentals, and lessons. ⊠ 2 Krylatskaya ul., ☎ 095/480–4308, Metro: Krylatskoye.

If you're without equipment, you can still join young Muscovites who buy very cheap plastic sheets called *ledyanki* from any sports equipment or toy store and head for the hills. The best are in Kolomenskoye (a five-minute walk from the metro station of the same name) or Neskuchny Sad (Metro: Leninsky Prospekt), right aross from the station entrance.

Swimming

Try the **Chaika Pool** (⊠ 1/3 Turchanynov per., ☎ 095/246–1344, Metro: Park Kultury). You can get the necessary health certificate there, and this heated, outdoor pool near the river is open all year round. You'll find a sauna, a café, and a small swimwear shop.

When it gets hot, people sunbathe and swim just about anywhere— even though the city health authorities have advised against swimming most places within the city. If you have Moscow friends and/or a car, or want to take the bus, you can join in a summer tradition by heading to **Serebryanny Bor** (Silver Pine Beach) for a dip in the Moskva River, where you'll encounter lots of interestingly clad, overheated city dwellers. You can also rent rowboats there. For other city pools, *see* the section on Fitness Centers, and the Luzhniki Sports Palace and Olympisky Sports compound, *above.*

Tennis

Courts are in scant supply and are usually reserved in advance by residents. The **Olympisky Sports** compound (⊠ 16 Olympisky per., ☎ 095/288–5663 or 095/288–5118, Metro: Prospekt Mira) rents courts at expensive rates. If you call shortly after 9 AM, you may be able to get a court at **Chaika** (⊠ 1/2 Korobeinikov per., ☎ 095/202–0474, Metro: Park Kultury), which has four indoor courts and one outdoor court.

Spectator Sports

Tickets for sporting events can be purchased at the sports arena immediately prior to the game or at any of the numerous theater box offices (teatralnaya kassa) located throughout the city. You can also ask your hotel's service bureau for assistance in obtaining tickets to sporting events, but the fee will probably far exceed the value of the ticket.

Horse-Racing

Races are held at the **Hippodrome** (✉ 22/1 Begovaya ul., ☎ 095/945–4516, Metro: Begovaya) weekends at 1 PM. Betting is in rubles. In winter troikas are sometimes raced.

Ice Hockey

Ice hockey matches are held at the **Dinamo Stadium** (✉ 36 Leningradsky Prospekt, ☎ 095/212–7092, Metro: Dinamo), which is Moscow's second-largest stadium, accommodating 60,000. Hockey matches are also held at Luzhniki's **Lenin Stadium** (☎ 095/201–0955, Metro: Sportivnaya), its largest, seating 100,000.

Soccer

The Russian national sport is soccer (in Russian, *futbal*), and it can ignite feverish passions. The city has several soccer teams, foremost among them Spartak and Dinamo. A game between them would be considered the team event of the year. Soccer matches are also frequently played at the Central Lenin Stadium and at the stadiums belonging to individual teams.

SHOPPING

It is time, at long last, to cast away cold-war images of long lines and empty shelves—it's simply no longer the case. Although the distribution of products can be uneven and unpredictable, there are nonetheless plenty of them and you should be able to locate most items you need, although perhaps in a more piecemeal way than at home. You will not go hungry or unclothed should you lose your shirt at one of Moscow's casinos. In fact, you'll find opportunities to buy something any way you turn.

The proliferation of new stores is matched only by an escalation in prices. Stores can be roughly divided into two types: Western-style and Russian-style, though this differentiation is fast fading into one of nice vs. not-so-nice, as the Russian-owned shops upgrade their service and presentation. There is an ever-changing array of kiosks, tabletops, and wooden stalls, combined with nicer, underground glassware boutiques and stores. The Western-style stores are more likely to carry familiar brands from the United States and Europe, especially Finland, at imported-goods prices. Russian-owned establishments tend to stock a mix of local and imported products.

In the past, special shops, called Beriozkas (Birch Trees), operated exclusively for foreigners. Stock was imported, payment was in hard currency only, and it was illegal for Soviet citizens to enter—let alone shop—in one. The Beriozka chain no longer exists, as it is now illegal in Russia to accept payment in currency other than rubles. Most "nice" food and consumer goods stores, however, will accept credit cards, payment being calculated at something close to that day's ruble exchange rate. (Be sure to check this rate, as stores often set very high rates—just like hotels—and it may well be better to be prepared to pay in cash rubles, acquired at a bank's more favorable rate.) Keep in mind that no stores take traveler's checks. Nationality, of course, is no longer relevant; wallet size is—anyone who can afford the higher prices is welcome.

There are still some "old-style" Russian stores hanging on, particularly outside the big cities. In Old World fashion, they tend to be denoted by their primary products (milk, bread, lights, women's shoes) but often carry more than their name implies, including a spate of imported Western goods, such as soft drinks, liquor, and chewing gum. The main stumbling block for foreigners in these places is the arduous method of purchase; it is time-consuming and quite trying. First you look for the item you want to buy and note its price (often asking the shop girl to wrap it up), then you go to the cashier and pay for it, indicating merely the price and department (*otdel*). Then, you take your receipt back to the shop girl and she gives you your goods in exchange. If you do not speak Russian and want to avoid this type of shopping (once the only way things were done), stick to Western-style stores or to street purchases, where you can use the universal language of finger-pointing and cash paid directly to the shop girl or vendor.

Russian-style service may be surlier than you are accustomed to, also. A few words spoken in Russian and a composed countenance may ameliorate this, but in any case, don't take it personally. Russians seem to have grown so inured to shoving and elbowing for position that they will display an indifference to rudeness that foreign visitors often find appalling. On the bright side, when you do encounter good manners, they are impeccable.

Assuming that, despite the improvements, one doesn't come to Moscow for the shopping, the following listings are intended to give a thumbnail sketch of places you may need to frequent as a tourist. You can find almost anything you want in Moscow these days, but the high prices on consumer goods almost demand that you delay purchases until you return home. (Which of course does not apply to souvenirs.) That said, if you must have something in a hurry, most of the stores listed are "nice" or "Western-style." If your schedule permits, it is interesting to browse in the shops that are frequented by locals, and it's a great way to take the pulse of a place, especially one in flux.

One caution: Before you spend a lot of money on a souvenir, think about how you will feel if you can't leave the country with it. Unfortunately, customs regulations are still vague and seem to change constantly and arbitrarily, depending on who is checking your luggage. The law basically disallows the export of anything of "cultural value to the Russian nation." In practical terms, this means anything older than 30–40 years is not allowed out without special permission of the Ministry of Culture or its local agent (and will be confiscated at the border if you lack this); anything prerevolutionary is simply not let out at all. If you are buying paintings or art objects, it's important to consult with the seller regarding the proper documentation of sale for export. Keep receipts of your purchases, wherever possible.

Please also exercise caution when shopping. You will stand out no matter what you do, and there are pickpocket and mugging rings, often operating in small bands (gypsy gangs are particularly pernicious). *Don't* be an easy target: Don't act flush with cash and don't stop if you encounter gypsies or bands of muggers. Swinging your arms or handbag and getting vocal often works to rout them.

Shopping Districts

Historically, the main shopping districts of Moscow have been concentrated in the city center, along Tverskaya ulitsa and Novy Arbat. Extend New Arbat through Kutuzovsky Prospekt and, on the other end, add the Old Arbat—which has been particularly spruced up for the tourist trade—these are your best bets. If you are willing to venture into distant regions outside the city, however, a brave new world of shopping awaits in Russia.

The closest thing to a mall in downtown Moscow is either **GUM,** pronounced "goom" (✉ Krasnaya ploshchad, 3, ☎ 095/929–3470, ☉ daily 9–8), a series of shops and boutiques inside a 19th-century shopping arcade, or the nearby **Manezh Underground Shopping Mall** complex (✉ Trade Center "Okhotny Ryad" Manezhnaya ploshchad, 1, ☉ daily 9–8), below the main square adjacent to the Kremlin, offering everything from designer clothing to gift items. GUM, which stands for State Department Store, is on Red Square, right across from the Kremlin.

Department Stores

Near Lubyanka Square you'll see **Detsky Mir** (✉ 2 Teatralny proyezd, ☎ 095/927–2007), the famous children's department store, which now also hawks cars and a wide assortment of toys for grown-ups.

Moskva Department Store (✉ Leninsky Prospekt 54, ☎ 095/137–0018) is a giant general store. **Petrovsky Passage** (✉ 10 ul. Petrovka, ☎ 095/928–5047), is home to a varied series of shops.**TsUM** (✉ ul. Petrovka 2, ☎ 095/292–1157 or 095/292–7600), open Monday–Saturday 9–8, Sunday 10–6, which translates as Central Department Store, is one of two large Russian department stores (the other being GUM, ☞ *above*). Russian consumers are also being treated to the "benefits" of superstores. A good example is the huge **Ramstore** (✉ ul. Yartsevskaya, 19, ☎ 095/937–0444), open weekdays 9–11 and weekends 9–10. Located not far from the metro Molodyozhnaya, this is a Russian version of Wal-Mart, with a huge parking lot, food supermarket, a wide selection of consumer goods, and an adjacent boutique mall. Its prices are also well below normal Moscow prices.

Specialty Stores

Arts and Crafts

Art boutiques of the Varvarka ulitsa Churches. These boutiques are located inside St. Maxim the Blessed, open daily 11–6, and St. George on Pskov Hill, open daily 11–7, and both offer a fine selection of handicrafts, jewelry, ceramics, and other types of Russian native art. (☞ Kitai Gorod, *above*). *Metro: Kitai-Gorod.*

Art Salon of the Arts Industry Institute. An excellent selection of artwork handcrafted by the institute's students and teachers is the draw here, including hand-painted trays, quilts, ceramics, and leather goods. ✉ *Povarskaya ul. 31, 2nd floor,* ☎ *095/290–6822.* ☉ *Daily 11–7, Fri. until 6. Metro: Arbatskaya or Barrikadnaya.*

Central Art Salon. This big salon sells just about everything you might be looking for—from handcrafted nesting dolls to ceramics, *khokhloma* (lacquered wood), and jewelry, all made by members of the Russian Union of Artists. Also on sale are beautiful Dagestani rugs. ✉ *Ukrainsky bulvar 6,* ☎ *095/243–9458.* ☉ *Sun.–Fri. 10–2, 3–7; Sat. 11–6. Metro: Kievskaya.*

Gzhel. If you are enamored of blue-and-white Gzhel ceramic ware, try their own shop, to find all manner of pieces. ✉ *22 ul. Petrovka,* ☎ *095/200–6137. Metro: Teatralnaya.*

Ikonnaya Lavka. This icon shop is just across the way from Russian Museum World (☞ *below*) and is set within the newly rebuilt Kazanskaya Church. It offers icons, religious books, silver crosses, and other Orthodox religious items. ✉ *Krasnaya ploshchad.* ☉ *Daily 9–8. Metro: Ploshchad Revolutsii.*

Museum of the Revolution Gift Shop A top spot for amber, nesting dolls, and other Soviet memorabilia such as pins, postcards, and T-shirts, this shop also features a store-within-a-store, **Linder,** which sells albums, catalogs, stamps, and vintage money for collectors. ⊠ *21 Tverskaya ul.,* ☎ *095/299–1695.* ☉ *Mon.–Sat. 10–5. Metro: Tverskaya.*

Russian Museum World. The art shop at the newly opened State Historical Museum, this place offers a wide gamut of souvenirs, ranging from replicas of museum pieces, khokhloma, jewelry, T-shirts, handmade crafts, Russian- and Ukrainian-style embroidered shirts, Gzhel, and more. As you enter Red Square through the newly rebuilt Vosskresenskiye Gates, it is on the right-hand side of the museum. ⊠ *Red Square, 1/2,* ☎ *095/292–1320.* ☉ *Daily 10–9. Metro: Ploshchad Revolutsii.*

Russkiye Souveniry. This state-run souvenir shop is easy to find and filled with handcrafted and mass-produced folk art, *palekh* (a school of colorful lacquered folkloric art) boxes, and jewelry, but its prices are very inflated. ⊠ *9 Kutuzovsky Prospekt,* ☎ *095/243–6496.* ☉ *Mon.–Sat. 11–2, 3–8. Metro: Kievskaya.*

Russkiye Uzory. The store name means Russian Patterns, and that's exactly what is on tap here, thanks to a beautiful and extensive selection of traditional Russian craft objects, most embellished with folkloric patterns. ⊠ *16 ul. Petrovka,* ☎ *095/923–1883. Metro: Teatralnaya.*

Skazki Starovo Arbata. This is another popular place for souvenirs, including amber, silver, crafts, nesting dolls, and lacquer boxes. ⊠ *Arbat 29,* ☎ *095/241–6135.* ☉ *Mon.–Sat. 10–5. MC, V. Metro: Arbat.*

Sofrino. You'll see occasional kiosks or counters in churches selling Russian Orthodox religious items—for an especially wide selection, venture here. ⊠ *11 Nikolskaya ul.,* ☎ *095/925–4480. Metro: Pl. Revolutsii.*

Food and Spirits

Caviar in Russia? Who can resist? Especially when you can buy it at the bargain rates now on offer in Moscow. Unlike vodkas, there are few concerns about counterfeiting and you can find authentic sturgeon caviar in any nice Russian food store. Expect to pay about $15 for 4 ounces of black caviar—it is best to purchase those already packed in export jars.

Buying liquor—especially **vodka**—in Russia is a de rigueur activity fraught with danger. Alcohol counterfeiting is a big problem and, if you don't follow safe buying practices, you could end up with a severe case of alcohol poisoning. Your best bet on price and safety is to buy at outlet shops of vodka distilleries. One conveniently located is the **Cristall outlet** (⊠ Zamorenova ul. 41, just behind the McDonald's restaurant), not far from the metro ulitsa 1905 Goda. Cristall is Moscow's biggest vodka producer and, in addition to about a dozen other unique brands, you can buy authentic Stolichnaya here in bottles that go for less than $5. Note: Every bottle of vodka sold in Russia must bear a white excise stamp, glued over the cap, and those sold in Moscow must also bear a bar-code stamp.

If you want to sample (or simply need) good **Russian bread,** there is no sense going to a posh Western-style supermarket. Instead, head for any *bulochnaya* (bakery). Here you can find a good loaf of bread for less than 50¢: *podmoskovny* sells for about 40¢ and is lighter than the stodgy white bread generally associated with Russia. Varieties of black rye bread (*borodinsky* and *khamovnichesky*) are the tastiest, but they still won't put you out more than 50¢.

Arbat Irish Store. An extremely well-stocked grocery store, this is also a small department store selling electronics, household goods, car accessories, and clothing (primarily jeans). The relatively reasonable prices here make for long lines, especially on the weekend. ⊠ *Novy Arbat 13,* ☎ *095/291–7641 or 095/291–7667* ⊙ *Daily 10–9, Sun. 10–8. Rubles downstairs; credit cards only upstairs. Metro: Arbatskaya.*

Danone. Health nuts take heart: This sleek shop on Tverskaya dishes out Dannon yogurt products—even six-packs. ⊠ *Tverskaya ul. 4,* ☎ *095/292–0512. Metro: Tverskaya.*

Global USA. Huge (billed as an American supershop, though Russian in its clientele and staffing), it's where you'll find almost every brand of every product you may be looking for. The quality of the imported clothing and footwear here is not high, but prices are low and discount sales are frequent. This chain is rapidly expanding and now counts six locations in Moscow. ⊠ *35 ul. Usacheva,* ☎ *095/245–5657,* ⊙ *Daily 10–10, Metro: Sportivnaya;* ⊠ *78 Leningradsky Prospekt,* ☎ *095/151– 3354,* ⊙ *Daily 10–8, AE, MC, V, Metro: Belorusskaya;* ⊠ *ul. Tver- skaya 6,* ☎ *095/229–8786;* ⊠ *Simonovsky Val, 12,* ☎ *095/274–5539 Metro: Proletarskaya;* ⊠ *Leningradsky Shosse, 112/1,* ☎ *095/451– 4001, on the way from/to Sheremetyevo 2 airport.*

Kalinka-Stockmann. This is a major supermarket chain, with four stores offering office supplies, electronics, and clothing; its grocery shop has a broad assortment, including fresh fruits and vegetables. The shops offering housewares and clothing are at separate locations. ⊠ *2/3 Zatsepsky Val,* ☎ *095/953–2602,* ⊙ *Daily 9–midnight, Grocery store, cosmetics, detergents; accepts all major credit cards., Metro: Paveletskaya;* ⊠ *Lyusinovskaya ul. 70/1,* ☎ *095/954–8234,* ⊙ *Daily 10-9, offers household appliances and linens;* ⊠ *Dolgorukovskaya ul. 2,* ☎ *095/978–2212,* ⊙ *Daily 10–9, clothing, footwear and cosmet- ics, Metro: Novoslobodskaya;* ⊠ *Leninsky Prospekt 73/8,* ☎ *095/134– 3546,* ⊙ *Daily 10-9, Boutique offering men's and women's clothing and footwear.*

Progress Trade House. This is a supermarket that invaded the second floor of the once-powerful foreign-language bookstore of the same name. ⊠ *Zubovsky bulvar 17,* ☎ *095/246–9078.* ⊙ *Mon.–Sat. 10–9, Sun. 11–8. AE, MC, V. Metro: Park Kultury.*

Sadko's Foodland. Moscow's first real Western-style supermarket, this has a large selection of imported grocery items, including cheese and other dairy products, alcohol, office supplies, and health and beauty products. They now have two shops. ⊠ *Bolshaya Doro- gomilovskaya ul. 6,* ☎ *095/243–6659 or 095/243–0319,* ⊙ *Daily 10– 10, accepts all major credit cards, Metro: Kievskaya;* ⊠ *Krasnopresnenskaya nab. 14,* ☎ *095/256–2213 or 095/256–7016,* ⊙ *Daily 10–10, Metro: ul. 1905 Goda.*

SAM Supermarkets. This is one of the leading Russian supermarket chains; they have several locations in Moscow. ⊠ *Vinokurova ul. 4,* ☎ *095/126–5800,* ⊙ *Daily 10 AM–midnight, Metro: Akademich- eskaya;* ⊠ *Leninsky Prospekt 7,* ☎ *095/930–1338,* ⊙ *Daily 24 hrs, Metro: Leninsky Prospekt;* ⊠ *Leninsky Prospekt 113/1,* ☎ *095/956– 5458,* ⊙ *Daily 8 AM–10:30 PM, Metro: Yugo-Zapadnaya.*

Seventh Continent. This leading chain of supermarkets features stores open 24 hours a day, 365 days a year. There are several locations: ⊠ *Arbat Ul. 54/2,* ☎ *095/241–0761, Metro: Smolenskaya;* ⊠ *Festival- naya ul. 8,* ☎ *095/454–3361, Metro: Vodny Stadion;* ⊠ *Mikhlukho- Maklaya 18-2,* ☎ *095/330–3030, Metro: Belyaevo;* ⊠ *ul. Serafimovicha 2,* ☎ *095/959–0342 or 095/959–3135, Metro: Polyanka or Bib- lioteka imeni Lenina;* ⊠ *Okhotny Ryad ul. 2,,* ☎ *095/292–2248 or 095/292–7202, Metro: Okhotny Ryad;* ⊠ *Leninsky Prospekt, 61/1,*

☎ *095/137–0093 or 095/137–0094, Metro: Leninsky Prospekt;* ✉ *Lubyanka Bolshaya ul. 12/1,* ☎ *095/928–9527 or 095/928–7221, Metro: Lubyanka. AE, MC, V accepted in all stores.*

Supersiwa. A classic, Western-style supermarket, this is a popular choice for food shopping and even takes credit cards. ✉ *Slavyansky bulvar 9, korpus 1,* ☎ *095/445–0570.* ◷ *Daily 9 AM–10 PM. AE, MC, V. Metro: Kutuzovskaya.*

Yeliseyevsky's. The most historic and sumptuous gourmeterie in all Moscow, this star of the Tverskaya ulitsa sparkles with chandeliers, stained glass, and gilt wall decorations. Luxe products abound, from cognac and Georgian wine (including Stalin's favorite Khvanchkava— still much touted even with its unsavory stamp of approval) to Russian chocolate and candy of all sorts. ✉ *14 Tverskaya ul.,* ☎ *095/ 209–0760* ◷ *Mon.–Sat. 8 AM–9 PM, Sun. 10-7. Metro: Tverskaya.*

Men's and Women's Clothing

Adidas. Three locations continue to draw crowds into this high-energy sports wear. ✉ *Novy Arbat 11, inside the Valday shopping center,* ☎ *095/291–1105;* ✉ *Solyanka 1, building 2,* ☎ *095/925–5987;* ✉ *Kamergersky per., not far from the MKhAT theater,* ☎ *095/229–7361.*

Benetton. The trademark line of sweaters, skirts, pants, and jeans are now a Moscow staple. Most stores are open daily 8–8. ✉ *Novy Arbat 13,* ☎ *095/291–1456;* ✉ *Manezhnaya Sq. 1,* ☎ *095/737–8397;* ✉ *GUM, first line,* ☎ *095/929–3217;* ✉ *Komsomolskaya Ploshchad 3 (inside the Moskovsky Univermag),* ☎ *095/204–5973.*

British House. Located just a few doors down Novy Arbat from Arbat Irish Store (☞ *above*), this place specializes in clothing, footwear, and household goods. ✉ *Novy Arbat, 15,* ☎ *095/967–1290.* ◷ *Mon.– Sat. 10–9, Sun. 10–8.*

Carlo Pazolini. This fashion designer has managed to amass five stores in Moscow, including this one near the U.S. Embassy. ✉ *Novinsky bulvar 1/2,* ☎ *095/241–4674.* ◷ *Daily 11–9, Sun. noon–8.*

Gallery of Fashion. Women interested in seeing the latest Russian haute couture may satisfy their curiosity at this designer house—no less than 18 different collections can be found here. ✉ *Pyatnitskaya ul. 11/ 23,* ☎ *095/233–2508. Metro: Novokuznetskaya.*

Hugo Boss. This high-profile fashion label now boasts two stores in Moscow, one on the Arbat, the other on the main shopping street of Tverskaya. ✉ *Arbat str. 15/43,* ☎ *095/913–6978,* ◷ *Mon.–Thurs. 10-9, Fri.–Sat. 10–10, Sun. 11–8;* ✉ *Tverskaya Yamskaya 1st ul., 13/ 1,* ☎ *095/250–3323,* ◷ *Weekdays 11–8, weekends noon–6.*

Levis. Once a quasi-currency in the USSR, they are now sold in three company outlet stores, one of which is open 24 hours. The most centrally located is in GUM. ✉ *Red Square, GUM, 1st line, 1st floor,* ☎ *095/929–3152;* ✉ *Sadovo-Spasskaya ul. 3,* ☎ *095/208–3825,* ◷ *Mon.–Sat. 10–8, Sun. 11–7;* ✉ *Stoleshnikov per. 14,* ☎ *095/733–9200,* ◷ *Daily 24 hrs.*

Nike. Nike fans can find its store across from Barrikadnaya subway station. There are two other Nike stores, but at less convenient locations. ✉ *Kundrinsky per. 1,* ☎ *095/255–4463. Metro: Barrikadnaya.*

Reebok. This big airy shop sells sports outfits, shoes, and equipment, and is located just across from the U.S. Embassy. ✉ *Novinsky bulvar 28/35,* ☎ *095/291–7873.* ◷ *Mon.–Thurs. 10–8, Fri.–Sat. 8 AM–9 PM, Sun. 11–7. Metro: Barrikadnaya.*

Stockmann Boutique. Those looking for high-fashion items might check out this swanky emporium. ⊠ *73 Leninsky Prospekt,* ☎ *095/ 134–3546. Metro: Paveletskaya.*

Yelena Pelyevina Salon. A wide array of women's fashions is to be found at this popular emporium, where Russian folk-inspired patterns and garments are the focus. ⊠ *Komsomolsky Prospekt 42,* ☎ *095/242– 3726. Metro: Park Kultury.*

Street Markets

Moscow's wave of reconstruction and renovation has also benefited fresh-food markets (but at the same time has closed many indefinitely, because of concerns over cleanliness and organized crime). The latest example is the old **Tishinka market,** which has been turned into a huge trade center, combining the elements of a green market and a supermarket. The supermarket is open 24 hours, the green market from 9 to 9. The second floor features boutiques and inexpensive Russian restaurants. ⊠ *Bolshaya Gruzinskaya ul. 50,* ☎ *095/254–1572.*

You might also try the **Dorogomilovsky Market** off Mozhaiska ulitsa, near the Kievsky train station. Beyond its outdoor "Veshchevoy Rynok" (literally, "market of things," which you'll see is certainly apt) is a large covered hall. Inside are rows of vendors hawking homemade cheese and milk products, honey, flowers, and produce of all kinds. Against one wall are sellers of pickled goods, an understandably popular form of food preparation in this part of the world; you may want to sample some of their cabbage and carrot slaws, salted cucumbers, or spiced eggplant or garlic. Tasting is free, but it's unlikely that you'll leave here without buying something. Remember to bargain. In another corner, you will also find tables of freshly cut meat, plucked chickens, and fish. The squeamish may want to avert their eyes from the whole suckling pigs and the occasional hare or goat, beheaded and proudly strung up for inspection.

Ptichy Rynok (Bird Market) is on Kalitnovskaya ulitsa. Open on Sundays only, this market offers a fascinating glimpse of Russians and their pets. The market is bustling with individuals selling adorable, furry animals—cats, dogs, and hamsters—as well as exotic birds and fish and, occasionally, a monkey. The softhearted should be forewarned that it is very difficult to leave this place without acquiring something. *Transportation: Metro to Taganskaya station. Exit from circle-line station, and from there take any bus or trolley from Marksistskaya ulitsa stop (across square from subway, near purple Tagansky department store). Bus line ends at pet market.*

Souvenirs

For good souvenir-hunting, you can certainly head straight to the **Arbat** (☞ The Arbat, Old and New, *above*). Stores here cater to tourists and Moscow's expatriate community, so you can expect good selection and service, but prices are on the high end. Its individual outdoor vendors invariably charge much more than they should, so stick to the stores.

You can spend a whole day at Moscow's **flea market** in Izmailovsky Park. Here you'll find hosts of reasonably priced used books, souvenirs and handicrafts, as well as Soviet memorabilia, such as army belts and gas masks, and *matryoshky* (nesting dolls), both classic and nouveau, with some bearing likenesses of recent Soviet leaders, others depicting American basketball stars. Nearby is the former royal residence of Izmailovo, situated in an old hunting preserve. The flea market is open weekends 9–6, but it's best to get there early. Many vendors close down by midday. Be sure to wrangle over prices. Bargaining is actually expected here, so it is advisable to take along a Russian friend with you to avoid over-paying. You can pay in dollars here if you come up short on rubles; this practice is technically illegal—but everybody does it. In fact, vendors are known to prefer hard currency and will usually offer a better price for *baksy* (new Russian lingo for "bucks"). *Transportation: subway to Iz-mailovsky Park station on the blue line (not to be confused with next stop, Izmailovskaya station), and follow the crowds as you exit.*

A great, unexpected souvenir from Russia is **Russian-made chocolates.** You can buy both individual candies—*krasnaya shapochka* (Little Red Riding Hood), *mishki* (little bears), and *melodiya* (melody)—and gift boxes. A nice box of *Nadezhda* chocolates sells for $7; a gift tin of *mishki* for about $12. Those from Moscow's Krasny Oktyabr (Red October) factory are the best. This dark, rich chocolate is widely available in stalls and kiosks as well as at the factory's corporate retail stores throughout Moscow (most are open 10–4). ⊠ *Ovchinnikovskaya nab. 22/24, Metro: Tretyakovskaya;* ⊠ *1st Tverskaya–Yamskaya ul. 12, Metro: Mayakovskaya;* ⊠ *Shabolovka, 17, Metro: Oktyabrskaya.*

For other souvenir resources, ☞ Arts and Crafts, *above.*

MOSCOW A TO Z

Arriving and Departing

By Boat

Moscow has two river ports: the **Northern River Terminal** (⊠ Severny Rechnoy Vokzal, 51 Leningradskoye Shosse, ☎ 095/457–4050) and the **Southern River Terminal** (⊠ Yuzhny Rechnoy Vokzal, 11 Andropov Prospekt, ☎ 095/118–7955). International cruise lines offering tours to Russia usually disembark in St. Petersburg and continue from there by land. It is possible, however, to book a two-way cruise from Moscow along the Moscow-Volga canal, which makes for a pleasant way to see the ancient cities of the Golden Ring. Some 129 km (80 mi) long, the canal links the Russian capital with the Caspian Sea, the Black Sea, the White Sea, and the Azov Sea. The Moscow port for long-distance passengers is the **Severny Rechnoy Vokzal** (northern port) on the Khimki reservoir.

By Car

You can reach Moscow from Finland and St. Petersburg by taking the Helsinki–St. Petersburg Highway (*shosse*) through Vyborg and St. Petersburg and continuing from there on the Moscow–St. Petersburg Highway. Be warned that driving in Russia is invariably more of a hassle than a pleasure. Repair shops are rare, and roads are very poorly maintained. In addition, you face the risk of car theft, a crime that is on the rise.

By Plane

AIRPORTS AND AIRLINES

As the single most important transportation hub in the CIS, Moscow has several airports. Most international flights arrive at **Sheremetyevo II** (☎ 095/956–4666), which currently handles an estimated 9 million passengers a year. One of the most modern in Russia, Sheremetyevo II was built in 1979, when there was much less international traffic; these days it is just barely coping. Expect to stand up to an hour or two at passport control. Disembarked passengers descend a long stair-case, then collect en masse in a large, dimly lit chamber to vie for the three or four lines to the passport officials' booths. Their legendary slow-ness is fact, not myth. The baggage area is located directly beyond. There may or may not be luggage carts. There's a bank in the waiting area where you can exchange money or traveler's checks while you're waiting for your luggage. After you have collected your bags, you'll go through customs. Finally, there are green and red aisles, so if you have nothing to declare, you frequently can walk right through the green aisle to the waiting area, where you will be greeted by mobs of Russians awaiting arriving passengers and eager gypsy cab drivers shouting *"Taksi! Taksi!"* Take a deep breath and plow straight through until you find your host or group. Welcome to the capital city!

In addition to its international airport, the city has four domestic terminals. **Sheremetyevo I** (☎ 095/578–9101), some 30 km (19 mi) northwest of the city center, services domestic flights to St. Petersburg and the former Baltic republics (Estonia, Latvia, and Lithuania). It has also been handling international flights of some new Russian airlines, so if you fly Transaero you may go here. **Domodedovo** (☎ 095/323–8903), one of the largest airports in the world, is located some 48 km (30 mi) southeast of Moscow; flights depart from here to the republics of Central Asia. **Vnukovo** (☎ 095/155–0922), 29 km (18 mi) southwest of the city center, services flights to Georgia, the southern republics, and Ukraine. **Bykovo** (☎ 095/155–0922), the smallest of the domestic terminals, generally handles flights within Russia and some flights to Ukraine. Be sure to find out from your travel agent which airport your flight is supposed to leave from.

For general information on arriving international flights, call the direct airline. For information on domestic Aeroflot flights, call 095/155–0922. Calling the airports directly is usually a complete waste of time; the line is almost always busy, and even if it's not, no one answers.

Aeroflot (☎ 095/156–8019; 095/155–0922 for information on domestic flights) operates flights from Moscow to just about every capital of Europe, as well as to Canada and the United States. **Transaero** (☎ 095/241–4800 or 095/241–7676), another Russian carrier, now has a large network of domestic flights as well as several international routes. Among the international airlines with offices in Moscow are **Air France** (☎ 095/237–2325); **Alitalia** (☎ 095/923–9856); **Austrian Airlines** (☎ 095/258–2020); **British Airways** (☎ 095/578–2923); **Delta** (☎ 095/578–2939); **Finnair** (☎ 095/292–8788 or 095/292–1762); **Japan Airlines** (☎ 095/921–6448); **KLM** (☎ 095/258–3600 or 095/578–3594); **Lufthansa** (☎ 095/975–2501 or 095/578–3151); **Malev** (☎ 095/232–3180); **SAS** (☎ 095/925–4747 or 095/578–2727); and **Swissair** (☎ 095/258–1888).

BETWEEN THE AIRPORT AND DOWNTOWN

You would be wise to make advance arrangements for your transfer from the airport. There are plenty of gypsy cabs available, but you should *not* take them; they are notorious for swindles and much, much worse. In a pinch, use the services offered on the airport's ground floor. These private firms are somewhat costly but less risky. Most hotels will provide airport transfers (for a fee) upon request by prior fax (which you should make sure is confirmed). All of the airports are serviced by municipal buses operating out of the **City Airport Terminal** (*Aerovokzal*) at 37 Leningradsky Prospekt, near the airport subway station. Service is somewhat unreliable and inconvenient, especially if you have any luggage, but very inexpensive. The schedule is slightly erratic, but theoretically a bus departs from Sheremetyevo II (International) Airport every two hours or so; service to Domodedovo and Vnukovo domestic airports is more frequent. The Sheremetyevo II bus stop is 300 ft to the right as you leave, at a small shelter that has a yellow bus-route sign on it for Bus 551, which is the one you take into Moscow. It *will,* inexorably, creep into the city.

By Train

Moscow is also the hub of the Russian railway system, and the city's nine railway stations handle some 400 million passengers annually. There are several trains daily to St. Petersburg, and overnight service is available to Helsinki, Riga, and Tallinn. All the major train stations have a connecting subway stop, so they are easily reached by public transportation. Please note that while we list phone numbers, they are all but impossible to get through to. For a visitor with limited time, it's best to ask your hotel service bureau or a travel agent for railway information and schedules. The most important stations are: **Belorussky Vokzal** (⊠ Belorussia Station, ☎ 095/973–8191, Metro: Belorusskaya), for trains to Belorussia, Lithuania, Poland, Germany, and France; **Kazansky Vokzal** (⊠ Kazan Station, ☎ 095/266–3181, Metro: Komsomolskaya), for points south, Central Asia, and Siberia; **Kievsky Vokzal** (⊠ Kiev Station, ☎ 095/240–1115, Metro: Kievskaya), for Kiev and western Ukraine, Moldova, Slovakia, the Czech Republic, and Hungary; **Kursky Vokzal** (⊠ Kursk Station, ☎ 095/924–5762, Metro: Kurskaya), for eastern Ukraine, the Crimea, and southern Russia; **Leningradsky Vokzal** (⊠ Leningrad Station, ☎ 095/262–9143), for St. Petersburg, northern Russia, Estonia, and Finland; **Paveletsky Vokzal** (⊠ Pavelets Station, ☎ 095/235–0527, Metro: Paveletskaya), for eastern Ukraine and points south; **Rizhksy Vokzal** (⊠ Riga Station, ☎ 095/971–1588, Metro: Rizhskaya), for Latvia; **Yaroslavsky Vokzal** (⊠ Yaroslav Station, ☎ 095/921–5914, Metro: Komsomolskaya), for points east, including Mongolia and China; the Trans-Siberian Express departs every day at 2 PM.

The past few years have witnessed increased crime on the most heavily traveled routes, and as a result many travelers to St. Petersburg now prefer the high-speed, day train *Avrora,* which makes the trip in just under six hours. Of the numerous overnight trains, the most popular is the *Krasnaya Strelka* (Red Arrow), which leaves Moscow at 11:55 PM and arrives the next day in St. Petersburg at 8:25 AM. Overnight trains are considered more dangerous than day trains, and if you are traveling alone, you should take added precautions. Experienced travelers in Russia bring their own lock and buy out the entire compartment so as not to risk their luck with unknown compartment mates. If that's not an option, you should stow your luggage in the bin under the lower bunk, and you should sleep with your money, passport, and other important items. While food and drink may be sold on trains, it is wise to bring a packed meal; most Russians will, and your compartment mates may offer to share (beware of offers of vodka, however; poison bootleg vodka is a big problem in Russia).

For information on train arrival and departure schedules, call 095/266–9333. For booking and ticket delivery, call 095/266–8333. Tourists must travel on a special, higher-priced ticket for foreigners. You can purchase it at the railway stations or at the **ticket offices** (⊠ 6 Griboyedova ul,, Metro: Chistiye Prudy or ⊠ 15/13 Petrovka ul., ☎ 095/929–8757, Metro: Teatralnaya). Bring your passport.

Getting Around

If you look at a map of Moscow, you will see that the city consists of a series of distinct circles with the Kremlin and Red Square at its center. The most famous and important sites are clustered within the first circle, which was once enclosed by the fortification walls of Kitai Gorod, the city's oldest settlement outside the Kremlin. This area can be easily covered on foot. Beyond that, the sights are more spread out and are best reached by subway. To get a sense of the city's geographic layout, you might consider hiring a car for a few hours and traveling around the main roads encircling the city—the Boulevard and Garden Rings.

By Bus, Tram, and Trolley

Buses, trams, and trolleys operate on the honor system. Upon boarding, you validate your ticket by punching it in one of the machines attached to a wall of the vehicle. The buses and trolleys are often overcrowded, and you may not be able to reach the canceling machine. Ask the person next to you to pass your ticket along; the canceled ticket will make its way back to you, and you should hold on to it until you get off. On some routes, particularly out of the city center, you may be the only person to pay for your ride. However, inspectors do sometimes board buses and may detain or fine you if you cannot show a canceled ticket.

You can purchase strips of tickets at subway stops and at kiosks throughout the city. The ticket is valid for one ride only; if you change buses you must pay another fare. Buses, trams, and trolleys operate from 5:30 AM to 1 AM, although service in the late-evening hours and on Sunday tends to be unreliable.

By Car

Your hotel may make arrangements for you. Otherwise, several international car-rental agencies have offices in Moscow. **Avis** (⊠ 24 Goncharnaya ul., ☎ FAX 095/915–0870) rents several European makes. **Budget** (⊠ 16 Verkhnaya Radishchevskaya ul., ☎ 095/915–5237 or 095/915–0870; ⊠ Sheremetyevo II airport, ☎ 095/578–7344) rents Fords that can be picked up at the airport or the Sheraton Palace Hotel. **Hertz** (⊠ 4 Chernyakhovskogo ul., ☎ 095/937–3274) rents Fords; for a fee they will deliver the car to you. All agencies require advance reservations (at least two–three days is a good idea), and you will have to show your driver's license, an international license, and a credit card.

Hertz and Budget also rent cars with drivers, which may be a better option unless you are a good and experienced driver; driving in Moscow is not unlike a big game of chicken. Budget has Lincoln Town Cars and minivans as well as smaller cars.

By Subway

The Moscow subway (in Russian, *metro*) ranks among the world's finest public transportation systems. Opened in 1935, the system's earliest stations—in the city center and along the circle line—were built as public palaces and are decorated with chandeliers, sculptures, stained-glass windows, and beautiful mosaics. With more than 200 km (124 mi) of track, the Moscow subway carries an estimated 8 million passengers daily. Even in today's hard economic times, the system continues to run efficiently, with trains every 50 seconds during rush hour. It leaves New Yorkers green with envy.

If you're not traveling with a tour group or if you haven't hired your own chauffeur, taking the subway is the best way to get around the Russian capital. You'll be doing yourself a great favor, though, and saving yourself a lot of frustration, if you learn the Russian alphabet well enough to be able to transliterate the names of the stations. This will come in especially handy at the transfer points, where signs with long lists of the names of subway stations lead you from one of the major subway lines to another. You should also be able to recognize the entrance and exit signs (☞ English-Russian Vocabulary, at end of this book) because going the wrong way could earn you a scolding from one of the many red-hatted women working in the stations.

The subway is easy to use and amazingly inexpensive. Stations are marked with a large illuminated "M" sign and are open daily 5:30 AM–

Moscow Metro

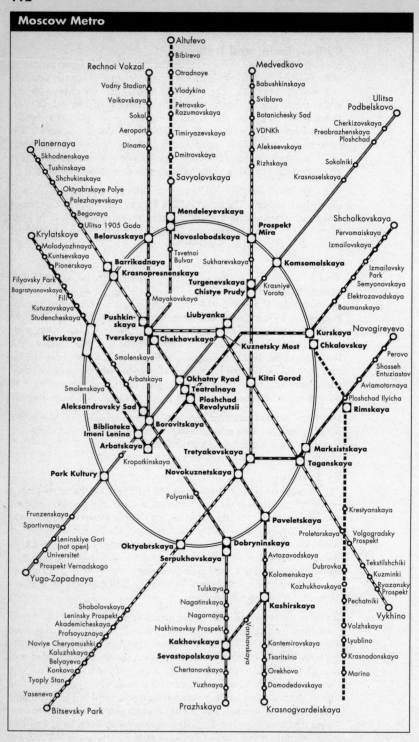

Altufevo
Bibirevo
Otradnoye
Rechnoi Vokzal
Vodny Stadion
Vladykino
Voikovskaya
Petrovsko-
Razumovskaya
Sokol
Aeroport
Timiryazevskaya
Dinamo
Dmitrovskaya
Savyolovskaya
Medvedkovo
Babushkinskaya
Sviblovo
Botanichesky Sad
VDNKh
Alekseevskaya
Rizhskaya
Ulitsa
Podbelskovo
Cherkizovskaya
Preobrazhenskaya
Ploshchad
Sokolniki
Krasnoselskaya
Planernaya
Skhodnenskaya
Tushinskaya
Shchukinskaya
Oktyabrskoye Polye
Polezhayevskaya
Begovaya
Ulitsa 1905 Goda
Mendeleyevskaya
**Prospekt
Mira**
Shcholkovskaya
Pervomaiskaya
Izmailovskaya
Krylatskoye
Molodyozhnaya
Kuntsevskaya
Pionerskaya
Belorusskaya
Novoslobodskaya
Tsvetnoi
Bulvar
Sukharevskaya
Komsomolskaya
Izmailovsky
Park
Semyonovskaya
Elektrozavodskaya
Baumanskaya
Filyovsky Park
Bagrationovskaya
Fili
Kutuzovskaya
Studencheskaya
Barrikadnaya
Krasnopresnenskaya
Turgenevskaya
Chistye Prudy
Krasniye
Vorota
Mayakovskaya
Liubyanka
**Pushkin-
skaya**
Tverskaya
Chekhovskaya
Kurskaya
Chkalovskay
Novogireyevo
Perovo
Shosseh
Entuziastov
Aviamotornaya
Kievskaya
Smolenskaya
Arbatskaya
Kuznetsky Most
Smolenskaya
Okhotny Ryad
Teatralnaya
**Ploshchad
Revolyutsii**
Kitai Gorod
Ploshchad Ilyicha
Rimskaya
Aleksandrovsky Sad
**Biblioteka
Imeni Lenina**
Borovitskaya
Arbatskaya
Tretyakovskaya
Marksistskaya
Taganskaya
Kropotkinskaya
Novokuznetskaya
Park Kultury
Polyanka
Krestyanskaya
Frunzenskaya
Sportivnaya
Paveletskaya
Proletarskaya
Volgogradsky
Prospekt
Leninskiye Gori
(not open)
Universitet
Prospekt Vernadskogo
Yugo-Zapadnaya
Oktyabrskaya
Serpukhovskaya
Dobryninskaya
Avtozavodskaya
Dubrovka
Tekstilshchiki
Kuzminki
Ryazansky
Prospekt
Kolomenskaya
Kozhukhovskaya
Pechatniki
Shabolovskaya
Leninsky Prospekt
Akademicheskaya
Profsoyuznaya
Noviye Cheryomushki
Kaluzhskaya
Belyayevo
Konkovo
Tyoply Stan
Yasenevo
Tulskaya
Nagatinskaya
Nagornaya
Nakhimovksy Prospekt
Kakhovskaya
Sevastopolskaya
Chertanovskaya
Yuzhnaya
Kashirskaya
Kantemirovskaya
Tsaritsino
Orekhovo
Domodedovskaya
Vykhino
Volzhskaya
Lyublino
Krasnodonskaya
Marino
Varshavskaya
Bitsevsky Park
Prazhskaya
Krasnogvardeiskaya

1 AM. The fare is the same regardless of distance traveled, and there are several stations where lines connect and you may transfer for free. You purchase a subway token (available at all stations) and insert it into the slot at the turnstile upon entering. Stations are built deep underground (they were built to double as bomb shelters); the escalators are steep and run fast, so watch your step. If you use the subway during rush hour (4–6 PM), be prepared for a lot of pushing and shoving. In a crowded train, just before a station, you are likely to be asked, *"Vyi khodyetye?"*, or whether you are getting off at the next station. If not, you are expected to move out of the way. Riders are expected to give up seats for older people and small children.

Pocket maps of the system are available at newspaper kiosks or sometimes from individual vendors at subway stations. Plan your route beforehand and have your destination written down in Russian and its English transliteration to help you spot the station. Each station is announced over the train's public address system as you approach it, and the name of the next one is given before the train moves off. Reminders of interchanges and transfers are also given.

If you want to avoid the lines for subway tokens, you can purchase a pass (*yediny bilyet*) that is valid for all modes of public transportation, and is sold by the calendar month. The passes are on sale at the same ticket windows as subway tokens. They are inexpensive and well worth the added expense for the convenience. When you have a pass, you must use a far turnstile. Before entering, you show it to the watchful matron standing guard; look for the crush of other passengers doing this. You can't go through the token turnstile with a pass, and if you try, two steel bars will slam closed on you. You can also buy 20-ride cards, which are inserted into slots at the turnstiles; be sure to take your ticket when it is ejected from the machine.

By Taxi

Foreign tourists should exercise caution when using taxicabs. There are standard taxis of various makes and colors but professional ones all have taxi lights on top and can easily be hailed in the city center. Official taxis have a T and checkered emblem on the doors (but there are not many of them). Generally, everyone with a car is a potential taxi driver in Moscow; it is very common for Muscovites to hail an ordinary car and negotiate a price for a ride. Of course, this is not recommended unless you speak some Russian. If you try it, never get in a car with more than one person inside, and if the driver wants to stop for another fare, say no or get out of the car. You can call cabs by phone or through your hotel's service bureau. **Maryino** (☎ 095/927–0000 or 095/348–8900) has 24-hour service. There is sometimes a delay, but the cab usually arrives within the hour. If you order a cab in this way, you pay the official state fare in rubles (which is very reasonable when calculated in dollars), plus a fee for the reservation. Drivers will appreciate and expect a tip of at least 20%. **Moscow Taxi** (☎ 095/238–1001) provides city cabs as well as airport service in vans or buses, picking up from hotels or privately. Their prices are higher than those of city cabs.

Contacts and Resources

Dentists

Russian dental facilities are as grim as other medical ones. Of the general service clinics, the **American Medical Center, European Medical Centre,** and **Mediclub Moscow** also offer dental services; the **International Medical Clinic** also has access to dental facilities. **U.S. Dental Care** (✉ 8 Shabolovka ul., Corpus 3, ground floor, ☎ 095/236–8106 or 095/236–5471, FAX 095/931–9909) is an independent clinic offering all types of dental treatment. Laboratories and pharmacy are on-site. Optional membership and all services are available to tourists. ☉ *Weekdays 8 AM–9 PM; after-hrs emergency. Metro: Shabolovskaya.*

The **Sofitel Dental Clinic** (✉ Sofitel Iris Hotel, 10 Korovinskoye Shosse, Room 18, ☎ 095/488–8279) also has a Western dental office, where Russian, English, French, and German are spoken. They offer a free shuttle service to and from Pushkin Square in the city center, since they are located outside of it. ☉ *Weekdays 10–5.*

Embassies
U.S. (✉ 19/23 Novinsky bulvar, ☎ 095/252–2451 through 095/252–2459). Unless you have official business or are met by embassy personnel or a compound resident, the embassy is off-limits, even to Americans. **Canada** (✉ 23 Starokonyushenny per., ☎ 095/956–6666). **U.K.** (✉ 14 Sofiyskaya nab., ☎ 095/956–7200). A new embassy is under construction near the foot of the Novy Arbat.

Emergencies
Ambulance (☎ 03). **Fire** (☎ 01). **Police** (☎ 02).

English-Language Bookstores
You'll pay a premium for most imported books, though books in Russian are remarkably inexpensive.

American Book Store (✉ 8/10 Denezhny per., ☎ 095/241–4224, Metro: Smolenskaya), open Monday–Saturday 10–3 and 4–7, is not far from the Old Arbat and sells some books at American prices.

Anglia British Bookshop (✉ 2/3 Khlebny per., ☎ 095/203–5802, Metro: Arbatskaya), open Monday–Saturday 10–7, is the sister store to American Book Store (☞ *above*). Bright and comfortable, it offers a good selection of literature and books about Russia—mostly books from Britain. It also holds readings and other events.

Dom Knigi (✉ The House of Books, 26 Novy Arbat, ☎ 095/290–4507, ☉ Mon.–Fri. 10–7:30, Sat. 10–7, Metro: Arbatskaya). Russia's largest bookstore has a small foreign-literature section (inside the doors, immediately to the right) and a large section for students of Russian language, but be sure also to examine the selection outside the front door, where individual sellers spread out their wares.

Shakespeare & Co. (✉ 5/7 Novokuznetsky Pervaya per., ☎ 095/951–9360, Metro: Paveletskaya), open Monday–Saturday 11–7, Sunday noon–6. A cozy branch of the famous Paris store, this has crammed shelves, helpful staff, literary readings, and good coffee. Shakespeare has a little of everything, including used books.

Zwemmer's (✉ 18 Kuznetsky most, ☎ 095/928–2021), open weekdays 10–7, Saturday 10–6. A British oasis, this is handily located, just around the corner from the Kuznetsky most metro station.

The English-language newspapers *The Moscow Times* (which publishes Tuesday–Saturday) and *The Moscow Tribune* (which publishes Tuesday, Wednesday, and Friday) carry world and local news. Pick them up in just about any Western store, restaurant, or major hotel.

Guided Tours
Every major hotel maintains a tourist bureau through which individual and group tours to Moscow's main tourist sights can be booked. In addition, there are numerous private agencies that can help with your sightseeing plans.

Intourist (✉ 13/1 Milyutinsky per., ☎ 095/232–2424 or 095/925–1300). This has a special travel department to provide you with any tour you want in Moscow; they also set up trips elsewhere in the CIS and help with visa support. They work within the system of Intourist offerings, so you'll be staying at their hotels, but because the network of their services is so extensive, you should be able to have whatever excursion you want.

Patriarshy Dom Tours (✉ 6 Vspolny per., ☎ 095/795–0927). A five-year-old company, Patriarshy Dom offers unusual day and overnight tours in and around Moscow and St. Petersburg for groups or individuals. Among the tours are the Red October chocolate factory, the KGB museum, literature or architectural walks, and the space flight command center. You can call for schedules or pick up copies in some hotels and Western stores. They have a phone number in the United States (☎ 413/584–9612).

Sputnik (✉ 15 Kosygina ul., ☎ 095/939–8580, FAX 095/956–1067). This is a company handling group and individual tours in Moscow and some day trips out of town. They can tailor plans to suit your needs.

VIP Service (✉ 3 Zubovsky proyezd, ☎ 095/247–0047). VIP can arrange a wide range of tours, including business trips. They will also make hotel, plane, and train reservations for other CIS destinations. Call at least a day in advance to make arrangements.

You should call around to get competitive rates. They can vary widely, depending on the trip you want, the number of people you have, and your transportation needs.

Hospitals and Clinics

With luck, you won't have to experience the medical system. It is plagued by a lack of medicines, low hygiene standards, and shortages of disposable needles and basic medical equipment. If you are ill, contact one of several Western clinics, which are used by the foreign community as well as Russians who can afford the higher fees. Some of these clinics are membership organizations, but all will provide service to tourists, though perhaps not with 24-hour access; costs will be higher than for members, too. Be sure to ask what payment method they accept. Usually it will be rubles or a credit card, and you will need to settle accounts up front.

In an emergency, you can also contact your country's consular section for help with the logistics of serious medical treatment. For U.S. citizens, contact **American Citizens Services** (☎ 095/956–4295; 095/956–4220 after-hrs emergency). **British citizens** can call their embassy, or during workdays get a referral from the embassy clinic (☎ 095/956–7269 or 095/956–7273). **Canadian citizens** should call the embassy number, where they will be connected to a duty officer.

The American Medical Center (✉ 10 Vtoroy Tverskoy-Yamskoy per., ☎ 095/956–3366, Metro: Belorusskaya or Mayakovskaya). This membership group offers full-range family practice and emergency services, including evacuation assistance. If treatment is needed outside their clinic, they use various hospitals, but primarily Kuntsevo Hospital (Kremlin VIP). The office is open 24 hours, and doctors make house calls 24 hours. Medicine can be provided at the clinic. A tourist plan is available.

The European Medical Centre (✉ 310 Vtoroy Tverskoy-Yamskoy per. 10, ☎ 095/251–6099, Metro: Belorusskaya or Mayakovskaya). This is not a membership group and offers a full range of services, including day and night house calls. Hospital referral is usually to the ZKB Presidential Hospital. English and French are spoken. Medicine can be provided at the clinic.

International Medical Clinic (✉ 31 Grokholsky per., 10th floor, ☎ 095/280–8388, 095/280–7177, or 095/280–8374; 095/280–8765 pharmacy, Metro: Prospekt Mira). This is a nonmember service that gives comprehensive care, hospitalization referral to the Kuntsevo (Kremlin VIP) Hospital, and evacuation via their in-house company (they are part of SOS International). In case overnight observation is necessary, they have on-site accommodations. English, French, and German are spoken. There is a pharmacy on site.

Mediclub Moscow (✉ 56 Michurinsky Prospekt, ☎ 095/931–5018 or 095/932–8653, Metro: Prospekt Vernadskovo). This is a Canadian clinic that provides full medical and ambulance service, hospital referral to Glavmosstroy Hospital, and assistance with evacuation. English and French are spoken. The pharmacy is stocked with Western and Russian medicines. Cash payment only. It's open weekdays 9–8 and Saturday 10–2; you may call after hours, but unless you are a member, it is not guaranteed that you will reach a doctor.

There is also a **Crisis Line** in English, operating 24 hours. It is free and confidential, for adults and children. The trained counselors are native English speakers and can help assist with personal problems such as depression, domestic abuse and suicidal feelings (☎ 095/244–3449 or 095/931–9682). When calling, ask for the Crisis Line, or give the code "crisis"; a pager service will take your phone number and a counselor will return your call as soon as possible.

An English-language **Alcoholics Anonymous** meets six evenings a week at various locations. Check the *Moscow Times* community bulletin board listings, published Wednesdays (☎ 095/243–1420 or 095/290–4814).

Late-Night Pharmacies

Pharmacies are plentiful and generally open only until 8 or 9 PM. Though they are becoming well stocked, Western-brand medicines may not be recognizable to you in their Russian packaging; however, you often can buy medicine over the counter that requires a prescription in the United States. For prescriptions, you can contact one of the foreign clinics' pharmacies, though prices will be high (☞ Emergencies, *above*). Some hotels also have small pharmacies.

Travel Agencies

There are many choices. Listed here are some Moscow travel agents, not local tour companies offering excursions. They can provide air (and sometimes train) ticketing for international travel and, as noted, travel to other points within Russia and the CIS.

American Express (✉ 21-A Sadovaya-Kudrinskaya ul., ☎ 095/755–9000 or 095/755–9001, ℻ 095/755–9003 or 095/755–9004), open weekdays 9–5, Saturday 10–2, handles arrangements for domestic and air tickets but not for trains. It will also help with car hire and hotel reservations. It is not necessary to be a member to receive these services. For members, it will replace your lost traveler's checks and credit cards, or issue you a cash advance against your credit card, provided you can write a personal check. The office has an ATM machine for its card holders; a commission is charged, the amount depending on the type of card you possess.

Apex Travel World (✉ 3 Zubovsky proyezd, ☎ 095/245–5438 or 095/247–0047). Though primarily a tour agency, this place may be able to arrange train ticketing in the CIS to points out of Moscow.

Intourist (✉ 13/1 Milyutinsky per., ☎ 095/232–2424 or 095/925–1300). This runs a special travel department. They can help with domestic and international air and train tickets, accommodations throughout the CIS as well as in Moscow, and visa support.

IRO Travel (✉ 13 Komsomolsky Prospekt, ☎ 095/234–6555, FAX 095/234–6556). An American-owned and -managed company, IRO can book domestic and international train and air tickets and hotel reservations, and provide visa support.

Sac-Voyage (✉ 16 Olympisky Prospekt, ☎ 095/281–6215, FAX 095/755–8824). This provides a full range of services, including airline bookings, hotel reservations, and visa support.

Slavyanka Tour (✉ Radisson Slavyanskaya Hotel, 2 Berezhkovsky nab., ☎ 095/941–8764, FAX 095/941–8765). They can arrange domestic and international tickets for both air and train travel. They'll also provide visa support and prepare excursion packages and make hotel reservations for business travelers and tourists.

SVO Travel (✉ 15 Novy Arbat, ☎ 095/202–6409 or 095/202–1328). This is a Canadian agency that handles ticketing on international flights. For CIS cities, it can book on Transaero, and handles Aeroflot ticketing only for domestic routes. Train tickets are booked only for corporate clients. Tickets are delivered for a fee.

Tour Service International (✉ 10 Tverskaya ul., ☎ 095/292-3556 or 095/747–3011). Useful for those wanting to go from Moscow or from elsewhere to Ukraine, this outfit offers visa support, including courier service (for which there is a fee) for its application, and hotel bookings. This may be your most expeditious route if you decide to visit Kiev only after you have arrived in Moscow.

VIP Service (✉ 5 Lubyansky proyezd, 3rd floor, ☎ 095/247–0047). This can book air tickets on international charters and on Transaero and Aeroflot in the CIS. Credit cards are accepted. They deliver tickets, for which service there is a fee.

For international plane tickets, you may also call the airlines directly. Ask them where you can pick up your tickets in Moscow.

Visitor Information

Moscow does not have a tourist information center *per se,* but the service bureaus of all the major hotels offer their guests (and anyone else willing to pay their fees) a wide variety of tourist services, including help in booking group or individual excursions, making a restaurant reservation, or purchasing theater or ballet tickets. You may also find help (as the hotels themselves often do) from the Intourist Service, today's reincarnation of the old Soviet tourist service (☞ Travel Agencies, *above*) or from some of the tour agencies (☞ Guided Tours, *above*). For the latest on what's happening in Moscow, check the listings in either of the two leading English-language newspapers—the *Moscow Times* or the *Moscow Tribune*. On Thursdays, the Russian newspaper *Moscow News* publishes an English-language translation of its paper, which includes a roundup of cultural events.

Where to Change Money

Most hotels have currency exchange bureaus, some operating 24 hours a day, where you can change your dollars for rubles. You can also use the Russian banks; while nowhere near as common as in U.S. cities, there are automatic teller machines around Moscow. Most of them will conduct transactions in English; some dispense dollars as well as rubles. Some serve only their own customers. In addition, you will find exchange bureaus all over the city, bearing the OBMEN VALUTY/EXCHANGE sign—these are often in Cyrillic, but just look for the signs with daily rates posted in easy view, often on freestanding sidewalk posters. Exercise reasonable caution when using them, and don't be surprised to find a security guard, who may let only one or two people inside at a time. By law it's required that you be issued a receipt, but you may find this erratic in practice; be sure to ask for one. You can exchange traveler's checks for rubles or dollars at any of the private banks. Try the **bank** offices in the Radisson Slavyanskaya Hotel (✉ 2 Berezhkovskaya nab., first floor, ☎ 095/941–8434) and in the Baltschug Kempinski (✉ 1 Balchug ul., first floor, ☎ 095/941–8020). The **American Express Office** (☞ Travel Agencies, *above*) will cash American Express traveler's checks for rubles and, if it has cash available, for dollars. You can also obtain dollars by writing the office a personal check and having the exchange charged to your American Express card.

3 Moscow Side Trips and the Golden Ring

Not far away from modern Moscow lies an ancient region enormously rich with historic sights—ranging from the Russian Versailles that is Kuskovo to Boris Godunov's tomb and the medieval town of Suzdal. For those who wish to stride back into the past, there are few other parts of Russia— and none so convenient to reach from Moscow—in which the sense of centuries unwinding is stronger.

By Paul E.
Richardson
and Mikhail V.
Ivanov

IN THE RIVER VALLEYS EAST AND NORTH of Moscow is a special realm you might call Russia's Capital-That-Might-Have-Been—Suzdalia, the region that encompassed the historic centers of Rostov, Vladimir, Suzdal, and Yaroslavl. These small towns—all within easy striking distance of Moscow—witnessed nothing less than the birth of the Russian nation nearly a millennium ago and, consequently, are home to some of the most beautiful churches and monasteries. But don't imagine that day trips from Moscow only provide glimpses of Old Russian religious splendor; magnificence can also be found at the palatial estates of Arkhangelskoye and Kuskovo. The list of sights goes on and on, and with romantic kremlins, famous monasteries, and famous works of art like "The Extraordinary"—Andrev Rublyev's frescoes in Vladimir's Cathedral of the Assumption—it is little wonder that the historic regions surrounding Moscow remain high on many sightseeing lists.

Many of these towns and districts have more than 10 centuries of history to share, but their history really begins early in the 12th century, when Prince Yuri Dolgoruky, son of Vladimir Monomakh, the Grand Prince of Kiev, was given control over the northeastern outpost of what was then Kievan Rus'. Dolgoruky built his power and authority, and founded the towns that would become Pereslavl-Zalessky and Kostroma. He also built frontier outposts to guard against his neighbors, including one on the southwest border, called Moscow.

Yuri Dolgoruky's son, Andrei Bogolyubsky, built considerable power within Kievan Rus', centered on his inherited lands of Suzdalia. He made Vladimir his capital and built up its churches and monasteries to rival those of Kiev. In 1169, unhappy with the pattern of dynastic succession in Kiev, Bogolyubsky sent his and allied troops to sack Kiev and placed his son on the throne as Grand Prince. From that point forward, political and ecclesiastical power began to flow toward the northeastern region of Rus'.

Had not the Mongol invasion intervened a century later, Vladimir might have continued to grow in power and be the capital of Russia today. But invade the Mongols did, and every town in the region was decimated, and remained subjugated for over 200 years. Moscow, meanwhile, with the cunning it is still known for today, slowly rose to prominence by becoming tax (or tribute) collector for the Mongols. Ivan Kalita ("Ivan Moneybags") was a particularly proficient go-between, and, as Mongol power receded in the 14th century, he began gathering together the lands surrounding Moscow, beginning with Vladimir.

The ancient Russian towns north and east of Moscow which make up what is most commonly called "The Golden Ring" seem quite unassuming now in comparison to the sprawling, bustling capital. But from the 12th to the middle of the 15th century, Rostov, Vladimir, Suzdal, and Yaroslavl were the centers of Russian political, cultural, and economic life. And while today they may lack some of the amenities travelers can easily find in Moscow, they have a provincial charm and aura of history that makes them an important stop for anyone seeking to become acquainted with Mother Russia. The towns lie on two main routes and most travelers divide the towns into two separate excursions—north of Moscow to Sergevev-Posad, Pereslavl-Zalessky, Rostov, Yaroslavl, and Kostromo, and east of Moscow to Vladimir and Suzdal.

Pleasures and Pastimes

Churches and Monasteries

With some exceptions, what you will be traveling to see in the Golden Ring region surrounding Moscow are churches and monasteries—the statement-making structures that princes, metropolitans, and merchants in old Russia built to display their largesse and power. And since most civil and residential buildings until the 18th century were constructed from wood, it turns out that these religious buildings, constructed of stone, have best survived the ravages of time, invading armies, and fire. Today, many are being returned to their original, ecclesiastical purposes, but most are still museums. In either instance, neglect and funding shortages have taken their toll on preservation and restoration efforts, and at times it can be difficult to imagine these historical monuments in their original glory.

Dining

Do not expect to find rows of quaint countryside cafés in Russian towns. While the tourist traffic to some towns near Moscow helps sustain a sufficient infrastructure, there are still few private restaurants—and this is largely because Russians themselves do not dine out that frequently. The most reliable restaurants are in hotels catering to tourists or, occasionally, in downtown locations near main tourist sites. This is slowly changing, and some of the restaurants outside hotels can be quite cozy. Happily, across the board, you will be surprised to find that restaurant prices here are considerably lower than in Moscow.

CATEGORY	COST*
$$$$	over $70
$$$	$40–$70
$$	$20–$40
$	under $20

*per person for a three-course dinner, excluding drinks and service

Lodging

None of the towns covered in this section has a long list of lodging options, and even fewer have good, tourist-class hotels. While basic amenities are not usually a problem, it will be some time before the hotels in these towns catch up with Moscow's two- and three-star hotels. But the good news is, as with restaurants, these hotels' prices are far below Moscow levels.

CATEGORY	COST*
$$$$	over $350
$$$	$250–$350
$$	$125–$250
$	$60–$125
¢	under $60

*All prices are for a standard double room, excluding service charge.

Great Itineraries

You need six to seven full days to really see this region well. There are bus tours (☞ Moscow Side Trips and Golden Ring A–Z, *below*) that can do the Golden Ring cities in less time, but these allow only limited options for exploring at your own pace. Be realistic about the time you have to explore and savor these rich, historical towns, alloting time to stop for a meal in a local restaurant or to linger in a 13th-century monastery.

Numbers in the text correspond to numbers in the margin and on the Moscow Side Trips and the Golden Ring map.

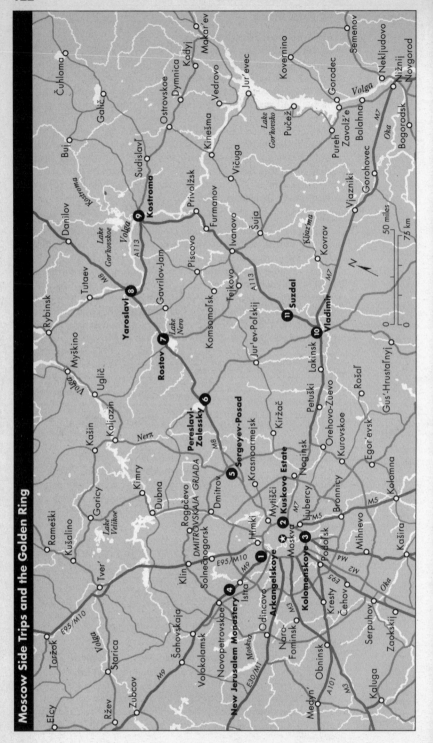

Moscow Side Trips and the Golden Ring

IF YOU HAVE 1 OR 2 DAYS

Arkhangelskoye ①, **Kuskovo Estate and Palace Museum** ②, **New Jerusalem Monastery** ④, and **Sergeyev-Posad** ⑤ can all be easily done as day trips from Moscow. By car and possibly by train, with an early start and a late return, Vladimir, Suzdal, or Pereslavl-Zalessky could all be sampled in a day trip.

If you have two days to explore the towns of the Golden Ring, drive or take a morning train (three hours) to **Vladimir** ⑩, explore the town, being sure to take in the Church of the Intercession on the Nerl, then travel on to ☷ **Suzdal** ⑪ and overnight in the beautiful Convent of the Intercession. This will put you right in the thick of things to start exploring Suzdal early the next morning. Return to Moscow via Vladimir late in the day.

Alternatively, take a morning train (five hours) to ☷ **Yaroslavl** ⑧ and spend the day and night there. The next morning, catch a return train on the same route, stopping off in **Rostov** ⑦ (1½ hours from Yaroslavl) to spend the day before catching a late afternoon train back to Moscow.

IF YOU HAVE 3 OR 4 DAYS

Follow either of the two-day itineraries above. But, for **Vladimir/Suzdal,** devote a second full day to **Suzdal** ⑪. For **Yaroslavl** ⑧, on the return, overnight in ☷ **Rostov** ⑦. On your final return on day three, stop for several hours in **Pereslavl-Zalessky** ⑥ before returning to Moscow.

MOSCOW SIDE TRIPS

Within easy reach of the city for half-day excursions are some majestic old palaces, estates and former noble residences, set in typical countryside. To see them to the best advantage you should try and time your visits to coincide with spring or summer.

Arkhangelskoye

❶ *26 km (15 mi) northwest of Moscow via Volokolamskoye shosse.*

The town of Arkhangelskoye, on the banks of the Moscow River, offers a beautiful example of a noble country palace of the late czarist era—the imposing estate of Prince Yusupov, whose Neoclassical palace forms the centerpiece of a striking group of 18th- and 19th-century buildings that artfully blends into the landscape. The palace but not the grounds of the **Arkhangelskoye Estate Museum** has been closed for several years for restoration work, and no date has been set for its official reopening, but excursions can still be made out there. Check first with your hotel's service bureau or the tour agency you have chosen for updated information.

The main palace complex was built at the end of the 18th century for Prince Golitsyn by the French architect Chevalier de Huerne. In 1810, the family fell upon hard times and sold it to the rich landlord Yusupov, onetime director of the Imperial theaters and of St. Petersburg's Hermitage Museum and ambassador extraordinary to several European lands (which is why his collection contained priceless furniture once belonging to Marie Antoinette and Madame de Pompadour). The estate became home to Prince Yusupov's extraordinary art collection.

The Classical palace's holdings included paintings by Boucher, Vigée-Lebrun, Hubert Robert, Roslin, Tiepolo, Van Dyck, and many others, as well as antique statues, furniture, mirrors, chandeliers, glassware, and china. The collection also includes samples of fabrics, china, and glassware, all of which were produced on the estate.

In the French Park are allées and strolling lanes; many still hold statues and monuments commemorating royal visits; there is also a monument to Pushkin, whose favorite retreat was Arkhangelskoye. In the western part is an interesting small pavilion, known as the Temple to the Memory of Catherine the Great, which depicts the empress as Themis, goddess of justice. It seems that Yusupov, reportedly a Casanova, had turned the head of Russia's empress, renowned herself for having legions of lovers. This "temple" was built as a compliment for a painting she had previously commissioned—one in which she was depicted as Venus, with Yusupov as Apollo. Overall, a definite sense of disrepair—with the exception of the closed palace with its ongoing reconstruction—pervades. Back outside the estate grounds, the Estate (Serf) Theater, on the right side of the main road, was built in 1817 by the serf architect Ivanov; it seated 400 and was the home of the biggest and best-known company of serf-actors. The well-preserved stage decorations are by the Venetian artist Pietrodi Gonzaga. As it turns out, Prince Yusupov was a kindly, paternalistic man and always opened his home to the public and allowed them to enjoy his palatial extravaganza. The Arkhangelskoye Estate Museum can be reached by Bus 541 from Moscow's Metro Station Sokolniki, or by car from the Rublevskoye Shosse (turn right at the Militia Booth toward Ilinskoe and take a right turn after you pass the Russkaya Izba restaurant). ⊠ *Arkhangelskoye.* ☉ *As the grounds are not officially open, there are no operating hrs.*

Dining and Lodging

$$ ✕ **Russkaya Izba.** A quaint and pricey option, this restaurant has a cottage style and rustic decor patterned on a Russian country home. ⊠ *In the village of Ilyinskoye, on the road to Arkhangelskoye, near the Moscow River,* ☏ *095/561–4244. Reservations essential. No credit cards.*

$ ✕ **Arkhangelskoye Restaurant.** Decorated inside with a Palekh motif, this is conveniently located directly across the road from the entrance to the museum. ⊠ *Arkhangelskoye,* ☏ *095/562–0328. AE, MC, V.*

Kuskovo Estate and Palace Museum

❷ *18 km (11 mi) southeast of the city center via Ryazansky Prospekt.*

In the 18th and 19th centuries, the country estate of Kuskovo was the Moscow aristocracy's favorite summer playground. It belonged to the noble Sheremetyevs, one of Russia's wealthiest and most distinguished families, whose holdings numbered in the millions of acres. (Today, Moscow's international airport, built on land once belonging to one of their many estates, takes their family name.) Kuskovo is located just outside the ring road marking the city boundary, but you can reach it by public transportation. Take the subway to Ryazansky Prospekt and then Bus 208 or Bus 133 six stops to Kuskovo Park. This is obviously not as accessible as Kolomenskoye (☞ *below*), and you may find it more convenient to book a tour that would include transportation. Whatever you do, be sure to phone ahead before making the trek out here, because the estate often closes in humid weather and when it is very cold.

The land of Kuskovo belonged to the Sheremetyevs as far back as the early 17th century, but the estate acquired its present appearance in the late 18th century. Often called a Russian Versailles, most work on it was commissioned by Prince Peter Sheremetyev, who sought a suitable place for entertaining guests in the summer. The park—one of the most beautiful spots in all of Russia—was created by Russian landscape artists who had spent much time in Europe studying their art. The French-style gardens are dotted with buildings representing the major

BONUS MILES MAKE GREAT SOUVENIRS.

Earn Miles With Your MCI Card.

Take the MCI Card along on this trip and start earning miles for the next one. You'll earn frequent flyer miles on all your calls and save with the low rates you've come to expect from MCI. Before you know it, you'll be on your way to some other international destination.

Sign up for MCI by calling 1-800-FLY-FREE

Earn Frequent Flyer Miles.

Is this a great time, or what? :-)

Easy To Call Home.

1. To use your MCI Card, just dial the WorldPhone access number of the country you're calling from.
2. Dial or give the operator your MCI Card number.
3. Dial or give the number you're calling.

# Austria (CC) ♦	022-903-012
# Belarus (CC)	
From Brest, Vitebsk, Grodno, Minsk	8-800-103
From Gomel and Mogilev regions	8-10-800-103
# Belgium (CC) ♦	0800-10012
# Bulgaria	00800-0001
# Croatia (CC) ★	0800-22-0112
# Czech Republic (CC) ♦	00-42-000112
# Denmark (CC) ♦	8001-0022
# Finland (CC) ♦	08001-102-80
# France (CC) ♦	0-800-99-0019
# Germany (CC)	0800-888-8000
# Greece (CC) ♦	00-800-1211
# Hungary (CC) ♦	00▼800-01411
# Iceland (CC) ♦	800-9002
# Ireland (CC)	1-800-55-1001
# Italy (CC) ♦	172-1022
# Kazakhstan (CC)	8-800-131-4321
# Liechtenstein (CC) ♦	0800-89-0222
# Luxembourg	0800-0112
# Monaco (CC) ♦	800-90-019
# Netherlands (CC) ♦	0800-022-9122
# Norway (CC) ♦	800-19912
# Poland (CC) ÷	00-800-111-21-22
# Portugal (CC) ÷	05-017-1234
Romania (CC) ÷	01-800-1800
# Russia (CC) ÷ ♦	
To call using ROSTELCOM ■	747-3322
For a Russian-speaking operator	747-3320
To call using SOVINTEL ■	960-2222
# San Marino (CC) ♦	172-1022
# Slovak Republic (CC)	00-421-00112
# Slovenia	080-8808
# Spain (CC)	900-99-0014
# Sweden (CC) ♦	020-795-922
# Switzerland (CC) ♦	0800-89-0222
# Turkey (CC) ♦	00-8001-1177
# Ukraine (CC) ÷	8▼10-013
# United Kingdom (CC)	
To call using BT ■	0800-89-0222
To call using C&W ■	0500-89-0222
# Vatican City (CC)	172-1022

CHASE

Flying to France on Friday? Get Francs from Chase on Thursday. Call Currency To Go at 935-9935 for overnight delivery.

CHASE CURRENCY TO GO 935-9935

O r pounds for London. Or Deutschmarks for Düsseldorf. Or any of 75 foreign currencies. Call **Chase Currency To Go**^{SM} at **935-9935** in area codes 212, 718, 914, 516 and Rochester, N.Y.; all other area codes call 1-800-935-9935. We'll deliver directly to your door.* Overnight. And there are no exchange fees. Let Chase make your trip an easier one.

CHASE. The right relationship is everything.^{SM}

architectural trends of Europe: the Dutch cottage, the Italian villa, the Grotto, and the exquisite Hermitage, where, in the fashion of the day, dinner tables were raised mechanically from the ground floor to the second-floor dining room.

The centerpiece of the estate is the **Kuskovo Palace,** built in the early Russian Classical style by the serf architects Alexei Mironov and Fedor Argunov—fronted by a grand horseshoe staircase and Greek temple portico, this building is the absolute quintessence of Russian Neoclassical elegance. The palace, which is made of timber on a white-stone foundation, overlooks an artificial lake. It has been a museum since 1918, and its interior decorations, including fine parquet floors and silk wall coverings, have been well preserved. The bedroom, with its fine canopy bed, was merely for show; the Sheremetyevs used the palace exclusively for entertainment and did not live here. The marvelous White Hall, with its parquet floors, gilt wall decorations, and crystal chandeliers, served as the ballroom. On display in the inner rooms are paintings by French, Italian, and Flemish artists, Chinese porcelain, furniture, ornaments, and other articles of everyday life from the 18th and 19th centuries. The palace also houses a collection of 18th-century Russian art and a rather celebrated ceramics museum with a rich collection of Russian, Soviet, and foreign ceramics.

Peter Sheremetyev owned more than 150,000 serfs, many of whom received architectural training and participated in the building of his estate. Serfs also constituted a theater troupe that gave weekly open-air performances, another common practice on nobles' estates, and the *crème de la crème* of Moscow society made it a point to attend these park performances. Today, of course, these vestiges of a spectacular lifestyle have disappeared, but the dreamlike park and palace remain as mute and eloquent testimony to a lifestyle long vanished. ⊠ *2 ul. Yunosti,* ☎ *095/370–0160.* ⊡ *$2.* ☉ *Nov.–Apr., Wed.–Sun. 10–4; May–Oct., Wed.–Fri. 11–7, weekends 10–6. Closed last Wed. of month.*

Kolomenskoye

★ ❸ *17 km (10.5 mi) south of the city center, via Kashirskoye shosse, and located on the western bank of the Moscow River.*

If you want to spend an afternoon in the great Russian outdoors without actually leaving the city, a visit to Kolomenskoye is a must. Situated on a high bluff overlooking the Moskva River, the estate was once a favorite summer residence of Moscow's grand dukes and czars. Today it is a popular public park with museums, a functioning church, old Russian cottages, and other attractions. Take the subway to the Kolomenskaya station on the green line; a walk of about 10 minutes up a slight hill will bring you to the park's entrance. ⊠ *Prospekt Andropova 39,* ☎ *095/112–0416.* ☉ *Tues.–Sun. 10–5.*

As you walk up the hill to Kolomenskoye, the first sight to greet you is a view of the striking blue domes of the **Church of Our Lady of Kazan.** The church is open for worship. A wooden palace once stood in the park opposite the church. It was built by Czar Alexei, Peter the Great's father, and Peter spent much time here when he was growing up. Nothing remains of this huge wooden palace (Catherine the Great ordered it destroyed in 1767), but there is a scale model at the museum. The exhibits of the museum, devoted to Russian timber architecture and folk crafts, are found in the old servants' quarters, at the end of the tree-lined path leading from the main entrance.

Most remarkable is the **Church of the Ascension,** situated on the bluff overlooking the river. The church dates from the 1530s and was restored in the late 1800s. Its skyscraping tower is an example of the tent or pyramid-type structure that was popular in Russian architecture in the 16th century. The view from the bluff is impressive in its contrasts, and there is always something happening. From your 16th-century backdrop, you can look across the river to the north, to the 20th-century concrete apartment houses that dominate the contemporary Moscow skyline. In summer you'll see Muscovites bathing in the river below the church, and in winter the area abounds in cross-country skiers.

Examples of wooden architecture from other parts of Russia have been transferred to Kolomenskoye, turning the estate into an open-air museum. In the wooded area near the site of the former wooden palace, you will find a 17th-century prison tower from Siberia, a defense tower from the White Sea, and a 17th-century mead brewery from the village of Preobrazhenskaya. One of the most attractive buildings to be seen in its original form is the wooden cottage where Peter the Great lived while supervising the building of the Russian fleet in Arkhangelskoye. It was moved here from that northern city in 1934.

New Jerusalem Monastery

4 *65 km (40.4 mi) northwest of Moscow via Volokolamskoye shosse and the M9.*

The **Novoierusalimsky Monastyr** (New Jerusalem Monastery) is located near the town of Istra, at a bend in the river of the same name. This is not the most visited place in Russia, and it is included in the standard offerings of tourist agencies only in the summer. In nice weather, it is a marvelous way to spend a day; its location in the picturesque Russian countryside—far from tourist crowds—only adds to its attraction. If you can't book a tour and are feeling adventurous, you could try an excursion on the commuter train. Trains leave from Rizhsky Vokzal (Riga Railroad Station) and take about an hour and a half. The best option of all would be to ask a Russian friend to guide you and make a day of it in the countryside. Be sure to pack your lunch; the best you'll find in Istra is an occasional cafeteria or outdoor café. ☉ *Wed.–Sun. 10–4; closed last Fri of month.* ▣ *$3.*

The monastery was founded in 1652 by Nikon, patriarch of the Russian Orthodox Church. It lies on exactly the same longitude as Jerusalem, and its main cathedral, **Voskresensky Sobor** (Resurrection Cathedral), is modeled after the Church of the Holy Sepulchre in Jerusalem. Nikon's objective in re-creating the original Jerusalem in Russia was to glorify the power of the Russian Orthodox Church and at the same time elevate his own position as its head. It was Nikon who initiated the great church reforms in the 17th century that eventually led to the *raskol* (schism) resulting in the Old Believer sects of the Russian Orthodox faith. As a reformer, he was progressive and enlightened, but he lusted for power, which eventually was his undoing. In 1658, before the monastery was even finished, the patriarch quarreled with the czar over Nikon's claim that the Church was ultimately superior to the State. Eventually Nikon was defrocked and banished to faraway Ferapontov Monastery. He died in virtual exile in 1681, then was buried in the monastery that was supposed to have glorified his power. You can find his crypt in the Church of St. John the Baptist, which is actually inside the Resurrection Cathedral. Ironically, the same church commission that defrocked Patriarch Nikon later voted to institute his reforms.

NORTH OF MOSCOW: THE GOLDEN RING

The towns of the historic region northeast of Moscow are commonly grouped together under the tourist agency rubric of "The Golden Ring of Russia." This means there are plenty of guided-tour options for independent travelers and groups, ranging from one-day outings to 1,000-km (3,000-mi) bus tours (☞ Moscow Side Trips and Golden Ring A–Z, *below*). But it also means that the independent traveler is likely to find these towns tourist-friendly, even if the transition to the market economy has them straining to keep their streets clean and museums open.

Sergeyev-Posad (Zagorsk)

★ ❺ *75 km (46 mi) northeast of Moscow via Yaroslavskoye shosse and the M8.*

Sergeyev-Posad is a comfortable, and popular, day trip from Moscow. The city's chief attraction is the Troitsa-Sergeyeva Lavra (Trinity Monastery of St. Sergius), which for 500 years has been the most important center of pilgrimage in Russia and remains one of the most beautiful of all monasteries—the fairytale gold and azure onion domes of its Assumption Cathedral are among the most photographed in the country. Until 1930, the town was known as Sergeyev, after the monastery's founder, and in 1991 it was officially renamed Sergeyev-Posad. But the Soviet name of Zagorsk—in honor of a Bolshevik who was assassinated in 1919—has stuck, and you are as likely to hear the town and the monastery itself called one as the other.

The ride to Sergeyev-Posad takes you through a lovely stretch of Russian countryside, dotted with colorful wooden cottages. As you approach the town, you see the sad and monolithic apartment buildings of the modern era. Then, peeking out above the sloping hills, the monastery's golden cupolas and soft-blue bell tower come into view.

The best way to visit Sergeyev-Posad is to join an organized tour, since it is a full-day affair, out of the city. All tour services offer day trips to Sergeyev-Posad. The cost usually includes lunch in addition to a guided tour and transportation. It is also possible to visit on your own by taking the commuter train from Moscow's Yaroslavsky Vokzal (Yaroslav Railroad Station). The ride takes about two hours; tickets are purchased at the train station for rubles. This is obviously much less expensive than an organized tour, but far from hassle-free. If you choose this alternative, be sure to pack your own lunch, since Sergeyev-Posad's only full-fledged restaurant fills up fast with prebooked tourist groups, especially in the summer. You must also take care to dress appropriately for your visit to the functioning monastery, to make certain you won't go all the way there only to be turned away at the entrance. (Russia is far stricter about enforcing dress codes at religious sites than are most similar places in Europe.) Men are expected to remove their hats, and women are required to wear below knee-length skirts or slacks (*never* shorts, even walking shorts) and bring something to cover their heads.

The heart of Holy Russia until 1920 (when the Bolsheviks closed down most monasteries and shipped many monks to Siberia), the **Troitsa-Sergeyeva Lavra** (Monastery of St. Sergius) was founded in 1340 by Sergius of Radonezh, who would later become Russia's patron saint. The site rapidly became the nucleus of a small medieval settlement, and in 1550 the imposing white walls were built to enclose the complex of buildings, whose towers and gilded domes make it a smaller,

128

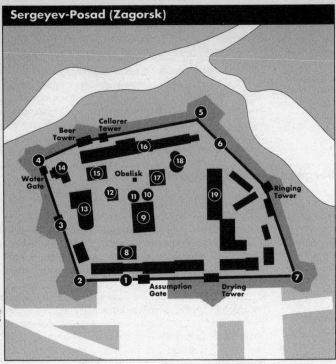

Sergeyev-Posad (Zagorsk)

but still spectacular, version of Moscow's Kremlin. The monastery was a Russian stronghold during the Time of Troubles and the Polish assault on Moscow in the early 17th century, and Peter the Great took refuge here during a bloody revolt of the *streltsy* (palace guard) that took the lives of some of his closest relatives and advisers. After the Bolshevik Revolution, the monastery was closed and turned into a museum. During World War II, however, in an attempt to mobilize the country and stir up patriotism, the Soviet government got the support of the Church by returning to religious purposes some of the Church property that had been confiscated earlier, including the Monastery of St. Sergius. Today the churches are again open for worship, and there is a flourishing theological college here. Until the reopening in 1988 of the Danilovsky Monastery in Moscow, this monastery was the residence of the patriarch and administrative center of the Russian Orthodox Church. ⊠ ▦ $3. ⊙ *Tues.–Sun. 10–5.*

You enter the monastery through the archway of the **Gate Church of St. John the Baptist,** which was erected in the late 17th century and is decorated with frescoes telling the life story of St. Sergius. One of the most important historical events in his life occurred prior to 1380, when the decisive Russian victory in the Battle of Kulikovo led to the end of Mongol rule in Russia. Before leading his troops off to battle, Prince Dmitri Donskoy sought the blessing of the peace-loving monk Sergius, a move that is generally thought to have greatly aided the Russian victory (☞ Donskoy Monastery *in* Chapter 2).

Although all of the monastery's cathedrals vie for your attention (and each visitor will have a different favorite), the dominating structure is the massive, blue-domed and gold-starred **Uspensky Sobor** (Assumption Cathedral) located in the center. Built in 1554–85 with money donated by Czar Ivan the Terrible—purportedly in an attempt to atone for murdering his own son—it was modeled after the Kremlin's Uspensky Sobor. Its interior boasts frescoes and an 18th-century iconostasis. Among the artists to work on it was Simon Ushakov, a well-known icon painter from Moscow. The cathedral is open for morning services.

The small building just outside the Uspensky Cathedral (near the northwest corner) is the **tomb of Boris Godunov** and his family. Boris Godunov died suddenly in 1605, during the Polish attack on Moscow led by the False Dmitri, the first of many impostors to claim he was the son of Czar Ivan the Terrible. The death of Boris facilitated the invaders' victory, after which his family was promptly murdered. This explains why Boris was not bestowed the honor of burial in the Kremlin normally granted to czars.

Opposite Boris Godunov's tomb is a tiny and colorful chapel built above a miracle-working fountain. It is called **Chapel-at-the-Well.** According to legend, the spring here appeared during the Polish Siege (1608–10), when the monastery bravely held out for 16 months against the foreign invaders (this time led by the second False Dmitri). You can make a wish by washing your face and hands in its charmed waters. Towering 285 ft above the monastery grounds is the five-tiered Baroque belfry. It was built in the 18th century to a design by the master of St. Petersburg Baroque, Bartolomeo Rastrelli.

Along the southern wall of the monastery, to your far left as you enter, is the 17th-century **Refectory and Church of St. Sergius.** The church is at the eastern end, topped by a single gilt dome. The long building of the Refectory, whose colorful facade adds to the vivid richness of the monastery's architecture, is where, in times past, pilgrims from near and far gathered to eat on feast days. The pink building just beyond the Refectory is the metropolitan's Residence.

A continual service in memoriam to St. Sergius is held all day, every day, in the white-stone **Troitsky Sobor** (Cathedral of the Holy Trinity), situated across the path from the metropolitan's Residence. The church, which is very beautiful inside, was built in the 15th century over the tomb of St. Sergius; over the centuries it has received many precious gifts from the powerful and wealthy rulers who have made the pilgrimage to the church of Russia's patron saint. The icons inside were created by famous master Andrey Rublyov and one of his disciples, Danil Chorny. Ryublov's celebrated *Holy Trinity,* now on display at the Tretyakov Gallery, originally hung here; the work you see is a copy.

The vestry, the building behind the Church of the Holy Trinity, houses the monastery's **Museum of Ancient Russian Art.** It is often closed for no apparent reason or open only to groups, which is yet another reason to visit Sergeyev-Posad on a guided tour. The museum contains a spectacular collection of gifts presented to the monastery over the centuries. On display are precious jewels, jewel-encrusted embroideries, chalices, and censers. Next door to the vestry are two more museums, which are open to individual tourists. The first museum contains icons and icon covers, portrait art, and furniture. The other museum (on the second floor) is devoted to Russian folk art, with wooden items and toys, as well as porcelain and jewelry. There is also a gift shop where you can pick up a souvenir of your visit to ancient Sergeyev-Posad.

The **Toy Museum** is evidence of Sergeyev-Posad's claim to fame as a center for toy-making. The world's first *matryoshka* (the familiar colorful, wooden nesting doll) was designed here at the beginning of the century, and most of the matryoshkas you see for sale in Moscow and St. Petersburg are made in Sergeyev-Posad. The museum is rarely included on organized tours, but it is located within walking distance of the monastery. The museum contains a collection of toys that amused, educated, and illuminated the lives of Russian children for generations. It is well worth an hour of your time, even if your interest is only casual. ✉ *136 Prospekt Krasnoi Armii.* 🎫 *$3.*

Dining and Lodging

$$$ ✕ **Skazka.** Since Soviet times, this has been a decent restaurant and a good place to stop on the road to or from Sergeyev-Posad. ✉ *42nd km, Yaroslavskoye shosse,* ☎ *095/584–3836. No credit cards.*

$$ ✕ **Russky Dvorik.** A nice café that is popular with tourist groups and close to downtown, the Russky Dvorik is situated right across from the Lavra. ✉ *134 ul. Krasnoy Army,* ☎ *254/45–114. AE, MC, V.*

$ ✕ **Zolotoye Koltso.** Considered the best restaurant in town, this place caters to tourist groups and has a good service record serving basic Russian fare. ✉ *121 ul. Krasnoy Army,* ☎ *254/41–517. No credit cards.*

$ 🛏 **Hotel Zagorsk.** Its location is its strongest suit, as it is right downtown, near the Lavra. Despite its decent restaurant and sauna, however, it still has a distinctive Soviet style. ✉ *171 ul. Krasnoy Army,* ☎ *254/25–926. 30 rooms with bath. Restaurant, sauna. No credit cards.*

Pereslavl-Zalessky

❻   *127 km (79 mi) northeast of Moscow via the M8, about half the distance to Rostov. The town cannot be reached by train, only by bus or car.*

Pereslavl-Zalessky was founded in 1157 by Yuri Dolgoruky for two very important reasons. The first was political: He sought to draw parallels between the power base he was building in northeast Rus' and the center of power in Kiev. So he named this town Pereyaslavl (meaning "to achieve glory," the "ya" was later dropped), after a town outside of Kiev, and he named the river alongside the town Trubezh, just as in the Kievan Pereyaslavl. The "Zalessky" appellation (added in the 15th century) means "beyond the forests" and was used to distinguish the town from many other Pereyaslavls (not least the one near Kiev).

The second reason was economic. The location of the town on the southern shore of Lake Pleshcheyevo was ideal for defending the western approaches to vital trade routes along the Nerl River to the Klyazma, Oka, and Volga rivers. The topography of the town only accentuates this role, with the impressive Danilovsky and Goritsky monasteries on the hills, peering down on the low wooden and stone buildings of the town.

The fortresslike **Goritsky Monastery** sits high on a hill south of the town center. It is now an art and history museum. Outside the entrance to the museum is a proud monument to the T-34 tank, which was the tank that saved Russia from the Germans in World War II. Inside is the large Assumption Cathedral (Uspensky Sobor). ✉ 🎫 *$2.* ☉ *Wed.–Mon. 10–5. Closed last Mon. of month.*

In the center of town, along Sovietskaya ulitsa, is the 12th-century limestone **Cathedral of the Transfiguration** (Spaso-Preobrazhensky Sobor). Building of this church began in the same year as the Church of Saints Boris and Gleb in Kideksha (☞ Suzdal, *below*), making it one of the oldest stone buildings standing in Russia.

Pereslavl-Zalessky is the birthplace of Alexander Nevsky and there is a small church in town honoring him. Alexander entered the pantheon of Russia's great heroes when, as Prince of Novgorod, he beat back invading Swedes in 1240, at the Battle of the Neva (thus his last name). For his victory, the Mongol Khan awarded Nevsky the title of Grand Prince of Vladimir.

Pereslavl-Zalessky's other claim to fame is that it is the birthplace of the Russian navy. In the **Botik museum** a few miles out of town is one of only two of the more than 100 boats Peter the Great built for the fleet he used to sail on Lake Pleshcheyevo. To get to the museum (3 km/2 mi away), you take a narrow-gauge train running south and west along the lake from the bus station, which is on ulitsa Kardovskovo, just below the Goritsky monastery. It departs the bus station at 9 AM, 1 and 4:30 PM and returns from the museum at 12:30, 4, and 8:30. The museum also has on display several naval guns, a triumphal arch, and a monument to Peter the Great. ⊠ *Near Veslevo village.* 🖼 *$2.* 🕐 *Tues.–Sun. 10-5.*

Dining and Lodging

$ ✕ **Bar Rita.** A nice restaurant, the Bar Rita is located in the Hotel Pereslavl and has a staff that prides itself on its service—the owner, as it turns out, learned quite a few things on his trips to the United States. ⊠ *27 Rostovskaya ul.,* ☎ *08535/21–633. No credit cards.*

$ 🏨 **Hotel Pereslavl.** A Soviet-style provincial hotel, this is conveniently located downtown. ⊠ *27 Rostovskaya ul.,* ☎ *08535/21–788. 59 rooms with bath. Restaurant, bar. No credit cards.*

Rostov

❼ *225 km (140 mi) northeast of Moscow via the M8 and 58 km (36 mi) southwest of Yaroslavl.*

Rostov, also known as Rostov-Veliky ("the Great"), so as not to confuse it with Rostov-on-the-Don, is one of the oldest towns in Russia. Founded even before Riurik came to rule Russia in the 9th century, it is first mentioned in historical chronicles in 862.

The town is small (population 36,000) and is beautifully situated on the edge of **Lake Nero,** with earthen ramparts and radial streets. At the center is the incomparable **Rostov kremlin** (fortress), with 6-ft-thick white stone walls and 11 circular towers topped with wood-shingled cupolas. The kremlin dates from 1631, but it was built to its present glory in 1670–90 by Rostov Metropolitan Jonah. Its main, practical purpose was as the court and residence for the metropolitan, though Jonah saw himself as creating an ideal type of self-enclosed city focused on the spiritual. As such, it was Russia's first planned city.

The huge, blue-domed **Uspensky Sobor** (Assumption Cathedral) stands just outside the walls of the kremlin—it was built about a century before. Inside are frescoes dating to 1675. But the truly memorable site is the adjacent four-towered **belfry.** The famous 13 bells of Rostov can play four tunes and chime on the half hour and full hour. It is said that the largest of the bells, which weighs 32 tons and is named Sysoi, for Jonah's father, can be heard from 19 km (12 mi) away.

You enter the kremlin through the richly decorated northern entrance, with its **Gate Church of the Resurrection.** Well-groomed pathways and a pleasant, tree-lined pond give the grounds a parklike atmosphere. Just to the right of the entrance into the kremlin is the Church of the Mother of God Hodegetria, with its faceted, baroque exterior and single onion dome.

Another gate church is on the west side of the kremlin, the **Church of John the Theologian.** Adjacent to this church is the two-story **Red Palace,** also once known as the "Chamber for Great Sovereigns." Built first for Ivan IV ("the Terrible"), on his visits to the town, it was later used by Peter the Great and Catherine the Great. It is now the International Youth Tourism Center, a hotel.

Adjacent is the **White Palace**—the metropolitan's residence. This is most notable for its large hall (3,000 square ft), supported by a single column. Connected to the residence is the private church of the metropolitan, the **Church of the Savior on the Stores,** which was actually built over a food-storage shelter. This church has the most beautiful wall paintings in the entire complex, as well as gilded columns and beautiful brass doors. The metropolitan's residence now houses a museum of icons and Rostov enamel (*finift*), a craft the town is famous for throughout Russia. ✉ *$3.* ☉ *Thurs–Tues. 9–5.*

Finally, in addition to other interesting towers and buildings, the southern portion of the kremlin features the tall Church of Grigory the Theologian.

On your way out of the kremlin complex, be sure to explore the **Trading Rows,** across the square from Uspensky Cathedral. In the early part of the 19th century, after Rostov had lost its metropolitanate to nearby Yaroslavl, it became an extremely important trading center. Its annual market was the third largest in Russia.

Southwest along the lakefront you will find **Yakovlevsky (Jacob) Monastery.** Dominating the rather eclectic ensemble is the huge, Romanesque Dmitriyev Church, with its large spherical central dome and four smaller corner domes. The monastery was founded in 1389.

At the other end of Rostov, northeast from the kremlin, but also on the lakefront, is the **Avraamiyev (Abraham) Monastery.** This is the oldest monastery in Russia, founded at the end of the 11th century. Interestingly, it was erected on the site of a former pagan temple to Veles, god of cattle. The five-domed Epiphany Cathedral in the monastery complex dates from 1553 and is the oldest standing building in Rostov.

Dining and Lodging

$ ✗ **Krasnaya Palata.** Located inside the kremlin, this is distinctively Russian dining, with a large, single hall (60 seats) decorated in old Russian style—in effect, a glorified cafeteria, but useful for those visiting the sights of historic Rostov. ✉ *Rostov kremlin. No credit cards.*

$ ✗ **Teremok.** Featuring good Russian cuisine, this is a nice, cozy restaurant, located just in front of the kremlin. ✉ *ul. Belinskovo 1,* ☏ *08536/31–648. No credit cards.*

$ 🏨 **Dom na Pogrebakh.** If you ever wanted to overnight in a kremlin, here is your chance. While a bit Soviet in style and presentation, rooms do have all the basic amenities. ✉ *Rostov kremlin, in the Red Palace,* ☏ *08536/312–59,* ℻ *08536/30–728. 13 rooms. Restaurant. No credit cards.*

Yaroslavl

❽ *282 km (175 mi) northeast of Moscow on the M8.*

Yaroslavl has had a very storied history, beginning with an apocryphal founding. It is said that local inhabitants set loose a bear to chase away Prince Yaroslav the Wise. Yaroslav wrestled and killed the bear. If true, it happened early in the 11th century; Yaroslav decreed the town's founding as a fortress on the Volga in 1010. Six hundred years later, in 1612, the town was the center of national resistance against the invading Poles, under the leadership of Kosma Minin and Dmitri Pozharsky.

The town rests at the confluence of the Volga and Kotorosl rivers, which made it a major commercial center from the 13th century through to 1937, when the Moscow-Volga canal was completed, allowing river traffic to proceed directly to the capital. This commercial heritage bequeathed the city a rich heritage that offers a glimpse of some of the finest church architecture in Russia.

The **Church of Elijah the Prophet,** on Sovietskaya Square, stands at the center of town, some say on the site of Yaroslav's alleged wrestling match with the bear (but which does not explain the monument down by the Volga, commemorating the spot of the town's founding). Its tall, octagonal belfry and faceted green onion domes make the church the focal point for the town. Inside the ornamental church are some of the best-preserved frescoes by Gury Nikitin and Sila Savin (1680), whose work also adorns Moscow Kremlin cathedrals, as well as churches throughout the region. The frescoes retell the Gospels, and the life of Elijah and his disciple Elisha. ⊠ *Sovietskaya Sq.* 🎫 *$4.* ☉ *Apr.–Oct., Thurs.– Tues. 10–1 and 2–6.*

Proceeding away from the river down ulitsa Nakhimsona toward the white, 10-ft-thick walls of the Monastery of the Transfiguration of the Savior, you will come to a statue of **Yaroslav the Wise,** unveiled in 1993. He is holding a piece of the kremlin and staring off in the direction of Moscow. The monastery is the site of northern Russia's first school of higher education (13th century), and houses several magnificent churches. It is also the place that Ivan IV ("the Terrible") took refuge in 1571, when the Mongols were threatening Moscow. The Holy Gates entrance to the monastery, on the side facing the Kotorosl River, is the oldest (1516) structure in the compound. Inside, the six-story belfry rises high above the round-domed **Cathedral of the Transfiguration of the Savior.** Climb to the top of the belfry for a panoramic view of the city. The clock in the belfry hung in the famous Spassky Tower of the Moscow Kremlin, until the merchants of Yaroslavl purchased it in 1624. ⊠ *Bogoyavlenskaya Pl.* 🎫 *Free. Individual museums in the monastery will charge a small fee.* ☉ *Tues.–Sun. 10–5. Closed 1st Wed. of month.*

Directly west of the monastery is the large, red-brick, blue-cupola **Church of the Epiphany.** Featuring beautiful decorative tiles and unusually tall windows, the church is renowned for its fine proportions. Inside are eight levels of wall paintings in the realistic style that began to hold sway in the late 1600s. ⊠ *Bogoyavlenskaya Pl.* 🎫 *$1.* ☉ *Wed– Mon. 10 AM–1 PM and 2–5 PM.*

From the monastery, it is a 1-km (½-mi) walk (or two stops on Bus 4) across the bridge and along the mouth of the Kotorosl to the 100-ft-tall "candle of Yaroslavl," which is actually a belfry for two churches, Ioann Zlatoust (St. John Chrysostum, 1649) and the miniature Church of the Vladimir Virgin. The former is a larger, summer church, ornately decorated with colorful tiles; the latter is the more modest and easy-to-heat winter church. On the same side of the Kotorosl, but west of the bridge by about 1 km (½ mi) is the 15-domed **Church of St. John the Baptist.** Fashioned from carved red brick, it looks as if it were carved from wood.

Back in the town center, proceed northwest along Pervomayskaya ulitsa, a favorite pedestrian area for locals that follows the semicircular path of the town's former earthen ramparts. Peruse the impressive, collonaded **trade rows** and walk on to the Znamenskaya watchtower, which in the middle of the 17th century marked the western edge of the town—another watchtower stands on the Volga embankment. The yellow building directly across the square is the **Volkov Theater.** Both the theater and square are named for Fyodor Volkov, who founded Russia's first professional drama theater here in 1750—the theater was the first to stage Hamlet in Russia. Continue along Pervomayskaya and it will take you to the banks of the Volga, which is 1 km (½ mi) wide at this point. Look for the monument to the great Russian poet Nikolai Nekrasov, who came from nearby Karabikha.

Dining and Lodging

$$ ✕ **Golden Bear Café.** Offering good Russian-style cooking, this is a pleasant café with a nice, modern interior and good service. ⊠ *3 Pervomayskaya ul.,* ☎ *0852/328–532. No credit cards.*

$ ✕ **Kotorosl.** In the hotel of the same name, it offers basic Russian fare with little luster. ⊠ *87 ul. Bolshaya Oktyabrskaya,* ☎ *0852/211–581. No credit cards.*

$ 🏨 **Kotorosl.** This is a decent, tourist class hotel, located not far from the city center and near the railway station. ⊠ *87 ul. Bolshaya Oktyabrskaya, 150000,* ☎ *0852/211–581,* FAX *. 70 rooms. Restaurant, bar, sauna, exercise room, currency exchange, meeting room. No credit cards.*

$ 🏨 **Yubileynaya.** A standard-fare Intourist-type hotel, the Yubileynaya has a convenient location near the monastery, overlooking the Kotorosl River. A nice plus is the hotel's restaurant, which serves European style cuisine. ⊠ *11a Kotoroslnaya nab., 150000,* ☎ *0852/297–435, 30 rooms. Restaurant, bar, currency exchange, meeting room. No credit cards.*

Kostroma

❾ *512 km (318 mi) northeast of Moscow via the M8 and the A113; 112 km (70 mi) east of Yaroslavl.*

Kostroma, a midsized (population 280,000) provincial town, owes its fame and beauty to two historical accidents, separated by 160 years. In 1612, the town unwittingly became the cradle of the Romanov dynasty—Mikhail Romanov and his family were in exile in the city when Mikhail was elected czar. Then, in 1773, a great fire decimated the town, after which a new building plan was implemented that rebuilt the center with radial streets converging on the waterfront.

The main attraction of Kostroma is actually outside the city center, across the Kostroma River (the town sits at the confluence of the Kostroma and Volga rivers)—the **Monastery of St. Ipaty.** Seen from the town side of the river, the beautiful, white-walled monastery perches on the water's edge, crowned with pine-green roofs, surrounded by lush foliage, with the faceted golden-domed towers of **Troitsky Sobor** (Trinity Cathedral) as a backdrop. Founded at the end of the 13th century, the monastery was patronized by Boris Godunov, who first was an able aide to Czar Ivan IV ("the Terrible"), then, from 1598 to 1605, ruled as czar before the Time of Troubles ensued. In 1586, Godunov commissioned the building of the Trinity Cathedral and it still contains the Godunov family burial chambers—but not the crypt of Boris Godunov; his tomb is found in Sergeyev-Posad. The cathedral was tragically destroyed in 1649, when some monks walked into the powder cellar with candles. It was rebuilt within three years and restored to better than new with the addition of frescoes by the Kostroma artist Gury Nikitin. ⊠ *Take Bus 8 from the city center directly to the monastery and museum.* 🎟 *Free.* ☉ *Sat.–Thurs. 9–4:30 (from 10 AM Oct.–May).*

Mikhail Romanov was crowned czar in Trinity Cathedral and there is a portrait of him and many other Russian princes and czars on the columns of the cathedral. As a result of this historical link, every Russian czar except Peter the Great visited the city, and the city enjoyed considerable royal patronage. The red **Romanov Chambers,** opposite the Cathedral, is where the Romanovs lived after Boris Godunov, on assuming control of Russia, exiled them to the town.

Adjacent to the monastery is a **Museum of Wooden Folk Architecture,** the oldest such museum in the country. Several of the buildings, including the **Transfiguration Church** and some bathhouses, are built on stilts, so as to protect them from spring flooding. They were moved here from villages in the surrounding area; many have been restored quite well, particularly the interiors.

Also buried in the monastery's Trinity Cathedral is a peasant named Ivan Susanin. Immortalized in the famous opera by Mikhail Glinka, *Life for the Tsar,* Susanin saved future czar Mikhail Romanov's life in 1613 by agreeing to lead a detachment of Polish enemy troops to Mikhail, then led them instead to a swamp where they and he drowned. There is a monument to Ivan at the very center of town; the central square is also named for him.

Flanking the monument to Ivan Susanin on Susanin square are the arched **Traders Arcades.** At the time of the Romanovs' ascension to the Moscow throne, Kostroma was the third-largest city in Russia and an economic powerhouse—from the 1850s on, the town was a center of the country's flax production. The arcades, excellent examples of Russian Classicism, are the oldest large town trade center to be found in Russia today, dating from the period after the great fire. Here you will find lots of souvenir, art, and antiques shops and an excellent food market. The quaint **Church of the Intercession** stands in the center of the southernmost arcade.

Across the main square, in the triangles separating the radial streets, are some of the fine buildings integral to the Romanov-financed rebuilding of the town at the end of the 18th century. The **fire tower** (leftmost, looking across the square from the arcades) is a UNESCO protected building. Near the central square on these radial streets are some fine brick houses from the early 1800s. Look for the **Nobles' House** at 22 ulitsa Ostrovskovo and Borshchov's House, next door.

Just south of the town center is the **Church of the Resurrection in the Thicket** (Tserkov Voskreseniya na Debre). A superb example of a church built by a local merchant—in this case in 1652 by a successful paint merchant—it is extremely decorative and stands in stark contrast to the simpler churches at St. Ipaty Monastery.

A block north of the main town square, at the corner of Simanovskaya ulitsa and the Pyatnitskaya ulitsa (ulitsa Simanovskaya 26) is the modest **Bogoyavlensko-Anastinsky Monastery** (Epiphany Monastery), which has just recently been reopened after restoration work. The most notable site here is the Icon of the Fyodorovsky Virgin, said to have worked miracles for Alexander Nevsky in his battles against the Swedes. The icon later became the Romanov family icon. The monastery was once a quite formidable fortress, and the huge **Epiphany Cathedral** (1559–65) is now brightly restored.

Dining and Lodging

$ ✕ **Berendeyevka.** A simple, wood-paneled decor and basic Russian-style cuisine are found here at this centrally located restaurant. ⊠ *150B ul. Lenina (in the park),* ☎ *094/550–781. No credit cards. Closed Tues.*

$ ✕ **Restoran Rus.** This is a reasonable dining solution, but don't expect anything fancy—just basic Russian fare. ⊠ *In the Hotel Volga, 1 ul. Yunosheskaya,* ☎ *0942/594–298. No credit cards.*

$ 🏨 **Hotel Volga.** Located on the banks of the Volga, this is a basic amenities/sufficient service type of hotel, not quite up to two-star Intourist standards. There is a casino on the premises. ⊠ *ul. Yunosheskaya 1 156000,* ☎ *0942/546–262, 90 rooms. Restaurant, bar, sauna, casino. No credit cards.*

$ ⊞ **Intourist Motel.** A new hotel and nearly the best option in town—
in fact, it's located 3 km (2 mi) from the center—this has 14 cottage-
style apartments with kitchens and 70 standard double rooms. ⊠ *40
ul. Magistralnaya 156000,* ☎ *0942/533–661,* FAX . *70 double rooms,
14 cottages. 2 restaurants, bar, pool, sauna, currency exchange, meeting room, car rental. No credit cards.*

EAST OF MOSCOW: THE GOLDEN RING

To the east of Moscow lies Vladimir and Suzdal, two towns which include some of Russia's most beautiful medieval kremlins and churches.

Vladimir

⑩ *190 km (118 mi) east of Moscow via the M7.*

While this fairly peaceful city of 350,000 seems unassuming today, half
a millennium ago it was the cultural and religious capital of northeastern
Rus'. Several of the monuments to this time of prosperity and prestige
remain, and a visit to this city, and nearby Suzdal, is vital to under-
standing the roots from which contemporary Russia grew.

Vladimir was founded in 1108 on the banks of the Klyazma by Vladimir
Monomakh, grandson of Yaroslav the Wise and father of Yuri Dolgoruky. But Yuri, as he increased his power en route to taking the throne
in Kiev, preferred Suzdal and made that town his de facto capital in
1152. On Yuri's death five years later, his son, Andrei Bogolyubsky,
moved the capital of Suzdalia to Vladimir and began a massive building campaign. ·

Two important city landmarks from Andrei's time are **Uspensky Sobor**
(Assumption Cathedral) and the **Golden Gates.** The cathedral, a working church, stands in the center of the town, at the corner of Murom-
skaya ulitsa and ulitsa Tretyevo Internationala, its huge, boxy outline
and golden domes rising high above the Klyazma. Rebuilt after a great
fire in 1185, it was again burned in 1237, when the Mongols attacked
the city. The town's residents took refuge in the church, hoping for mercy.
Instead, the invaders burned them alive. The cathedral was again restored and, in 1408, the famous artist Andrei Rublyev repainted the
frescoes of the *Last Judgment,* which alone makes this impressive
monument worth a visit. It was this cathedral that Ivan the Great had
his architects use as the model when rebuilding the Assumption Cathedral in the Moscow Kremlin. It is also worth noting that the cathedral
houses a replica of Russia's most revered icon, **Our Mother of Vladimir**—
the original was moved from here to Moscow in 1390. ⊠ ☞ *$3 for
foreigners.* ☉ *Daily 1:30–4:30.*

Originally, Vladimir had four gates guarding the main approaches to the
town. The Golden Gates, which stand in the middle of Moskovskaya
ulitsa, a few hundred yards west of the Cathedral, guarded the western
approach. The main road from Moscow to Siberia passed through these
gates, which, starting in the 1800s, became a significant monument on
the infamous "Vladimirka"—the road prisoners took east to Siberia.

The main focus of Andrei Bogolyubsky's construction activities were
in **Bogolyubovo,** 10 km (6 mi) east of Vladimir. Here, near the con-
vergence of the Nerl and Klyazma rivers, he built an impressive fort
and living compound. The dominant building in the compound today
is the richly decorated **Uspensky Sobor** (Assumption Cathedral), rebuilt in the 19th century. But remnants of his quarters—a tower and
an archway—still stand as well. It was on the stairs of this tower that

Andrei, despised by many for his authoritarian rule, was stabbed to death by several members of his inner circle. In the 13th century, Bogolyubovo became a monastery. In 1702, Andrei was canonized.

Less than a 2 km (1 mi) from Bogolyubovo is Andrei's greatest creation and, some feel, the most perfect medieval Russian church built— the **Church of the Intercession on the Nerl.** A few hundred yards west of the monastery, walk down ulitsa Frunze and under a railway bridge, then follow the path through a field to the church. Perched on a massive limestone foundation covered with earth, the church sits near the confluence of the Nerl and Klyazma rivers and appears to be rising out of the water that surrounds it. Andrei built the church in memory of his son, Izyslav, who was killed in a victorious battle with the Bulgars. Look for the unique carvings of King David on the exterior, the earliest such iconographic carvings in this region. Inside, the high, narrow arches give an impressive feeling of space and light.

Andrei was succeeded by Vsevolod III, also known as "the Great Nest," because of the great number of his progeny. While he focused much of his energy in the neighboring regions of Ryazan and Murom, he was instrumental in rebuilding the town center in 1185 after the great fire. He also built the remarkable **Cathedral of St. Dmitri.** The cathedral stands adjacent to Vladimir's much larger Uspensky Sobor and is covered in ornate carvings with both secular and religious images. Both Vsevolod and Andrei are buried in Uspensky Sobor.

Dining and Lodging

$ ✕ **Tri Peskarya.** The name means "three minnows." This is a cozy place with good service, nice cuisine and an attractive decor. ⊠ *88 ul. 3-Internationala,* ☏ *09222/93–078. No credit cards.*

$ 🏨 **Klyazma.** A basic, tourist-class hotel located 2 km (1 mi) from the city center, the Klyazma is set in a nice, green area of the city. The hotel is now under new management and struggling to offer the best hotel service in town. ⊠ *15 Sudogorskoye shosse 600000,* ☏ *09222/29– 413,* 🇫🇦🇽 *09222/23–829. 48 double rooms, 29 single rooms. Bar. No credit cards.*

$ 🏨 **Zolotoye Koltso.** Newly built and the best in town, offering all the basic amenities (TV, phone, in room refrigerators) and a pleasant decor. ⊠ *27 ul. Chaikovskovo 600000,* ☏ *9222/48–807, 45 rooms with bath. Restaurant, bar, sauna, casino, nightclub, currency exchange. No credit cards.*

Suzdal

⓫ *Via Vladimir, Suzdal is 190 km (118 mi) east of Moscow on the M7, then 26 km (16 mi) north on the A113.*

Suzdal is the crowning jewel of the Golden Ring. With over 200 historical monuments and some of the most picturesque churches in Russia, this quiet tourist town of 12,000 on the Kamenka River can be visited entirely on foot, but to do it justice, give it two days.

One of the earliest settlements in central Russia, Suzdal has been inhabited since the 9th century and was first mentioned in the Russian Chronicle in 1024. In 1152, Yuri Dolgoruky made Suzdal the capital of his growing fiefdom in northeastern Russia, and built a fortress in nearby Kideksha (the town, just 4 km/2½ mi to the east, is home to the oldest stone church in northeastern Russia—the **Church of Saints Boris and Gleb,** dating to 1152). His son, Andrei Bogolyubsky, preferred nearby Vladimir and focused much of his building efforts there. Still, Suzdal remained a rich town, largely because of donations to the many local monasteries and church building commissions. Indeed, medieval Suzdal had only about 400 families, but some 40 churches.

The **Suzdal kremlin** sits on an earthen rampart, with the Kamenka River flowing around all but the east side (demarcated by ulitsa Lenina). The dominant monument in the kremlin (and indeed the town) is the **Sobor Rozhdestva Bogorodnitsy** (Cathedral of the Nativity of the Virgin), with its deep blue cupolas, festooned with golden stars. It has been subjected to many calamities and reconstructions, yet original limestone carvings can still be found on its corners and on its facade, and its beautiful bronze entry doors are the oldest such doors in Russia, having survived since the 13th century. Inside, the brilliant and colorful frescoes dating from the 1230s and 1630s are without compare.

The long, white, L-shape three-story building which the cathedral towers over is the **Archbishop's Chambers.** Behind its broad windows you will find the beautiful cross-chamber (named for its shape), which is a large hall without any supporting pillars—the first hall of its type in all Russia. In the kremlin, there are also museums of antique books and art. ▧ *$2. ☉ Wed.–Mon. 10–4. Closed last Fri. of month.*

Just below the kremlin and across the river to the south is the **Museum of Wooden Architecture.** It contains interesting wooden buildings moved here from around the region. The buildings can be viewed from the outside any time of year, but from the inside only in summer. Of particular interest here is the ornate **Church of the Transfiguration,** dating from 1756 and moved from the village of Kozlyatievo. To get to the museum, you'll need to go south on ulitsa Lenina, cross the river, and turn right on Pushkarskaya ulitsa. ▧ *$2. ☉ Wed.–Mon. 9:30–4. Closed last Fri. of month.*

Walking north from the kremlin on ulitsa Lenina, you will pass several churches on your left and the pillared trading arcades. Just beyond the arcades are the beautiful **Churches of St. Lazarus and St. Antipy** and their colorful bell tower with a unique, concave tent-roof design. This ensemble is also a good example of Russian church architecture, where a summer church (St. Lazarus, with the shapely onion domes) adjoins a smaller, easier-to-heat and more modest winter church (St. Antipy).

Next on your left, across from the post office, is **Rizopolozhensky monastyr** (Monastery of the Feast of the Deposition of the Robe). The bell tower in this complex is the tallest building in Suzdal (236 ft)—it was built by local residents in 1819 to commemorate Russia's victory over Napoléan. Proceed along ulitsa Lenina until you reach the impressive **Spaso–Yefimiyev monastyr** (St. Yefimy monastery), which dates from 1350. With its tall brick walls and 12 towers, the monastery has often been a cinematic stand-in for the Moscow Kremlin. ▧ *$1.50; museums in the complex charge an additional $1–$3 each. ☉ Tues.–Sun. 10–4. Closed last Thurs. of month.*

The main church in the monastery, the **Church of the Transfiguration of the Savior,** is distinctive for its extremely pointed onion domes and its beautiful frescoes by Gury Nikitin and Sila Slavin, the famous 17th-century Kostroma painters. There is a museum in the monastery devoted to their life and work. Inside the church you will also find a tomb containing the remains of Dmitri Pozharsky, one of the resistance leaders against the Polish invaders in the Time of Troubles (Moscow's Red Square holds a famous monument to Pozharsky and Kosma Minin). Adjoining the church is a single-dome nave church. In actuality, this is the original Church of the Transfiguration, built in 1509, constructed over the grave of St. Yefim, the monastery's founder. Every hour on the hour there is a wonderful chiming of the church's bells.

The **Uspenskaya tserkov** (Church of the Assumption), just next to the larger Church of the Transfiguration, is one of the earliest examples of tent-roof architecture in Russia. In the middle of the 18th century, the monastery became, in part, a place for "deranged criminals," many of whom were political prisoners. The prison and hospital are along the north wall and closed to visitors.

Interestingly, Suzdal's other monastery, **Pokrovsky monastyr** (Convent of the Intercession), was also a place for political incarcerations. The Convent sits across the Kamenka River from St. Efimy, in an oxbow bend of the river. (To get there, you will have to return down ulitsa Lenina, turn east [right] on ulitsa Stromynka and north [right again] on Pokrovskaya ulitsa). Basil III divorced his wife Solomonia in 1525 and banished her here when she failed to produce a male heir. This monastery may have been chosen because, in 1514, Basil had commissioned the beautiful octagonal, three-domed Cathedral of the Intercession here, as supplication for a male heir (interestingly, local legend has it that Solomonia subsequently gave birth to a boy and then staged his death to hide him from Basil). Basil subsequently married Yelena Glinskaya, who did give him an heir: Ivan IV, who would be know as "the Terrible." Ivan, in turn, banished his wife Anna here. And when Peter the Great, after returning from Europe in 1698, finally decided that he wanted to rid himself of his wife Evdokia, he forced her to take the veil and live out her life in this convent. A fine view of the monastery can be had from across the river, from the sparse remains of **Alexander Nevsky monastery.** You can also overnight in cozy *izbas* (wooden cabins) inside the convent; one of the town's best restaurants is also located on the convent grounds. ⌧ *$1.50.* ☉ *Wed.–Mon. 9:30 AM–4 PM. Closed last Fri. of month.*

Dining and Lodging

$ ✕ **Trapeznaya.** Excellent Russian fare, reputedly real "old-style" Russian cuisine, all served in the Intercession Convent itself—obviously this place remains one of the best options around. ⌧ *In the Intercession Convent. No credit cards.*

$ ✕ **Trapeznaya Kremlya.** Not to be confused with the restaurant in the Intercession Convent of the same name, this is an equally nice Russian-style restaurant, located in the Suzdal kremlin. ⌧ *In the Archibishop's Chambers on the 1st floor of the kremlin. No credit cards.*

$$ ▥ **Intercession Convent.** These are cozy accommodations in 19th-century izba-like log cabins—but note the decorous strictures of overnighting in a convent do apply. ⌧ *Inside Pokrovsky monastery. 601260,* ☎ *09231/208–89, 30 rooms. Restaurant. No credit cards.*

$ ▥ **Dom Kuptsa Likhonina.** A cozy B&B option in a centrally located 17th-century house, this was formerly the abode of a rich merchant. Unfortunately, the architecture of the structure does not allow bathrooms in every room. ⌧ *34 ul. Slobodskaya 601260,* ☎ *09231/219–01. 5 rooms. No credit cards.*

$ ▥ **GTK Tourist Complex.** This large complex was recently divided into three separately functioning units. The GTK is a rather basic, Soviet style hotel with middling service. The Motel offers two story rooms with separate street entrances; some even have garages. The Rezolit has big, cozy rooms and charming personal service. ⌧ *7 ul. Korovniki 601260,* ☎ *09231/215–30,* ⅎ𝖠𝖷 *09231/206–66. 430 rooms. Restaurant, pool, sauna, shops, currency exchange. No credit cards.*

MOSCOW SIDE TRIPS AND GOLDEN RING A TO Z

Arriving and Departing

By Boat

It is possible to book a cruise from Moscow to St. Petersburg along the Moscow-Volga canal, but these cruises (which, including airfare from the United States, can cost as little as $1,000) visit just one city of the Golden Ring, Yaroslavl. For cruise companies, see the listing in the Gold Guide.

By Bus

Travel by bus can be a comfortable way to travel as long as it is not the height of summer, when it can be exceedingly stuffy. But it is not as comfortable or secure-feeling as travel by train. Buses run on direct routes to all the towns of the Golden Ring. And, to get to two towns—Pereslavl-Zalessky and Suzdal—by public transport, you will need to travel by bus at least part of the way.

Kostroma: Nine hours from Moscow's Shchyolkovsky station.

Pereslavl-Zalessky: Three hours from Moscow's Shchyolkovsky station. There are four buses daily that run between the capital and this town; there are also many other buses that travel farther on and simply stop here. There are also four buses each day between Pereslavl-Zalessky and Sergeyev-Posad (about a 1-hour ride).

Rostov: Five hours from Moscow's Shchyolkovsky station.

Sergeyev-Posad: 1–1½ hours from Moscow's Shchyolkovsky station.

Suzdal: Just one daily bus goes direct to Suzdal from Moscow, departing Shchyolkovsky station at 5 PM and taking five hours. It is best to take the train or bus to Vladimir and then change to a bus (running nearly every hour) between Vladimir and Suzdal.

Vladimir: Four hours from Moscow's Shchyolkovsky station.

Yaroslavl: Six hours from Moscow's Shchyolkovsky station.

By Car

By far, for the towns of the Golden Ring, which lie in relatively close proximity to one another and are connected by some of Russia's better paved roads, travel by car is the most flexible option. Of course, all the caveats to renting a car (☞ the Gold Guide) apply. But if you rent a car (with or without driver) for the weekend, you will find you are happily independent of public transport. Gas supplies in these towns is not a problem.

By Metro

Three of the locations covered in this section are traveled to mainly by metro.

Arkhangelskoye: Take the metro to Tushinskaya station (purple, or Tagansko-Krasnopresnenskaya line), then take Bus 549 to the estate.

Kuskovo: Take the metro to Ryazansky Prospekt station (purple, or Tagansko-Krasnopresnenskaya line), then Bus 208 or Bus 133 six stops to the park.

Kolomenskoye: Take the metro to Kolomenskaya station (green, or Gorkovsko-Zamoskvoretskaya line). The entrance to the museum is just a 10-minute walk.

By Plane

None of these towns are far enough away from Moscow to warrant the hassle and undependability of air travel. All are efficiently served by train and bus.

By Train

There are two types of trains that will get you to most of these towns, *elektrichkas* (suburban trains) and normal long-distance trains. Elektrichkas have the advantage of running more frequently and are less expensive. But they are also a bit less comfortable and there is no reserved seating. The towns served by trains and the originating Moscow stations are indicated below, with the travel times. Check with a local travel agent (☞ Contacts and Resources, *below*) or at the station itself for train schedules. With the exception of traveling by elektrichka at busy times (Friday evenings and weekends), you should not have trouble getting a ticket the same day as you wish to travel.

Kostroma: Seven hours by long-distance train from Moscow's Yaroslavsky train station.

New Jerusalem Monastery: Take an elektrichka from Rizhsky train station and get off at Istra. From there take any local bus to the "muzey" (museum) stop.

Rostov: Four hours by long-distance train from Yaroslavsky station in Moscow. Five hours by elektrichka (changing in Aleksandrov). Elektrichkas also run regularly between Rostov and Yaroslavl, originating in the Yaroslavsky station—the trip lasts 1-1½ hours.

Sergeyev-Posad: One and one-half hours by elektrichka from Yaroslavsky train station.

Suzdal: You cannot take the train to Suzdal. Simply take the train to Vladimir, then catch one of the frequent buses to Suzdal from there.

Vladimir: It is a three- to four-hour train ride by long-distance train from Moscow's Kursky train station.

Yaroslavl: Five hours by long-distance train from Moscow's Yaroslavsky station.

Getting Around

By Bus

For short-distance travel between towns, buses can't be beat. But, in these difficult economic times for Russia, buses are the most unreliable form of long-distance transport. Be sure to check schedules before leaving to make sure that there are plenty of return buses if you need one.

By Car

As noted above, travel by car is a convenient way to get around these towns, as well as between them.

By Taxi

You will usually have no trouble getting a taxi at a train or bus station in these towns, which is important, because the stations are often far from the town center. Most of the towns are small enough to be navigated easily on foot, but a taxi may be a desirable alternative to short bus trips (e.g., from Vladimir out to Bogolyubovo, from Vladimir to Suzdal).

By Train

There are plenty of trains running on the main routes (Moscow–Yaroslavl and Moscow–Nizhny Novgorod) on which most all these towns lie, so this is a good way to get between towns in this region, as well as to and from Moscow. Most elektrichkas will stop in all these towns; you will want to double-check if long-distance trains stop along the way.

Contacts and Resources

Guided Tours

There are several local and international travel agents who specialize in tours to the Golden Ring or in travel for foreigners. The two below have several years' experience leading foreign tourists in the region.

Mir Corporation (☏ 800/424–7289) is based in Seattle and is a highly experienced travel agent in the countries of the former Soviet Union. It is particularly good at independent travel arrangements and also conducts regular tours to Russia that include the Golden Ring.

Patriarchy Dom offers a variety of one- and multi-day tours throughout the Golden Ring at very reasonable rates. (☏ FAX in Moscow, 095/ 795–0927, email: alanskaya@co.ru).

Visitor Information

Unfortunately, there is no regional tourist office dealing with the Golden Ring region. Any questions should be directed to officials at the travel agencies and guided tour companies listed in Moscow A to Z (☞ Chapter 2).

Changing money has gotten much easier in Russia in recent years. In Moscow and St. Petersburg, you can find exchange offices on nearly any downtown street. But there are far fewer such offices per capita in smaller towns. Here, look for exchange bureaus in the larger hotels or in larger banks downtown. Communication with the capital is fairly good, and you should be able to get rates of exchange essentially equivalent to Moscow rates.

4 St. Petersburg

A powerful combination of East and West, of things Russian and European, St. Petersburg was born of the passion of its founder, Czar Peter the Great, to bring an unwilling Russian nation into the fold of Europe. Today, it remains an Imperial city of golden spires and gilded domes, of pastel palaces and candlelit cathedrals. Pleasures and treasures beckon: Feast on the Hermitage's 35 Matisses, take a Neva river cruise, then saunter through the stately streets—still peopled by the spirits of Dostoyevsky, Fabergé, Diaghilev, and Tchaikovsky.

By Lauri del
Commune

Updated by
Pierre Noel

BORN IN THE HEART OF AN EMPEROR, St. Petersburg is Russia's adopted child. So unlike the Russian cities that came before it, St. Petersburg—with its strict geometric lines and perfectly planned architecture—is almost too European to be Russian. And yet it is too Russian to be European. A powerful combination of both East and West, of things Russian and things European, St. Petersburg is, more than anything, a city born of the passion of its founder, Czar Peter the Great, to bring an unwilling Russia into the fold of Europe and into the mainstream of history. That he did, and more.

"The most abstract and intentional city on earth"—to quote Fyodor Dostoyevsky—became the birthplace of Russian literature, the setting for Dostoyevsky's Raskolnikov and Pushkin's Eugene Onegin. From here, Tchaikovsky, Rachmaninov, Prokofiev, and Rimsky-Korsakov went forth to conquer the world with Russian music. It was in St. Petersburg that Petipa invented—and Pavlova, Nijinsky, and Ulanova perfected—the ballet, that most aristocratic of all dance forms. Later, Diaghilev and his Ballets Russes departed St. Petersburg to sweep the western world at the start of the 20th century. It was here that great architects were summoned by 18th-century empresses to build palaces that transformed the city into a symphony of marble, malachite, and gold. And, a century later—perhaps not surprisingly—it was here that Fabergé craftsmen created splendid objects, fit to adorn the collections of royalty and millionaires.

It was in 1703, just a little less than 300 years ago, that the grand, new capital of the budding Russian empire was built to face Europe, its back to reactionary Moscow. Unlike some cities, it was not created by a process of gradual, graceful development but was forcibly constructed, stone by stone, under the force and direction of Peter the Great, for whose patron saint the city is named. Just as that other great capital, Washington, D.C., rose from a swamp, so did Peter's New Town. It was nearly an impossible achievement—so many men died laying the foundations of the city that it was believed to have been built on bones, not log posts. "The founding of St. Petersburg is the greatest proof of that ardor of the Russian will which does not know anything is impossible," to quote Madame de Staël.

But if Peter's exacting plans called for his capital to be the equal of European ones, they always took into account the city's unique attributes. Peter knew that his city's source of life was water, and whether building palace, fortress, or trading post, he never failed to make his creations serve it. With most of the city nearly at sea level (there is a constant threat of flooding), it seems to rise from the sea itself. Half of the River Neva lies within the city's boundaries. When, outward bound, it reaches the Gulf of Finland, it subdivides into the Great and Little Neva and the Great and Little Nevka. Together with numerous affluents, they combine to form an intricate delta.

Water weaves its way through the city's streets as well. Covering more than 100 islands and crisscrossed by more than 60 rivers and canals, St. Petersburg can be compared to that other great maritime city, Venice, but the Russian one has a uniquely northern appeal. Even during periods of economic hardship and political crisis, its Imperial palaces sparkling on the embankments maintain the city's regal bearing, especially in the cold light of the Russian winter. In the long days of summer, the colorful facades of its riverside estates glow gently, in harmony with the dark blue of the Neva's waters. Between June and

July, when the city falls under the spell of the White Nights, the fleeting twilight imbues the streets and canals with an even more delicate charm.

St. Petersburg is not just about its fairy-tale setting, however, for its history is integrally bound up in Russia's dark side too—a centuries-long procession of wars and revolutions. In the 19th century, the city witnessed the struggle against czarist oppression. Here the early fires of revolution were kindled, first in 1825 by a small band of starry-eyed aristocratic officers, the so-called Decembrists, and then by organized workers' movements in 1905. The full-scale revolutions of 1917 led to the demise of the Romanov dynasty, the foundation of the Soviet Union, and the end of the city's role as the nation's capital. But the worst ordeal by far came during World War II, when the city—then known as Leningrad—withstood a 900-day siege and blockade by Nazi forces. Nearly 650,000 people died of starvation, and more than 17,000 were killed in air raids and by indiscriminate shelling.

St. Petersburg has had its name changed three times during its brief history. With the outbreak of World War I, it became the more Russian-sounding Petrograd. After Lenin's death in 1924, it was renamed Leningrad in the Soviet leader's honor. Following the failed coup d'etat of August 1991, which hastened the demise of the Soviet Union and amounted to another Russian revolution, its original name was restored. A sign of the changing times is that—for the first time—the city's residents were given a choice in the matter. Many people opposed the change, primarily because memories of the siege of Leningrad and World War II had become an indelible part of the city's identity. But for all the controversy surrounding its name, many residents have always referred to the city simply—and affectionately—as Peter.

Pleasures and Pastimes

Dining

Dining out in St. Petersburg is an experience all visitors must have. For years the dining scene was shamefully limited for such a large, cosmopolitan city. Today, you can enjoy a Cordon Bleu meal at the Tea Pavilion of the Yusupov Palace, complete with a gâteau on which the opening notes of Tchaikovsky's No. 1 Piano Concerto are outlined in chocolate. A slew of top-grade, privately owned restaurants and cafés have taken over from their jaded state-run predecessors. Western-style bar food, such as hamburgers and pizza, is available from fast-food joints all over the city. Russian-style restaurants have also been multiplying and those in search of traditional Russian cuisine will easily find better options than in your regular McDonalds. The main meal of the day is served in mid-afternoon and consists of a starter, soup, and a main course. Russian soups are excellent, including *borshch* (beet soup), *shchi* (cabbage soup), and *solyanka,* a spicy, thick stew made with vegetables and meat or fish. Delicious and filling main courses include Siberian *pelmeni* (tender meat dumplings) or *beef stroganov* (beefsteak in mushroom–sour cream sauce). If you are looking for Russian delicacies, try the excellent smoked salmon, blini with caviar, or the famous Kiev cutlet, a butter-filled chicken breast covered with crisp crust. Order a shot of vodka, local beer, or a bottle of Georgian wine to accompany your meal. Daytime reservations are not usually necessary, but you must plan ahead for an evening meal, as restaurants are usually always full. Ask your hotel or tour guide for help and bear in mind that eating out in St. Petersburg is often an all-night affair, with a lot of drinking and dancing.

Farmers' Markets

The city's farmers' markets are a true St. Petersburg experience that should not be missed. Inside these large covered halls you'll find rows of stalls packed with dairy produce, honey, flowers, fine cuts of fresh and cured meats and fish, and fresh fruit and vegetables. Pickled goods are popular in St. Petersburg, and you will most likely be invited to taste the cabbage and salted cucumbers.

Palaces

During the 18th century, St. Petersburg was transformed into an Imperial city of dazzling palaces. Outstanding examples of Russian Baroque are the Winter Palace and the Stroganov Palace, both created by the Italian architect Rastrelli. The Classical style, which supplanted the Baroque as the favored style of the city's greatest architects, is also well represented, with such exceptional mansions as the Mikhailovsky Palace and the Taurida Palace. Two suburban palaces, the Catherine Palace in Pushkin and the Great Palace in Peterhof, were the summer residences of the Imperial family from the days of Peter the Great, but lay in ruins after the 900-day siege of Leningrad. Museum workers had managed to evacuate much of the art housed in the suburban palaces before the German occupation. These magnificent palaces have been restored, so you can now see them in their former splendor. Even more spectacular are the vast palace estates built in the suburbs of St. Petersburg—Pavlovsk, Lomonosov (Oranienbaum), and Gatchina are all reachable by commuter train and almost out-Versailles Versailles for sheer grandeur.

Performing Arts

St. Petersburg's reputation as Russia's cultural capital is well deserved. The city is home to countless museums, art galleries, scientific institutions, libraries, archives, and historic buildings. Its rich musical heritage is on show all over the city, with concerts, recitals, and a multitude of other musical programs given daily; the last two weeks in June are particularly rich, as the city hosts an international festival of culture. The famous St. Petersburg Philharmonic, housed in the magnificent Bolskoy Zal located in the Nobles' Club on Ploshchad Isskustv, has superb acoustics and a history of collaborating with some of Russia's finest composers, including Anton Rubinstein and Tchaikovsky. But it is ballet that the city is most famous for: The Mariinsky Theater (formerly the Kirov) has produced some of the world's greatest dancers, among them Nureyev and Barishnikov. A night at the Mariinsky Theater or the Mussorgsky Theater of Ballet and Opera (formerly the Maly Theater) can be one of the highlights of your stay. Unfortunately, the Mariinsky is too keen on cashing on its reputation and does not hesitate to put on lackadaisical performances for audiences that often completely consist of foreign tourists. Amateurs of ballet should also look out for the Boris Eifman Ballet Theater, St. Petersburg's only professional contemporary ballet troupe.

EXPLORING ST. PETERSBURG

Commissioned by Peter the Great as "a window looking into Europe," St. Petersburg is a planned city whose elegance is reminiscent of Europe's most alluring capitals. Built on more than a hundred islands in the Neva Delta linked by canals and arched bridges, it was first called the "Venice of the North" by Goethe, and its elegant embankments are reminiscent of those of Paris. The city's focal point is the Admiralty; its most-visited attraction, a stone's throw away, is the Winter Palace. Three major avenues radiate outward from the Admiralty: Nevsky Prospect (St. Petersburg's main shopping street), Gorokhovaya ulitsa, and Voznesensky Prospect. Most visitors begin, however, at Palace Square, home to the fabled Hermitage. The square is possibly one of the best starting points for exploring the city, and not just for geographical reasons: In a way it symbolizes the city's past, the transition years, and the present. Here was not only the center of power—the czar's residence and the great offices of state—but also the splendid art collections of the Imperial family. In the twilight of the czar's empire, it was here that troops were ordered to disperse a workers' demonstration on Bloody Sunday in 1905—sealing the fate of the Imperial family and ushering in the 1917 Revolution. Wherever you go exploring in the city, remember that an umbrella often comes in handy. In winter be prepared for rather cold days that often alternate with warmer temperatures bringing heavy snowfalls.

Great Itineraries

IF YOU HAVE 3 DAYS

If you have only three days, begin your visit of the city on **Vasilievsky Island** and the left bank. You will find most of the historical sights on the eastern edge of the island: the **Rostral Columns,** the old **Stock Exchange,** and the **Kunstkammer.** On the left bank of the Neva is **Decembrists' Square,** site of the Bronze Horseman, the **Admiralty,** and **St. Isaac's Cathedral.** After lunch is the right time to tackle the gargantuan **Hermitage,** one of the world's richest repositories of art. Spend the rest of the afternoon wandering through its vast galleries; you will leave feeling that your visit was incomplete, but remember that it would take at least a month to visit the museum properly. Devote the morning of your second day to visiting the **Peter and Paul Fortress** and the Petrograd Side. The main attraction of the Fortress is the Cathedral of Sts. Peter and Paul, which served as the Imperial burial grounds. Near the Fortress you'll find **Peter the Great's Cottage.** Not far away the cruiser **Avrora** lies at anchor. Spend the afternoon in the **Russian Museum,** one of the country's most important art galleries with more than 300,000 works of art. On your third day, we recommend that you make an excursion to **Pushkin** (formerly Tsarskoye Selo), 24 km (15 mi) south of St. Petersburg. Tsarskoye Selo was the summer residence of the Imperial family and a popular summer resort for the Russian aristocracy. The main attraction here is the **Catherine Palace,** with its magnificent treasures and the surrounding park filled with waterfalls, boating ponds, and marble statues. Should you choose to spend the whole day here, you can have lunch and then visit the **Lyceum,** formerly a school for the Russian nobility. The most famous graduate of this school, which is now a museum, was Alexander Pushkin, Russia's greatest poet.

IF YOU HAVE 7 DAYS

Follow the three-day itinerary described above. Devote your fourth day to St. Petersburg's inner streets, squares, and gardens. Start at the Square of the Arts. Here you can visit the **Ethnography Museum** and its unique collection of applied art, national costumes, and weapons of the various ethnic groups of the former Soviet Union. When you leave the museum, walk to the colorful **Khram Spasa na Krovi** (Church of the Savior of the Spilled Blood), now open after decades of renovation. Your next stop is the **Marsovo Pole** (Field of Mars), used primarily for military exercises. After the February and October revolutions of 1917, it was turned into a burial ground for 180 people who had perished in the armed struggle against the aristocracy. Finish your walk at the **Letny Sad** (Summer Garden) with its famous railing designed by Yuri Felten in 1779. After lunch, visit the **Kazan Cathedral.** Czar Paul I commissioned this copy of St. Peter's in Rome after a visit to the Eternal City. On the fifth day, you should visit **Peterhof** (Petrodvorets), accessible by hydrofoil. The best time to visit is in summer, when the fountains adorned by 144 gilt statues, monumental cascades, lush parks, and the magnificent Great Palace are at their best. Devote the morning of your sixth day to a visit of the **Pushkin Apartment Museum,** where the beloved poet died. After lunch, visit the **Menshikov Palace,** the first stone building in St. Petersburg. Devote your seventh day to an excursion to **Pavlovsk,** only 5 km (3 mi) from the Catherine Palace in Pushkin and 32 km (20 mi) south of St. Petersburg. See the **Great Palace** with its splendid interiors featuring gilt ceilings and marble pillars. Enjoy the famous park with its numerous pavilions, waterways, and statues. After lunch, visit the **Zoology Museum,** one of the largest of its kind in the world.

IF YOU HAVE 10 DAYS

Follow the itineraries described above, and on your eighth day, travel 40 km (26 mi) west of St. Petersburg to reach the town of **Lomonosov.** This luxurious summer residence is the only one to have survived World War II intact. With its seaside location and splendid park it is an ideal place to spend a summer's day. On your ninth day, you may want to visit the **Yusupovsky Palace**—formerly the home of Russia's wealthiest family and now a museum with a concert hall and a theater—on the banks of the Moika River. It was in this beautiful prerevolutionary mansion that the "mad monk," Rasputin, was killed. Devote your last day in St. Petersburg to the **Piskaryevskoye Cemetery,** a mass burial ground for more than half a million victims of the 900-day siege of Leningrad during World War II. Visit the museum and its collection of memoirs and photographs documenting that terrible time. It is perhaps fitting that you should finish your visit to this extraordinary city here, a place where memories of the past have become an indelible part of the city's identity.

Imperial Splendor: Palace Square, the Winter Palace, and the Hermitage Museum

The place where you must begin to get to know St. Petersburg is the elegant Dvortsovaya Ploshchad or Palace Square. In its scale alone, it can hardly fail to impress. But there can be no better reason for coming to St. Petersburg than to visit the Hermitage. Renowned as one of the world's leading picture galleries, it is also a treasure house of ancient cultures. In addition, the Hermitage is an extension of the Winter Palace, the former residence of the Russian Imperial family, and provides a setting of unparalleled opulence for its various dazzling collections.

Numbers in the text correspond to numbers in the margin and on the St. Petersburg map.

A Good Walk

Begin at **Dvortsovaya Ploshchad** (Palace Square) ①. Extending the length of the western side of the square, with its back to the river, is the **Zimny Dvorets** (Winter Palace) which, along with the **Ermitazh** ② art gallery, constitute the legendary Hermitage museum. In the center of the square is the **Alexander Column,** which commemorates the Russian victory over Napoléon in 1812. Dominating the eastern side is the **Glavny Shtab,** formerly the army's general staff headquarters. No matter what your plans are while in St. Petersburg, make sure you set aside at least half a day for a visit to the Hermitage.

TIMING

With more than 400 exhibit halls, the Hermitage cannot possibly be seen in a single day. It has been estimated that in order to spend one minute on each object on display, a visitor would have to devote an entire year to the museum. Official guided tours tend to be rushed, and you will probably want to return on your own. If you have limited time, concentrate on the Antiquities and Italian Art rooms, which will take at least a couple of hours to view properly. Devote another couple of hours to the extraordinary collection of Impressionist and Postimpressionist art on the third floor. It is best to begin your tour around 11:30 AM, when the early-morning crowds have dispersed. During peak tourist season, or when there is a special exhibition, you may encounter long lines at the museum entrance. Don't forget your umbrella, no matter what the time of year or what the weather forecast. It rains at some point almost every day in St. Petersburg, and you don't need to get off to a wet start. Note that the Hermitage is closed on Mondays.

Sights to See

Aleksandrovskaya Kolonna (Alexander Column). The centerpiece of Palace Square is a memorial to Russia's victory over Napoléon. Measuring 155.8 ft from the pedestal to the top, the Alexander Column was commissioned in 1830 by Nicholas I in memory of his brother, Czar Alexander I, and was designed by August Ricard de Montferrand. The column was cut from a single piece of granite and, together with its pedestal, weighs more than 650 tons. It stands in place by the sheer force of its own weight; there are no attachments fixing it to the pedestal. When it was erected in 1832, the entire operation took only an hour and 45 minutes, but 2,000 soldiers and 400 workmen were required, using an elaborate system of pulleys and ropes. It is crowned by an angel (symbolizing peace in Europe) crushing a snake, an allegorical depiction of Russia's defeat of Napoléon.

★ ☞ ❶ **Dvortsovaya Ploshchad** (Palace Square). One of the world's most magnificent plazas, the square is a stunning ensemble of buildings and open space that manages to combine several seemingly incongruous architectural styles in perfect harmony. It is where the city's Imperial past has been preserved in all its glorious splendor, but it is also resonant with the revolutionary history that followed. Here, the fate of the last Russian czar was effectively sealed, on Bloody Sunday in 1905, when palace troops opened fire on peaceful demonstrators, killing scores of women and children. It was across Palace Square that the Bolshevik revolutionaries stormed the Winter Palace in their successful attempt to overthrow Kerensky's provisional government in October 1917, an event that led to the birth of the Soviet Union. Almost 75 years later, it was also on Palace Square that during tense days, a huge crowd rallied in support of perestroika and democracy. Beautiful Palace Square is today a bustling hubbub of tourist and marketing activity, lively yet seemingly imperturbable as ever. Children will enjoy the horseback and carriage rides for hire.

★ ❷ **Ermitazh** (Hermitage Museum). Leonardo's *Benois Madonna* . . . Rembrandt's *Danaë* . . . Matisse's *The Dance* . . . you get the picture. As the former private art collection of the czars, this is one of the world's most famous museums, virtually wallpapered with celebrated paintings. In addition, the walls are works of art themselves, for this collection is housed in the lavish Winter Palace, one of the most outstanding examples of Russian Baroque magnificence. The museum gets its name from Catherine the Great, who used it for her private apartments, meaning them to be a place of retreat and seclusion; "Only the mice and I can admire all this," the empress once declared. Between 1764 and 1775, the empress undertook, in competition with rulers whose storehouses of art greatly surpassed Russia's, to acquire some of the world's finest works of art. In doing so, sometimes acquiring entire private collections outright, she quickly filled her gallery with masterpieces from all over the world. This

150

Dvorets = palace
Ploshchad = square
Sobor = cathedral

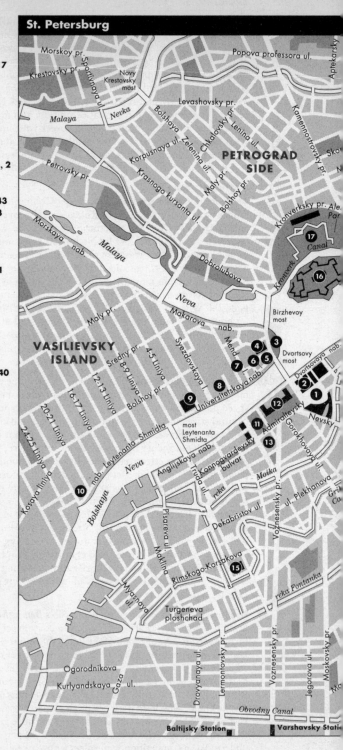

St. Petersburg

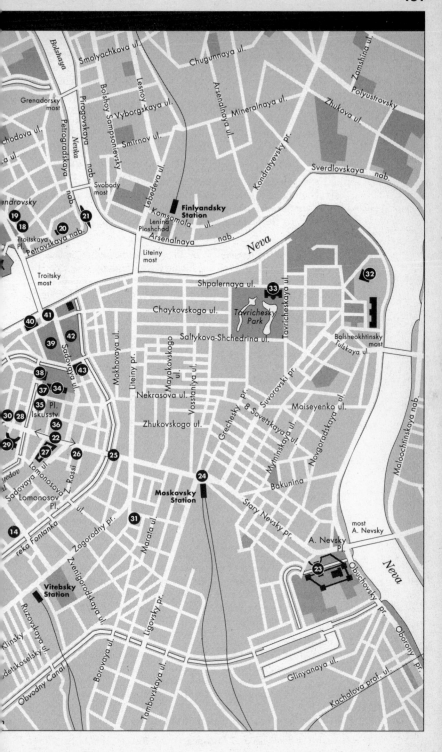

section of the Hermitage Museum, completed in 1770 by Vallin de la Mothe, is now known as the Maly (Little) Hermitage. It is attached to the Stary (Old) Hermitage, which was built in 1783 by Yuri Felten to house the overflow of art, and also contained conference chambers for the czar's ministers. Attached to the Hermitage by an arch straddling the Winter Canal is the **Hermitage Theater** (1783–87), created for Catherine the Great by the Italian architect Giacomo Quarenghi. Yet another addition, the New Hermitage, was added between 1839 and 1852 under Catherine's grandson, Nicholas I; it became Russia's first public museum, although admission was by royal invitation only until 1866. Its facade is particularly striking, with ten male figures cut from monolithic gray granite supporting the portico.

Today's Hermitage Museum is one of the world's richest repositories of art, continuously enlarged with czarist treasures and acquisitions, all later confiscated and nationalized, along with numerous private collections, by the Soviet government after the 1917 Bolshevik Revolution.

The entrance to the museum is on the side of the Winter Palace that faces the Neva River, not the one facing Palace Square. When you first enter the Hermitage, the *kassa* (ticket window) is ahead of you, slightly to the left. Once you have your tickets, you can check your belongings and then return to enter the hall that was to your left as you came in. Be forewarned that the ticket-takers are strict about oversize bags and about foreigners trying to enter on Russian-rate tickets.

Through this hall you reach the second-floor galleries by way of the **Jordan Staircase,** a dazzling creation of marble, granite, and gold. The staircase was once used by the Imperial family in processions down to the Neva River for christenings. The masterwork of Count Bartolomeo Rastrelli—Empress Elizabeth I's favorite architect—the Jordan Staircase shows how theatrical Russian taste could be. In fact, art historians now point to the famous 17th-century scenographic engravings of the Bibiena brothers as one of Rastrelli's main sources of inspiration.

Although the museum is divided into eight sections, they are not clearly marked, and the floor plans available are not terribly useful, though they are in English as well as Russian. All of this makes it easy to get lost in the mazelike complex of the Hermitage, but do not despair. Enjoy your wander, and don't be shy about asking the special assistants placed throughout the museum to point you in the right direction.

There are three floors in the museum. In brief, the **ground floor** covers prehistoric times, showing discoveries made on former Soviet territory, including Scythian relics and artifacts; art from the Asian republics, the Caucasus, and their peoples; and Greek, Roman, and Egyptian art and antiquities.

On the **second floor** you will find many rooms that were part of the former Winter Palace. One of the first you pass through is the **Malachite Room,** with its displays of personal items from the Imperial family. In the White Dining Room the Bolsheviks seized power from the Provisional Government in 1917. Balls were held in the small Concert Hall (which now also holds the silver coffin of the hero Alexander Nevsky) and, on grand occasions, in the Great Hall.

A wealth of Russian and European art is also on this floor: Florentine, Venetian, and other Italian art through the 18th century, including Leonardo's *Benois Madonna* and *Madonna Litta* (Room 214); Michelangelo's *Crouching Boy* (Room 229); two Raphaels; eight

Titians; and works by Tintoretto, Lippi, Caravaggio, and Canaletto. The Hermitage also boasts a superb collection of Spanish art, of which works by El Greco, Velázquez, Murillo, and Goya are on display. Its spectacular presentation of Flemish and Dutch art includes roomfuls of Van Dycks, including portraits done in England when he was court painter to Charles I; the Hermitage has more than 40 canvases by Rubens (Room 247) and an equally impressive number of Rembrandts, including *Flora, Abraham's Sacrifice* and *The Prodigal Son* (Room 254). The famous *Danae,* which was multilated by a knife- and acid-wielding lunatic in 1985, is back on exhibition once again. There is a smattering of excellent British painting, extending also to the next floor, with works by Joshua Reynolds, Thomas Gainsborough, and George Morland.

Reflecting the Francophilia of the Empresses Elizabeth and Catherine, the museum is second only to the Louvre in its collection of French art. The scope is so extraordinary it has to be housed on both the second and third floors. Along with masterpieces by Lorrain, Watteau, and Poussin—including his *Tancrède et Herminie* (Room 279)—you will also find early French art and handicrafts, including some celebrated tapestries.

On the **third floor,** you can start with the art of the 19th century, where you will find Delacroix, Ingres, Corot, and Courbet. You then come to a stunning array of Impressionists and Postimpressionists, originally gathered mainly by two prerevolutionary industrialists and art collectors, Sergei Shchukin and Ivan Morozov. They include Monet's deeply affecting *A Lady in the Garden,* Sisley, Pissarro, Renoir, and Degas' *Woman at Her Toilette* and *After the Bath.* Sculptures by Auguste Rodin and a host of pictures by Cézanne, Gauguin, and Van Gogh are followed by Picasso and a lovely room of Matisse, including one of the amazing *Joys.* Somewhat later paintings—by the Fauvist André Derain and by Cubist Fernand Léger, for example—are also here. Rounding out this floor, if your senses can absorb any more, is the museum's collection of Oriental and Middle and Near Eastern art; its (small) American collection; and two halls of medals and coins.

Possibly the most prized section of the Hermitage—and definitely the most difficult to get into—is the **Treasure Gallery,** also referred to as the *Zolotaya Kladovaya* (Golden Room). This spectacular collection of gold, silver, and royal jewels is well worth the hassle and expense of admission. Special tickets, which include entry to the "regular" Hermitage Museum, are sold in limited quantities. Go early to be sure you get one. The collection is divided into two sections. The first section, covering prehistoric times, includes Scythian gold and silver treasures of striking simplicity and refinement recovered from the Crimea, Ukraine, and Caucasus. The second is a dizzying display of precious stones, jewelry, and such extravagances as jewel-encrusted pillboxes and miniature clocks, from the 16th through the 20th centuries. You can also purchase tickets for the Winter Palace of Peter the Great, accessible through a tunnel (the site historians believe is where Peter died). They do not include the Hermitage and they also sell out early. ⊠ *36 Dvortsovaya nab.,* ☎ *812/311–3420.* ⊠ *60 rubles; 84 rubles for the Treasure Gallery.* ☉ *Tues.–Sun. 10:30–6 (kassa open until 5). Exchange office and theater ticket office on the premises.*

NEED A BREAK?

The **Literary Café** (⊠ 18 Nevsky Prospect, ☎ 812/312–6057) is a short walk from the Hermitage Museum. The menu offers classic Russian fare, with, alas, service to match, but the café stands out for its pleasant atmosphere and 19th-century decor; live chamber music adds to the Old

World atmosphere. In 1837 the beloved Russian poet Alexander Pushkin was served his last meal here before setting off for his fatal duel. To reach the café, walk across Palace Square, through the arch of the General Staff Building, and then take a left onto Nevsky Prospect. It is open daily from noon to midnight.

Glavny Shtab (General Staff Building). The eastern side of Palace Square is formed by the huge arc of this building whose form and size give Palace Square its unusual shape. During czarist rule the army headquarters and the ministries of foreign affairs and finance were situated here. Created by the architect Carlo Giovanni Rossi in the Neoclassical style and built between 1819 and 1829, the General Staff Building is actually two structures connected by a monumental archway. Together they form the longest building in Europe. The arch itself is another commemoration of Russia's victory over Napoléon. Atop it is an impressive 33-ft-tall bronze of Victory driving a six-horse chariot, created by the artists Vasily Demut-Malinovsky and Stepan Pimenov. The passageway created by the arch leads from Palace Square to St. Petersburg's most important boulevard, Nevsky Prospect.

Shtab Gvardeiskovo Korpusa (Headquarters of the Guard Corps). Just to the left, this structure serves as an architectural buffer between the Neoclassical General Staff Building and the Baroque Winter Palace. Designed by the architect Alexander Bryullov and built between 1837 and 1843, this modest building is noteworthy for the very fact that it easily goes unnoticed. Instead of drawing attention to itself, it leads the eye to the other architectural masterpieces bordering Palace Square. The restraint show in Bryullov's creation was considered the ultimate architectural tribute to the masters who came before him.

★ **Zimny Dvorets** (Winter Palace). This magnificent palace, the residence of Russia's rulers from Catherine the Great (1762) to Nicholas II (1917), is the focal point of Palace Square. It is built in the ornate style of Russian Baroque, adorned with rows of columns and outfitted with 2,000 heavily decorated windows. The roof balustrade is topped with statues and vases. Created by the Italian architect Bartolomeo Francesco Rastrelli, the Winter Palace stretches from Palace Square to the Neva River embankment. It was the fourth royal residence on this site, the first having been a wooden palace for Peter the Great (today, a remnant of this palace exists and has been restored; it can be visited as an independent excursion). Oddly enough, the all-powerful czar had to observe some bureaucratic fine print himself. Since it was forbidden to grant land from this site to anyone not bearing naval rank, Peter had to obtain a shipbuilder's license before building his palace. The present palace was commissioned in 1754 by Peter's daughter Elizabeth. By the time it was completed, in 1762, Elizabeth had died and the craze for the Russian Baroque style had waned. Catherine the Great (ruled 1762–96) left the exterior unaltered but had the interiors redesigned in the Neoclassical style of her day. In 1837, after the palace was gutted by fire, these were revamped once again. The Winter Palace contains more than 1,000 rooms and halls, three of the most celebrated of which are the **Gallery of the 1812 War,** where portraits of Russian commanders who served against Napoléon are on display; the **Great Throne Room,** richly decorated in marble and bronze; and the **Malachite Hall,** designed by the architect Alexander Bryullov and decorated with columns and pilasters of malachite. Today the only parts of the Winter Palace on view to the public are those that form a part of the Hermitage Museum. When touring the museum, you must therefore think of portions of it as the Imperial residence it once was.

Around the Admiralty: Vasilievsky Island and the Left Bank

Vasilievsky Ostrov, the largest island in the Neva Delta, is one of the city's oldest developed sections and is where Peter the Great wanted his city's center. His original plans for the island called for a network of canals for the transport of goods from the main sea terminal to the city's commercial center at the opposite end of the island. These plans to re-create Venice never materialized, although some of the smaller canals were actually dug (and later filled in). These would-be canals are now streets, and are called "lines" (*liniya*). Instead of names, they bear numbers, and they run parallel to the island's three main thoroughfares: the Great, Middle, and Small avenues (or prospects, to use the Russian lingo). Now the island is a popular residential area, with most of its historical sites concentrated on its eastern edge. The island's western tip, facing the Gulf of Finland, houses the city's main sea terminals. Also on the island are the city's most renowned academic institutions, including the St. Petersburg branch of the Academy of Sciences, St. Petersburg University, the Repin Art Institute (formerly St. Petersburg Academy of Arts), and the city's oldest institution of higher learning, the St. Petersburg Institute of Mining Technology.

A Good Walk

Begin your tour of Vasilievsky Island at its easternmost tip, which is known colloquially as the **Strelka** ③. It is most easily reached by crossing the Dvortsovy most (Palace Bridge), the one in front of the Hermitage, or by taking Trolley 1 or 7 from any stop on Nevsky Prospect. As you stand in Birzhevaya Square, as the park on the Strelka is called, you will be between two thick, brick-red columns, known as the **Rostralnyie Kolonny.** The columns frame the most significant architectural sight on this side of the river, the **Stock Exchange** ④. Flanking the Stock Exchange are the almost identical Dokuchayev Soil Museum and, to the south, the **Zoologichesky Musey** ⑤.

Continue along the Universitetskaya naberezhnaya (University Embankment), which leads away from the Strelka (the Neva will be to your left). The next building you encounter is the **Kunstkammer** ⑥. Continue along the embankment, crossing Mendeleyevskaya liniya and passing an imposing statue of the 18th-century Russian scientist Mikhail Lomonosov. You soon come to the main campus of **St. Petersburg University** ⑦. Farther up the embankment, after passing on the left a monument that marks the location of the first (floating) bridge of the city, stands one of St. Petersburg's grandest—and oldest—buildings, the **Menshikovsky Dvorets** (Menshikov Palace) ⑧. As you leave Menshikov Palace, crossing Syezdovskaya liniya, you come upon **Rumyantsev Square** to your right. Another notable building farther up the embankment is the **Repin Institute of Painting, Sculpture, and Architecture** ⑨. On the landing in front of the Institute are the Egyptian Sphinxes, among the city's most memorable landmarks. For the sake of completeness, let us mention the **Gorny Institut** ⑩, situated at the end of the embankment, at the corner of 21 liniya. It can be reached either by walking (some distance!) or by taking any of the trams that stop at the corner of 11 liniya and the embankment.

At this point you conclude your tour of Vasilievsky Island by crossing the bridge called **most Leytenanta Shmidta,** which will take you back across the Neva and toward the city center. Once across, you may tour the **Anglijskaya naberezhnaya,** the left bank of the Neva. Continue down the embankment with the Neva on your left. You pass the former **Senate and Synod.** Across the street from it, if you continue going straight, is **Dekabristov Ploshchad** ⑪, a large open square on your right. The golden yellow building on the other side is the **Admiralty** ⑫.

Proceed through the park in front of the Admiralty and you will come out on Admiralteysky Prospect, the eponymous avenue running parallel to it. Ahead of you is the back of massive **Isaakievsky Sobor** (St. Isaac's Cathedral) ⑬. Its entrance is on the other side, so go right on the prospect a bit to take a left and go around the cathedral's side. Where the prospect meets Konnogvardysky bulvar is the gracefully designed Manège. On the opposite side of the square, directly across from, is the **Mariinsky Dvorets** (Maria's Palace). To the left, past the Nicholas Statue and in front of the palace, is the short **Siniy most** (Blue Bridge). Passing over the Moika via the Blue Bridge, you will spot a stone column. Its marks show the different water levels of the many floods that have plagued the city over the years. November 19, 1824, when water went up 13 ft and killed at least 200 people, is still a sad and memorable day in the history of St. Petersburg. Turn to the right and continue down the Moika embankment. The elegant yellow building is the **Yusupovsky Dvorets** (Yusupovsky Palace) ⑭. You can end your tour here, perhaps choosing to return to the Astoria for coffee or a snack. If you prefer to end up on Nevsky Prospect, follow the Moika embankment a few blocks down to where they intersect. Going this way, shortly before you reach Nevsky, on the right-hand side behind a tall fence, is the **Pedagogical Institute.** If you have time, continue along the Moika away from Nevsky and turn left at the next bridge. What you will see in front of you is **St. Nicholas Cathedral** ⑮, also well worth a visit. From there, you will probably want to go back downtown using public transportation. In that case, walk the last 100 yards to Sadovaia ulitsa, where any tram except the 11 will take you back to Nevsky.

TIMING

This is a long walk, divided into two sections, though there is (literally) a bridge between them. If you have the time and want to linger in each place, you may choose to do them as two excursions. If not, do plan a lunch break midway.

Sights to See

⑫ **Admiralty.** The Admiralty is considered the city's architectural center, and its flashing spire—visible at various points throughout the city— is one of St. Petersburg's most renowned emblems. To get the picture-perfect first impression, walk around to the front of this lovely golden-yellow building by crossing the square diagonally.

A series of important constructions, all related to the naval industry, predate the present building. The first was a shipyard of Peter's, followed by an earthen fortress that guarded the port; after these came the first Admiralty, made of stone and topped by the famous spire that has endured to grace each successive structure.

The current building was designed by Andrei Zakharov and was built between 1806 and 1823, after it was decided that the city required a much grander Admiralty to match its more impressive buildings. It is adorned with Classical sculptures glorifying Russia's naval prowess, including a frieze of Neptune handing his trident to Peter. Used as a shipbuilding center through the 1840s, it has belonged to the Higher Naval Academy since 1925 and is not open to the public.

An Admiralty Lawn once adorned its front expanse, but in Alexander's time it was turned into a small park bearing his name (to which it has been returned, after having been named for Maxim Gorky under the Communists). As you walk through it, you'll see various statues, mostly of artists such as the composer Mikhail Glinka and the writer

Mikhail Lermontov; the one accompanied by the delightful camel is of Nikolai Przhevalsky, a 19th-century explorer of Central Asia.

Anglijskaya naberezhnaya (English Embankment). Before the 1917 Revolution this was the center of the city's English community. Here one can find some of St. Petersburg's finest aristocratic estates—cum—overcrowded communal apartments. For instance, as you take a left off the bridge and follow the embankment, you come to No. 28, formerly the mansion of Grand Duke Andrei Vladimirovich Romanov. Today it is a so-called Wedding Palace, the only place under Communism where marriages could be performed; the state-run, secular ceremonies, still the usual type held here, are perfunctorily recited with assembly-line efficiency. A lot of these mansions are being renovated and destined to become once again luxury real estate, whether office space or housing.

⓫ **Dekabristov Ploshchad** (Decembrists' Square). First called Senatskaya Ploshchad (Senate Square), the square was renamed earlier this century. Officially it has returned to its original name, but it is hardly ever used. It holds one of St. Petersburg's best-known landmarks, the gigantic equestrian statue of Peter the Great. The square took its new name from the dramatic events that unfolded there on December 14, 1825, when, following the death of Czar Alexander I, a group of aristocrats staged a rebellion on the square in an attempt to prevent the crowning of Nicholas I as the new czar, and perhaps do away with the monarchy altogether. Their coup failed miserably, as it was bloodily suppressed by troops already loyal to Nicholas, and those rebels who were not executed were banished to Siberia. Although the Decembrists, as they came to be known, did not bring significant change to Russia in their time, their attempts at liberal reform were often cited by the Soviet regime as proof of deep-rooted revolutionary fervor in Russian society. In 1925 the square was renamed in their honor.

In the center is the grand statue called the **Medny Vsadnik** (Bronze Horseman), erected as a memorial from Catherine the Great to her predecessor, Peter the Great. (The simple inscription on the base reads, "To Peter the First from Catherine the Second, 1782.") Created by the French sculptor Etienne Falconet and his student Marie Collot, the statue depicts the powerful Peter, crowned with a laurel wreath, astride a rearing horse that symbolizes Russia, trampling a serpent representing the forces of evil. The enormous granite rock on which the statue is balanced comes from the Gulf of Finland. Reportedly, Peter liked to stand on it to survey his city from afar. Moving it was a herculean effort, requiring a special barge and machines and nearly a year's work. The statue was immortalized in a poem of the same name by Alexander Pushkin, who wrote that the czar "by whose fateful will the city was founded beside the sea, stands here aloft at the very brink of a precipice, having reared up Russia with his iron curb."

⓾ **Gorny Institut** (Mining Institute). Founded in 1773 by Catherine the Great, this is St. Petersburg's oldest technical institution of higher learning and well worth the visit if you have time. The present building, in the Neoclassical style, was built between 1806 and 1811 by Andrei Voronikhin, architect of the Kazan Cathedral on Nevsky Prospect. The main entrance is supported by 12 Doric columns and is lined with statues designed by Demut-Malinovsky and Pimenov (creators of the bronze sculpture above the General Staff Building). The institute boasts an unusual museum of precious stones and minerals, including a piece of malachite weighing over a ton and an iron meteorite. ⊠ *21 liniya*, ☎ *812/218–8429.* ⊙ *Not open to individual visitors.*

★ ⓭ **Isaakievsky Sobor** (St. Isaac's Cathedral). Of the grandest proportions, St. Isaac's is the world's third-largest domed cathedral and the first monument the traveler sees of the city when arriving by ship. Its architectural distinction is a matter of taste; some consider the massive design and highly ornate interior to be excessive, while others revel in its opulence. Commissioned in 1818 by Alexander I to celebrate his victory over Napoléon, it took more than 40 years to build. The French architect Auguste Ricard de Montferrand devoted his life to the project, and died the year the cathedral was finally consecrated, in 1858. Enter St. Isaac's through the front portal and buy your tickets inside (Russians purchase lower-rate tickets at the kassa outside). Follow the signs in English. Tickets are sold both to the church ("the museum") and/or to its outer colonnade; the latter affords a walk on the upper balustrade, where you will get an excellent view of the city.

The interior is lavishly decorated with malachite, lazulite, marble, and other precious stones and minerals. Gilding the dome required 220 pounds of gold. The church can hold up to 14,000 people. After the 1917 Revolution it was closed to worshipers and in 1931 was opened as a museum. Since 1990, as in many other churches in the city, services have been resumed. The Foucault pendulum that hung there to demonstrate the axial rotation of the earth was taken away in 1991. St. Isaac's was not altogether returned to the Orthodox Church, but Christmas and Easter are celebrated here (note that orthodox holidays follow the Julian calendar and fall about 13 days after their Western equivalents). When the city was blockaded during World War II, the gilded dome was painted black to avoid its being targeted by enemy fire. Despite efforts to protect it, the cathedral nevertheless suffered heavy damage, as bullet holes on the columns on the south side attest.

Opening up in front of the eponymous cathedral, **Isaakievsky Ploshchad** (St. Isaac's Square) is the city's most recent square, having been completed only after the cathedral was built. In its center stands a **statue of Czar Nicholas I** (1825–55). Unveiled in 1859, the Nicholas Statue was commissioned by the czar's wife and three children, whose faces are engraved (in the allegorical forms of Wisdom, Faith, Power, and Justice) on its base. It was designed, like St. Isaac's Cathedral, by Montferrand. The statue depicts Nicholas I mounted on a rearing horse. Other engravings on the base describe such events of the czar's reign as the suppression of the Decembrists' uprising and the opening ceremonies of the St. Petersburg–Moscow railway line.

To one side of the cathedral, where the prospect meets Konnogvardysky bulvar, is the gracefully designed **Manège.** Another Quarenghi creation, this former barracks of the Imperial horse guards is used as an art exhibition hall. Every January, it houses an exhibition of new works by St. Petersburg artists. ✉ *1 Isaakievskaya Pl.,* ☎ *812/315–9732.* ✉ *For the church: 50 rubles; for the colonnade: 18 rubles.* ☾ *Mon., Tues., Thurs.–Sun. 11–6 (kassa open until 5).*

❻ **Kunstkammer.** The Chamber of Art, also called the Chamber of Curiosities, is another fine example of the Russian Baroque. Painted bright azure with white trim, the building stands out from the surrounding classically designed architecture. Its playful character seems to reflect its beginnings; it was originally commissioned in 1718 to house Peter the Great's collection of oddities, gathered during his travels. Completed by 1734, the Kunstkammer (from the German *Kunst,* "art," and *Kammer,* "chamber") was destroyed by fire in 1747 and almost entirely rebuilt. Today it houses the Museum of Anthropology and Ethnography but still includes a room with Peter's original collection, a truly bizarre assortment ranging from rare precious stones to preserved human organs and fetuses. The museum is enormously popular, so purchase entrance tickets early in the day. ⊠ *3 Universitetskaya nab.,* ☏ *812/218–1412.* ▣ *15 rubles.* ⊙ *Fri.–Wed. 11–6 (kassa open until 4:45). Closed last Wed. of month.*

Mariinsky Dvorets (Maria's Palace). Completed in 1844 by Andrey Stakenschneider for the eldest and favorite daughter of Nicholas I, Grand Duchess Maria Nikolayevna, this palace was subsequently used briefly as the residence of the Provisional Government and as the seat of the Leningrad Soviet's Executive Committee; today, it is the home of the St. Petersburg City Council. In August 1991, it was also on this square, in front of the palace, that citizens put up barricades and held all-night vigils to demonstrate their commitment to democracy. The facade is still adorned with Soviet regalia, although the flag and the double eagle above it are actually reclaimed Russian emblems. Since this is a working government building, public access is restricted; however, group tours can be arranged by special request after 6 PM on weekdays or during the day on weekends. ⊠ *6 Isaakievskaya Pl.,* ☏ *812/319–9012.* ▣ *35 rubles per person for groups of 10 or more. A surcharge applies to groups of fewer than 10; the fee includes a guide.*

⑧ Menshikovsky Dvorets (Menshikov Palace). Alexander Menshikov, St. Petersburg's first governor, was one of Russia's more flamboyant characters. A close friend of Peter the Great (often called his favorite), Menshikov rose from humble beginnings as a street vendor, reportedly getting his start when he sold a cabbage pie to the czar—or so the legend goes. Eventually becoming one of Russia's most powerful statesmen (he was granted the entire island outright for a while), Menshikov was famous for his corruption and political maneuvering. His palace, the first stone building in St. Petersburg, was, at the time of its completion in 1720, the city's most luxurious building. Although only a portion of the original palace has survived, it easily conveys a sense of Menshikov's inflated ego and love of luxury. Particularly noteworthy is the tilework in the restored bedrooms, whose walls and ceilings are completely covered with handcrafted ceramic tiles. The story goes that Peter had them sent home from Delft for himself, but Menshikov liked them and appropriated them. After Peter's death and Menshikov's subsequent exile to Siberia in 1727, his palace was turned over to a military training school and was significantly altered over the years. In June 1917 it served as the site of the First Congress of Russian Soviets. Neglected until 1967, when badly needed restoration work was launched, the Menshikov Palace is today a branch of the Hermitage Museum. In addition to the restored living quarters of the Menshikov family, there is an exhibit devoted to early 18th-century Russian culture. ⊠ *15 Universitetskaya nab.,* ☏ *812/213–1112.* ▣ *30 rubles, includes guided tour; MC, V accepted when the machine works.* ⊙ *Tues.–Sun. 10:30–4:30.*

Most Leytenanta Shmidta (Lieutenant Schmidt Bridge). Built in 1842–50, this was the first stationary bridge to connect Vasilievsky Island with the left bank of the Neva; it was renamed in honor of the naval officer who was a leader of the Black Sea Fleet mutiny during the 1905–07 Revolution.

⑮ Nikolsky Sabor (St. Nicholas Cathedral). This turquoise-and-white extravaganza of a Russian Baroque cathedral was designed by Rastrelli's pupil, S. I. Chevakinsky. A theatrical showpiece, its artistic inspiration was in part derived from the 18th-century Italian prints of the Bibiena brothers, designs meant for opera and theater presentations. Surrounded by picturesque canals and green spaces, flanked by an elegant campanile, the church's wedding-cake silhouette, marked by a forest of white Corinthian pilasters and columns, closes Glinka Street and makes it a natural pole of attraction if you find yourself in the vicinity. Inside, there a lower church (low, dark, and warm for the winter) and an upper church (high, airy, and cool for the summer) typical of Russian orthodox sanctuaries. It is no less picturesque than the outside and is a vivid example of an orthodox church that stayed open under Soviet power. If you go during a service, you will also hear the beautiful choir, but whenever you go, there always seems to be a priest celebrating some ritual for a few parishioners gathered around him. ✉ *1/3 Nikolskaya Ploshchad,* ☎ *812/114–0862.* ☉ *Morning services at 7 and 9* AM, *vespers at 6* PM.

Pedagogical Institute. The grounds belonged to Count Razumovsky, who had his palace here in the late 18th century. The adjacent house, dating from the early 1750s, belonged to the merchant Stegelmann, who was in charge of selling supplies to the royal court. Both houses were later taken over, linked, and made into a foundling hospital and orphanage. Today they house the Pedagogical Institute.

OFF THE
BEATEN PATH

DOSTOYEVSKY LITERARY MUSEUM – This was the writer's last residence, where he wrote *The Brothers Karamazov.* Dostoyevsky preferred to live in the part of the city inhabited by the ordinary people he wrote about. He always insisted that the windows of his workroom be opposite a church, as they are in this simple little house. ✉ *5/2 Kuznechny pereulok,* ☎ *812/311–4031.* ✲ *16 rubles.* ☉ *Tues.–Sun. 11–5:30. Closed last Wed. of month.*

❾ Repin Institute of Painting, Sculpture, and Architecture. Like architects, artists began equally abruptly–and perhaps still more slavishly—to imitate Western models during the reign of Peter the Great. In order to enforce the "right" Western standards, Peter set up a school of drawing in St. Petersburg which was later elevated by Catherine the Great to the Russian Academy of Fine Arts in 1757. The success of this Westernizing policy was complete—excessively so. Russian artists started painting portraits in the Gainsborough mode and imitated the French and German Romantics, but unlike native architects, Russian painters failed to put their own stamp on the foreign styles they had imported. Finally, in 1863, a number of talented painters broke away from the Academy and began to foster the idea that art should serve a social purpose. The supreme artist among this group was Ilya Repin (1844–1930), whose most famous works, such as the *Volga Bargemen,* are in Moscow museums. Along with Repin, other famous graduates of the institute include Dmitri Levitsky and Orest Kiprensky. Today, the Repin Institute maintains a public museum of graduation works from the original Academy. The rarest thing to be seen in the Academy, however, is probably a foreign tourist. Do not expect any kind of sign in English, except the one that tells you to pay six times more than a Russian to gain admission to this temple of culture. You might just as well go all the way and spend an extra 70 rubles for a guided tour, since the names and the significance of the artists will probably be unknown to you. This place is one of the last to have Socialist Realistic Art (most famously seen in the the graduation works of the current academicians and authorities of the Institute). It is also bustling with the activity of aspirant artists. As you make your way to the museum on the second floor, have a look through the balcony to the interior circular courtyard, for which an international design competition was recently held as a prelude to its rehabilitation. The building itself was built between 1764 and 1788 and designed by Alexander Kokorinov and Vallin de la Mothe. It remains a fine example of early Russian Classicism. ✉ *17 Universitetskaya nab.,* ☎ *812/213–6496.* ✲ *30 rubles (100 for a guided tour).* ☉ *Wed.–Sun. 11–6 (kassa open until 5).*

On the landing in front of the Repin Institute, leading down to the Neva, stand two of St. Petersburg's more magnificent landmarks, the famous **Egyptian Sphinxes.** These twin statues date from the 15th century BC and were discovered during an excavation at Thebes in the 1820s. They were apparently created during the era of Pharaoh Amenhotep III, whose features they supposedly bear.

NEED A BREAK?	If you want a rest and a bite to eat at a popular local establishment, try **Lukamorye** (✉ 19 nab. Leytenanta Shmidta, ☎ 812/218–5900). It's a short walk (four blocks) up the embankment from the Academy of Arts and is located on the corner of the 13 liniye and the embankment. The *griby v smetane* (mushrooms in cream) is good and filling, as are the solyanka and the borshch. As in most cafés, expect to pay 50 rubles per person for a two-course lunch. It's open daily noon–11.

Rostralnyie Kolonny (Rostral Columns). Erected between 1805 and 1810 in honor of the Russian fleet, the name of these columns on Birzhevaya Square comes from the Latin *rostrum,* meaning "prow." Modeled on similar memorials in ancient Rome, the columns are decorated with ships' prows, with sculptures at the base depicting Russia's main waterways, the Dnieper, Volga, Volkhov, and Neva rivers. Although the columns originally served as lighthouses—until 1855 this was St. Petersburg's commercial harbor—they are now lighted only on special occasions. They were designed to frame the architectural centerpiece of this side of the embankment—the old ☞ **Stock Exchange** (Birzha), now the Naval War Museum.

Rumyantsev Square. This square was established in honor of the 18th-century general who led Russia to victory in the Russo-Turkish wars of 1768–74. Its obelisk, designed by Vikenty Brenna, originally stood in the Field of Mars (Marsovo Pole) and was moved to its present site in 1818. The new site was chosen for its proximity to the military school in the former Menshikov Palace, where Rumyantsev once studied.

Russian Academy of Sciences. Located next to the **Kunstkammer** (☞ *above*), this is the original building of the Russian Academy of Sciences. Erected on strictly Classical lines in 1783–89, it is considered Giacomo Quarenghi's grandest design, with an eight-column portico, a pediment, and a double staircase. The administrative offices of the academy, founded in 1724 by Peter the Great and known as the Russian Academy of Sciences until the 1917 Revolution, were transferred to Moscow in 1934. The building now houses the St. Petersburg branch of the Russian Academy of Sciences and is not open to the public.

⑦ St. Petersburg University. One of Russia's leading institutions of higher learning, with an enrollment of over 20,000, St. Petersburg University was founded by Alexander I in 1819. Its campuses date from the time of Peter the Great. The bright red Baroque building to your immediate right is the **Twelve Colleges Building,** named for the governmental administrative bodies established during Peter's reign. Designed by Domenico Trezzini and completed 16 years after Peter's death, in 1741, the building was transferred to the university at the time of its establishment and today houses the university library and administrative offices. It is not officially open to the public, but no one will stop you from looking around.

The next building in the university complex is the **Rector's Wing,** where a plaque on the outside wall attests that the great Russian poet Alexander Blok was born here in 1880. The third building along the embankment is a former palace built for Peter II, Peter the Great's grandson, who ruled only briefly. Completed in 1761, the building was later given to the University.

Senate and Synod. This long, light-yellow building, built along Classical lines, housed Russia's highest judicial and administrative body before the revolution. Designed by Carlo Rossi and erected between 1829 and 1834, it now contains state historical archives and is closed to the public.

Siniy most (Blue Bridge). The bridge, which spans the Moika River and is so called because of the paint on its underside, is so wide (328 ft) and stubby that it seems not to be a bridge at all but rather a sort of quaint raised footpath on St. Isaac's Square.

❹ **Stock Exchange.** Erected in 1804–10 and, like the Rostral Columns, designed by the Swiss architect Thomas de Thomon, the Neoclassical Stock Exchange was modeled on one of the Greek temples at Paestum. It was intended to symbolize St. Petersburg's financial and maritime strength. Since 1940, the building has housed the **Voenno-Morskoy Muzey** (Central Naval Museum), which itself founded in 1805. Its collections date from Peter's reign and include, in accordance with his orders, a model of every ship built in Russian shipyards since 1709. On display are exhibits of Russia's naval history to the present. The collections also contain a 3,000-year-old dugout found on the bottom of the Bug River as well as Peter the Great's personal belongings, including his first boat and the ax he used in building it. ✉ *4 Birzhevaya Ploshchad, Vasilievsky Ostrov,* ☎ *812/218–2502.* 🎫 *20 rubles.* ☉ *Wed.–Sun. 10:30–5:30 (kassa open until 4:45). Closed last Thurs. of month.*

NEED A BREAK?	The **Café Idiot** (✉ Moika, 82, ☎ 812/315–1675), halfway between Maria's Palace and the Yusopov Palace, on the Moika, has become a favorite among St. Peterburg expatriates since its opening in 1997. Its entrance is the second door from the corner, marked by a discreet white globe with *Idiot* inscribed on it—it may be this discretion that explains why it is not patronized by the somewhat forbidding types (fancy leather jackets, ponytails, and cellular phones) often found in more ostentatious hangouts. The Idiot serves hearty Russian vegetarianized food and good cappuccino. The cozy decor reminds one of a New York East Village joint; the background music leans heavily to the Russian taste for French singers like Aznavour, Adamo, and Patricia Kaas.

❸ **Strelka.** The Strelka (arrow or spit) affords a dazzling view of both the Winter Palace and of the Peter and Paul Fortress, off to its left (☞ Peter and Paul Fortress and the Petrograd Side, *below*), and reveals the city's triumphant rise from a watery outpost to an elegant metropolis. Seen against the backdrop of the Neva, the brightly colored houses lining the embankment seem like children's toys—the building blocks of a bygone aristocracy. They stand at the water's edge, supported not by the land beneath them but seemingly by the panorama of the city behind them. Gazing at this architectural wonder, you begin to understand the scope of Peter the Great's vision for his country. The view is also revealing because it makes clear how careful the city's founders were to build their city not despite the Neva but around and with it. The river's natural ebb and flow accords perfectly with the monumental architecture lining its course.

⓮ **Yusupovsky Dvorets** (Yusupov Palace). Set on the bank of the Moika River, this elegant yellow palace belonged to one of Russia's wealthiest families, the Yusupovs. On the cold night of December 17, 1916, it became the setting for one of history's most melodramatic murders. Prince Yusupov and others loyal to the czar spent several frustrating and frightening hours trying to kill Rasputin, who had strongly influenced the czarina during the tumultuous years leading up to the Bolshevik Revolution. To their horror, the courtiers found the "mad monk" nearly invincible: When he did not succumb to the arsenic-laced cake given to him, the conspirators proceeded to shoot him several times (thinking him dead after the first shot, they had left the room, only to return and find he'd staggered outside—whereupon they shot him again). They then dumped him, still living, into the icy waters of an isolated section of a nearby canal, where he finally succumbed, only due to being trapped under a floe of ice. On display are the rooms in which Rasputin was (or began to be) killed, as well as a waxworks exhibit of Rasputin and Prince Yusupov (who was forced to flee the country when the monk's murder was uncovered). They are only visible on an organized tour given once daily in the late afternoon. The other organized tour (given several times daily during the afternoon) takes you through the former reception rooms of the second floor. As for the scenes where the final acts of the drama were played out—the palace's underground tunnel and Turkish bath—they are ostensibly off-limits, but you may be able to view them if you can avail yourself of the bathroom facilities on the lower level of the mansion. On a lighter note, the showpiece of the palace remains the jewel-like rococo theater, whose stage was once graced by Liszt and Chopin; today, concerts are still presented here, as well as in palace's august and elegant White-Columns Room (concert tickets usually have to be purchased just before performance time). ⊠ *94 nab. Moiki,* ☎ *812/314–8893.* ⊡ *Rasputin Rooms, 20 rubles; Reception Rooms, 30 rubles.* ⊙ *By guided tours only. The Rasputin Rooms: daily, 4:40; Reception Rooms: daily, noon, 1, 2, 3.*

❺ Zoologichesky Musey. The prize of this zoological museum's unusual collection, which contains over 40,000 species, is a stuffed mammoth recovered from Siberia in 1901. ⊠ *1 Universitetskaya nab.,* ☎ *812/ 218–0112.* ⊡ *$4.* ⊙ *Sat.–Thurs. 11–5. Closed holidays.*

The Petrograd Side: From the Peter and Paul Fortress to Leo Tolstoy Square

St. Petersburg was born in the battles of the Northern Wars with Sweden, and it was here, on Zayachy Ostrov (Hare Island), where it all began: In 1703, Peter laid the foundation of the first fortress to protect the mainland and to secure Russia's outlet to the sea. Ever since, the small hexagonal island forms, as it were, the hub around which the city revolves. The showpiece of the island is the Petropavlovskaya Krepost (Peter and Paul Fortress), the starting point for any tour of this section of the city, which actually consists of a series of islands, and is commonly referred to as the Petrogradskaya Storona (Petrograd Side). Hare Island and the fortress are almost directly across the Neva from the Winter Palace. Cut off from the north by the moatlike Kronverk Canal, the island is connected by a footbridge to Troitskaya Ploshchad (Trinity Square, sometimes still referred to by its Soviet name, Revolution Square) on Petrogradsky Ostrov (Petrograd Island). Along with its famous monuments, this part of the city is also one of its earliest residential areas and Trinity Square, named for the church that once stood here (demolished in 1934), is the city's oldest square.

A Good Walk

You can reach Hare Island, site of the **Peter and Paul Fortress** ⑯, from central St. Petersburg by crossing the Troitsky most from the Palace embankment. It is also easy to reach by subway; the closest station is Gorkovskaya. After exiting the station, walk through the small park in front of you, heading in the direction of the Neva. The fortress will emerge through the trees to your right. If you want to make your visit to this famed monument complete, you may want to also head to a building associated with the fortress but situated outside its walls: Across the Kronverk Canal to the north of the fortress is the horseshoe-shape **Artillery Museum** ⑰. Leaving the fort by its western end and crossing the footbridge there, bear right; leaving by the way you came in and crossing its footbridge, bear left. The large museum, devoted to the history of Russia's weaponry, will soon be visible.

Return now to Trinity Square. At the northern edge of the square, at the corner of Kuybysheva ulitsa and Kamennostrovsky Prospect, stands the **Russian Political History Museum** ⑱. As you leave the museum, take a right, and then turn right again onto Kronversky Prospect. It's hard to miss the bright azure domes of St. Petersburg's only mosque—the **Mechet** ⑲—above the trees. Now head back (left) in the direction of the Neva River. When you reach the waterfront, turn left again, to walk along Petrovskaya naberezhnaya (Peter Embankment). A few minutes away, you'll find the **Domik Petra Pervovo** ⑳, Peter the Great's Cottage. Keep walking east along the embankment. When you reach the corner where the Petrovskaya and Petrogradskaya embankments meet (and the Great Nevka converges with the Neva River), you'll be in front of a blue-and-white building in the Russian Baroque style (although built only in 1911 by a certain Aleksandr Dmitriev). This is the Nakhimov Academy of Naval Officers, in front of which is anchored the cruiser **Avrora** ㉑. Across the river stands the enormous **St. Petersburg Hotel.** From here you can return to your starting point by retracing your steps along the embankment. If you want to see more of the Petrograd Side's residential areas, take the longer route back via Kuybysheva ulitsa. Walk down to the bridge to your left (as you face the cruiser *Avrora*) and turn left onto Kuybysheva. This will take you back to Trinity Square. From here the Trinity Bridge is to your left and the Gorkovskaya subway stop a short walk to your right. If you turn right, the straight avenue opening up before you (Kamennoostrovsky Prospect) was the most fashionable and modern avenue at the end of the 19th century and goes all the way to Kamenny Ostrov (Stone Island), where the well-to-do families of the day had their dachas built. If you're an architecture buff and want a delicious feast of Northern Art Nouveau, walk to the next subway station (Petrogradskaya) along the avenue and pay attention on the way to buildings No. 1–3, 9, 13, 16, 20, 24 and 26–28 (where Kirov lived). Your effort will finally be rewarded by the sight of the "house with towers," which gives shape to the intersection of Kamennoostrovsky and Bolshoi Prospekts, on Ploshchad Lva Tolstovo (Leo Tolstoy Square), and which is also where you should take the subway back to downtown and enjoy some well-deserved rest.

TIMING

You'll need to devote two to three hours to simply walking this route—more time will be needed if you plan to visit the sights. The main attraction, the Peter and Paul Fortress, can easily eat up an afternoon. Note that the Cathedral of Sts. Peter and Paul is closed on Wednesday.

Sights to See

⑰ **Artileriysky Muzey** (Artillery Museum). This building once served as the city's arsenal and was turned over to the Artillery Museum in 1872. The museum itself dates from the days of Peter the Great, who sought to present the entire history of weaponry, with a special emphasis on Russia. Today the Artillery Museum is St. Petersburg's main army museum. ✉ *7 Alexandrovsky Park,* ☎ *812/232–0296.* 🎫 *25 rubles.* ☉ *Wed.–Sun. 11–6 (kassa open until 5). Closed last Thurs. of month.*

NEED A
BREAK? If you have walked all the way over to the Artillery Museum or come out of the Peter and Paul Fortress through the western entrance, you may as well walk a bit farther and try out St. Petersburg's floating café, the **Petrovsky** (⊠ 3 nab. Mytninskaya, ☎ 812/325–4204). It is located on a ship permanently moored (the third in the row) in the Kronverk Canal, just south of the Artillery Museum. It may look gloomy, particularly if the weather is bad, but down below is a snug bar where you can enjoy a cup of strong coffee, pastry, or even a shot of cognac. The café has live music on Fridays and Saturdays.

☝ ㉑ **Avrora.** This historic cruiser is permanently moored in front of the **Nakhimov Academy of Naval Officers.** Launched in 1903, it fought in the 1904–05 Russo-Japanese War as well as in World War II, but it is best known for its role in the Bolshevik Revolution. At 9:40 PM on November 7, 1917, the cruiser fired the shot signaling the storming of the Winter Palace. A cherished relic in the Soviet era, the *Avrora* was carefully restored in the 1980s and opened as a museum. Although the revolution it launched brought itself under fire in the end, the cruiser is still a favorite place to bring children, and on weekends you may encounter long lines. On display are the crew's quarters and the radio room used to broadcast Lenin's victory address. ⊠ *4 Petrogradskaya nab.,* ☎ *812/ 230–8440.* ☜ *Free; price for guided tours depending on the group.* ⊙ *Tues.–Thurs., weekends 10:30–4.*

Botanical Gardens. Founded as an apothecary garden for Peter the Great, the grounds display millions—literally—of different forms of plant life. ⊠ *2 ul. Professora Popova,* ☎ *812/234–1764.* ☜ *24 rubles.* ⊙ *Hothouses Sat.–Thurs. 11–4.*

㉒ **Domik Petra Pervovo** (Peter the Great's Cottage). Built in just three days in May 1703, this cottage was home to Peter the Great during construction of the Peter and Paul Fortress. It is made of wooden logs painted to resemble bricks. Inside, 18th-century furniture is on display, arranged as it might have been in Peter's day, along with a few of Peter's personal effects. The stone structure enclosing the cottage was erected in 1784 by Catherine the Great to protect the structure from the elements. The cottage consists of just three rooms, whose ceilings are surprisingly low—considering that Peter the Great was nearly 7 ft tall. In the courtyard in front of the cottage stands a bronze bust of the czar. The large stone sculptures of the Shi-Tsza (Lion-Frogs) flanking the stairwell leading down the embankment side were brought to Russia from Manchuria in 1907. ⊠ *6 Petrovskaya nab.,* ☎ *812/232–4576.* ☜ *15 rubles.* ⊙ *Wed.–Mon. 11–6. Closed last Mon. of month.*

Kirov Museum. This is the home of the former head of the city's Communist Party, whose murder by Stalin in 1934 marked the beginning of the infamous purges. Look for a red sign "musei Kirova" and take the elevator to the fourth floor. The rest of the building is currently occupied by the administration of the Petrograd district. ⊠ *26/28 Kamennostrovsky Prospect,* ☎ *812/346–0217.* ☜ *3 rubles.* ⊙ *Mon., Tues., Thurs.–Sun. 11–5. Closed last Tues. of month.*

㉑ **Mechet** (Mosque). Built in 1910–14 to serve St. Petersburg's Muslim community, the Mosque was designed after the Gur Emir in Samarkand, where Tamerlane is buried. ⊠ *7 Kronversky Prospect,* ☎ *812/233– 9819.* ⊙ *Daily 10–4. Services daily at 1:30.*

★ ⑯ **Petropavlovskaya Krepost** (Peter and Paul Fortress). The fortress was the first building in Sankt-Piter-Burkh, as it was then named, and erected in just one year, between 1703 and 1704, to defend this location in the Great Northern War against Sweden. It was never used for its intended purpose, however, since the Russian line of defense quickly moved farther north, and, in fact, the war was won before the fortress was mobilized. Instead, it has served mainly as a political prison, primarily under the czars. Today, 1703 is celebrated as the official year of the foundation of the city; grand city-wide celebrations are already being planned for 2003.

Cross the footbridge and enter the fortress through **Ioannovskyie Vorota** (St. John's Gate), the main entrance to the outer fortifications. Once inside, you will need to stop at the ticket office, which is inside the outer fortification wall on the right (the ticket booth to your immediate left sells only theater tickets). Although entry to the fortress grounds is free, you must buy tickets here for the exhibits or you will be sent back for them. ✉ *Kronverskaya nab.,* ☎ *812/238–4540.* 🖂 *18 rubles.* ⊘ *Mon., Tues., Thurs.–Sun. 11–6 (kassa open until 5, until 4 on Tues.). Closed last Tues. of month.*

Entrance to the inner fortress is through the **Petrovskyie Vorota** (St. Peter's Gate). Designed by the Swiss architect Domenico Trezzini, it was built from 1717 to 1718. Its decoration includes the double-headed eagle of the Romanovs and a wooden bas-relief depicting the apostle Peter prevailing over Simon Magus. The allegory was meant to inspire confidence in Peter the Great's impending victory over Charles XII of Sweden, which did not come until 1721.

After you pass through St. Peter's Gate, the first building to your right is the **Artillery Arsenal,** where weaponry was stored. Just to your left is the **Inzhenerny Dom** (Engineer's House), which was built from 1748 to 1749. It is now a branch of the Museum of the History of St. Petersburg (as are all exhibits in the fortress) and presents displays about the city's prerevolutionary history. The small building right after the Engineer's House is the **Gauptvakhta** (Guardhouse), built in 1743 and later reconstructed. Today it houses the museum's administrative offices and is not open to the public.

As you continue to walk down the main center lane, away from St. Peter's Gate, you soon come to the main attraction of the fortress, the **Petropavlovsky Sobor** (Cathedral of Sts. Peter and Paul). Constructed between 1712 and 1733 on the site of an earlier wooden church, it was designed by Domenico Trezzini and later embellished by Bartolomeo Rastrelli. It is highly unusual for a Russian Orthodox church. Instead of the characteristic bulbous domes, it is adorned by a single, slender, gilded spire whose height (400 ft) made it the city's tallest building. The spire is identical to that of the Admiralty across the river, except that it is crowned by an angel bearing a golden cross. The spire remained the city's highest structure—in accordance with Peter the Great's decree—until 1962, when the television tower was erected (greatly marring the harmony of the city's skyline).

The interior of the cathedral is also atypical. The Baroque iconostasis, designed by Ivan Zarudny and built in the 1720s, is adorned by freestanding statues. Another uncommon feature is the pulpit. According to legend, it was used only once, in 1901, to excommunicate Leo Tolstoy from the Russian Orthodox Church.

Starting with Peter the Great, the cathedral served as the burial place of the czars. You can identify Peter's tomb—a place of his own choosing, to the far right as you face the iconostasis—by the czar's bust on the railing. Nearly all of Peter's successors had been ceremoniously buried in the cathedral as well, with a few notable exceptions: Peter II, Ivan VI, and the last czar, Nicholas II, who was executed with his family in Ekaterinburg in 1918. In 1998, the remains of the czar and his family were officially identified (with Alexei, the czarevich, and one of the three daughters still missing) and were solemnly given a final resting place in the Peter and Paul Fortress on July 17. Already in 1992, in recognition of Russia's Imperial past, the most recent Romanov pretender, Grand Duke Vladimir, had been bestowed the honor of burial here, although not in the royal crypt.

You may exit the cathedral through the passageway to the left of the iconostasis. This leads to the adjoining **Usypalnitsa** (Grand Ducal Crypt), built between 1896 and 1908. It contains an exhibit on the architectural history of the fortress.

As you leave the cathedral, you will notice a small Classical structure to your right. This is the **Botny Domik** (Boathouse), built in 1762–66 to house Peter the Great's boyhood boat. The boat has since been moved to the Central Naval Museum on Vasilievsky Island (☞ Vasilievsky Island and the Left Bank, *above*), and the building is not open to the public. The wooden figurine on its roof is meant to symbolize navigation.

The long pink-and-white building to your left as you exit the cathedral is the **Komendantsky Dom** (Commandant's House). Erected between 1743 and 1746, it once housed the fortress's administration and doubled as a courtroom for political prisoners. The Decembrist revolutionaries were tried here in 1826. The room where the trial took place forms part of the ongoing exhibits, which deal with the history of St. Petersburg from its founding in 1703 to 1917.

Across the cobblestone yard, opposite the entrance to the cathedral, stands the **Monetny Dvor** (Mint), which dates from 1716. The present building was erected between 1798 and 1806. The mint is still in operation, producing coins, medals, military decorations, and *znachki*, or Russian souvenir pins. The coins that were taken along on Soviet space missions were made here.

Take the pathway to the left of the Commandant's House (as you are facing it), and you will be headed right for the **Nevskyie Vorota** (Neva Gate), built in 1730 and reconstructed in 1787. As you walk through its passageway, note the plaques on the inside walls marking flood levels of the Neva. The most recent, from 1975, shows the river more than 9 ft above normal. The gate leads out to the **Komendantskaya Pristan** (Commandant's Pier). It is this side of the fortress that was meant to be seen by would-be invaders and convince them to turn back. Up above to the right is the **Signal Cannon,** fired every day at noon. From this side you get a splendid view of St. Petersburg. You may want to step down to the sandy beach, where even in winter hearty swimmers enjoy the Neva's arctic waters. In summer the beach is lined with sunbathers, standing up or leaning against the fortification wall (supposedly this allows for a more even tan).

Returning back inside the fortress, consider that it was also through the Neva Gate that prisoners were led to their execution. Several of the fortress's bastions, concentrated at its far western end, were put to use over the years mainly as political prisons. One of them, **Trubetskoi Bastion,** is open to the public as a museum. If you turn left from the gate and walk the length of the fortification wall, you can identify the museum by the diagonal stripes on its door and the iron gate enclosing the entrance. Aside from a few exhibits of prison garb, the only items on display are the cells themselves, restored to their chilling, prerevolutionary appearance.

The first prisoner confined in its dungeons was Peter the Great's own son, Alexei, who was tortured to death in 1718, allegedly under the czar's supervision. The prison was enlarged in 1872, when an adjacent one, Alexeivsky Bastion, which held such famous figures as the writers Fyodor Dostoyevsky and Nikolai Chernyshevsky, became overcrowded by the swelling numbers of dissidents of the czarist regime. A partial chronology of revolutionaries held here includes some of the People's Will terrorists, who killed Alexander II in 1881; Lenin's elder brother Alexander, who attempted to murder Alexander III (and was executed for his role in the plot); and Leon Trotsky and Maxim Gorky, after taking part in the 1905 Revolution. The Bolsheviks themselves imprisoned people here for a short period, starting with members of the Provisional Government who were arrested and "detained for their own safety" for a few days, as well as sailors who mutinied against the Communist regime in Kronstadt in 1921. They were apparently the last to be held here, and in 1925 a memorial museum (to the prerevolutionary prisoners) was opened instead. Some casements close to the Neva Gate have been renovated in 1997 and converted into a printing workshop (the **pechatnya**), where you can appreciate and buy good-quality graphic art in a broad range of prices. Original late-19th-century presses are used to create lithographs, etchings, and linocuts depicting, most often, urban St. Petersburg landscapes. In the basement, the original foundations were excavated; different layers of the history of the fortress can thus be seen. The pechatnya comes as a welcome alternative to the stuff usually proposed to tourists. ☎ 812/238–4742. ☉ *Daily 11–5, 10–6 in high season.*

⑱   Russian Political History Museum. This elegant house is the former mansion of Mathilda Kshesinskaya, a famous ballerina and mistress of the last Russian czar, Nicholas II, before he married Alexandra. She left Russia in 1917 for Paris, where she married a longtime lover (another Romanov), Andrei Vladimirovich (the one who owned the current Palace of Marriages on Angliyskaya Embankment). Margot Fonteyn was one of her pupils. Built in the Art Nouveau style in 1905 by Goguen, the mansion served as Bolshevik committee headquarters in the months leading up to the October Revolution. In 1957 it was linked to the adjoining town house by a rather nondescript central wing and turned into the Museum of the Great October Socialist Revolution; in 1991 it was given its current name. It offers temporary exhibits on Russian political movements, both before and after the 1917 Revolution, and one room is dedicated to Kshesinskaya and her parents and siblings, all dancers. All that is left of the original interiors is the reception hall. As for the museum, you will not be missing much if you skip it. ⊠ *2/4 ul. Bolshaya Dvoryanskaya (ul. Kuybysheva),* ☎ *812/233–7052.* ▣ *12 rubles; with a Russian guide, 25 rubles per person; with an English-speaking guide, 35 rubles per person.* ☉ *Fri.–Wed. 10–6 (kassa open until 5).*

St. Petersburg Hotel. Before 1992, this enormous hotel across the river from the **Avrora** was named the Leningrad, which was probably a more appropriate name since this Intourist outpost clearly belongs to the Soviet era. Built in the monotonous style of a Brezhnev-era high-rise, the concrete-and-steel structure seems horribly out of place among the prerevolutionary architecture lining the embankment.

The Inner City: The Nevsky Prospect and the Alexander Nevsky Lavra

"There is nothing finer than Nevsky Prospect, not in St. Petersburg at any rate, for in St. Petersburg it is everything . . ." wrote the great Russian author Nikolai Gogol more than 150 years ago. Today it may not be as resplendent as it was in the 1830s, when noblemen and ladies strolled along the elegant avenue or paraded by in horse-drawn carriages. It still remains, however, its main thoroughfare, unquestionably the pulse of the city. Through the 18th century it was built up with estates and manors of the gentry, most of which still stand as testimony to the city's noble past. The next century saw a boom of mercantile growth that added sections farther south as centers for commerce, finance, and trade. Under the Communists, few new sites were planned on the Prospect. Instead, old structures found new uses, and the bulk of the Soviets' building was directed outside the city center.

A Good Walk

To explore the inner city and St. Petersburg's most famous avenue, **Nevsky Prospect** ㉒, start at the relatively peaceful **Alexander Nevsky Lavra** ㉓, which is at the southeastern end of Nevsky Prospect. It can be reached by taking the subway to the Ploshchad Alexandra Nevskovo station, which comes out at the foot of the Moskva Hotel, one of Intourist's gargantuan complexes. The entrance to the Lavra is across the square from the subway exit. After visiting the monastery, return to Alexander Nevsky Square. The bridge to your right, also named for Alexander Nevsky, is the city's longest; it leads to some of St. Petersburg's main bedroom communities, where, these days, most of the city's residents live. You should take the subway one stop north to the Mayakovskaya station, and at that stop, follow the signs for the adjacent Vosstaniya exit to emerge at a better location for viewing the next sights. It is at this point that the avenue's most interesting architecture begins, starting at **Ploshchad Vosstaniya** (Insurrection Square) ㉔. Head west, away from the monastery and the railway station, and after three blocks you'll reach the **Fontanka River** and one of the city's most beautiful bridges, the **Anichkov most** ㉕; over the river, on the opposite corner, stands the **Anichkov Palace.** The next stop is **Ploshchad Ostrovskovo** (Ostrovskovo Square), dominated by the city's oldest theater, the **Pushkin Drama Theater** ㉖. Before moving beyond Ostrovsky Square, step around to the back of the Pushkin Theater, where the **ulitsa Zodchevo Rossi**—a street whose every proportion has been carefully detailed—begins.

Back at Ostrovskovo Square, take note of the Neoclassical building to your left, on the west side of the square. This is the **Russian National Library,** the nation's largest after the State Library in Moscow. You may want to cross Nevsky at this point to peek inside the **Yeliseyevsky Food Emporium.** As you pass Sadovaya ulitsa, taking up the entire block on the other side of the street is the huge **Gostinny Dvor** ㉗ department store. On the same side as Yeliseyevsky, between Nos. 40–42, is the blue-and-white Armenian **Church of St. Catherine.** At the corner of Mikhailovskaya ulitsa is the **Grand Hotel Europe.** You will next notice, at No. 34, another recessed church, the **Catholic Church,** also dedicated to St. Catherine. Across on the corner, at No. 33, stands the former city hall under the czars, the **Gorodskaya Duma** (City Duma). Cross the short Kazan Bridge over the Griboyedov Canal, and you'll come to the city's largest bookstore, **Dom Knigi** ㉘. Across the street is one of the city's more resplendent works of architecture, the **Kazansky Sobor** (Kazan Cathedral) ㉙. Crossing the street and continuing one block down Nevsky, you'll reach the **Lutheran Church,** another church on a recessed lot, at Nos. 22–24.

Return now to the other side of the street. Before you cross the little bridge spanning the Moika Canal, you'll be at a magnificent green building overlooking the embankment. This is the former **Stroganov Palace** ㉚. The golden building of the **Admiralty** marks the end of Nevsky Prospect. To return to the subway, take trolleybus 1, 5, 7, 10, or 22 one stop to Nevsky Prospect Station, although since trolleybuses on Nevsky are notoriously overcrowded you might prefer to walk. Palace Square and the Winter Palace, if you somehow haven't noticed, are nearby, across from the street flanking the Admiralty's right side. If you have the time and are interested in farmers' markets, you can easily include **Kuznechny Rynok** in your tour; this is one of St. Petersburg's most popular markets, and is only 10 minutes away from Nevsky, walking along Vladimirsky Prospekt (Metro: Vladimirskaya). Other worthwhile sites in the area include **Smolny,** ㉜ the great convent and cathedral on the left bank of the Neva, and the **Taurida Palace,** ㉝ on Shpalernaya Street, both reachable from Nevsky Prospekt by Trolleybus 5 or 7 (get off at Tulskaya Street).

TIMING

Your best bet to avoid the crowds that pack the trolleybuses and the trains is to visit in the morning. However, if you take the subway or the trolleybus rather than walk from one sight to the next you will save at least a couple of hours, hours that you can then devote to a little shopping; most of the souvenir shops are on and around Nevsky Prospekt.

Sights to See

★ ㉓ **Alexander Nevsky Lavra.** The monastery complex includes the Church of the Annunciation—converted under the Soviets into the Museum of City Sculpture—the Holy Trinity Church, a theological seminary, and several cemeteries. Entrance to the monastery grounds is free, but you must purchase a ticket for the two most interesting cemeteries and the museum. There are ticket kiosks outside the two paying cemeteries, after the gate, and inside the Tikhvin cemetery, on the right side. ⊠ *1 Pl. Alexandra Nevskovo,* ☎ *812/274–1612.* ⊑ *For the 2 necropolis (including the exhibition of urban sculpture) 10 rubles.* ☾ *Fri.– Wed. 11–6.*

The word *lavra* in Russian is reserved for a monastery of the highest order, of which there are just four in all of Russia and Ukraine. Named in honor of St. Alexander Nevsky, this monastery was founded in 1710 by Peter the Great and given lavra status in 1797. Prince Alexander of Novgorod (1220–63), the great military commander, became a national hero because he halted the relentless eastward drive for Russian territory by the Germans and the Swedes. Peter chose this site for the monastery, thinking that it was the same place where the prince had fought the battle in 1240 that earned him the title Alexander of the Neva (Nevsky), though the famous battle actually took place some 20 km (12 mi) away. Alexander Nevsky had been buried in Vladimir, but in 1724, on Peter's orders, his remains were transferred to the monastery that was founded in his honor.

Entrance to the monastery is through the archway of the elegant **Gate Church,** built by Ivan Starov in 1783–85. The walled pathway is flanked by two cemeteries, whose entrances are located a short walk down the path. To the left lies the older Lazarus Cemetery. The list of famous people buried here reads like a catalog of St. Petersburg architecture and includes Quarenghi, Rossi, Voronikhin, and Thomas de Thomon. The cemetery also contains the tombstone of the father of Russian science, Mikhail Lomonosov. The **Tikhvin Cemetery,** on the opposite side, is the final resting place of a number of St. Petersburg's great literary and musical figures. The grave of Fyodor Dostoyevsky, located in the northwestern corner, is easily identified by the tombstone's sculpture, which portrays the writer with his flowing beard. Continuing along the path you'll soon reach the composers' corner, where Rimsky-Korsakov, Mussorgsky, Borodin, and Tchaikovsky are buried. The compound includes an exhibition hall with temporary exhibits of "urban sculpture."

Having pondered St. Petersburg's cultural legacy, return to the path and cross the bridge spanning the quaint **Monastyrka Canal.** As you enter the monastery grounds, the **Church of the Annunciation** greets you on your left (under renovation). The red-and-white rectangular church was designed by Domenico Trezzini and built between 1717 and 1722. The Museum of City Sculpture inside contains models of St. Petersburg's architectural masterpieces as well as gravestones and other fine examples of memorial sculpture. Also in the church are several graves of 18th-century statesmen. The great soldier, Generalissimo Alexander Suvorov, who led the Russian army to numerous victories during the Russo-Turkish War (1768–74), is buried here under a simple marble slab that he purportedly designed himself. It reads simply: "Here lies Suvorov." Opposite the church, a shop sells religious items and souvenirs. ⊘ *Daily, 9:30–7:30; lunch break 1–2* PM.

Continuing along the same path, you'll reach the monastery's main cathedral, the **Troitsky Sobor** (Trinity Cathedral), which was one of the city's few churches allowed to function during the Soviet era. Designed by Ivan Starov and completed at the end of the 18th century, it stands out among the monastery's predominantly Baroque architecture for its monumental Classical design. Services are held here daily, and the church is open to the public from 6 AM until the end of the evening service around 7 PM. The magnificent interior, with its stunning gilded iconostasis, is worth a visit. The large central dome, adorned by frescoes designed by the great architect Quarenghi, seems to soar toward the heavens. It is in this church that the main relics of Alexander Nevsky are kept.

As you leave the church, go through the gate on the right. There is a door on the left with a simple inscription by hand, SVEZHY KHLEB. That is where the delicious bread baked on the premises can be bought. After the gate comes a courtyard and in the back of the church, a gate to yet another burial ground: **Nikolskoye kladbishche** (St. Nicholas Cemetery), opened in 1863 and one of the most prestigious burial grounds of the time; it's open daily, 9–8. It was decided in 1927 to close it down and the remains of prominent people buried there, including novelist Goncharov and composer Rubinstein, were transferred to the Volkovskoye Cemetery and the Necropolis of Masters of Arts (Tikhvin Cemetery). This pilferage of the tombs went on until the 1940s, by which time valuable funeral monuments had already been irremediably lost. As you reach the steps of the little yellow-and-white church in the center (which gave its name to the graveyard), take a turn right and walk to a derelict chapel of yellow brick, which has been turned into a makeshift **monument to Nicholas II,** the czar-martyr. Photocopies stand in for photographs of the Imperial family; pro-monarchy white, yellow, and black flags hang from the ceilings; and passionate adherents have added primitive frescoes to the scene. Nearby, in front of the Trinity church, is yet another final resting place on the lavra's grounds—the **Kommunisticheskaya Ploshchadka** (Communist Burial Ground), where, starting in 1919, defenders of Petrograd, victims of the Kronstadt rebellion, old bolsheviks, and prominent scientists, were buried. The last to receive that honor were people who took part in the Siege of Leningrad.

OFF THE
BEATEN PATH

CHESMENSKAYA TSERKOV – Surrounded by dreary Soviet high-rises in a remote residential area, this bright red-and-white-striped church is a delightful surprise. A rare example of pseudo-Gothic Russian architecture, the church was built to accompany the **Chesma Palace** (across the street), which served as a romantic staging post for the Imperial court en route to the summer palaces of Tsarskoye Selo (now Pushkin) and Pavlovsk. Catherine the Great renamed the palace (originally called

Kekerekeksinensky, which means "frog swamp" in Finnish) to commemorate the Russian naval victory at Chesma in the Aegean in 1770. Both buildings were constructed between 1774 and 1780 by Yuri Felten, designer of the famous Summer Gardens fence. The palace was rebuilt as a hospice in the 1830s by A. E. Shtaubert, upon instructions from Nicholas I, to house invalid veterans of the Patriotic War of 1812. The two wings that he attached to the main building destroyed the charm of the original equilateral triangle, and the rare toothed parapets were demolished. Today it is a unique training school for aircraft designers, but is in dire disrepair and just another example of what happens when one city has too many moldering landmarks to preserve. The church had been made into a branch of the city's Naval Museum, but is once again a place for services. Not far from the Pulkovskaya Hotel, the Chesma Church is within walking distance of the Moskovskaya subway stop; it is accessible as a regular church, but the palace remains closed to the general public. ✉ *12 ul. Lensoveta,* ☎ *812/293–6114.* ⊙ *Services at 10 AM.*

㉕ Anichkov most. Each corner of this beautiful bridge spanning the **Fontanka River** (the name means "Fountain") bears one of a quartet of exquisite equestrian statues. Designed by Peter Klodt and erected in 1841, the bronze sculptures depict phases of horse taming. Taken down and buried during World War II, the beautiful monuments were restored to their positions in 1945. The bridge was named for Colonel Mikhail Anichkov, whose regiment had built the first wooden drawbridge here. At that time, early in the 18th century, the bridge marked the city limits, and the job of its night guards was much the same as that of today's border guards, to carefully screen those entering the city. As you cross the bridge, pause for a moment to look back at No. 41, on the corner of Nevsky and the Fontanka. This was formerly the splendiferous **Palace of Prince Beloselsky-Belozersky**—a highly ornate neo-Baroque pile, its facade of blazing red stonework and whipped-cream stucco trim remains the most eye knocking in St. Petersburg. Finished in 1848 by Stackenschneider, who wanted to replicate Rastrelli's Stroganov Palace, this lavish building, once opulent inside and out, housed the local Communist Party headquarters during the Soviet era. Today it is the setting for classical music concerts. The interiors have unfortunately been largely destroyed and are no longer nearly as magnificent as the facades.

OFF THE
BEATEN PATH

BOAT RIDES – A float down the Neva or through the city's twisting canals is always a pleasant way to spend a summer afternoon. For trips through the canals, take one of the boats at the pier near Anichkov Bridge on Nevsky Prospect. Boats cruising the Neva leave from the pier outside the Hermitage Museum. Both boat trips have departures early morning to late afternoon from mid-May through mid-September. Smaller boats that you can hire on demand also leave from the Moika River, opposite Marsovo Pole, two steps away from the Spas na Krovi Church.

Anichkov Palace. This palace was named for the colonel whose regiment built the **Anichkov most.** It was built by Empress Elizabeth for her lover, Alexei Razumovsky, between 1741 and 1750. As if to continue the tradition, Catherine the Great later gave it to one of her many favorites, Grigory Potemkin. An able statesman and army officer, Potemkin is famous for his attempts to deceive Catherine about conditions in the Russian south. He had fake villages put up for her to view as she passed by during her 1787 tour of the area. The term "Potemkin village" has come to mean any impressive facade that hides an ugly interior.

The Anichkov Palace was originally designed by Mikhail Zemtsov and completed by Bartolomeo Francesco Rastrelli. The building has undergone a number of changes, and little now remains of the elaborate Baroque facade. This was once a suburban area, which explains why its main entrance faces the Fontanka rather than Nevsky, where there is only a side entrance. Today it houses the Youth Palace (once the Pioneer Palace), which offers activities for young people.

Armenian Church. This blue-and-white church set back from the street was built by Velten between 1771 and 1780. A fine example of the early Classical style, the church fell into disrepair and is now under full restoration, but it is holding some services and is open to the public. ✉ *Nevsky Prospect, between 40 and 42.*

Church of St. Catherine. Built between 1762 and 1783 by Vallin de la Mothe and Antonio Rinaldi, it is done in a mixture of the Baroque and the Classical, styles that were then converging in Russia. The grave of the last king of Poland (and yet another lover of Catherine the Great), Stanislaw Poniatowski, is here. St. Catherine's is one more sanctuary that was given back to its original function at the beginning of the '90s; Services are held in a chapel at the back while restoration continues. ✉ *34 Nevsky Prospect.*

28 **Dom Knigi** (House of Books). The city's largest bookstore still goes by its generic Soviet name. Before the revolution, it was the offices of the Singer Sewing Machine Company, whose distinctive globe trademark still adorns the roof. Here one finds Peterburgers in a favorite pursuit, perusing and buying books. ✉ *28 Nevsky Prospect.* ☉ *Mon.–Sat. 9– 8; Sun. 11–7.*

Gorodskaya Duma (City Duma). This building with a notable red-and-white tower was the city hall under the czars. Its clock tower, meant to resemble those in European cities, was erected by Ferrari between 1799 and 1804. It was equipped with signaling devices that sent messages between the Winter Palace and the royal summer residences. ✉ *1 ul. Dumskaya.*

27 **Gostinny Dvor.** Taking up an entire city block, this is St. Petersburg's answer to the GUM department store in Moscow. Initially constructed by Rastrelli in 1757, it was not completed until 1785, by Vallin de la Mothe, who was responsible for the facade with its two tiers of arches. When it was erected, traveling merchants were routinely put up in guest houses (called *gostinny dvor*), which, like this one, doubled as places for doing business. This arcade was completely rebuilt in the 19th century, by which time it housed some 200 general-purpose shops that were far less elegant than those in other parts of the Nevsky. It remained a functional bazaar until alterations in the 1950s and 1960s connected most of its separate shops into St. Petersburg's largest department store. Gostinny Dvor is undergoing what Russians call "capital" repairs and, tellingly enough enough, fashionable boutiques are opening on the second floor, while Carroll's, one of the city's biggest fast-food chains, has taken over almost the entire ground floor along Nevsky. Virtually across the street is the city's other major "department store," also an arcade, called **Passazh** (Passage) and built in 1848.

NEED A BREAK?

Nevsky Prospect 40 offers a soothing place to take a break. It is a German venture and includes a restaurant and bar. The wood-paneled interior and parquet ceilings have been restored to their original, prerevolutionary appearance. Coffee, ice cream, and scrumptious cakes are available in a no-smoking environment (in the restaurant part, through the left entrance).

OFF THE
BEATEN PATH

KIROVSKY PARK ON YELAGIN OSTROV – Yelagin Ostrov (island) is named after its 18th-century aristocratic owner. The park covers most of the island and has an open-air theater, boating stations, a beach, and the Yelagin Palace, designed by Carlo Rossi for Alexander I, who then presented it to his mother, Catherine the Great. The palace contains a number of fine rooms, including the Porcelain Room, beautifully decorated with painted stucco by Antonio Vighi, and the Oval Hall. If you walk along Primorsky Prospekt for about 1 km (½ mi) to the *strelka* (spit), you can catch a view of the sunset over the Gulf of Finland. To reach the park, take the subway to the Chyornaya Rechka station, then take any tram on Savushkina street (i.e., heading West) and get off at the Buddhist temple. As you reach the embankment, you will see a bridge to the island. ✉ *4 Yelagin Ostrov,* ☎ *812/239-1411.* ◷ *Wed.–Sun. 10–6.*

RAILWAY MUSEUM – Farther down Sadovaya, this museum displays Russia's railroad history. Complete with moving model trains, this museum is a hit with kids and parents alike. ✉ *50 ul. Sadovaya,* ☎ *812/315-1476.* ▨ *Free.* ◷ *Sun.–Thurs. 11–5:30. Closed last Thurs. of month.*

㉙ **Kazansky Sobor** (Kazan Cathedral). Czar Paul I commissioned this magnificent cathedral after a visit to Rome, wishing to copy—and perhaps present the Orthodox rival to—that city's St. Peter's. Erected between 1801 and 1811 from design by Andrei Voronikhin, the huge cathedral is approached through a monumental, semicircular colonnade. Inside and out, the church abounds with sculpture and decoration. On the prospect side the frontage holds statues of St. John the Baptist and the apostle Andrew as well as such sanctified Russian heroes as Vladimir and Alexander Nevsky. Take note of the enormous bronze front doors. They are exact copies of Ghiberti's Gates of Heaven at Florence's Baptistery.

In 1932 the cathedral, which was closed right after the Revolution, was turned into the Museum of Religion and Atheism, with emphasis on the latter. The history of religion was presented from the Marxist point of view, essentially as an ossified archaeological artifact. The museum still operates here, in one half of the church (it has dropped the "Atheism" from its name, but it remains an odd sight, needless to say). It is due to move to new premises opposite the main post office (the *pochtamt*) at a future date. As for the cathedral proper, it is again open as a place of worship; on March 29, 1998, it was solemnly rededicated by Vladimir, Metropolitan of St. Petersburg and Ladoga.

Back outside the church, have a look at the square that forms its front lawn. At each end are statues of a military leader, at one end, one of Mikhail Barclay de Tolly, at the other, Mikhail Kutuzov. They reflect the value placed in the 19th century on the cathedral as a place of military tribute, especially following Napoléon's invasion in 1812. Kutuzov is buried in the cathedral's northern chapel, where he is supposed to have prayed before taking command of the Russian forces. ✉ *2 Kazanskaya Pl.,* ☎ *812/311–0495 or 812/312–3586.* ▨ *Museum 18 rubles.* ◷ *Mon., Tues., Thurs., Fri. 11–6; weekends 12:30–6 (kassa open until 5). The church is open daily 8:30–8 and services are held weekdays at 8:30 AM and 5 PM, weekends and holidays at 9 AM and 5 PM.*

Lutheran Church. Designed by Alexander Bryullov in 1833 to replace an older church that had become too small, this church follows the Romanesque tradition of rounded arches and simple towers. It suffered the same fate as the giant Cathedral of Christ Our Savior in Moscow: During the years when religion was repressed, it was converted into a municipal swimming pool. Now, the upper floor is once again a church full of light. Farther down, at No. 20, is the **Dutch Church** (currently a library), yet another reminder of the many denominations that once peacefully coexisted in old St. Petersburg.

★ ㉒ **Nevsky Prospect.** St. Petersburg's Champs-Élysées, Nevsky Prospect was laid out in 1710, making it one of the city's first streets. Just short of 5 km (3 mi) long, beginning and ending at different bends of the Neva River, St. Petersburg's most famous street starts at the foot of the Admiralty building and runs in a perfectly straight line to the Moscow Railway Station, where it curves slightly before ending a short distance farther at the Alexander Nevsky Lavra, or monastery. Because St. Petersburg was once part of the larger lands of Novgorod, the road linking them was known as Great Novgorod Road, and trade and transport traveled over it. By the time Peter the Great built the first Admiralty, however, another major road clearly was needed to connect the Admiralty directly to the shipping hub. It was decided to begin the new avenue at the Admiralty. Originally this new street was called the Great Perspective Road, and later, the Nevsky Perspektiv, and finally Nevsky Prospect.

On the last few blocks of Nevsky Prospect are a few buildings of historical importance. No. 18, on the right-hand side, is the **Literary Café.** Originally a private dwelling, Kotomin's house, it subsequently held a café called Wulf and Beranger. Reportedly, it was here that Pushkin ate his last meal before setting off for his fatal duel (☞ Dining, *below*). Called **Chicherin's House,** No. 15 was one of Empress Elizabeth's palaces before becoming the Nobles' Assembly and, in 1919, the House of Arts. Farther down, at No. 14, is one of the rare buildings on Nevsky Prospect built *after* the Bolshevik Revolution. The blue sign on the facade dates from World War II and the siege of Leningrad; it warns pedestrians that during air raids the other side of the street is safer. The city was once covered with similar warnings; this one was left in place as a memorial.

OFF THE
BEATEN PATH

PUSHKIN APARTMENT MUSEUM – In this rental building (which, at the end of the 18th century, had been the palace of Prince Volkhonsky) the beloved Russian poet Alexander Pushkin died on January 27, 1837, after fighting a duel to defend his wife's honor. He actually lived at this address less than a year and the apartment/museum has been restored to give it the appearance of an upper-middle-class dwelling typical of the beginning of the 19th century. Pushkin had a family of six to support with his writing, so it's no surprise to learn that his apartment was actually less luxurious than it looks now. Although few of the furnishings are authentic, his personal effects (including the waistcoat he wore during the duel) and those of his wife are on display. The library, where Pushkin actually expired, has been rebuilt according to sketches made by his friend and fellow poet, Vasily Zhukovsky, who was holding vigil in his last hours. A moving account leads you through the apartment and retells the events leading up to the poet's death. The museum is a short walk from the corner of Nevsky Prospect and the Moika embankment. ✉ *Nab. Moiki, 12,* ☎ *812/314–0006.* 🎟 *12 rubles; recorded tape in English, German, or French for an extra 15 rubles.* ☉ *Wed.–Mon. 10:30–5. Closed last Fri. of month.*

KONYUSHENNAYA CHURCH – Since you have seen Pushkin's deathbed, you should not miss the small church around the corner, where his funeral was held on February 1, 1837. Coming out of Moika 12, turn right, and right again at the bridge, to have the Imperial stables and the Konyushennaya square on your left. The door to the left of the passageway in the central portion of the stables is the entrance to the church. Pushkin's funeral was held there, some say to keep it low profile (Pushkin had had sympathy for the Decembrists and the church was too small for a big crowd to attend), some say as a special favor from Emperor Nicholas I, since the church was attached to the Palace and not open to the public. Built in 1816–23 by Stassov, its coziness, light, and warmth make it a very tranquil stop. ⊠ *1 Konyushennaya Pl.. ⊙ Daily 9–7.*

㉔ **Ploshchad Vosstaniya** (Insurrection Square). Originally called Znamenskaya Ploshchad (Square of the Sign) after a church of the same name that stood on it, the plaza was the site of many revolutionary speeches and armed clashes with military and police forces—hence its second name. Like Decembrists' Square, it's now officially back to its first name, but it's still unusual to hear it called that. (The subway station of the same name hasn't changed.) The busy Moscow Railroad Station is here, and from this point, the street is lined with almost every imaginable kind of shop, from fruit markets to art salons to bookstores. A stroll here is not a casual affair, for Nevsky is almost always teeming with bustling crowds of shoppers and street artists. Budding entrepreneurs, who sell their wares on the sidewalk on folding tables, further obstruct pedestrian traffic. Here you will also see an increasingly rare sight, the old men of the Great Patriotic War (the Russian name for World War II) still proudly wearing their medals.

OFF THE
BEATEN PATH

PISKARYEVSKOYE KLADBISHCHE – The extent of this city's suffering during the 900-day siege between 1941 and 1944 becomes clear after a visit to the sobering Piskaryevskoye Cemetery. Located on the northeastern outskirts of the city, the field here was used, out of necessity, as a mass burial ground for the hundreds of thousands of World War II victims, some of whom died from the shelling, but most of them from cold and starvation. The numbingly endless rows of common graves carry simple slabs indicating the year in which those below them died. In all, nearly 500,000 people are buried here, and individual graves were an impossibility. The cemetery, with its memorial monuments and an eternal flame, serves as a deeply moving historical marker. Inscribed on the granite wall at the far end of the cemetery is the famous poem by radio personality Olga Bergholts, which ends with the oft-repeated phrase, "No one is forgotten, nothing is forgotten." The granite pavilions at the entrance house a small museum with photographs and memoirs documenting the siege. (Start with the one on the right side; the pavilions are open until 5 and admission is free.) On display is Tanya Savicheva's diary, scraps of paper on which the young schoolgirl recorded the death of every member of her family. The last entry reads, "May 13. Mother died. Everyone is dead. Only I am left." (Later, she too died as a result of the war.) Visiting this cemetery today gives you a taste of what the current rupture of the subway line 1 means for the locals: Go to Lesnaya stop, then follow the crowd and take the free shuttle bus 80 to Ploshchad Muzhevstva subway station (which the transit authority promised to reconnect to the rest of the network by the year 2000); there, walk back 20 yards to the other side of the avenue and take regular Bus 123 to the cemetery. On the way back, Bus 123 will leave you at the exact same bus stop where you will board Bus 80 to Lesnaya. A moving context for a visit to this cemetery is provided by the *Blockade Diary* of Lidya Ginzburg (Harvill Press, 1995). ⊠ *74 Nepokorennykh,* ☎ *812/247–5716.*

RIMSKY-KORSAKOV MUSEUM – From Insurrection Square (Ploshchad Vosstania) go south and west to Vladimirsky, then to Zagorodny Prospect where you'll find this small museum. Classical concerts are held twice a week in the small concert hall of the composer's former home. ⊠ *28 Zagorodny Prospect, Apt. 39,* ☎ *812/113-3208.* 🎫 *20 rubles. ⊙ Wed.–Sun. 11–6. Closed last Fri. of month.*

26 **Pushkin Drama Theater.** The most imposing building on **Ploshchad Os-trovskovo** (Ostrovsky Square, although you may hear it referred to as Ploshchad Alexandrinskaya) was originally named the Alexandrinsky Theater (for the wife of Nicholas I) and built in Classical style between 1828 and 1832. Six Corinthian columns adorn the Nevsky facade. Apollo's chariot dominates the building, with statues of the muses Ter-pischore and Melpomene to keep him company. In the small garden in front of the theater stands the **Catherine Monument,** which shows the empress towering above the principal personalities of her famous reign. Depicted on the pedestal are Grigory Potemkin, Generalissimo Suvorov, the poet Gavril Derzhavin, and others. Among the bronze fig-ures is the Princess Dashkova, who conspired against her own sister's lover—who just happened to be Catherine's husband, Peter III—to help the empress assume the throne.

Russian National Library. Opened in 1814 as the Imperial Public Library, it was Russia's first built for that purpose and today is known fondly as the "Publichka." It has over 20 million books and claims to have a copy of every book ever printed in Russia. Among its treasures are Voltaire's personal library and the only copy of *Chasovnik* (1565), the second book printed in Russia. The building comprises three sections. The main sec-tion, on the corner of Nevsky Prospect and Sadovaya ulitsa, was designed by Yegor Sakolov and built between 1796 and 1801. The wing nearest you, built between 1828 and 1832, was designed by Carlo Rossi as an integral part of Ostrovsky Square. True to the building's purpose, the facade is adorned with statues of philosophers and poets, including Homer and Virgil, and the Roman goddess of wisdom, Minerva.

32 **Smolny.** Confusion abounds when you mention the Smolny, for you can mean either the beautiful Baroque church and convent or the clas-sically designed institute that went down in history as the Bolshevik headquarters in the 1917 Revolution. It doesn't help matters much that the two architectural complexes are right next door to each other, on the Neva's left bank. Construction of the Smolny Convent and Cathe-dral began under Elizabeth I and continued during the reign of Cather-ine the Great, who established a school for the daughters of the nobility within its walls. The centerpiece of the convent is the magnificent five-domed **Cathedral of the Resurrection,** which was designed by Bartolomeo Rastrelli. Some say it is his greatest creation. At first glance, the highly ornate blue-and-white cathedral seems to have leapt off the pages of a fairy tale. Its five white onion domes, crowned with gilded globes supporting crosses of gold, convey a sense of magic and power. Begun by Rastrelli in 1748, the cathedral was not completed until the 1830s, by the architect Vasily Stasov. It is now open to the public, but few traces of the original interior have survived. It is currently used for con-certs, notably of Russian sacred music, and rather insignificant exhibits. For an admission fee, you can also climb up the tower for beautiful views of the city. ⊠ *3/1 Pl. Rastrelli,* ☎ *812/271–9421 guided tours, 812/271–9182 box office.* ⊠ *Free; $2. to cathedral tower.* ☉ *Fri.– Wed. 11–4:30.*

The **Smolny Institute,** just south of the cathedral, is a far different struc-ture. Designed by Giacomo Quarenghi in 1806–08, the Classical building was done in the style of an imposing country manor. The Smolny Institute will long be remembered by the Russian people as the site where Lenin and his associates planned the overthrow of the Kerensky gov-ernment in October 1917. Lenin lived at the Smolny for 124 days. The rooms in which he resided and worked are now a memorial museum. Today the building houses the offices of the mayor of St. Petersburg and can be visited only by special request. ⊠ *1 Proletarskoy Diktatury,*

☎ 812/276–1461. ▨ *20 rubles.* ⊙ *Lenin memorial museum: week-days 10–5 on appointment (call at least a day in advance).*

㉚ **Stroganov Palace.** This palace, completed in 1754, is an outstanding example of the Russian Baroque and one of Rastrelli's finest achievements. Its entrance is unique, in that it faces Nevsky Prospect. Above the archway you still see the family coat of arms: two sables holding a shield with a bear's head above. It symbolizes the Stroganovs' source of wealth—vast holdings of land, with all its resources, including furs—in Siberia. You can go into the courtyard and even peek inside, for there is a small branch of the applied arts section of the Russian Museum operating here; the renovation is extensive but far from complete. Unfortunately, most of the palace's interior was ravaged by fire at the end of the 18th century, though the outside remained intact. Before you leave, you may find it amusing to remember that this was the birthplace of beef Stroganov.

㉝ **Taurida Palace** (Tavrichesky Dvorets). Built in 1783–89 on the orders of Catherine the Great for her court favorite, Count Grigory Potemkin, the palace is one of St. Petersburg's most magnificent buildings. Potemkin had been given the title of the Prince of Taurida for his annexation of the Crimea (ancient Taurida) to Russia. The Taurida Palace is a splendid example of Classicism, the main trend in Russian architecture in the late 18th century. The luxurious interior decor contrasts with its modest exterior. For a long period after Potemkin's death the palace remained inhabited. Later, in 1906 it was partially rebuilt for the State Duma, Russia's parliament. During the February Revolution of 1917 the Taurida Palace became a center of revolutionary events. Today the palace is used for international conferences and meetings, and houses the Interparliamentary Assembly of the Commonwealth of Independent States (CIS). It is not open to the public. ✉ *47 Shpalernaya ul.*

Ulitsa Zodchevo Rossi. Once world famous as "Theater Street," this thoroughfare has extraordinary proportions. It is bounded by two buildings of exactly the same height, its width (72 ft) equals the height of the buildings, and its length is exactly 10 times its width. A complete view unfolds only at the end of the street, where it meets Lomonosov Square. The perfect symmetry is reinforced by the identical facades of the two buildings, which are painted the same subdued yellow and decorated with impressive white pillars. One of the buildings here is the legendary **Vaganova Ballet School** (founded in 1738), whose pupils included Karsavina as well as Pavlova, Nijinsky, Ulanova, Baryshnikov, and Nureyev.

Yeliseyevsky Food Emporium. The name has finally been returned to this famous store, after having been officially called Gastronome No. 1 under the Communists. It is located directly across the street from the Catherine Monument. Built at the turn of the century for the immensely successful grocer, Yeliseyev, it is decorated in the style of early Art Nouveau, with colorful stained-glass windows, gilded ceilings, and brass chandeliers. Before the revolution it specialized in imported delicacies, and after several lean decades, goods again overflow its shelves. (The Moscow branch is on Tverskaya ulitsa.) ✉ *56 Nevsky Prospect.*

OFF THE **ANNA AKHMATOVA LITERARY MUSEUM** – Opened in 1989, the museum
BEATEN PATH is located in the former palace of the Count Sheremetyev and is accessible either from 53 Liteyny Prospect or from the Fontanka, through the palace hall and the garden. The famous St. Petersburg poet lived for many years in a communal apartment in a wing of the palace. Born in 1888 in Odessa, she was published for the first time in 1910. She did not leave Petrograd after the October Revolution, but remained silent be-

tween 1923 and 1940. She died in 1966 and is remembered as one of the greatest successors to Pushkin. ✉ *34 nab. Fontanki,* ☎ *812/272–2211 or 812/272–5895.* 💰 *12 rubles.* ⊙ *Tues.–Sun. 10:30–5:30. Closed last Wed. of month.*

On the Road to the Summer Gardens: From the Square of the Arts to the Field of Mars

This walk takes you to some of St. Petersburg's prettiest inner streets, squares, and gardens, starting at Ploshchad Iskusstv (Square of the Arts). Along the route are several squares and buildings of historical interest: It was in this area of the city that several extremely important events in Russian history took place, including the murder of czars Paul I, who was assassinated in the Mikhailovsky Castle by nobles opposed to his rule, and of Alexander II, killed when a handmade bomb was lobbed at him by revolutionary terrorists as he was riding in a carriage along the Griboyedov Canal.

A Good Walk

Go down Nevsky Prospect to ulitsa Mikhailovskaya, opposite Gostinny Dvor. Walking up this short street will take you past the handsome Grand Hotel Europe, built in the 1870s, and given its Art Nouveau facade in 1910. It remains one of St. Petersburg's most elegant lodging places. Straight up this street is **Mikhailovsky Dvorets** ㉞, at the far end of Ploshchad Iskusstv. The building to the right of the palace appears to be an extension of its right wing but is a different building entirely; it is the **Ethnography Museum.**

If you stand in front of the palace and turn to survey the entire square, the first building on your right, with old-fashioned lanterns adorning its doorways, is the **Maly Theater** ㉟. The next one, No. 3, is the **Isaac Brodsky Museum.** Bordering the square's south side, on Mikhailovskaya ulitsa's east corner, is the former Nobles' club, now the **Philarmonia** ㊱, home to the St. Petersburg Philharmonic. The buildings on the square's remaining side are former residences and school buildings, including a special school, funded and staffed since perestroika by the **Russian Museum** ㊲, for pupils interested in history and culture. One of the entrances to the museum is around the corner, through **Korpus Benois.** To find it, leave the Square of the Arts and go down ulitsa Inzhenernaya toward the Griboyedov (Ekaterininsky) Canal. Take a right and you find the entrance a few steps away. Go right when you leave the museum, and straight ahead is the almost outrageously colorful **Khram Spasa na Krovi** ㊳.

To the right as you walk past the church is a small park behind a lovely wrought-iron fence. Known as Mikhailovsky Sad (Mikhail Garden), it forms the back of Grand Duke Mikhail's former estate. On the other side of this pleasant park runs Sadovaya ulitsa. Follow the street you're on, however, as it curves around gently to the right. Opposite the gardens, across the street, spreads **Marsovo Pole** ㊴.

The long line of buildings flanking the left side of Marsovo Pole are the former Barracks of the Pavlovsky Guards Regiment. They were completed in 1819, in homage to the regiment's victories in the war against Napoléon. Go down this side of the street, and you will reach Millionaya ulitsa (Millionaire's Street), which, as the name implies, was once one of St. Petersburg's swankest addresses.

On this street, in front of you, is the **Mramorny Dvorets** ㊵, a noted governmental palace. Take a right and walk down Millionaya ulitsa the length of the Field of Mars. On the left you pass **Suvorovskaya**

Ploshchad ㊶. Walk up to the river and continue going east (right). Very soon you will find yourself in front of the marvelous grille that marks the entrance to **Letny Sad** ㊷, the Yuri Felten–designed summer gardens. You enter at the far left end of the railing. Exiting at the south end of the park will bring you out in front of the former castle of Czar Paul I, across the street, the **Inzhenerny Zamok** ㊸. The tour ends here. From the castle, you can walk down ulitsa Sadovaya until it intersects with Nevsky Prospect. If you take the first right off it, you will return to the Square of the Arts. If you like, you can stop in the Mikhail Garden now; there is an entrance on this side, to the right.

TIMING

Including stops, this walk should take between two and three hours. Letny Sad, Mikhailovsky Sad, and Marsovo Pole are worth visiting at any time of the year. Note that the Neva is very close here and it is windy year-round.

Sights to See

Ethnography Museum. This museum contains a fascinating collection of applied art and many sociological displays about peoples of the 19th and 20th centuries, including the various ethnic groups of the former Soviet Union. ✉ *4/1 Inzhenernaya ul.,* ☎ *812/219–4320.* 🎫 *$3.50.* 🕐 *Tues.–Sun. 11–6. Closed last Fri. of month.*

㊸ **Inzhenerny Zamok** (Engineer's Castle). This orange-hued building belonged to one of Russia's stranger and more pitiful leaders. Paul I grew up in the shadow of his powerful mother, Catherine the Great, whom he despised; no doubt correctly, he held her responsible for his father's death. By the time Paul became czar, he lived in terror that he, too, would be murdered. He claimed that, shortly after ascending the throne, the Archangel Michael appeared to him in a dream and instructed him to build a church on the site of his birthplace (hence the other name of this landmark: Mikhailovsky Castle, not to be confused with the Mikhailovsky Palace). Paul then proceeded to erect not just a church but a castle, which he tried to make into an impenetrable fortress. Out of spite toward his mother, he took stones and other materials from castles that she had built. The Fontanka and Moika rivers cut off access from the north and east; and for protection everywhere else, he installed secret passages, moats with drawbridges, and earthen ramparts. All of Paul's intricate planning, however, came to naught. On March 24, 1801, a month after he began living there, he was murdered—suffocated with a pillow in his bed. Historians speculate that his own son, Alexander I, knew such a plot was underway and may even have participated. After Paul's death, the castle stood empty for 20 years, then was turned over to the Military Engineering Academy. One of the school's pupils was Fyodor Dostoyevsky, who as a novelist was absorbed with themes of murder and greed. Since 1991, the building has belonged to the Russian Museum (☞ *below*), which has been renovating the chapel, the grand staircase, and the rooms of Grand Dukes Nicholas and Konstantin Pavlovich; it houses a collection of formal portraits from the 18th to the early 19th centuries. ✉ *2 Sadovaya ul.,* ☎ *812/210–4173.* 🎫 *48 rubles.* 🕐 *Mon. 10–5, Wed.–Sun. 10–6 (kassa open until 1 hr before closing time).*

NEED A BREAK?

The **Grand Hotel Europe** has a lovely mezzanine café, where you can relax and enjoy a pot of tea or a glass of champagne, served with bowls of strawberries. While there, take a peek at the beautifully renovated Art Nouveau lobby, replete with stained-glass windows and antique furnishings.

Isaac Brodsky Museum. This structure was built in the 1820s for the Golenishchev-Kutuzovs, a high-ranking military family. The painter Isaac Brodsky lived here from 1924 to 1939, and it is now a memorial museum to him. On view are some of his works as well as some from his private collection, which included pieces by Ilya Repin and Valentin Serov. ✉ *3 Pl. Iskusstv,* ☎ *812/314–3658.* ☉ *Wed.–Sun. 11–7.*

OFF THE BEATEN PATH	**JACQUOT'S HOUSE** – No. 5 Ploshchad Iskusstv had a famous café cum art salon in its basement from 1911 to 1915, called the Stray Dog. A diverse range of painters, writers, and musicians, including Anna Akhmatova, Nikolai Gumilev, and Osip Mandelstam, used it as a creative meeting point.

★ ❸❽ **Khram Spasa na Krovi** (Church of the Saviour on the Spilled Blood). The highly ornate, old Russian style seems more befitting to Moscow than St. Petersburg, where the architecture is generally more subdued and subtle; indeed, the architect Alfred Parland was consciously aiming to copy Moscow's St. Basil's. The drama of the circumstances leading to the church's inception more than matches the frenzy of its design, however. It was commissioned by Alexander III to memorialize the shocking death of his father, Alexander II, who was killed on the site in 1881 by a terrorist's bomb.

The church opened in 1907 but was closed by Stalin in the 1930s. It suffered damage over time, especially throughout World War II. After meticulous reconstruction for decades (painstaking attempts have been made to replace all original components with identically matched materials), it finally reopened in 1997. The interiors are as extravagant as the exterior, with glittering stretches of mosaic from floor to ceiling (70,000 square ft in total). Stone carvings and gold leaf adorn the walls, the floors are of pink Italian marble, and the remarkable altar is made entirely of semiprecious gems and supported by four jasper columns. Blinded by all this splendor, you nearly overlook the painted scenes of martyrdom, including one that draws a parallel between the czar's death and the crucifixion of Christ. You can also see a small exhibit dedicated to Alexander II in an annex of the church; head to the other side of the bridge over the canal. ✉ *Kanal Griboyedova, 2a,* ☎ *812/315–1636.* ▣ *100 rubles (the kassa for foreigners is inside the church); exhibit on Alexander II, 20 rubles.* ☉ *Thurs.–Tues. 11–7 (admittance until 6).*

★ ❹❷ **Letny Sad** (Summer Garden). Inspired by Versailles, the Summer Garden was another of Peter the Great's passions. When first laid out in 1704, it was given the regular, geometric style made famous by Louis XIV's gardener, Andre Le Nôtre, and decorated with statues and sculptures as well as with imported trees and plants. Grottoes, pavilions, ponds, fountains, and intricate walkways were placed throughout, and the grounds are bordered on all sides by rivers and canals. In 1777, however, disastrous floods did so much damage (entirely destroying the system of fountains) that the Imperial family stopped using the garden for entertaining. When they decamped for environs farther afield, they left the Summer Garden for use by the upper classes. Today it is a popular park accessible to everyone, but you will have to imagine the first formal garden, for it is no longer there. The graceful wrought-iron fence that marks the entrance to the garden was designed in 1779 by Yuri Felten, and is supported by pink granite pillars decorated with vases and urns.

Just inside this southeastern corner is Peter's original Summer Palace, **Letny Dvorets.** Designed by Domenico Trezzini and completed in

1714, the two-story building is quite simple in design, as most of Peter's dwellings were. The walls are of stucco-covered brick, painted primrose yellow. Open since 1934 as a museum, it has survived without major alteration. Two other attractive buildings nearby are the **Coffee House** (built by Rossi in 1826) and the **Tea House** (by L. I. Charlemagne in 1827), neither of which, alas, serves the beverage for which it is named.

As you walk through the park, have a look at some of its statues, of which more than 80 still exist. You can see *Peace and Abundance*, sculpted in 1722 by Pietro Baratta, an allegorical depiction of Russia's victory in the war with Sweden. Another statue, just off the main alley, is of Ivan Krylov, "Russia's La Fontaine." It is by Peter Klodt (who also did the Anichkov Bridge horse statues) and was unveiled in 1855. Scenes from Krylov's fables, including his version of "The Fox and the Grapes," appear on the pedestal. As in many other parks and public places, the sculptures are protected from the harsh weather by wooden covers from early fall to late spring. There is an admission fee to the park on weekends in the summer.

㉟ Maly Theater (Little Theater). This historic theater is better known as the Maly, the name given it during the Communist era. Before the Revolution it was the Mikhailovsky Theater, but French companies performed here so often that it was more commonly referred to as the French Theater. Since 1991 it is officially the **Mussorgsky Theater of Opera and Ballet,** St. Petersburg's second most important theater, after the Mariinsky (Kirov).

★ **㊲ Marsovo Pole** (Field of Mars). The site was once a marsh, from which both the Mya and the Krikusha rivers began. Peter the Great had it drained (and the rivers linked by a canal), and the space was subsequently used for parades and public occasions. The field acquired its present name around 1800, when it began to be used primarily for military exercises. Shortly after 1917 it was turned into a burial ground for Red Army victims of the Revolution and ensuing civil war. The massive granite **Monument to Revolutionary Fighters** was unveiled here on November 7, 1919, with an eternal flame lit 40 years later, on the Revolution's anniversary.

㉞ Mikhailovsky Dvorets (Mikhailovsky Palace). The square in front of the palace was originally named Mikhailovsky Ploshchad for Grand Duke Mikhail Pavlovich (1798–1849), the younger brother of Alexander I and Nicholas I and resident of the palace. The square's appearance is the work of Carlo Rossi, who designed the facade of each building encircling it as well as the palace. Each structure, as well as the plaza itself, was made to complement Mikhail's residence on its north side. Built between 1819 and 1825, it comprises a principal house and two service wings. The central portico with eight Corinthian columns faces a large courtyard now enclosed by a fine Art Nouveau railing, a late (1903) addition. The statue of Alexander Pushkin in the center of the plaza was designed by Mikhail Anikushin and erected in 1957 (☞ *below,* under Russian Museum, for service information).

㊵ Mramorny Dvorets (Marble Palace). One of Catherine the Great's favorite palaces, this was designed for Count Grigori Orlov, one of the empress's more famous amours, by Arnoldo Rinaldi and built between 1768 and 1785. Its name derives from its pale pink-purple marble facing. From 1937 to 1991, it housed the Lenin Museum; in the courtyard was the armored automobile from which he made his revolutionary speech at the Finland Station. Today, instead of Lenin's automobile you can see an equestrian statue of Czar Alexander III first erected in 1909 on

Znamenskaya Ploshchad (by the Moscow railway station). The statue survived under the Soviets hidden in the Russian Museum's courtyard. The palace now belongs to the Museum (☞ *below*) and houses three main collections: On the second floor, you will find works by foreign artists who worked in Russia in the 18th and early 19th centuries, which will expand as renovation continues, as well as a collection of contemporary art by 33 artists (including Rauschenberg, Lichtenstein, and Warhol), donated to the Russian Museum by the world famous German collectors Peter and Irene Ludwig. You may also wish to have a look at the Marble Hall, covered with lazurite and marbles from the Urals, Northern Russia, and Italy; enjoy the superb views of *both* the Peter and Paul Fortress and the Engineer's Castle; check out the curious *Peter the Great as a child, saved by his mother from the fury of the Streltsy* by Ch. Steuben; and then head to the third floor. The gallery here is called "A museum in the museum"; it contains the collection of paintings and drawings by people like Puni, Altman, Tatlin, Malevich, and Matiushin, put together in 1918–22 for the MKhK (Museum of Fine Arts). Known in art history as leaders of the the Russian avant-garde movement called Constructivism, which developed on a par with French Cubists and other European movements of the early 20th century, these works were deemed politically incorrect under the Soviets and kept in storage until perestroika. A separate ticket is required for a guided tour of his private quarters (groups of 10 people maximum). ✉ *5/1 Millionnaya ul.,* ☎ *812/314–3448.* 🎟 *48 rubles.* ☉ *Mon. 10– 5, Wed.–Sun. 10–6 (kassa open until 1 hr before closing time); K. R. tour on weekdays except Tues. at noon and 3.*

❸❻ Philarmonia. The former private Nobles' Club is now home to the **St. Petersburg Philharmonic.** Its main concert hall, the Bolshoy Zal, with its impressive marble columns, has been the site of many celebrated performances, including the first presentation of Tchaikovsky's Sixth (*Pathetique*) Symphony, his final masterpiece, with the composer conducting. (He died nine days later.) More recently, in 1942, when Leningrad was completely blockaded, Dmitri Shostakovich's Seventh (*Leningrad*) Symphony premiered here, an event broadcast in the same spirit of defiance against the Germans in which it was written. Later the concert hall was officially named for this composer. A smaller hall, the Maly Zal, located on Nevsky, is also part of the Philarmonic complex and is named after Glinka.

★ ❸❼ Russian Museum. One of the country's most important art galleries has been housed in the Mikhailovsky Palace since 1898, when Nicholas II turned it into a museum. He did so in tribute to his father, Alexander III, who had a special regard for Russian art and regretted, after seeing Moscow's Tretyakov Gallery, that St. Petersburg had nothing like it. In 1991–92, the Marble Palace, the Engineer's Castle, and the Stroganov Palace became branches of the Russian Museum. On March 19, 1998, the museum celebrated its 100th anniversary with much pomp; a treasure gallery was inaugurated (guided tours only; you need a special ticket that you can get before noon) and it was announced that the "museification" of the Marble Palace and the Engineer's Castle would be completed by 2003, the 300th anniversary of the founding of St. Petersburg. Directors of major Moscow, New York, and Paris museums made the trip to St. Petersburg for the occasion.

Officially named the *Gosudarstvenny Muzey Russkovo Iskusstva* (State Museum of Russian Art), its collection is four times greater than Moscow's Tretyakov Gallery, with scores of masterpieces on display. Outstanding icons include the 14th-century *Boris and Gleb* and the 15th-century *Angel Miracle of St. George*. Seventeenth- and 18th-century paintings are also well represented, especially with portraiture. One of the most famous 18th-century works here is Ivan Nikitin's *The Field Hetman*. By far the most important cache, however, comprises 19th-century works—huge canvases by Repin, many fine portraits by Serov (his beautiful *Countess Orlova* and the equally beautiful, utterly different portrait of the dancer Ida Rubinstein), and Mikhail Vrubel's strange, disturbing *Demon Cast Down*. Since so little of this work was heretofore known in the West, it is fascinating to see the stylistic parallels and the incorporation of outside influences into a Russian framework. Painters of the World of Art movement—Bakst, Benois, and Somov—are also here. There are several examples of 20th-century art, with works by Kandinsky and Kazimir Malevich. Natan Altman's striking portrait of the poet Anna Akhmatova is in Room 77. The museum usually has at least one excellent special exhibit in place. ✉ *4/2 Inzhenernaya ul.*, ☎ *812/314–3448*, ᖴᴀX *812/314–4153.* 🎫 *48 rubles.* ◷ *Mon. 10–5, Wed.–Sun. 10–6 (kassa open until 1 hr before closing time.*

㊶ **Suvorovskaya Ploshchad** (Suvorov Square). In the middle of this square there is a statue of the military commander Alexander Suvorov, cast as Mars, god of war. Appropriately enough, when first unveiled in 1801, the statue stood in Marsovo Pole, but in 1818 it was moved to its present location.

OFF THE
BEATEN PATH

ST. PETERSBURG CIRCUS – Though perhaps not as famous as the Moscow Circus, the St. Petersburg Circus dates from 1867 and remains a popular treat for children. Avid young circus fans may get a kick out of its adjacent **Circus Art Museum** (☎ 812/210–4413), as well, with displays about the world of the circus. ✉ *3 nab. Fontanki*, ☎ *812/210–4198.* ◷ *Performances daily 7 PM; matinees at 11 AM and 3 PM on weekends. Museum weekdays only noon–6. Closed Mon. and Thurs.*

MONUMENT TO THE HEROES OF THE DEFENSE OF LENINGRAD DURING WORLD WAR II – You are likely to see this on the way from the airport or if you visit the Park Pobedy region. Financed and built by city residents, it faces the southern part of St. Petersburg, which saw the fiercest fighting. The center obelisk inside a broken ring symbolizes the breaking of the enemy blockade. Surrounding it are groups involved in the battles—sailors, partisans, soldiers, and people's volunteers. Underneath is a memorial hall museum. ✉ *Pl. Pobedy*, ☎ *812/293–6563.* 🎫 *Free.* ◷ *Thurs.–Tues. 11–5. Closed last Tues. of month.*

DINING

For those who knew Leningrad in the 1980s, few other aspects of the city have changed as radically as the restaurant scene. Not only do new places pop up constantly, but they can often include such erstwhile rare species as Chinese, Korean, or Japanese restaurants. Needless to say, prices have been going up—not just in rubles, but also in their dollar equivalent. Most restaurants are simply out of reach for the average Russian citizen, and when you inquire about a place, try to understand who patronizes it. The arrogance and the cellular telephone habit of "New" Russians can spoil a meal.

Remember that landing a table in a good restaurant is still not done on a whim: You must plan ahead. Reservations are almost always essential, especially in the evening, partly because there just aren't *that* many good places. You may have better luck if you ask your hotel or tour guide for help. Keep in mind that at restaurants featuring floor shows, dining out will be an all-night affair, involving drinking and dancing the night away. Although you may find it in poor taste, the entertainment usually entails exceptionally loud music (perennial favorites are played over and over again), colored disco-light shows, and scantily clad dancers. To boot, few restaurants offer no-smoking sections. Remember that most restaurants stop serving food between 11 and midnight, although some cater to all-night dancing.

Credit cards were on their way to becoming commonly accepted but the recent economic crisis and ruble devaluation has made credit card companies leery of extending privileges at many places; we list credit cards as taken before the crisis, but keep in mind it is difficult to find dining spots today which still extend credit card privileges. If paying in cash, remember that only rubles will be accepted. What follows is a sampling of old-era restaurants, well established post-perestroika eateries, and places that cater to foreigners; it is no longer possible to enumerate all of them. The under-$10 category does not offer much in terms of real restaurants anymore. You will find cafés that still accommodate small budgets at night, but don't expect them to offer a culinary experience.

CATEGORY	COST*
$$$$	over $40
$$$	$25–$40
$$	$10–$25
$	under $10

per person, excluding drinks and service

WHAT TO WEAR

Dress at the restaurants reviewed below is casual, unless noted otherwise.

$$$$ ✕ **Europe.** This elegant restaurant in the Grand Hotel Europe is in a
★ category all its own. It offers luxury and fine dining of a kind that St. Petersburg has not seen since before the 1917 Revolution. Like the dining room at the Metropole in Moscow, this has a breathtaking interior, complete with stained-glass roof and private balconies, and seems fit for a czar. But then, so do the prices. The menu, which features European and Russian cuisines, is exotic by local standards. For starters, try the fresh goose liver, served with a honey-and-wine sauce. The main dishes vary, but a highlight is the fillet of salmon, filled with cream cheese and served with a wine-and-herb sauce. If you're not up to an opulent dinner, you may enjoy the popular Sunday-morning Classic Brunch. Don't hesitate for long, though, because tables book up fast, especially in the summer. ✉ *1/7 Mikhailovskaya ul., in Grand Hotel Europe,* ☎ *812/329–6000. Reservations essential. Jacket and tie. AE, MC, V.*

$$$$ ✕ **Imperial.** This is the Nevsky Palace Hotel's swank restaurant, and whereas the Europe (☞ *above*) emphasizes Old World grandeur, the Imperial settles for sleek comfort. It, too, is a top-class spot, nicely nestled above Nevsky Prospect, so at some tables you can watch the Russian world go by. The changing dishes are strong on good Continental fare, with meat the house specialty: beef, pork, lamb, and chicken, all grilled with vegetables. In the evening there's a buffet, which includes an assortment of the meats on the menu. There's usually a jazz trio livening things up in the background. ✉ *57 Nevsky Prospect,* ☎ *812/275–2001. Reservations essential. Jacket and tie. AE, MC, V.*

$$$$ ✕ **Nevsky Melody.** This Russo-Swedish venture ranks among St. Petersburg's finest gourmet experiences. The menu is exquisite, the atmosphere is elegant, and the wine list is superb. The restaurant offers beautifully prepared Russo-European as well as Mexican dishes. The restaurant opens at 12, but stays open until 6 AM. ✉ *62 Sverdlovskaya nab.,* ☎ *812/227–1596. Jacket and tie. AE, MC, V.*

186

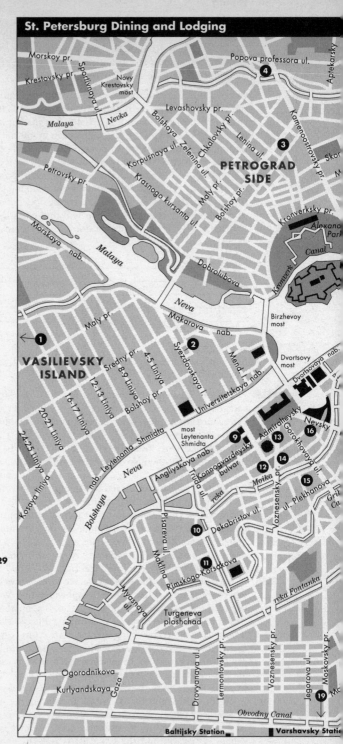

St. Petersburg Dining and Lodging

$$$$ ✕ **Senat Bar.** Housed in the famous Senate building, this delightful restaurant serves exquisite European cuisine in an elegant atmosphere highlighted by a stylized interior with crystal chandeliers and old-fashioned chairs. The menu, a mix of Russian and Continental dishes, offers up such appetizers as black and red caviar, crab, and spicy chicken in a walnut sauce. For a main course, try the excellent *Kievskaya kotleta* (chicken Kiev). The staff cultivates a high level of service and foreign visitors are always welcome. Excellent wines from France, Spain, Germany, and Argentina stock the extensive cellar, and there is a large choice of beers from Holland and Belgium. ✉ *1 ul. Galernaya,* ☎ *812/314–9253 or 812/314–4920. Reservations required. Jacket and tie. AE, MC, V.*

$$$ ✕ **Angleterre.** This pretty restaurant off the main lobby of the Astoria Hotel offers average food at above-average prices. Though it advertises European cuisine, the unimaginative menu is dominated by standard Russian dishes, such as borshch, herring, and beef stroganov. The food, once it actually makes it to your table, is quite good, if unsurprising. What the restaurant lacks in speed and innovation, however, it does make up for in atmosphere. The lovely all-white room is lit by crystal chandeliers, and light from the exquisite lobby outside also filters through its discreetly curtained glass walls. The piano music tinkling in the background is a carryover of the hotel's better days at the turn of the century. The restaurant also offers a popular buffet breakfast, which comes with all the blini you can eat and at a more reasonable prix fixe than the prices found on the lunch and dinner menus. The kitchen closes at 11 PM. ✉ *39 Bolshaya Morskaya ul.,* ☎ *812/210–5906. Reservations essential. AE, MC, V.*

$$$ ✕ **Aphrodite.** This Russo-Finnish restaurant has a decidedly Scandinavian slant, serving lots of fish and seafood along with equally interesting Russian dishes. Its two white rooms, graced with archways and filled with soft, filtered light, provide a soothing place to unwind after a day of touring. Talk is quiet (it's a good choice for dinner *à deux*), background music is light (Sinatra classics are a favorite), and service is attentive—even deferential. The amusingly eccentric array of appetizers includes smoked reindeer salad, oysters on the half shell, and warm frogs' legs. The excellent selection of fish dishes features salmon, sturgeon, turbot, and perch. You may want to try the red perch in paper with ginger and bacon or the wolffish in spices with vegetables. Heartier appetites can order a beefsteak but may want to try the rabbit stew or elk steak. The wine list is small but decent. ✉ *86 Nevsky Prospect,* ☎ *812/275–7620. AE, MC, V.*

$$$ ✕ **Austeria.** This restaurant inside the Peter and Paul Fortress actually dates from the reign of Peter the Great, though altered somewhat over the centuries. Originally an officer's club (hosteria), the restaurant continues to offer Russian cuisine in an 18th-century setting, now altered after renovation. Handcrafted cast-iron chandeliers provide the lighting while somber draperies typical of the era of Soviet "chic" have at last been retired. Specialties of the house include pancakes stuffed with mushroom and liver as an hors d'oeuvre and "Catherine's legs" (chicken legs stuffed with turkey and walnuts) as a signature entrée. The menu also offers a few fish dishes, including flounder. Service and music still need fine tuning, but the restaurant is altogether quite user-friendly for foreigners. The restaurant is located inside the fortress's outer fortification wall, a short walk to your left after entering through the Ivan Gate. Whatever you may be told, the Neva is *not* visible from where you eat. You can also drive in through the eastern entrance (by the gas station) and park in front of the restaurant. ✉ *St. John's Ravelin, Peter and Paul Fortress,* ☎ *812/238–4262. MC, V.*

$$$ ✕ **Brasserie.** This restaurant off a ground-floor wing of the Grand Hotel Europe is the perfect place for a refreshing Caesar salad or a well-prepared steak. The menu has some nice Russian standbys but aims toward bistro exotic—try the garlicky snails with tomato bread. There is always a satisfying plat du jour as well. The relaxed atmosphere is enhanced by the efficient and excellent service: Come to the Brasserie if the outside world has been getting you down. ✉ *1/7 Mikhailovskaya ul.,* ☎ *812/329–6000. AE, MC, V.*

$$$ ✕ **Dvoryanskoye Gnezdo** (Noblemans' Nest). Tucked away in the
★   garden pavilion of the amazing Yusupovsky Palace, this very chic spot is particularly attractive to the after-theater crowd—the Mariinsky is not far away—and the international set, who most often use the restaurant's English name. Formal attire matches its service, decor, and food, which is mainly of the European, French-influenced variety. You may be able to close your eyes and imagine the carriages waiting beyond the door. ✉ *21 ul. Dekabristov,* ☎ *812/312–3205. Reservations essential. Jacket and tie. AE, MC, V.*

$$$ ✕ **Kalinka.** In this restaurant on Vasilyevsky Island you can enjoy Russian cuisine with European service. Kalinka's excellent soups include solyanka, a spicy thick stew made with vegetables and meat or fish, and borshch. Kalinka recommends the *griby v smetane* (mushrooms baked in sour cream sauce) and blinis served with black or red caviar. ✉ *9 Syezdovskaya linya,* ☎ *812/218–2866. MC, V.*

$$ ✕ **Cat.** A popular café with the young and trendy, on a side street off Nevsky Prospect, it has Russian food all the same, solid and predictable. You may be better off dropping in at lunch, when it's a convenient place to unwind and recharge, and just order rounds of appetizers. ✉ *24 ul. Karavannaya,* ☎ *812/315–3800. MC, V.*

$$ ✕ **Chopsticks.** It doesn't seem quite fair that the Grand Hotel Europe, among its other excellent offerings, also has the best Chinese food in town. With Chinese chefs and authentic ingredients (most supplies are imported), Chopsticks is in a league of its own. Its emphasis is on the sweet-and-sour dishes from the north, tangy but not too hot. If you crave American-style Chinese food, this is a gold mine. One word of advice: Don't count on nabbing one of its few tables if you just drop by; the cozy restaurant is always full. ✉ *1/7 Mikhailovskaya ul.,* ☎ *812/329–6000. Reservations essential. AE, MC, V.*

$$ ✕ **The City Restaurant.** This is on the second floor of the Kapella, where once the buffet of this beautiful concert hall used to be. Obviously, it is a great spot for a pre- or post-concert meal or drink (the space is about equally divided between restaurant and bar). What is offered on the menu is not necessarily available and service can be somewhat peculiar, but the waitresses are usually charming. The pork chops with thyme and sage are tasty and filling; the whitefish stuffed with spinach, walnuts, and raisins could be more subtle to the palate. Crème brûlée should not taste burnt, despite its name. That should not discourage you from going: It will not be easy to find another place that is so cozy, relaxed, and friendly, and in such a beautiful setting. The wine list includes Californian and French wines. ✉ *20 Moika,* ☎ *812/314-1037. MC, V.* ☺ *Daily noon–11.*

$$ ✕ **John Bull Pub.** As easy to get to as it is on the nerves, this English pub serves Russian food in its dining hall and standard snacks at the bar. For a bowl of borshch, or just a foamy mug of beer and refuge from architectural overload, try this cozy inn. Just next door is a more ambitious John Bull restaurant. ✉ *79 Nevsky Prospect,* ☎ *812/164–9877. MC, V.*

$$ ✕ **Krunk.** Halfway between Hotel Rus and Hotel Europe, in a particularly atmospheric neighborhood, Krunk caters Armenian food in a pleasant setting. It has been operating for a number of years in a small basement, like many pioneer private ventures, and is patronized by Armenians, too. Service is friendly; have them slow down so the entrée doesn't come when you are still eating soup. Try the flounder or sturgeon *shashlyk*, which you can match with a decent Moldavian wine. They play taped music, but will spare you the usual Russian *pop-muzyka* and let you listen to Armenian music if you ask. ⊠ *14 Solyanoi pereulok,* ☎ *812/273–3830. No credit cards.*

$$ ✕ **Literary Café.** You may have encountered this slice of history on one of your walks. Famous as the site of Pushkin's last meal (it was then a confectionery), it is imbued with a melancholy air of the past. The old-fashioned dining rooms, adorned with white linen and old silver, draw a cultured crowd. You'll find only Russian food, but there's a lot to choose from. Service is the weak point: Waiters are frequently testy but still can't spoil the pleasantly hushed ambience. There's usually a small entrance fee, because of the attendant classical musicians. The kitchen stays open until 2 AM. ⊠ *18 Nevsky Prospect,* ☎ *812/ 312–6057. AE, MC, V.*

$$ ✕ **Metropole.** Centrally located near Gostinny Dvor and just off Nevsky Prospect, this faded, state-run restaurant was once one of St. Petersburg's finest. Today it faces stiff competition, and the kitchen is having trouble keeping up with the city's better-run and -funded ventures. The menu offers standard Russian fare, such as chicken Kiev and fried perch. The selection of *zakuski* (hors d'oeuvres) is good, but the main courses tend to be heavy on the sauces and fried potatoes. Where the Metropole has the city's shiny cafés beat is in ambience. Opened in 1898, it's the city's oldest restaurant, and its atmosphere can't be reproduced with substitute decor—no matter how tastefully done. Although it has clearly seen better days, the marble pillars, ceiling moldings, and crystal chandeliers still exude elegance. For a price, you can reserve one of the private balcony rooms (which accommodate up to 30 people) overlooking the main dining hall. Russian pop bands provide nightly entertainment. If you want to mingle and dance with the locals, ask for a table in the main hall. There is a limited selection of wine—but plenty of Russian vodka and champagne. Except for the unpleasant reception you might get from the grouchy man guarding the front door, service here is pleasant, although typically slow. ⊠ *22 ul. Sadovaya,* ☎ *812/310–1845. No credit cards.*

$$ ✕ **Nikolai.** Located in the House of Architects and previously open only
★   to members of the Architects' Union, this little-known restaurant is in a beautiful 18th-century mansion just off St. Isaac's Square (opposite is No. 47, which belonged to the Nabokov family before the October Revolution). The dazzling interior features carved oak paneling, ceiling paintings, brass chandeliers, and gilt window frames. Its astounding beauty has somehow remained a secret, and unlike other elegant dining establishments, the place is not swarming with tourists. The cuisine, unfortunately, is far less appealing than the decor. The kitchen offers simply prepared meat and fish appetizers, as well as standard Russian dishes. The house specialty, *myaso po Arkhitektorsky,* is a beef dish baked in a mayonnaise sauce and topped with thinly sliced potatoes. Gourmands obviously won't rave, but with interiors like these it doesn't matter. If you're nice to the friendly waitresses, they may let you take a peek upstairs at the oak-paneled library and gilt ballroom. You can dance out the night to the sound of DJ music (no techno here) in the basement, where a nightclub called Matador is open daily from 7 PM on. ⊠ *52 ul. Bolshaya Morskaya,* ☎ *812/311–1402. Reservations essential. AE, MC, V.*

$$ ✕ **Sadko.** This lively and comfortable restaurant-bar is another pleasant eating establishment of the Grand Hotel Europe, minus its pomp and circumstance. Check your tie at the door and sit down for a re-

freshing (imported) draft beer and pizza. The blackboard menu, which changes daily, offers satisfying Western-style bar food, such as hamburgers, spareribs, and pasta. The good food, fun atmosphere, and nightly entertainment (the place closes at 1 AM), which usually features popular local performers and up-and-coming new bands, make this a good choice if you just want to kick back and settle in. You can also get a good view of life on the Nevsky Prospect. ⊠ *1/7 Mikhailovskaya ul. (separate entrance from Grand Hotel Europe)*, ☎ *812/329–6000. AE, MC, V.*

$$ ✕ **Saigon.** Don't be fooled by the name—you'll find nothing but Russian cooking at this pleasant restaurant just a block off St. Isaac's Square. And don't be fooled by the finely remodeled interior. The Vietnamese partners in this restaurant pulled out at the last minute, but the Saigon opened anyway. It's a lovely, quiet place in which to take a break from the hustle and bustle of downtown St. Petersburg. The varying selection of Russian main dishes, although pleasantly prepared, is heavily laden with french fries and oily vegetables. The appetizers and soups are better choices. Try the house specialty, *griby po Domashnemy* (homestyle mushrooms), served with a heavy sauce inside light pastry shells. If you like squid, you'll enjoy the *stolichnyi salat,* garnished with onions and radishes in a mayonnaise base. The chicken soup comes with a tasty open-faced grilled-cheese sandwich. ⊠ *33 ul. Kazanskaya,* ☎ *812/315–8772. No credit cards.* ⊙ *Mon.–Sat. noon–11, Sun. 2–11.*

$$ ✕ **Shvabsky Domik.** You can tell the food here is authentic by the crowds of German expatriates who keep coming back for the schnitzel and wurst. The simple decor, with heavy wood paneling and long wooden benches, makes for a relaxed and pleasant atmosphere. The waitresses, all in German national dress, aim to please, and offer a pleasant change of pace from the usual harried service. Unlike most restaurants in St. Petersburg, advance reservations aren't necessary. Combine that with the quick service and location—right outside the Novocherkasskaya subway station—and this becomes a good stop for a quick meal on those days when you haven't planned ahead. A German-Russian joint venture, the restaurant specializes almost exclusively in German cuisine, with a few Russian appetizers like blini with caviar or cabbage soup thrown in for variety. The kitchen produces its own homemade pretzels, the *Shvabski Brezel.* Wash down your sausage and sauerkraut with a cold mug of refreshing German draft beer, while you listen to the balalaika-strumming folk trio. ⊠ *28/19 Novocherkassky Prospect,* ☎ *812/528–2211. AE, DC, MC, V.*

$$ ✕ **Tandoor.** This restaurant, specializing in the cuisine of Northwest India, gets high marks across the board and is a good find for vegetarians. Among the many tandooris and excellent fish and meat dishes (try the lamb kurma or chicken tikka masala), you'll find plenty of paneer, lentil, and vegetable-only dishes. The friendly atmosphere is inviting, the service solicitous. Its location is good, too—at the foot of Voznesensky Prospect, which converges with Nevsky and Moskovsky prospects at the Admiralty. After touring St. Isaac's or the nearby Palace Square, you may want to drop by here. ⊠ *2 Voznesensky Prospect,* ☎ *812/312–3886. AE, MC, V.*

$$ ✕ **Tête-à-Tête.** As its name suggests, this exclusive private restaurant,
★ which has just one small dining room, specializes in French cuisine. Tables are available only by advance booking, and the front door is bolted shut to keep customers from entering "off the streets." (If you have a reservation, ring the bell.) Although the chef is clearly not from Paris, the kitchen does a creditable job of producing French dishes using locally procured ingredients. For starters, try the rich and creamy onion soup or the *julienne s gribami,* mushrooms served in a cream sauce with onions. The French menu also features a savory grilled beef

wrapped inside a cheese omelet and served with a mushroom cream sauce. The classically designed interior suits the restaurant's exclusive image well. In the evenings, the grand piano tucked in a corner provides light background music. The fully draped windows and dim lighting add to the intimate atmosphere. Just don't go in groups larger than four. ⊠ *65 Bolshoi Prospect, near Petrogradskaya metro station,* ☎ *812/232–7548. Reservations essential. Jacket and tie. No credit cards.* ⊙ *Daily 1–11.*

$$ ✕ **Tschaika.** This lively, smoke-filled restaurant and bar is popular with young locals and expatriates alike. A German-Russian venture, it offers good, hearty North German food and great German beer (which you can enjoy until 3 AM). The dark wood interior, with lots of booths, long tables, and paneling, is right out of Germany, and the food, except for such Russian delicacies as caviar, is dominated by dishes like frankfurters with sauerkraut. It's a great place to come on a rainy day for a piping-hot bowl of French onion soup or Hungarian goulash. The system of taking orders is a bit odd: You're handed a punch card on entering, on which your waiter records your order. When you leave you present it to the cashier. The staff seems studiously blasé but gets the job done. ⊠ *14 Kanal Griboyedova,* ☎ *812/312–4631. Reservations not accepted. AE, MC, V.*

$ ✕ **Don Quixote.** This café is housed in the Home of Friendship with Foreign Countries. Expect the *garnir* accompanying your pork cutlet to be canned food and the Spanish twist to the menu rather fake. However, their dry red wine imported from Spain is indeed red and dry—and not overpriced, as French wines often are. You can order pastries or a full meal, according to the time of the day and your appetite. Its location on Fontanka (two steps from Nevsky), the live music—most often jazzy and never intrusive—and its late hours (until 6 AM) make it a perfect landing spot before or after a show around Nevsky. ⊠ *21 Fontanka,* ☎ *812/210–4517. No credit cards.*

$ ✕ **Lagidze.** As Metekhi next door, this is a Georgian café, where you can try *kupaty* (a sort of sausage), *satsivi* (cold chicken in a walnut sauce) and *lobio* (spicy beans). They naturally also offer the well known shashlyk, and there is dark tap beer and maybe *tarkhun* (a green bitterish beverage) to help you gulp down the whole thing. Bread here is called *lavash*. Both Lagidze and Metekhi look the same and taste the same; choose according to where you find room. A plus with Metekhi is that they have an English menu, but since it is a café, open from 11 to 9, expect to share a table with other patrons and not to be invited to linger more than necessary. You have to order at the counter and pick up your silverware, but the food is brought to your table when it is ready. ⊠ *3 Belinskogo ul. No credit cards.*

LODGING

St. Petersburg's hotel industry has undergone considerable change in recent years. Until the late 1980s, all of the city's hotels were controlled by Intourist, the Soviet agency that enjoyed a monopoly over the tourist trade. Rates for foreign tourists were standardized, and there were few distinctions in service and facilities from one hotel to the next. Perestroika—and St. Petersburg's sudden rise in popularity as a tourist destination—changed this. The influx of tourists prompted foreign contractors to launch a number of renovation projects, with the result that two of the city's most prestigious hotels, the Grand Hotel Europe and the Astoria Hotel, reopened to luxury-class status after major reconstruction; a third, the Nevsky Palace Hotel, joined their ranks as a brand-new contender.

The choices are still limited, however. As in Moscow, but with fewer offerings, hotels fall into two groups, separated by a wide gulf. Since the least expensive way to come to Russia is on an organized tour, you are likely to land in one of the old Intourist standbys, whose quality has hardly improved. Most U.S. and British tour operators take advantage of the deeply discounted rates available to them at these hotels and usually place groups at the Moskva, the Pribaltiskaya, the Pulkovskaya, or the St. Petersburg (formerly Leningrad). These hotels were built in the late 1970s and early '80s, though they look at least 30 years older. Their facilities are fairly uniform. They would be considered inferior by Western standards. The service, though mildly unpredictable, is perfectly acceptable, however, provided you are not expecting royal treatment. The main reason to choose them is their vastly lower rates. You probably should opt for those with the best location for you, for in addition to their other inconveniences, only one or two are close to the major attractions.

If your surroundings don't affect you, and especially if you plan to have a car or easy access to group transport, you'll probably want to save on hotel rates and make do with one of the less expensive hotels. If you want insulation from the uglier sides of life here, however, plan to pay up in order to stay at an accommodation in the better category.

CATEGORY	COST*
$$$$	over $200
$$$	$140–$200
$$	$65–$140
$	under $65

All prices are for a standard double room for two, excluding service charge.

$$$$ ▦ **Astoria.** Reopened in 1991 after major reconstruction, the Astoria is actually two hotels: It interconnects with the old Angleterre, a hotel with enduring "fame" because it's where the much-loved poet Sergei Yesenin committed suicide in 1925. Originally built in the Art Nouveau style in 1910–12, the Astoria was one of St. Petersburg's most renowned hotels before the 1917 Revolution. Its renovation by Finnish contractors was bitterly opposed by many residents, as plans to merge the two hotels called for the complete destruction of the original building where Yesenin died. The contractors won out, and their renovations produced a fine hotel: Not a trace of St. Petersburg's dusty streets can be found. The splendid interiors have been decorated using antiques retrieved from various museums. Adding to the hotel's attraction is its convenient location in the heart of downtown St. Petersburg, directly across the street from St. Isaac's Cathedral and a 10-minute walk from the Hermitage. Among the top three hotels here, this one is the least expensive. ✉ *39 Bolshaya Morskaya ul.,* ☎ *812/210–5757,* ℻ *812/210–5133. 436 rooms with bath. 3 restaurants, 2 cafés, bar, pool, exercise room, sauna, nightclub, business services, travel services. AE, MC, V.*

$$$$ ▦ **Grand Hotel Europe.** This five-star hotel is without question the
★ finest in town. Reopened in 1991 after extensive renovations, it offers the elegance of prerevolutionary St. Petersburg along with every modern amenity. Its stunning Baroque facade has been carefully restored, and the Art Nouveau interior, with its stained-glass windows and authentic antique furniture, brings back its past glory. The stylish and comfortable rooms, done in pleasing tones of mauve, cream, and gold, verge on luxurious. The hotel is operated as a Russo-Swedish venture and is managed by Reso Hotels of Sweden. The Russian staff is held to European standards of excellence, and the service shines. The Swedish management has thought of everything: 24-hour room service, direct-dial international telephone, mail service via courier to Helsinki, and

satellite TV and radio, with CNN and MTV programming. The central location can't be beat: Nevsky Prospect, the Hermitage, and the Square of the Arts are all within walking distance. If money is no object, this is the place to stay. ✉ *1/7 Mikhailovskaya ul.,* ☎ *812/329–6000,* FAX *812/329–6002. 211 rooms with bath, 17 junior suites, 18 terrace rooms, 23 penthouse suites, 26 two-room suites, 4 executive suites, 2 deluxe suites. 4 restaurants, bar. café, sauna, health club, nightclub, meeting rooms. Metro: Nevsky Prospect, Gostinny Dvor. AE, MC, V.*

$$$$ ⊞ **Nevsky Palace Hotel.** Sister to the Palace Hotel in Moscow and owned by Sheraton, this modern and spacious five-star establishment was re-fashioned on the site of an old building but is completely new. The top-notch service caters to the business elite who are looking for no fuss and serious comfort. Well situated not far from the Moscow Rail Station, it's accessible to everything you're likely to want to see. ✉ *57 Nevsky Prospect,* ☎ *812/275–2001,* FAX *812/301–7323. 287 rooms with bath. 3 restaurants, 2 bars, coffee shop, sauna, shops, business services, meeting rooms, service bureau. Metro: Mayakovskaya. AE, DC, MC, V.*

$$$$ ⊞ **Northern Crown** (Severnaya Korona). When it eventually opens by the end of 1999, this hotel will be the largest hostelry in the luxury category. Fetchingly, it is located in the district with the highest density of Art Nouveau buildings, close to Ploshchad Lva Tolstovo, on the picturesque river Karpovka. At press time (winter 1998), it was still fenced off. ✉ *37 Karpovki reki nab.,* ☎ *812/329–7000,* FAX *812/329–7001. 256 rooms with bath. 4 restaurants, café, pool, sauna, Turkish bath, exercise room, business services, meeting rooms. Metro: Petrogradskaya.*

$$$ ⊞ **Deson-Ladoga.** Located on the right bank of the Neva, five minutes from the Novocherkasskaya metro station, this Russo–Hong Kong joint venture was opened after reconstruction in September 1994. The rooms (of which 10 are designated for nonsmokers) are furnished with direct-dial satellite telephone and television. The decor is modest but very fresh. ✉ *26 Shaumyana Prospect,* ☎ *812/528–5393,* FAX *812/528–5448. 95 rooms with bath. Beauty salon, sauna, nightclub. Metro: Novocherkasskaya. MC, V.*

$$$ ⊞ **Pribaltiskaya.** Swedish-built but Soviet-designed, this huge 16-story skyscraper is frequently booked by tourist groups. Opened in 1978, it was once considered the city's top hotel. The rooms are clean and all come with cable television (including CNN and MTV). The modest furnishings are adequate, although slightly worn. Its first major drawback is the location: Far out on the western tip of Vasilievsky Island, the hotel is a good 20-minute drive from downtown St. Petersburg, and the closest subway station is several bus stops away. The predominantly residential area offers rows and rows of benumbing Soviet-era highrises—but very few shops and restaurants. If you can stand the isolation, the views of the Gulf of Finland are phenomenal, especially at sunset (ask for a room on the western side of the hotel). Another disadvantage is its increasing appeal to unsavory crowds, which may particularly bother single travelers. One plus is the hotel's well-stocked "Baltic Store," where you can pick up bottled water, imported snack foods, and a fairly recent copy of the *International Herald-Tribune* or *USA Today.* ✉ *14 ul. Korablestroiteley,* ☎ *812/356–0263 or 812/356–0001,* FAX *812/356–4496. 1200 rooms with bath. 11 restaurants, 5 bars, 10 snack bars, sauna, bowling, shop, convention center, travel services, parking (fee). AE, MC, V.*

$$$ ⊞ **Pulkovskaya.** Opened in 1981, this Finnish-built hotel has withstood
★ heavy tourist traffic, and its attractive Scandinavian-designed interior is still surprisingly well maintained. Accommodations are on the same level as the Pribaltiskaya (☞ *above*), although the rooms are slightly

cleaner and more attractive. Service is friendly and efficient by local standards. Unusual for a Russian hotel, the curtains and bedspreads actually match the upholstery; and the bathrooms, complete with Finnish plumbing, are relatively large. Again, the disadvantage here is location. The hotel is not near the city center and is convenient only to the airport; the subway is a 10-minute walk away, and the ride into town takes at least 20 minutes. But in contrast to the Pribaltiskaya's surroundings, the area around the Pulkovskaya is mainly residential, with plenty of shops and even a restaurant or two. The views from the rooms, though, can depress you: you have a choice between gloomy high-rises and smokestacks or the severe, very Soviet, Victory Square monument outside the hotel's main entrance. ⊠ *1 Pl. Pobedy,* ☎ *812/123–5022 or 812/123–5122,* FAX *812/123–5856 or 812/123–5845. 850 rooms with bath, telephone, TV, refrigerator. 2 restaurants, 6 bars, 6 snack bars, beauty salon, 2 saunas and dipping pool, shops, business services, travel services, car rental. Metro: Moskovskaya. AE, DC, MC, V.*

$$ 🖭 **Moskva.** The unimaginative and depressing decor at this enormous, visibly aging hotel is yet another prime example of Brezhnev-era design. Store up on patience before checking in, because the lackluster service can make even paying your bill a frustrating experience; the desk clerks spend more time at lunch and on the phone than they do attending to guests. The dreary rooms and public areas show obvious signs of neglect, but the hotel management keeps making stabs at renovations. The hotel's reputation for seedy mobs hanging out at the main entrance seems to have improved. Perhaps because this is the best located of the Intourist hotels, many groups stay here, and while they may sometimes remind you of the crowds at Disneyland, at least you will feel safe. Location is good here: It is literally on top of the subway and faces the entrance to the 18th-century Alexander Nevsky Monastery. This is at one end of Nevsky Prospect, which is still the center of town. Another plus is that rates are on the low end of the $$ category. ⊠ *2 Pl. Alexandra Nevskovo,* ☎ *812/274–3001 or 812/274–4001,* FAX *812/274–2130. 770 rooms with bath. Restaurant, 5 bars, 7 snack bars, shops, business services, travel services. AE, DC, MC, V.*

$$ 🖭 **Okhtinskaya.** The location, directly across the river from the Baroque
★ Smolny Sobor, is great for views but terribly inconvenient if you plan on going anywhere by public transportation. St. Petersburg's museums and tourist attractions are all on the other side of the river, and the subway (Novocherkasskaya) is several bus stops away. Canadian-built and opened in 1991, the hotel is now run as a French-Russian venture. Service is unusually friendly, and the rates are extremely reasonable. Although the interior features the usual marble-and-chrome decor, the public areas are cheery and bright and, most important, devoid of the ubiquitous slot machines. The rooms are clean and well appointed, with imported furnishings and pretty flowered wallpaper. While almost all the rooms come with balconies, only the suites have full baths. Unfortunately only one room on every floor faces the cathedral, but the views of the urban landscape on this side of town are more refreshing than most. ⊠ *4 Bolsheokhtinsky Prospect,* ☎ *812/227–4438 or 812/227–3767,* FAX *812/227–2618. 204 rooms with bath or shower. 2 restaurants, 2 bars, snack bar, sauna, shops, meeting rooms. AE, DC, MC, V.*

$$ 🖭 **Rus.** The name of this hotel refers to the first medieval Russian state,
★ but forget about any fantasies about onion domes and Tartary trim. Many Petersburgers say this is the most hideous building in town—and that the architect should be banished forever for creating such a modern eyesore in an otherwise charming and quiet neighborhood, which is home to many consulates and cultured expatriates. Inside, there is no Petersburg flair to it at all—yet the hotel's perfect location (two steps away from Liteiny Prospect and in walking distance of the Cherny-

shevskaya subway stop)—and its price scheme make it all in all an excellent option. If you find yourself on Liteiny, look for No. 26; it is a useful shortcut to the hotel. Inside, a helpful staff awaits (once you pass the somewhat somber doorman). It is popular, so book early. All rooms come with telephone and TV. ⊠ *1 Artilleriyskaya ul.,* ☎ *812/279–5003,* 𝔽𝔸𝕏 *812/279–3600. 165 rooms with bath. Bar, café, beauty salon, sauna, shop, exchange office, business services, travel services. Metro: Chernyshevskaya. AE, DC, MC, V.*

$$ ▦ **St. Petersburg.** Formerly called the Leningrad, this aging hotel of-
★ fers both the best and worst views of contemporary St. Petersburg. Although the rooms overlooking the Neva have magnificent vistas of the city's waterfront architecture, the other half have a depressing view. Although this is definitely not the luxury hotel it once was, if you can land a waterfront room, it is the only place to stay during the White Nights. The Finnish-decorated interior is faded and the furnishings are a bit worn, but the rooms and public areas are clean and not nearly as shabby as the Moskva's. The vast lobby holds a host of stores, including souvenir and gift shops. The location, however, is good only for the views. The Finland railway station and subway are within walking distance, but the route is unpleasant and takes you along a busy highway. ⊠ *5/2 Pirogovskaya nab.,* ☎ *812/542–9411,* 𝔽𝔸𝕏 *812/248–8002 or 812/542–8149. 410 rooms with bath. 2 restaurants, 3 bars, 3 snack bars, sauna with dipping pool, shops, business services, meeting rooms, travel services. Metro: Ploshchad Lenina. AE, DC, MC, V.*

$$ ▦ **Sovietskaya.** The name says it all: This is a Soviet hotel with the typically slow and disgruntled service of a state-run enterprise. Yet another concrete-and-steel monstrosity, the hotel is in an unattractive section of downtown St. Petersburg. Although the location allows for some good views of St. Petersburg's canals, it's still a long walk to just about anywhere, including the subway. There are two buildings, both built in the late 1960s, but the "newer wing" (the part called Fontanka) was recently remodeled. All rooms in both wings are relatively clean and have decent views, but accommodations in the "new" wing are generally in better shape and come with Finnish furnishings (and higher rates). ⊠ *43/1 Lermontovsky Prospect,* ☎ *812/329–0186 or 812/329–0182,* 𝔽𝔸𝕏 *812/329–0188. 1,099 rooms with bath. 3 restaurants, 3 bars, café, 4 snack bars, sauna, business services, travel services. Metro: Baltiskaya. MC, V.*

$ ▦ **Holiday.** The "Holiday" hostel opened in 1993 on the Neva embankment (Petrograd Side) and is a five-minute walk from the Finland railway station. There is a pier in front of the building where you can arrange a sightseeing tour through the rivers and canals of the city. The hostel can accommodate from 70 people in winter to 100 in summer. Two- to six-bed rooms have the Neva river view. Showers and toilets are in the corridor on each floor. The hostel is open 24 hours and there is a bar on the fourth floor in summer. This is a good choice for budget-minded tourists who want to get closer to real life in Russia. ⊠ *1 Mikhailova ul.,* ☎ 𝔽𝔸𝕏 *812/542–7364. Accommodates 70–100 people. Metro: Ploshchad Lenina. MC, V.*

$ ▦ **St. Petersburg International Hostel.** This joint Russian-American project launched by young enthusiasts in the early '90's was one of the first to freshen up the entrepreneurial landscape of the city. It is a converted dormitory, which means you book not a room, but a "place," of which there are 55 in total, distributed in rooms holding three to five beds. Showers and toilets are on the floor and it costs just under $20 a night to stay here (especially attractive since St. Petersburg has so few budget options). The location is excellent (walking distance from the Moscow railway station) and the staff is as friendly as advertised. The premises also house the Sindbad travel office (☎ 812/327-8384), which caters to budget travelers, facilitates visa support, and is the starting point of walking tours of the city. The major drawback is the curfew from 1 AM to 8 AM. Needless to say, the hostel fills up very quickly in the summer. ✉ *3rd Sovietskaya ul, 28,* ☎ *812/329–8018,* FAX *812/ 329–8019. Accommodates 55 people. Metro: Ploshchad Vosstanya, Mayakovskaya. No credit cards.*

NIGHTLIFE AND THE ARTS

The Arts

St. Petersburg's cultural life is one of its top attractions. Except for the most renowned theaters, tickets are easily available and inexpensive. You can buy them at the box offices of the theaters themselves, at theater kiosks (*teatralnaya kassa*) located throughout the city—Central Box Office No. 1 is at 42 Nevsky Prospect (☎ 812/311–3183) and is open daily from 11 to 7—and at service bureaus in hotels, most of which post performance listings in their main lobby. The Mariinsky Theater (better known in the West by its Soviet name, Kirov) and the Mussorgsky Theater of Ballet and Opera (also known as the Maly) charge different prices for Russians and foreigners. However, it is much easier to sneak in with a Russian ticket here than at the Hermitage or the Russian Museum.

Your best sources of information are the local English-language publications, *Neva News* and *The St. Petersburg Times*. The latter is a fullfledged newspaper; it comes out on Tuesdays and Fridays and is widely distributed (free). Pick up a copy at the Hotel Europe if you have not yet found one by hanging out around Nevsky Prospect. The Friday edition has an excellent "All About Town" section, with theater and concert listings, and a restaurant column. There is also a new glossy edition of *Where St. Petersburg,* a franchise of the Los Angeles–based Where International, that you can pick up for free in hotels and other places patronized by foreigners. Last but not least, the monthly *Pulse* (available in English and Russian) also has extensive listings. Copies of all these can be picked up at Western airline offices, and bars, clubs, hotels, cafés, and other places generally patronized by foreigners. In another genre, it will be useful to invest about $5 in *The Traveller's Yellow Pages for Saint Petersburg* if you are spending some time in the city. It is a compact telephone book and handbook written in English, with indexes in English, Russian, German, French, Swedish, and Finnish. For the latest information, look at *The Traveller's Yellow Pages On-Line* at www.infoservices.com.

All sorts of special arts performances are organized for the White Nights' Festival, held in the last two weeks of June. After that, most major theaters close down for the summer and start up again in mid-September.

Concerts

Classical music can be enjoyed all over the city. The famous **Philharmonic** (✉ 2 ul. Mikhailovskaya, ☎ 812/311–7333) offers excellent performances in its concert hall (*Bolshoi zal*) on the Square of the Arts, located in the former Nobleman's Club, opposite the Russian Museum. Concerts are also given in the Philharmonic's smaller concert hall (*Maly zal*); ✉ 30 Nevsky Prospect, ☎ 812/311–8333), around the corner. One of St. Petersburg's best-kept secrets is the lovely **Kapella** (✉ 20 nab. Moiki, ☎ 812/314–1159), which presents not only choral events but also symphonic, instrumental, and vocal concerts. Hidden in a courtyard and with an entrance that could not be less conspicuous, this concert hall dates from the 1780s, and many famous musicians, including Glinka and Rimsky-Korsakov, have performed here.

For a relaxing evening of classical music in a prerevolutionary setting, try the concert halls in some of St. Petersburg's mansions, palaces, and churches. Performances are held regularly at: the **Beloselsky-Belozersky Palace** (✉ 41 Nevsky Prospect, ☎ 812/315–4076); the **Bosse Mansion,** the chamber concert hall of the Kapella (✉ 15/4 liniya, Vassily Island, ☎ 812/213–3488); **Kochnevaya's House** (✉ 41 Fontanka, ☎ 812/110–4032 or 812/110–4042); the **Kshesinskaya Mansion** (✉ 2/4 Bolshaya Dvoryanskaya, ☎ 812/233–7052); the **Lutheran Church St. Catherine** (✉ 1-A Bolshoi Prospect, Vassily Island, ☎ 812/213–1852); **Samoilovs' appartment** (Entrance from the back side of the Nevsky Palace Hotel, ✉ 8 ul. Stremyannaya); the **Sheremetyev Palace** (✉ 34 Fontanka, ☎ 812/272–5818 or 812/272–2123); the **Smolny Cathedral** (✉ 3/1 Pl. Rastrelli, ☎ 812/271–9182); and the **Yusupov Palace** (tickets available only on the spot; ✉ 94 nab. Reki Moiki, ☎ 812/314–8893). Many of the concerts organized at these addresses are run by Peterburg-Kontsert; if you want quality and real contact with local musical life, they are a much better bet than most of the events organized especially for tourist groups. The offices of Peterburg-Kontsert are located in Kochnevaya's House (Dom Konchevoi; ☞ *above*), and tickets can be bought there, too. The entrance is rather inconspicuous: Look for a door on the right side in the passageway at 41 Fontanka (after the restaurant Cucaracha, coming from Nevsky).

Opera and Ballet

The world-renowned **Mariinsky Theater of Opera and Ballet** (✉ 1/2 Teatralnaya Pl., ☎ 812/114–4344 or 812/114–1211) should not be missed. Its elegant blue-and-gold auditorium has been the main home of the Russian ballet—the Kirov—since the 1880s. The lesser-known **Mussorgsky Theater of Opera and Ballet** (✉ 1 Pl. Iskusstv, ☎ 812/219–1949 or 812/219–1978), also known as the Maly, offers outstanding performances but at much lower prices than the Kirov. Two more addresses to remember are the opera and ballet theater of the **Konservatoria** (✉ 3 Teatralnaya Ploshchad, ☎ 812/312–2519), opposite the Marinsky, and the **St. Petersburg Opera,** which, at the time of writing, had just been assigned the former mansion of Baron Derviz (better known to Peterburgers as the Palace of Culture "Mayak" (✉ 33 Galernaya ul.) as its permanent location. Operas are usually sung in Russian, and the repertoire is dominated by Russian composers.

Theater

St. Petersburg also offers some excellent dramatic theaters, with performances almost exclusively in Russian. Even if you can't understand the dialogue, you may want to visit the famous **Bolshoi Drama Theater** (✉ 65 nab. Fontanki, ☎ 812/310–0401). Russia's oldest theater is the elegant **Alexandra Theater**—known as the Pushkin Drama Theatre under the Soviet regime (✉ 2 Pl. Ostrovskovo, ☎ 812/312–1545), where the repertoire is dominated by the classics.

CHILDREN'S THEATER

St. Petersburg's puppet theaters all perform regularly for children: **Bolshoi Puppet Theater** (✉ 10 ul. Nekrasova, ☎ 812/273–6672); **Puppet-Marionette Theater** (✉ 52 Nevsky Prospect, ☎ 812/311–1900).

Talented skaters perform at the **Improvisational Children's Theater on Ice** (✉ 148 Ligovsky Prospect, ☎ 812/112–8625), whose office is open weekdays 11–5. Children may enjoy a show at the **Through the Looking-Glass Children's Theater** (✉ 13 ul. Rubinsteina, ☎ 812/164–1895), one of the city's best, open Friday–Sunday.

Nightlife

Compared with Moscow, which is bursting at the seams with hot new nightspots, St. Petersburg borders on the tame. Yet it can outdo its rival in trendiness. Maybe it's simply that St. Petersburg looks so arty, but it's always been considered the style capital, and is also inarguably the home of Russian rock and roll. So when you're stepping out for the latest music, you will have a good time here. Just remember the floor shows that Intourist-associated clubs traditionally arrange are a deafening assault on the senses, so if you want something else, you'd better look well outside their doors for entertainment. Once again, your best companions are the Friday edition of the *St. Petersburg Times*—which also makes excellent reading about the economic and political life of the city and the region—and *Pulse.*

A note about security: Though media reports on increased crime in Russia tend to exaggerate the situation, foreigners in this economically strapped country are easy prey for robbers and muggers. Use common sense and stay away from sleazy bars and clubs, where prostitution can thrive and the main goal of guests seems to be reaching a state of drunken bliss. If you plan to spend the evening away from your hotel, you'll be glad if you made arrangements for the trip home before setting out. Although there are virtually no after-dark hours during the White Nights, a too-late evening stroll down Nevsky Prospect may be an invitation to trouble.

Bars and Lounges

All the major hotels have bars and nightclubs, but except for the Astoria and Grand Hotel Europe, the local clientele is often of questionable intention and the atmosphere tends to get boorish as the night wears on.

One of the better spots in town is **Sadko** (⊠ Grand Hotel Europe, 1/7 ul. Mikhailovskaya, ☎ 812/329–6000). Nightly entertainment often features top local performers, such as a Russian reggae band. The crowds are mostly foreign tourists and Russian students, with a few *novye russkye,* or new Russians (BMW-owning, free-spending locals) mixed in. In the summer **The Beer Garden** (⊠ 86 Nevsky Prospect, ☎ 812/275–7620) is a good spot for a large mug of beer.

Casinos

Casino fever is lower in St. Petersburg than in Moscow and Kiev, but high rollers can still have fun. Some casinos are coupled to restaurants like the Nevsky Melody of the Venice; the hotels Astoria and Pribaltiskaya have their own. **Conti** (⊠ 44 Kondratievsky, ☎ 812/540–8130) and **Fortuna** (⊠ 71 Nevsky Prospect, ☎ 812/164–2087), in the city center, are two more addresses out of a dozen. The latest place to have opened is the **Taleon Club,** in the former mansion of the Yeliseyevs, on the corner of Moika and Nevsky (⊠ 59 Moika, ☎ 812/315–7645). This entertainment complex, where artists and writers were housed under the Soviet regime, includes a restaurant (open until 3 AM), a casino, a bar (both open until 6 AM) and a fitness center; it claims to cater to the local high society and politicians and to businessmen from home and abroad.

Comedy Clubs

The **Chaplin Club** is one of the few cabarets of this kind in town and conveniently located around the corner from the subway station Chernyshevskaya. The name describes the decoration adequately, as well as the spirit. From Friday to Sunday, the small stage is most often occupied by the *Litsedeyi,* a pantomime troop that also fills up the biggest concert halls of the city and has established its home base here. There is a cover charge of 50 rubles when there is a performance, and prices for food and beverages remain reasonable. Small bands play live music when there is no show. ☒ *59 ul. Chaikosvkogo,* ☎ *812/272–6649. Closed Tues. No credit cards.*

In the category of Art Clubs—as the local bohemians like to call them—you may wish to check out **Manhattan** (☒ 90 nab. Fontanki, ☎ 812/113–1945), designed as a boiler room as a reminder of the days when decent intellectuals refused to cooperate with the authorities and thus worked as *kotelniki,* (boiler-room operators and other lowly positions) and **Liverpool** (☒ 16a ul. Mayakovskogo, ☎ 812/279–2054), entirely dedicated to the memory of the Beatles.

Dance Clubs

For performance art, live rock, and the very trendy, there was the legendary Pushkinskaya 10 commune; this artists' squat is finally to be given a face-lift. Of this sanctuary for alternative culture, at present there remains **Fish Fabrique,** with its deliberately destroyed interior, on the fourth floor. You can hear pop, techno, or reggae—or most likely, a concoction of all three—at **Domenico's** (☒ 70 Nevsky Prospect, ☎ 812/272–5717). That it takes its artiness seriously is reflected in its steep cover charge. **Luna** (☒ 46 Voznesensky Prospect, ☎ 812/310–1616) is no less expensive to enter (120 to 150 rubles) and has the inevitable erotic show at midnight. A new techno venue has replaced the now defunct Tunnel; it is called **Mama** (☒ 3B Malaya Monetnaya ul.) and operates on Fridays and Saturdays from 11:50 PM on. The noisy and lively **Wild Side** (☒ 12 nab. Bumazhnovo Kanala, ☎ 812/186–3466) accompanies its blasting music with lots of lights. **Port** is the latest venture to have opened and another techno venue, with two halls—huge! (☒ 2 Pereulok Antonenko, ☎ 812/314–2609). It operates daily, from 3 PM to 6 AM. **Metro** (☒ 174 Ligovsky Prospect, ☎ 812/166–0204) is a two-floor discotheque sponsored by Coca-Cola, with a dance hall for Russian pop dance music and one for techno/rave music. It has the advantage of being open daily from 11 PM to 6 AM, but its clientele consists largely of teenagers. If, like Cinderella, midnight is the latest you can stay out, there is the **Monroe Club** (in a basement at ☒ 8 Kanal Griboyedova, ☎ 812/312–1331). The music is Russian pop and the clientele is young, but not overwhemingly so, and more on the gay side on Sundays. No live shows here, but trendiness always seems to rhyme with sex in post-perestroika Russia; there are booths outfitted with erotic video channels in the rear. They are easy to ignore, though, and the whole thing is more bizarre than sleazy. **Matador** (☒ 52 ul. Bolshaya Morskaya, ☎ 812/311–1402), in the basement of the Architects' House, is another escape from techno music. In four vaulted rooms, the central one being the dance floor, a DJ plays Russian and foreign popular music until 6 AM every day except Monday (no cover charge unless there is a performance). They also serve food.

The Russo-Swedish venture **Nevsky Melody** (☒ 62 nab. Sverdlovskaya, ☎ 812/227–1596) has a hopping dance floor and an erotic floor show that is definitely a matter of taste. This nightspot is popular with St. Petersburg's nouveaux riches.

Club 69 (☒ 2nd Krasnoarmeiskaya, 6, ☎ 812/259–5163, Tekhnologichesky Institut subway stop) is the first gay club to be openly visible and that seems to be here to stay. It is open daily from 10 PM (9 PM on Saturdays) and has diverse music and male striptease and drag shows. There is also a bar. The extreme right political leader Vladimir Zhirinovsky paid an official visit to the club—one still wonders why. So did new-wave rocker Bryan Ferry. Women pay double the cover charge to get in.

Jazz, Rock, and Blues

To hear Russia's top jazz musicians, head for the St. Petersburg **Jazz Philharmonic Hall** (✉ 27 Zagorodny Prospect, near the Dostoyevskaya metro station, ☎ 812/164–8565). Regular performances by the likes of the world-renowned Leningrad Dixieland Band and David Goloshchokin's Ensemble make this a favorite nightspot. Serious jazz lovers will enjoy the fantastic atmosphere in this turn-of-the-century building. It makes for a classy night out. The **JFC Jazz Club** (✉ 33 ul. Shpalernaya, ☎ 812/272–9850) is a less emphatically highbrow jazz venue. It is small and reservations are recommended. **Kvadrat** (Palace of Culture Pishchevikov, ✉ 10 ul. Pravdy, ☎ 812/164–8508) operates on Tuesdays, from 8 to 11 PM.

The **Gora Club** (✉ 153 Ligovsky Prospect) showcases local rock bands. Rockabilly fans will find their fellows at the **Money Honey Saloon** (✉ Block 14, Apraksin Dvor, ☎ 812/310–0147), but pay heed: Although the music may be good, the neighborhood is not. On the Petrograd island, at walking distance from the new subway station Chkalovskaya, you may wish to check out the club **Rio** (✉ corner of Maly Prospect and Gatchinskaya ul.). The entrance fee is very reasonable (15 to 20 rubles); and so is the beer (10 rubles for a pint of Baltika). The place is not too small, not too big, with a mixed and unthreatening audience, and a different band plays live rock and roll, blues, rockabilly, and country every night. Just remember that at 2 AM between May and November, bridges go up and you may then have to swing on the dance floor until 5.

OUTDOOR ACTIVITIES AND SPORTS

Participant Sports

Unfortunately, athletic facilities available to tourists in St. Petersburg are rather limited. As in Moscow, access to municipal facilities is restricted and requires a special "doctor's certificate" attesting to the user's health needs. These are possible to get, but you'd have to spend at least a few hours at a Russian clinic to do so. Most hotels have their own athletic facilities, however, and sometimes they are open to nonguests; these spots do not require a doctor's certificate.

Fitness Centers and Sports Complexes

The **Army Sports Club** (✉ 13 ul. Inzhenernaya, ☎ 812/219–2967) has a pool and both volleyball and basketball courts. The **Dinamo Sports Center** (✉ 44 Dinamo Prospect, ☎ 812/235–4717) has a range of facilities, including volleyball courts and running tracks. Weightlifters can try the **Olympia Fitness Center** (✉ 14 ul. 6th Krasnoarmeiskaya, ☎ 812/110–1887); a one-month package here is very reasonable, so you may simply want to purchase one, even if your stay will be shorter.

If your own hotel doesn't have a place to work out, the fitness center at the **Astoria Hotel** is open to nonguests. Its pool (10 meters/33 ft) is by far the largest in the city's hotels. ☎ 812/210–5869. ☉ *Weekdays 9 AM–10 PM, weekends 9–9; call in advance to check availability.* ▦ *Fee for use of gym, pool, and sauna for 2 hrs, $20.*

Running

Runners, like cyclists, can find some lovely spots to exercise. You might stick to the Neva embankments or head for gardens like Letny Sad or the Field of Mars. It's easier here than in Moscow to avoid huge clumps of traffic and the attendant congestion. And though you'll still be in a minority, you probably won't feel as conspicuous if you just put on those track shoes and go.

Skating

You can skate at the following rinks: **Moskovsky Park Pobedy** (✉ 25 ul. Kuznetsovskaya, ☎ 812/298–4521), open daily 2–9 in winter; **Yubileyny Palace of Sports** (✉ 18 ul. Dobrolyubova, ☎ 812/119–5609), by advance booking only.

Swimming

The fitness centers listed above have pools. The **World Class Fitness Center** (✉ 6 Vyborgskoye Shosse, ☎ 812/554–4147) also offers a 25-meter (82-ft), six-lane pool. Onetime use is an option, but at twice the members' price. More central, **Hotel Moskva** (✉ 2 Ploshchad Aleksandra Nevskogo, ☎ 812/274–3001) also offers a convenient swimming pool.

Tennis Courts

Tennis players should be able to find an open court. Public indoor courts are located at **Dinamo Stadium** (✉ 44 ul. Dinamo, ☎ 812/235–0055). The stadium can be reached by Tram 21 or 34. There are also **municipal courts** (37 ul. Kazanskaya, ☎ 812/315–6220). Outdoor **public courts** are across the street from the Field of Mars at 16 Aptekarsky pereulok. The **World Class Fitness Center** (☞ *above*) has tennis courts available for rental if they aren't previously reserved. If these options don't pan out, check with the **Lawn Tennis Sports Center** (✉ 116 Metallistov Prospect, ☎ 812/540–1886).

Spectator Sports

Tickets for sporting events can be purchased at the sports arena immediately prior to the game or at one of the many theater box offices (teatralnaya kassa) located throughout the city, notably on Nevsky Prospect at No. 22–24, 39, 42, and 74. Stadiums may be housing commercial fairs and exhibits; here are a few addresses that you can check out: **Kirov Stadium** (✉ 1 Morskoi Prospect, Krestovsky Ostrov, ☎ 812/235–5452), **Peterburgsky Sports and Concert Complex** (✉ 8 Yuri Gagarin Prospect, ☎ 812/298–2164), **Petrovsky Stadium** (✉ 2-g Petrovsky Ostrov, ☎ 812/233–1752), **SKA Sports Palace** (✉ 2 Zhdanovskaya nab., ☎ 812/237–0073), and **Yubilyeiny Sports Palace** (✉ 19 Prospect Dobrolyubova, ☎ 812/119–5612). Two names to remember: Zenith and SKA, respectively the St. Petersburg teams of soccer and hockey.

SHOPPING

If you have come to St. Petersburg to shop, you will probably be disappointed. Although there have been improvements, they consist mostly of bringing in a solid array of products that are considered "normal" – juice, cosmetics, socks—elsewhere. In other words, apart from certain arts and crafts, there is nothing to whet your appetite for the unusual or exquisite; you'll have to let your experience of St. Petersburg alone fulfill that. The good news, of course, is that basic items are no longer scarce. Also, stores have considerably extended their opening hours and many will be open until 8 or 9 PM, or on Sundays.

The same sense of a two-tiered system of stores exists in St. Petersburg as in Moscow and Kiev. "Western-style" shops taking credit-card payment have effectively replaced the old Beriozkas, which were stocked only for foreigners. With increased competition, some of their prices have gone down, and they are open to anyone who can afford them.

State-run shops are better stocked now than before, and you might as well look into some of these groceries and department stores if you don't want anything too fancy. Only rubles are accepted here, however, and you'll have a tough time maneuvering through the cashiers if you don't speak some Russian.

Kiosks, tables on the street, and impromptu markets offer a colorful jumble of junk most of the time. But this mini-industry of individual entrepreneurs, which mushroomed wildly in the first years of glasnost, is on the wane. Everything's being tidied up and taken back inside. Another new phenomenon is the "24 chasa" stores (i.e. open 24 hours a day). They vary from smallish to big, but there will always be one near you, stocked with alcohol, cigarettes, and groceries.

Shopping Districts

Historically, St. Petersburg's main shopping districts are Nevsky Prospect and Gostinny Dvor. Located smack in the center of town, at 35 Nevsky Prospect, Gostinny Dvor is easily reached by subway; a station right outside its doors is named in its honor. Some sections of Gostinny Dvor have been entirely renovated to attract upscale boutiques, but many remain empty since most inhabitants of the city can only stare in awe at the price tags.

Department Stores

The patient shopper may chance upon some tremendous bargains at **DLT** (*Dom Leningradskoi Torgovly*), just off Nevsky Prospect, at 21/23 Bolshaya Konyushennaya ulitsa. **Passage,** at 48 Nevsky Prospect, caters primarily to the local population. The souvenir sections, however, are often a shopper's paradise as prices, in rubles, are significantly lower here than in the souvenir shops around hotels and in other areas frequented by tourists. At 25 Nevsky, in another renovated building intended to become the most sophisticated business center in town, a boring **Britansky Dom** (A BHS venture) tries hard to give a Western touch to the scene.

Outside the large department stores of Nevsky Prospect, you will find some boutiques and lots of "variety shops"—part souvenir oriented, part practical—which can be a bit bewildering. Look in them if you have time; you never know what you may find.

Specialty Stores

Art Galleries

The art-gallery culture developed enormously in Russia in 1991 and the years following. Both foreign and domestic collectors, including banks, were hungry for Russian contemporary art. It has notably faltered since; buyers have either retreated or fallen back on more established values. In St. Petersburg, works offered for sale tend to be unimaginative urban landscapes. You will also note that sculpture, photography, and room installations are absent—a lack explained by economic realities.

Nevsky Prospect is lined with art shops, where local artists sell their wares on commission. Before making a major purchase at these stores, be sure to ask if they will take care of the paperwork necessary to allow you to take the item out of the country. It's also a good idea to inquire whether they charge an additional fee for this service. Some of the best art shops are: **Art Collegium** (⌧ 64 Ligovsky Prospect, ☎ 812/164–9564)); **Borey** (⌧ 58 Liteyny Prospect, ☎ 812/273–3693), with both avant-garde and academic artists, painting, graphics, and applied art; **Guild of Masters** (⌧ 82 Nevsky Prospect, ☎ 812/279–0979), which offers paintings, graphics, applied art, and items of jewelry; **Lavka Khudozhnika** (⌧ 8 Nevsky Prospect, ☎ 812/312–6193), whose stock includes paintings, graphics, ceramics, and textiles; **Palitra** (⌧ 166

Nevsky Prospect, ☎ 812/277–1216), which carries primarily the work of young Russian artists; **Pechatnya** (⊠ Peter and Paul Fortress, ☎ 812/238–4742), which offers exhibition and sale of works of lithography, xylography, etchings, and linocuts; **Petropol** (⊠ 27 Millyonnaya ul., ☎ 812/315–3414), which sells items made of mammoth ivory; and **Society of Free Artists** (look for the words "Art Gallery" on the window, ⊠ 20 Nevsky Prospect, ☎ 812/311–7777), founded in October 1988. Right in the Nevsky Palace Hotel you will find **Anna Gallery** (☎ 812/310–0777); its founder, Anna Hachaturian, was the first person to open a private gallery in 1989.

Clothing Stores

Presumably, you aren't here to find clothes, but if you are, try the department stores listed above. Chic boutiques in the better hotels have some designer pieces, usually at higher-than-designer prices. Go to the **Fashion House** (⊠ 21 Nevsky Prospect, ☎ 812/312–5307) for local designers like Larissa Pogoretskaya, Olga and Andrei Yanov, or Bunakova Hokhloff. **Tatyana Parfyonova** has her own boutique at ⊠ 51 Nevsky Prospect, ☎ 812/113–1415. The Moscow-based and Russia's "king of fashion," Valentin Yudashkin, is said to be looking for a location to open a satellite store in the city.

Craft and Souvenir Shops

Besides the counters in hotel lobby shops, where prices are often wildly inflated, you can find tasteful gifts at **Khudozhestvennye Promysly** (⊠ 51 Nevsky Prospect, ☎ 812/113–1495), including hand-knitted scarves and mittens, hand-painted trays, and ceramics; **Guild of Masters** (⊠ 82 Nevsky Prospect, ☎ 812/279–0979) sells jewelry, ceramics, and other types of Russian native art, all made by members of the Russian Union of Artists; **Khudozhestvenny Salon** (⊠ 8 Nevsky Prospect, ☎ 812/312–6193) stocks ceramics, boxes, jewelry, painting, dolls, and a fine selection of handicrafts; and **Nasledie** (⊠ 116 Nevsky Prospect, ☎ 812/279–5067) carries *palekh* and *khokhloma* (different types of hand-painted lacquered wood), samovars, nesting dolls, amber, and hand-painted trays. For china made at the Lomonosov China Factory (LFZ), once a purveyor to the czars, go to the **Farfor** (i.e., "china") store (⊠ 64 Nevsky Prospect, ☎ 812/314–4263 or 7 Vladimirsky Prospect, ☎ 812/113–1513).

Farmers' Markets

The farmers' markets in St. Petersburg are lively places where a colorful array of goods and foods are sold by individual farmers, often from out of town and sometimes from outside the Russian republic. In recent years the variety of goods available at the market (in Russian, *rynok*) has increased tremendously. Because markets are much cleaner and better lit here than in Moscow, it can also be fun just to visit and browse. In addition to the fine cuts of fresh and cured meat, dairy products, and homemade jams and jellies, piles of fruits and vegetables can be found, even in winter. Try some homemade pickles or pickled garlic, a tasty local favorite. You can also find many welcome surprises like hand-knitted scarves, hats, and mittens. Farmers' markets are generally open daily from 8 AM to 7 PM and usually close at 5 PM on Sundays.

St. Petersburg's most popular markets are: **Kuznechny Rynok** (⊠ 3 Kuznechny pereulok), just outside the Vladimirskaya metro station; **Sytny Rynok** (⊠ 3/5 Sytninskaya Pl.), in the Petrograd Side district, not far from the Gorkovskaya subway station; and the huge, sprawling flea market known as **Sennoi Rynok** (⊠ Sennaya Pl.), at the exit from the subway station of the same name. The latter was closed for renovation at press time (winter 1999).

Grocery Stores

For those looking for a big Western supermarket that takes credit cards, try **Kalinka-Stockmann** (⊠ 1 Finlandsky Prospect, ☎ 812/542–2297), open daily 9–10. **Super Babylon** (⊠ 54/56 Maly Prospect, Petrograd Side, ☎ 812/230–8096), is a superstore open daily 24 hours. For imported cheese and excellent fruit and vegetables, try **Supermarket** (⊠ 48 Nevsky Prospect, ☎ 812/219–1732), open Monday–Saturday 10–9 and Sundays 11–9. Another option is the **Jinn** supermarket (⊠ 61 Sredny Prospect, Vassily Island, ☎ 812/218–0469), open daily 10–10. Otherwise, have a go at the local *dieta* (dairy-food store), *gastronom* (food store), and *produkty* (hard food products).

Music

The closest thing to a Western music store is the Saigon store, on the corner of Nevsky Prospect and Vladimirsky Prospect. Their selection of classical music is nonexistent, but they will be able to brief you on Russian pop music. You will find a more user-friendly branch in the renovated part of the Gostinny Dvor (on the side of Nevsky Prospect, ground floor), where you can freely roam between the shelves. Otherwise, keep an eye open throughout the city, as CDs and tapes can be found in many kiosks and the choice will never be twice the same.

SIDE TRIPS FROM ST. PETERSBURG

Several extraordinary palaces are located in the suburbs of St. Petersburg. Following the 1917 Revolution, these former summer residences of the czars were nationalized and turned into museums.

Of all the palaces you will see in Russia, one that will make a distinct and lasting impression is Peterhof, on the shore of the Baltic Sea, some 29 km (18 mi) from St. Petersburg. It is more than just a summer palace; it is an Imperial playground replete with lush parks, monumental cascades, and gilt fountains. In czarist times, Tsarskoye Selo, now renamed Pushkin, was a fashionable haunt of the aristocracy, who were anxious to be near the Imperial family and to escape the noxious air and oppressive climate of the capital. After the Revolution of 1905 Nicholas II and his family lived here, more or less permanently. Pavlovsk, the Imperial estate of Paul I (in Russian Pavel, hence Pavlovsk) is some 30 km (18 mi) south of St. Petersburg and only 5 km (3 mi) from Pushkin and the Catherine Palace. Because of the proximity of the two towns, it's often suggested that tours to them be combined. If you decide to do this, make sure to give yourself enough time to do justice to both. The estate of Lomonosov, on the Gulf of Finland, some 40 km (25 mi) west of St. Petersburg and about 9 km (5½ mi) northwest of Peterhof, is perhaps the least commanding of the suburban Imperial palaces. It is, however, the only one to have survived World War II intact.

Except for Kronstadt, all the destinations in this section can be reached by commuter train (*elektrichka*), but the simplest way to see the palaces is to book an excursion (available through any tour company). The cost is reasonable and covers transportation, guided tour, and admission fees. An organized excursion to any of the suburban palaces will take at least four hours. If you travel on your own, it's likely to take up the entire day. Although you'll find some cafeterias and cafés, they're nothing special, so you may prefer to pack a lunch or bring a snack with you.

Peterhof (Petrodvorets)

The visitor to Peterhof and to the other Imperial residences nearby will find it difficult to believe that when the Germans were finally dirven out of the area toward the end of World War II, everything (or almost everything) was in ruins. Many priceless objects had been removed to safety before the Germans advanced, but a great deal had to be left behind for the invaders to loot and destroy. Now, after decades of pains-taking work, art historians and craftsmen, using pieces of fabric, pho-tographs, and written descriptions, have returned the palaces to their former splendor. Peterhof and its neighboring palaces are so vast, how-ever, that renovation work will be ongoing for many years to come.

An integral part of visiting any museum-palace in Russia is encoun-tering the autocratic *babushki* who now control them. In this, Peter-hof is no exception. No matter how annoying, they deserve respect, for they survived the 900-day siege of Leningrad, witnessed the palaces' destruction, and saw them rise again, almost miraculously, from the ashes. As you enter the palace, you will be given tattered shoe covers so as to protect the highly polished floors as you walk through the splen-did halls. One cautionary note: On most occasions, flash photography is not allowed, although for a fee, fast-film and videotaping may be used. Sometimes the babushki aren't aware of the difference. So hang on tight to your equipment to avoid having it confiscated by an overzealous custodian of Peter's treasures.

★ **Peterhof** is best visited in summer. A winter visit can be quite disap-pointing, as from late September to early June the fountains and cas-cades are closed down and take on the depressing look of a drained pool. You can reach the palace by commuter train from St. Petersburg but, minimal fog permitting, the best way to go is by hydrofoil, from which your first view is the panorama of the grand palace overlook-ing the sea. Be aware that the lines to get into the palace can be ex-cruciatingly long in summer. Sometimes guided tours get preferential treatment. ⊠ *2 ul. Razvodnaya, town of Peterhof,* ☎ *812/427–9527.* ▨ *Palace and park $12, plus separate admission fees for park pavil-ions; park grounds only, $5.* ☉ *Great Palace Tues.–Sun. 10:30–6. Closed last Tues. of month. Transportation: commuter train from Baltisky Vokzal (Baltic Station) to Novy Peterhof station, approximately 40 mins from St. Petersburg. From station take Bus 351 to Dvorets. In sum-mer, hydrofoils to Peterhof leave from pier outside the Hermitage Mu-seum approximately every 30 mins. Ride takes about ½ hr.*

The complex of gardens and residences at Peterhof was masterminded by Peter the Great, who personally drew up the first plans, starting around 1720. His motivation was twofold. First, he was proud of the capital city he was building and wanted its new-made Imperial grandeur showcased with a proper summer palace. Second, he became attached to this spot while erecting the naval fortress of Kronstadt on a nearby island across the Gulf of Finland; because it lay in easy view, he often stayed here during the fort's construction. When it was finished, by which time he had had a series of naval victories (including the North-ern War against the Swedes), he threw himself into establishing many parts of the grounds that would be called Peterhof (Peter's Court), a German name changed to Petrodvorets after World War II.

If you travel by hydrofoil, you will arrive at the pier of the Lower Park, from which point you work your way up to the Grand Palace. If you arrive by land, you'll simply go through the process in reverse. Either way, the perspective always emphasizes the mightiness of water. Half encircled by the sea, filled with fountains and other water monuments,

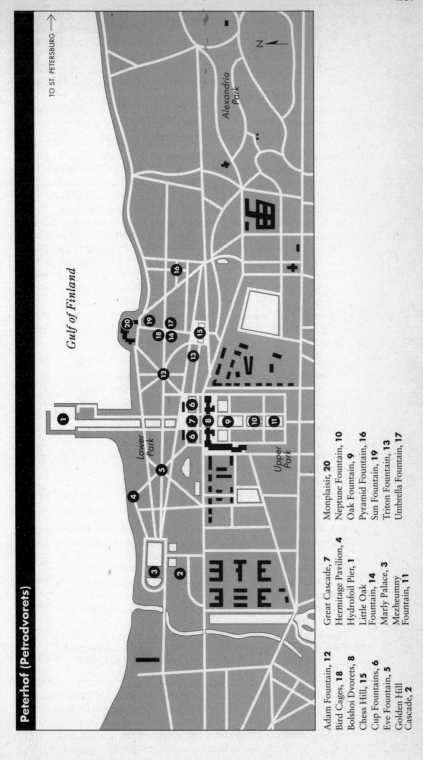

Peterhof (Petrodvorets)

TO ST. PETERSBURG →

Gulf of Finland

Alexandria Park

Lower Park

Upper Park

Adam Fountain, **12**
Bird Cages, **18**
Bolshoi Dvorets, **8**
Chess Hill, **15**
Cup Fountains, **6**
Eve Fountain, **5**
Golden Hill
Cascade, **2**

Great Cascade, **7**
Hermitage Pavilion, **4**
Hydrofoil Pier, **1**
Little Oak
Fountain, **14**
Marly Palace, **3**
Mezheumny
Fountain, **11**

Monplaisir, **20**
Neptune Fountain, **10**
Oak Fountain, **9**
Pyramid Fountain, **16**
Sun Fountain, **19**
Triton Fountain, **13**
Umbrella Fountain, **17**

with the Marine Canal running straight from the foot of the palace into the bay—Peter's place was also his loving tribute to the role of water in the life, and strength, of his city. The Lower Park was a formal Baroque garden in the French style, adorned with statues, fountains, and cascades. Peter's playful spirit is still very much in evidence here. The fun-loving czar installed "trick fountains"—hidden water sprays built into trees and tiny plazas and brought to life by stepping on a certain stone or moving a lever, much to the surprise of the unsuspecting visitor and the delight of the squealing children who love to race through the resulting showers on hot summer days.

Located in the eastern half of Lower Park is the oldest building at Peterhof, **Monplaisir** (literally "My Pleasure"). This is where Peter the Great lived while overseeing construction of the main Imperial residence, and, as was typical with Peter, he greatly preferred this modest Dutch-style villa to his later, more extravagant living quarters. The house is open to the public and makes a pleasant tour. Some of its most interesting rooms are the **Lacquered Study,** decorated with replicas of panels (the originals were destroyed during World War II) painted in the Chinese style; **Peter's Naval Study**; and his bedroom, where some personal effects, such as his nightcap and a quilt made by his wife, are on display. Attached to Peter's villa is the so-called **Catherine Wing,** built by Rastrelli in the mid-18th century in an utterly different style. The future Catherine the Great was staying here at the time of the coup that overthrew her husband and placed her on the throne; it was later used mainly for balls.

In the western section of the Lower Park is another famous structure, the **Hermitage.** This two-story pavilion gives new meaning to the concept of a movable feast. The building, which was used primarily as a banqueting hall (for special guests), was at one time equipped with a device that would lift the dining table area—diners and all—from the ground floor to the private dining room above. A slightly different system was put in place after Czar Paul I's chair broke during one such exercise. The center part of the table could be lifted out, and guests would write down their dinner preferences and then signal for their notes to be lifted away. Shortly thereafter, the separated section would be re-lowered, complete with the meals everyone had ordered. The only way to the Hermitage was over a drawbridge, so privacy was ensured.

A walk up the path through the center of the Lower Park (along the Marine Canal) leads you to the famous **Great Cascade.** Running down the steep ridge separating the Lower Park and the Grand Palace towering above, the cascade comprises three waterfalls, 64 fountains, and 37 gilt statues. The system of waterworks has remained virtually unchanged since 1721. The ducts and pipes convey water over a distance of some 20 km (12 mi). The centerpiece of the waterfalls is a gilt Samson rending the jaws of a lion, from which a jet of water spurts into the air. The statue represents the Russian victory over the Swedes at Poltava on St. Samson's day. The present figure is a meticulous replica of the original, which was carried away by the Germans.

Crowning the ridge above the cascade is the magnificent **Bolshoi Dvorets** (Great Palace). Little remains of Peter's original two-story house, built between 1714 and 1725 under the architects Leblond, Braunstein, and Machetti. The building was considerably altered and enlarged by Peter's daughter, Elizabeth. She entrusted the reconstruction to her favorite architect, the Italian Bartolomeo Rastrelli, who transformed the modest residence into a sumptuous blend of medieval architecture and Russian Baroque. Before you begin your tour of the palace interiors, pause for a moment to enjoy the breathtaking view from the marble terrace. From here a full view of the grounds below unfolds, stretching from the cascades to the Gulf of Finland and on to the city horizon on the shore beyond.

As for the main palace building, the lavish interiors are primarily the work of Rastrelli, although several of the rooms were redesigned during the reign of Catherine the Great to accord with Classicism, the architectural style of her day. Of Peter's original design, only his **Dubovy Kabinet** (Oak Cabinet) survived the numerous reconstructions. The fine oak panels (some are originals) lining the walls were designed by the French sculptor Pineau. The entire room and all its furnishings are made of wood, with the exception of the white marble fireplace, above which hangs a long mirror framed in carved oak.

One of the largest rooms in the palace is the **Tronny Zal** (Throne Room), which takes up the entire width of the building. Classically designed, this majestic room—once the scene of great receptions and official ceremonies—features exquisite parquet floors, elaborate stucco ceiling moldings, and dazzling chandeliers. The pale-green and dark-red decor is bathed in light, which pours in through two tiers of windows (28 in all) taking up the long sides of the room. Behind Peter the Great's throne at the eastern end of the room hangs a huge portrait of Catherine the Great. The empress, the epitome of confidence after her successful coup, is shown riding a horse, dressed in the uniform of the guards regiment that supported her bid for power.

Next to the Throne Room is the **Chesmensky Zal** (Chesma Hall), whose interior is dedicated entirely to the Russian naval victory over the Turks in 1770. The walls are covered with 12 huge canvases depicting the battles, which were created by the German painter P. Hackert at Empress Catherine's behest. According to legend, the artist explained that he could not paint a burning ship, since he had never seen one. Catherine arranged to have ships blown up for him to use as models. Such were the privileges of divine right. Arguably the most dazzling of the rooms is the **Audients Zal** (Audience Hall). Rastrelli created the definitive Baroque interior with this glittering room of white, red, and gold. Gilt Baroque bas-reliefs adorn the stark white walls, along which tall mirrors are hung, further reflecting the richness of the decor.

Other notable rooms include the **Kitaiskye Kabinety** (the Chinese Study Rooms), designed by Vallin de la Mothe in the 1760s. Following the European fashion of the time, the rooms are ornately decorated with Chinese motifs. Finely carved black-lacquered panels depict various Chinese scenes. Between the two rooms is the **Kartinny Zal** (Picture Hall), whose walls are paneled with 368 oil paintings by the Italian artist Rotari. The artist used just eight models for these paintings, which depict young women in national dress.

After a tour of the palace interiors, a stroll through the **Upper Park** is in order. Lying on the south side of the palace, this symmetrical formal garden is far less imaginative than the Lower Park, with its playful fountains and cascading waterfalls. Its focal point is the Neptune Fountain, made in Germany in the 17th century and bought by Paul I in 1782. During the war the three-tiered group of bronze sculptures was carried away by the Germans. It was eventually recovered and reinstalled in 1956.

Pushkin (Tsarskoye Selo)

The town of **Pushkin,** 24 km (15 mi) south of St. Petersburg, was the summer residence of the Imperial family from the days of Peter the Great right up to the last years of the Romanov dynasty. Formerly known as

Pushkin

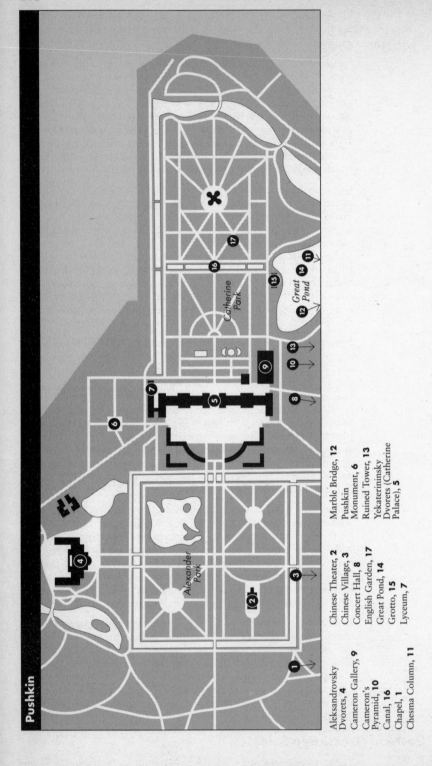

Aleksandrovsky Dvorets, **4**
Cameron Gallery, **9**
Cameron's Pyramid, **10**
Canal, **16**
Chapel, **1**
Chesma Column, **11**

Chinese Theater, **2**
Chinese Village, **3**
Concert Hall, **8**
English Garden, **17**
Great Pond, **14**
Grotto, **15**
Lyceum, **7**

Marble Bridge, **12**
Pushkin Monument, **6**
Ruined Tower, **13**
Yekaterininsky Dvorets (Catherine Palace), **5**

Tsarskoye Selo (The Czar's Village), its name was changed after the 1917 Revolution, first to Detskoye (Children's) Selo and then to Pushkin, in honor of the great Russian poet who studied at the lyceum here. During the 18th and 19th centuries, Tsarskoye Selo was a popular summer resort for St. Petersburg's aristocracy and well-to-do. Not only was the royal family close by, but it was here, in 1837, that Russia's first railroad line was opened, running between Tsarskoye Selo and Pavlovsk, followed three years later by a line between here and St. Petersburg.

★ Pushkin's main attraction is the dazzling **Yekaterininsky Dvorets** (Catherine Palace), a perfect example of Russian Baroque. The exterior is painted bright turquoise and features row after row of white columns and pilasters with gold Baroque moldings alternating the entire length (985 ft) of the facade. Although much of the palace's history and its inner architectural design bears Catherine the Great's stamp, it is for Catherine I, Peter the Great's second wife, that the palace is named. Under Empress Elizabeth, their daughter, the original modest stone palace was completely rebuilt. The project was initially entrusted to the Russian architects Kvasov and Chevakinsky, but in 1752 Elizabeth brought in the Italian architect Bartolomeo Rastrelli (who went on to build the Winter Palace in St. Petersburg). Although Catherine the Great had the interiors remodeled in the Classical style, she left Rastrelli's stunning facade untouched. ⊠ *7 ul. Sadovaya, town of Pushkin,* ☎ *812/465–5308.* ▧ *$10.* ☺ *Wed.–Mon. 10–5; park open daily. Closed last Mon. of month. Transportation: commuter train from Vitebsky Vokzal (Vitebsk Station) to Pushkin–Detskoe Selo, approximately 30 mins from St. Petersburg. From station take Bus 371 or 382 to Dvorets (palace).*

You'll enter the palace grounds through the gilded black iron gates designed by Rastrelli. The *E* atop is for Catherine (Ekaterina in Russian). To your right, a visual feast unfolds as you walk the length of the long blue-and-gold facade toward the museum entrance. Sparkling above the palace at the northern end are the golden cupolas of the Palace Church. The interiors are just as spectacular; many of the rooms are famous in their own right. Although little of Rastrelli's original design remains, the many additions and alterations made between 1760 and 1790 under Catherine the Great do; these were carried out by noted architects, the Scottish Charles Cameron and the Italian Giacomo Quarenghi.

Entering the palace by the main staircase, which was not added until 1861, you will see displays showing the extent of the wartime damage and of the subsequent restoration work. Like Peterhof, the palace was almost completely destroyed during World War II. It was used by the occupying Nazi forces as an army barracks; as the Germans retreated, they blew up what remained of the former Imperial residence. Today the exterior of the palace again stands in all its glory, while work on the interior is proceeding.

The largest and arguably most impressive room is the **Bolshoi Zal** (Great Hall), which was used for receptions and balls. The longer sides are taken up by two tiers of gilt-framed windows. Tall, elaborately carved and gilt mirrors have been placed between them. Light pouring in through the windows bounces off the mirrors and sparkles on the gilt, amplifying the impression of spaciousness and brilliance. The huge ceiling painting, depicting Russian military victories and accomplishments in the sciences and arts, makes the room seem even larger. Here it is easy to imagine the extravagant lifestyle of St. Petersburg's prerevolutionary elite.

On the north side of the State Staircase is one of the palace's most famous rooms, the **Yantarnaya Komnata** (Amber Room), so named for the engraved amber panels that once lined its walls. A treaty gift to

Peter the Great from the king of Prussia in 1716, the panels were stolen by the Nazis and their fate has remained unknown for decades. In 1979 the Soviet government finally gave up hope of ever retrieving them and began the costly work of restoring the room. The work is far from complete, but the few restored panels—and a prewar black-and-white photograph of the room—give you some idea of how marvelous the original interior was. In the meantime, one of the four Florentine mosaic panels that originally adorned the Amber Room was found in Bremen, where a German pensioner whose father had fought in the Soviet Union was trying to sell it.

Leaving the Amber Room, you will come to the large **Kartinny Zal** (Picture Gallery), which runs the full width of the palace. The paintings are all from Western Europe and date from the 17th to the early 18th century.

Highlights among the other splendid rooms on the north side include the Blue Drawing Room, the Blue Chinese Room, and the Choir Anteroom, all of which face the courtyard. Each has pure silk wall coverings. The Blue Chinese Room, originally designed by Cameron, has been restored on the basis of the architect's drawings. Despite its name, it is a purely Classical interior, and the only thing even remotely Chinese is the Oriental motif on the silk fabric covering the walls. The fine golden-yellow silk of the Choir Anteroom is from the same bolt used to decorate the room in the 18th century. When the postwar restoration began, an extra supply of the original silk was discovered tucked away in a storage room of the Hermitage.

Having savored the treasures inside the palace, you can now begin exploring the beautiful **Yekaterininsky Park** outside, with its marble statues, waterfalls, garden alleys, and boating ponds, pavilions, bridges, and quays. The park is split into two sections. The inner, formal section, known as the French Garden, runs down the terraces in front of the palace's eastern facade. The outer section centers around the Great Pond and is in the less rigid style of an English garden. If you follow the main path through the French Garden and down the terrace, you will eventually reach Rastrelli's Hermitage, which he completed just before turning his attention to the palace itself. Other highlights of the French Garden include the Upper and Lower Bath pavilions (1777–79) and Rastrelli's elaborate blue-domed Grotto.

There is much to be seen in the English Garden, too. A good starting point is the **Cameron Gallery,** which actually forms a continuation of the palace's parkside frontage. It is off to the right (with your back to the palace). Open only in summer, it contains a museum of 18th- and 19th-century costumes. From its portico you get the best views of the park and its lakes—which is exactly what Cameron had in mind when he designed it in the 1780s. The double-sided staircase leading majestically down to the Great Pond is flanked by two bronze sculptures of Hercules and Flora.

From here, go down and begin your exploration of the park. Just beyond the island in the middle of the Great Pond, which is actually an artificial lake, stands the **Chesma Column,** commemorating the Russian naval victory in the Aegean in 1770. At the far end of the pond is **Cameron's Pyramid,** where Catherine the Great reportedly buried her beloved greyhound dogs.

If you follow around the pond's right side, you will come to the pretty blue-and-white **Marble Bridge,** which connects the Great Pond with a series of other ponds and small canals. At this end, you can rent rowboats. Farther along, up to the right, you come to the **"Ruined Tower."**

It's not authentic or old, just built to enhance the romantic ambience of these grounds.

Outside the park, just north of the Catherine Palace, stands yet another palace, the **Alexandrovsky Dvorets,** a present from Catherine to her favorite grandson, the future Czar Alexander I, on the occasion of his marriage. Built by Quarenghi between 1792 and 1796, the serene and restrained Classical structure was the favorite residence of Russia's last czar, Nicholas II. The left wing of the building has been open to the public since 1997. Most interiors were lost, with the notable exception of Nicholas' cabinet, a fine example of Art Nouveau furniture and design. A visit is most interesting in the context of the ongoing rehabilitation of Nicholas II in Russia.

Built in 1791 and originally intended for the education of Catherine the Great's grandchildren, the **Lyceum** later became a school for the nobility. Its most famous student, enrolled the first year it opened, was the adored Alexander Pushkin. The building now serves as a museum; the classroom, library, and Pushkin's bedroom have been restored to their appearance at the time he studied there. In the school's garden is a statue of the poet as a young man, seated on a bench, presumably deep in creative meditation. The building is attached to the Catherine Palace.

Pavlovsk

The estate grounds of Pavlovsk had always been the royal hunting grounds, but in 1777 Catherine the Great awarded them to her son Paul I, upon the birth of his first son (the future czar, Alexander I). Construction of the first wooden buildings started immediately, and in 1782 Catherine's Scottish architect Charles Cameron began work on the Great Palace and the landscaped park. In contrast to the dramatically Baroque palaces of Pushkin and Peterhof, Pavlovsk is a tribute to the reserved beauty of Classicism. Paul's intense dislike of his mother apparently manifested itself in determinedly doing exactly what she would *not*—here, visitors agree, with gratifying results. The place is popular with St. Petersburg residents, who come to stroll through 1,500-acre park, with its woods, ponds, alleys, and pavilions. ⊠ *20 ul. Revolutsiy, town of Pavlovsk,* ☎ *812/470–2156.* ➥ *$9.* ☉ *Sat.–Thurs. 10–5. Closed 1st Mon. of month. Transportation: commuter train from Vitebsky Vokzal (Vitebsk Station) to Pavlovsk, approximately 25–35 mins from St. Petersburg. From station walk to palace, or take Bus 370 or 383.*

★ A tour of Pavlovsk begins with the **Bolshoi Dvorets (Great Palace),** which stands on a high bluff overlooking the river and dominates the surrounding park. The building is painted golden yellow and crowned with a flat, green dome supported by 64 small white columns. Built in 1782–86 as the summer residence of Paul and his wife, Maria Fyodorovna, the stone palace was designed in imitation of a Roman villa. It was enlarged by Vincenzo Brenna in 1796–99, when a second story was added to the galleries and side pavilions. Despite a devastating fire in 1803 and further reconstruction by Voronikhin in the early 19th century, Cameron's basic design survived.

In front of the palace stands a statue of the snub-nosed Paul I, a copy of the statue at Gatchina, Paul's other summer residence. When you enter, you'll find many rooms on view, and you may start on either the ground or the second floor. The splendid interiors, with their parquet floors, marble pillars, and gilt ceilings, were created by some of Russia's most outstanding architects. Besides Cameron, Brenna, and Voronikhin, the roll call includes Quarenghi, who designed the interiors of five rooms on the first floor, and Carlo Rossi, who was responsible for the library, built in 1824. The state apartments on the ground floor include the pink-and-blue **Ballroom**; the formal **Dining Hall**, where the full dinner service for special occasions is set out; and the lovely **Corner Room**, with walls of lilac marble and doors of Karelian birch. Among the lavishly decorated state rooms on the second floor is the famous **Greek Hall**, whose layout is that of an ancient temple. Its rich green Corinthian columns stand out against the white of the faux marble walls. The hall, which also served as a small ballroom, linked the state rooms of Paul I to those of his wife, Maria. The last room on his side, leading here, was the **Hall of War.** Her private suite, called the **Hall of Peace**, was designed to correspond to it. The gilt stucco wall moldings are decorated with flowers, baskets of fruit, musical instruments, and other symbols of peace.

Beyond the empress's apartments is the light-filled **Picture Gallery**, with its floor-length windows and eclectic array of paintings. From it, via a small, pink marble waiting room, you reach the palace's largest chamber, **Throne Hall.** It once held Paul I's throne, which was removed for a victory party after Napoléon's defeat and somehow never returned.

Leave the palace to explore its grounds. Covering over 1,500 acres, Pavlovsk's splendid park boasts numerous pavilions, tree-lined alleys, waterways, and statues. Like the palace, the design of the park was shared by the leading architects of the day—Brenna, Cameron, Voronikhin, and Carlo Rossi. Once again, the Pavlovsk park differs greatly from park designs of the other Imperial palaces; those applied strict rules of geometrical design, whereas at Pavlosk nature was left unfettered, with simple beauty, instead of precisely determined effect, the result.

The combined length of the park's paths and lanes is said to equal the distance between St. Petersburg and Moscow (656 km/410 mi). Since you can't possibly cover the entire territory in one day anyway, you might just want to see where your whim leads you. If you walk down the slope just behind the palace to the **Czar's Little Garden (Sobstvenny Sadik)**, you can see the Three Graces Pavilion. Created by Cameron, the 16-columned pavilion encloses a statue of Joy, Flowering, and Brilliance. A stone staircase, decorated with lions, is directly behind the palace and will take you to the Slavyanka Canal. On the canal's other side, down to the left, is the graceful **Apollo Colonnade**, whose air of ruin was not entirely man made; built in 1783, it was struck by lightning in 1817 and never restored. If you bear right at the end of the stairs, you come to the **Temple of Friendship**, meant to betoken the friendship between Empress Maria and Catherine the Great, her mother-in-law. Beyond it is a monument from the empress to her own parents; the center urn's medallion bears their likenesses. Of the other noteworthy pavilions and memorials dotting the park, the farthest one up the bank is the **Mausoleum of Paul I.** Set apart on a remote and overgrown hillside toward the center of the park, it was built by Maria for her husband after he was murdered in a palace coup. Paul was never interred here, however, and lest his death appear too heartrending for his widow (portrayed as inconsolable in a statue here), historical evidence indicates she was well aware of the plot to kill her husband.

Lomonosov (Oranienbaum)

Renamed for the 18th-century scientist Mikhail Lomonosov, Lomonosov was originally named Oranienbaum, after the orangery attached to its palace. It was the property of Alexander Menshikov, Peter the Great's favorite, who, following Peter's lead, in 1710 began building his own luxurious summer residence on the shores of the Baltic

Sea. Before his plans could be realized, however, Peter died and Menshikov was stripped of his formidable political power and exiled, leaving his summer estate half finished. The palace reverted to the crown and was given to Peter III, the ill-fated husband of Catherine the Great. Most of the buildings on the grounds were erected during his six-month reign, in 1762, or completed later by Catherine. ⊠ *48 ul. Yunovo Lenintsa, town of Lomonosov,* ☏ *812/422–4796.* 🖾 *$9.* ☾ *Wed.– Mon. 11–5. Closed last Mon. of month; some of the buildings are also closed on Mon. Transportation: commuter train from Baltisky Vokzal (Baltic Station) to Oranienbaum-1 (not II), approximately 1 hr from St. Petersburg.*

Menshikov's Great Palace, the original one here, is also its biggest. It is situated on a terrace overlooking the sea. Built between 1710 and 1725, it was designed by the same architects who built Menshikov's grand mansion on Vasilievsky Island, Giovanni Fontana and Gottfried Schaedel. The Great Palace has been under reconstruction for some time and is currently closed to the public.

Nearby is **Peterstadt Dvorets.** the modest palace that Peter III used, a two-story stone mansion built between 1756 and 1762 by Arnoldo Rinaldi. Its interior is decorated with very handsome lacquered wood paintings. That it seems small, gloomy, and isolated is perhaps appropriate since it was here, in 1762, that the czar was arrested, then taken to Ropsha and murdered in the wake of the coup that placed his wife, Catherine the Great, on the throne.

The building that most proclaims the estate's Imperial beginnings, however, is unquestionably Catherine's **Kitaisky Dvorets (Chinese Palace),** also designed by Rinaldi. Intended as one of her private summer residences, it is quite an affair—Rococo inside, Baroque without. Lavishly decorated, it has ceiling paintings created by Venetian artists, inlaid-wood floors, and elaborate stucco walls. The small house outside served as the kitchen. At press time (winter 1999), unfortunately, the place was closed for restoration.

Down the slope to the east of the Great Palace is the curious **Katalnaya Gorka (Sledding Hill).** All that remains of the slide, which was several stories high, is the pavilion that served as the starting point of the ride, where guests of the empress could catch their breath before tobogganing down again. Painted soft blue with white trim, the fanciful pavilion looks like a frosted birthday cake. Also on the premises, near the pond, is a small amusement park offering carnival rides.

Kronstadt

Located on the Kotlin Island, **Kronstadt** can be seen from Peterhof and Lomonosov, but it is reached by bus from the other side of the Gulf of Finland, on a titanic dike erected in 1979 (meant to prevent flooding of St. Petersburg) just south of where the Finnish border was until 1939. Kronstadt remains a myth; it is a picturesque town, although in a dire condition, built in 1703 by Peter the Great and was for a long time the only military harbor of the Empire. That is also why it was off-limits to all but its permanent residents; visitors had to stop at special checkpoints as late as 1996. Today anyone can board bus 510 or the boat *meteor* and visit this historic place. Along with its artistic delights—the Summer Garden, the Gostinny Dvor, and the Menshikov Palace—Kronstadt is famed as the hometown of Aleksandr Popov, inventor of the radio antenna in 1889, and as the center of the historic antibolshevik rebellion of 1921. The Kronstadt "Commune" aimed to break the monopoly of the Communist Party and to give back to peasants the right to use freely their land; the revolt lasted two weeks, nearly put Lenin's power in peril, but, in the end, was bloodily repressed. Tellingly, the streets of Kronstadt have not recovered their prerevolutionary names and are still named after Karl Marx and Lenin. A rousing finale to any trip to Kronstadt is its Church of Seamen, built in 1902–13 by Vassili Kosyakov and the finest example of neo-Byzantine architecture in Russia. *To reach Kronstadt, take the subway to the Chernaya Rechka station; walk across Savushkina street to the embankment of the Chernaya Rechka river and take Bus 510 (regular, express, or collective taxi; 5 and 6 rubles respectively) to the very end. The trip takes about 1 hr and buses leave every 20 mins. In the summer, there is a fast boat that leaves from* ✉ *nab. Makarova (*☎ *812/ 218–2223; 812/236–3317 in Kronstadt), near the Tuchkov bridge.*

ST. PETERSBURG A TO Z

Arriving and Departing

By Boat

Call the **Baltic Line** (☎ 812/355–1616) for the latest information on boats that call at St. Petersburg. Kiel, Germany, is not a departure option anymore. Freight ships that also take passengers and their cars may be available from Sweden. Arriving in or departing from St. Petersburg by boat from the Kotlin border is 1½ hours of sheer pleasure: The boat passes the island of Kotlin (Kronstadt), then along the coastline where Lomonosov, Peterhof, and Strelna can be successively seen with the aid of binoculars. Finally, it makes it into the huge city harbor, with the St. Isaac Cathedral as a constant focus. Recently, passenger boats from Russia to Sweden have keep highly erratic schedules so always keep in mind the option of driving to Helsinki to board a boat there to Stockholm. The **sea passenger terminal** is on Vasilievsky Island at Morskoi Slavy Ploshchad (☎ 812/355–1310). The **river passenger terminal** is at 195 Obukhovskoi Oborony Prospect (☎ 812/262–0239, Proletarskaya subway stop); boat trips to Valaam, Kizhi, and other destinations leave from here (June through September).

By Bus

The Russian firm **Sovavto St. Petersburg** (☎ 812/298–1352, ℻ 812/ 298–7760) offers daily departures to Helsinki from the following hotels: Astoria, Grand Hotel Europe, Pulkovskaya, and St. Petersburg. The Finnish bus company **Finnord** (☎ 812/314–8951, ℻ 812/314– 7058) offers daily service to Vyborg and Helsinki, leaving from hotel Pulkovskaya and 37 ulitsa Italyanskaya.

By Car

You can reach St. Petersburg from Finland via the Helsinki–St. Petersburg Highway through the border town of Vyborg; the main street into and out of town for Finland is Kamennoostrovsky Prospect. To reach Moscow, take Moskovsky Prospect; at the hotel Pulkovo roundabout, take Mosvoskoye Shosse (M-10/E-95), slightly to the left of the road to the airport.

By Plane

AIRPORTS AND AIRLINES

St. Petersburg is served by two airports, **Pulkovo I** (domestic) and **Pulkovo II** (international), located just 5 km (3 mi) apart and 12 km (7 mi) south of downtown St. Petersburg. The runways of the two Pulkovos interconnect, so it's possible you could land at Pulkovo I and taxi over to Pulkovo II.

Compared to Moscow's Sheremetyevo II, Pulkovo II is a breeze. It's compact and well lit, with signs in both Russian and English. Remember that on departure you will need to fill out a final customs declaration (available at all the long tables) before proceeding through the first checkpoint. To be there 1½ hours in advance is not overdoing it.

For domestic flight information, call 812/104–3822. For international information, call 812/104–3444.

Aeroflot (☎ 812/315–0072) offers direct flights to more than 20 countries out of Pulkovo II. **Transaero** (☎ 812/279–1974), the "new airline in town," is now a tough Russian competitor to Aeroflot, including on some international routes, but it only flies to Moscow from St. Petersburg. **Pulkovo** is the latest carrier to be born out of Aeroflot (☎ 812/311–8093 for domestic flights, including CIS; 812/315–0072 for international flights). Other international airlines with offices in St. Petersburg include: **Air France** (☎ 812/325–8252); **Austrian** (☎ 812/325–3260); **Balkan** (☎ 812/315–5030); **British Airways** (☎ 812/329–2565); **CSA (Czech airlines)** (☎ 812/315–5259); **Delta** (☎ 812/311–5819); **Finnair** (☎ 812/315–9736); **KLM** (☎ 812/325–8989); **LOT** ☎ 812/272–2982); **Lufthansa** (☎ 812/314–4979); **Malev** (☎ 812/315–5455); **SAS** (☎ 812/325–3255);and **Swissair** (☎ 812/314–5086).

BETWEEN THE AIRPORT AND DOWNTOWN

From Pulkovo I, Municipal Bus 39 will take you to the Moskovskaya subway stop on Moskovsky Prospect; the stop at the airport is right outside the terminal. Tickets are sold on the bus, which runs every 20 minutes during the day. From Pulkovo II, the service is less reliable and more inconvenient. If you have any luggage, the only realistic way to reach downtown St. Petersburg is by car. If you are traveling with a tour package, all transfers will have been arranged. Independent tourists are advised to make advance arrangements with their hotels for transfers from the airport. There are plenty of taxis available, but for safety reasons non-Russian speakers should not pick up a cab on their own. Foreign tourists, especially passengers arriving at train stations and airports, are prime crime targets. Cab fare from the airport will depend entirely on your negotiating skills; the range is $30 to $50. The airport is about a 40-minute ride from the city center. When you return to the airport, a regular **cab** that you order by phone (☎ 812/312–0022) will only cost you $10.

By Train

Train travel is by far the most convenient and comfortable mode of travel in Russia. St. Petersburg has several train stations, the most important of which are **Finlandsky Vokzal** (Finland Station), for trains to Finland; **Moskovsky Vokzal** (Moscow Station), at Ploshchad Vostania, off Nevsky Prospect, for trains to Moscow and points east; **Varshavsky Vokzal** (Warsaw Station) for trains to the Baltic countries; and **Vitebsky Vokzal** (Vitebsk Station) for trains to Ukraine and points south. All the major train stations have a connecting subway stop, so they are easily reached by public transportation.

There are several trains daily from Moscow to St. Petersburg, the most popular of which is the **Red Arrow,** a night train that departs from one end at 11:55 PM and arrives at the other at 8:25 AM the next day. During the day travelers prefer the high-speed **Avrora,** which makes the trip in less than six hours. There are two trains daily to and from Helsinki; the trip takes 6½ hours.

For information on train arrival and departure schedules, call 812/168–0111. Train tickets may be purchased through the tourist bureau in your hotel or at the Central Railway Agency Office at 24 Kanal Griboyedova (off Nevsky Prospect, adjacent to the Kazan Cathedral; ☎ 812/201, an unusual three-digit number). Tickets for trips other than same-day departures are *not* for sale at the train stations.

A reminder about train travel: You must travel on an Intourist train ticket or risk being fined by the railway. As a foreigner you pay the special higher price for train travel and, in return, usually get above-average service (the best trains are still reserved for foreign tourists).

Long-distance travelers should be aware that trains can often lack heat and hot water, a result of feuds between rail administrations in different republics. To avoid discomfort, be sure to bring along some drinking water whenever traveling by train. You are also advised to carry a personal supply of toilet tissue.

Getting Around

Although St. Petersburg is spread out over 650 square km (150 square mi), most of its historic sites are concentrated in the downtown section and are best explored on foot. The historic sites are often not well served by the extensive public transportation system, so be prepared to do a lot of walking.

By Bus, Tram, and Trolley

You must purchase a ticket from the conductor after you have boarded. At press time, a ticket valid for one ride costs 1 ruble; if you change buses, you must pay another fare. Buses, trams, and trolleys operate from 5:30 AM to midnight, although service in the late evening hours and on Sundays tends to be unreliable.

St. Petersburg has an elaborate surface transportation system, but in contrast to the subway, service has deteriorated in recent years. Vehicles tend to be dilapidated and extremely overcrowded during rush hours; people with claustrophobia should avoid them. In the last years of the Soviet regime, Russia depended on Hungary for buses, but in today's economic order, these are no longer forthcoming. It is not uncommon to ride buses with holes in the ceiling and doors that will not properly close, or that keel to the side when turning corners, like a sailboat in rough seas.

By Subway

Although St. Petersburg's metro does not boast the elaborate design and decoration common in the Moscow subway system, its good qualities are still substantial. Despite economic hardships, St. Petersburg has managed to maintain efficient, inexpensive service; the only drawback is that the stops tend to be far apart.

To use the subway, you must purchase a token or a magnetic card (available at stations) and insert it, upon entering, into the slot at the turnstile. The fare is the same regardless of distance. Alternatively, you may purchase a pass valid for an entire month and good for transport on all modes of city transportation. The cost is insignificant and well worth the convenience if you plan to use the subway a lot. The subway operates from 5:30 AM to midnight, but is best avoided during rush hours. Stations are deep underground, necessitating long escalator rides. Some of them have encased landings so that entry is possible only after the train has pulled in and the secondary doors are opened. Note that a section between Lesnaya Station and Ploshchad Muzhestva Station is out of service due to an accident. The repair work began in 1997 and should be completed by the year 2000. In the meantime a free shuttle operates between the two stations. On the yellow line, two stations

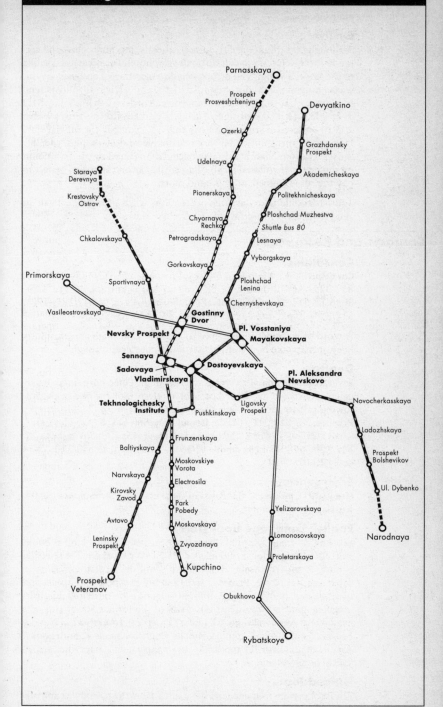

opened in 1997 on the Petrograd side and two more farther north are promised for 1998, to provide better access to Krestovsky and Yelagin islands.

By Taxi

Although taxis roam the city quite frequently, it is far easier—and certainly safer—to order a cab through your hotel. Fares vary according to the driver's whim; you are expected to negotiate. Foreigners are always charged much more than Russians, and oblivious tourists tend to be gouged. If you speak Russian, you can order a cab by dialing 812/312–0022. There is sometimes a delay, but usually the cab arrives within 20–30 minutes. If you order a cab this way, you pay the official state fare, which turns out to be very reasonable in dollars, plus a fee for the reservation. No other tip is expected than rounding up the amount on the meter. If you hail a cab or a private car on the street, expect to pay the ruble equivalent of $3 and more.

Tourists should take the same precautions when using taxicabs in St. Petersburg as in Moscow.

Contacts and Resources

Consulates

Canada (⊠ 32 Malodetskoselsky Prospect, ☎ 812/325–8448, FAX 812/325–8393). **U.K.** (⊠ 5 Pl. Proletarskoi Diktatury, ☎ 812/325–6036, FAX 812/325–6037). **U.S.** (⊠ 15 Furstadtskaya, ☎ 812/275–1701, 812/274–8568, and 812/274–8689, FAX 812/110–7022).

A word of warning: Phone lines to the U.S. Consulate are constantly busy. It may take hours of persistent dialing to get through.

Dentists

Several private dental practices operate in St. Petersburg. In an emergency, you could ask your hotel for a referral, or try one of the following private clinics: **Clinic Complex St. Petersburg** (22 Moskovsky Prospect, ☎ 812/316–6272); **Dental Polyclinic No. 3** (12, 21st liniya, ☎ 812/213–7551 or 812/213–5550); **Medi** (13, 10th Sovietskaya, ☎ 812/274–6480); or **Nordmed** (12/15 ul. Tverskaya, ☎ 812/110–0654 or 812/110–0401).

Emergencies

Fire (☎ 01). **Police** (☎ 02, Russian speakers only). **Ambulance** (☎ 03, Russian speakers only).

English-Language Bookstores

For English-language publications, try St. Petersburg's largest bookstore, **Dom Knigi** (House of Books), at 28 Nevsky Prospect. The selection is nothing to write home about, but it's still the largest bookstore in town and fun to see. **Planeta,** at 30 Liteiny Prospect, has a selection of imported books, too. A limited selection of outdated English-language guidebooks on various parts of the former Soviet Union is available at **Akademkniga** (57 Liteiny Prospect). **Iskusstvo** (52 Nevsky Prospect), like Akademkniga, stocks English-language guidebooks. American and British paperbacks, newspapers, and magazines are on sale in hotel gift shops.

Guided Tours

A host of private tour agencies have surfaced in the past few years, primarily because tourism is now seen as an easy source of foreign currency. Keep in mind that whatever the price quoted for a tour, it may very well be negotiable. In addition to the private agencies, every major hotel has a tourist bureau through which individual and group tours can be booked.

St. Petersburg Tourist Company, formerly Intourist (✉ 60 nab. Moiky, ☎ 812/315–5129, FAX 812/312–2558) offers group or individual excursions to all of the major sites and suburban palaces.

The **St. Petersburg City Excursion Bureau** (✉ 56 Angliskaya nab., ☎ 812/311–4019, FAX 812/311–2445) arranges sightseeing trips throughout the city. Specially tailored tours can be made by **Staraya Derevnya** (✉ 72 ul. Savushkina, ☎ FAX 812/239–0000).

Hospitals and Clinics

Public medical facilities in St. Petersburg still are poorly equipped and short on supplies. However, as with dentistry, private clinics are proliferating, which offer a higher level of treatment. As in the other cities, it is recommended that tourists seek emergency medical help at Western-style clinics. The **American Medical Center** (✉ 10 Serpukhovskaya ul., ☎ 812/325–6101, FAX 812/325–6120) is open weekdays 8:30 to 6, and offers 24-hour comprehensive care. **The Clinic Complex** has been around for years as the St. Petersburg Polyclinic No. 2 (✉ 22 Moskovsky Prospect, ☎ 812/316–6272, FAX 812/316–5939); it is open weekdays 9–9, Saturdays 9–3. A doctor is on call 24 hours a day. Another possibility, still in the same neighborhood, is the **Emergency Medical Consulting** (✉ 14 Izmaylovsky Prospect, entrance from Sovietsky pereulok, ☎ 812/112–6510, FAX 812/112–6508), a European medical center. If you are unfortunate enough to be hospitalized while in St. Petersburg, you will probably be placed in **Hospital No. 20** (✉ 21 ul. Gastello, ☎ 812/108–4808 or 812/108–4066).

Pharmacies

Most pharmacies in St. Petersburg close by 8 or 9 PM. **PetroFarm** (22 Nevsky Prospect, ☎ 812/164–4410) has a pharmacist on call daily 9–3.

Pharmacies that regularly stock imported and Western medicines are: **Pharmacy Damian** (✉ 22 Moskovsky Prospect, ☎ 812/110–1744, FAX 812/110–1240); **PetroFarm** (also at 83 Nevsky Prospect, ☎ 812/277–7966); and **Pharmadom** (✉ 5 Nevsky Prospect, ☎ 812/312–7078). The **American Medical Center** and the **Clinic Complex** listed under Hospitals and Clinics also have pharmacies stocked with Western drugs.

Travel Agencies

For international travel help, **American Express** operates an office in the Grand Hotel Europe. Besides ticketing, the office replaces lost traveler's checks and credit cards. ✉ *1/7 ul. Mikhailovskaya, just off Nevsky Prospect,* ☎ *812/329–6060.* ☉ *Weekdays 9–5.*

Avista Tours (✉ 7 ul. Millionaya, ☎ 812/275–6635, FAX 812/275–3488) arranges international bookings. **Sindbad Travel,** at the Russian International Hostel, is friendly and helpful (✉ 28, 3rd Sovietskaya, ☎ 812/327–8384, FAX 812/329–8019). There are many more agencies and it would be impossible to list them all; this is probably where the change is most notable compared to pre-perestroika years.

Visitor Information

You may consult the **St. Petersburg Council for Tourism** (✉ 3 ul. Italianskaya, ☎ 812/314–8786 office, 812/110–6739 foreign section; FAX 812/110–6824 or 812/311–9381). The **St Petersburg City Tourist Information & Services Center (TISC)** has a database on cultural and sports events, hotels, major tourist attractions, and so on (☎ 812/210–4527 or 812/276–1365, FAX 812/210–4927). You can also call the **Infoline** (☎ 812/325–9325) 24 hours a day; they may not have the answer to your question, but they will tell you so nicely.

Your most expeditious route is your hotel, for virtually all of them have established tourist offices for their guests. These offices, which provide a wide variety of services, will help you book individual and group tours, make restaurant reservations, or purchase theater tickets. Even if you are not a hotel guest, you are usually welcome to use these facilities, provided you are willing to pay the hefty fees for their services.

Where to Change Money

Exchange bureaus, which are generally open from 9 AM to 6 PM, with an hour's break for lunch in the afternoon, are now all over the place. ATM machines, with access to Cirrus, Visa, Mastercard and Plus, pop up by the day. Look for them in subway stations and in the exchange bureaus. There is one at the **Passazh,** the department store on Nevsky Prospect opposite the Gostinny Dvor (not accessible at night), and another one, also centrally located on Nevsky, between Rubinshteina ulitsa and Vladimirsky Prospect. It is accessible at all times, but you should exercise caution if withdrawing money here at a late hour. Naturally, your hotel will also have an exchange office, which may be the safest and most convenient option for you.

5 Portrait of Moscow and St. Petersburg

Russia Without Tears

RUSSIA WITHOUT TEARS

YOU KNOW YOU WILL RETURN to Paris. You know there will be another trip to London. Russia, your heart tells you, you will see only once. Once is not much for a country shrouded in melodrama and mythology. Once is rather a gamble when the country is so large, its language so utterly foreign, its reputation somewhat less than reliable.

Once, on the other hand, can be unforgettable.

This was a trip I did not trust myself to plan. But who wouldn't trust the Finns? So decent, efficient, dependable, the Finns have been putting together escorted tours of Russia for 10 years. Norvista Finn Way has an entire bookful of tours, and one in particular promised eight fairly complete, reasonably priced, smoothly run days in Moscow and St. Petersburg.

The day before I was to leave, I collected my envelope of tickets and vouchers from Norvista Finn Way. As I examined them I mumbled something about finally getting to see the Summer Palace.

"I am very sorry," the agent said. "The Summer Palace will be closed for the three days you are in St. Petersburg."

Silence.

"You must not let this upset you."

She'd noticed.

"There are other palaces."

I don't want to see other palaces.

"You must believe me. The palaces are not what you will remember."

Arriving at Sheremetyevo airport in Moscow is the first thing you will remember. It's the crossroads of every place you have never heard of. I had landed on the dark side of the moon. And I had worked myself up into quite a state. What if the Norvista Finn Way guide wasn't there? Where would I go? What would I do? What if . . .? What if . . .?

"You must be . . .," said a woman of about 50 with Geraldine Ferraro hair and an Hermès scarf, who approached me as I stepped through passport control. How she knew who I was, I can't say.

"Welcome. My name is Natasha."

Natasha. She must be kidding.

From the airport chaos Natasha continued to pick out our group of 12 travelers, through which no common thread seemed to run. We were young and we were old. We wore teal nylon track suits and we carried shopping bags from Henri Bendel.

Quickly Natasha had us on our way. There is no greater thrill than that first drive from the airport to a new city in a new country. While our shabby gray Mercedes-Benz bus passed through the shabby brown streets of Moscow, every dreary Soviet building was an occasion for a lively story, one that I was too tired to absorb but delighted to hear. Clearly Natasha was not going to waste a minute of our week.

"Tonight Swan Lake is at the Bolshoi," she said. "It is performed very rarely. You must stay awake. You must go."

Six hours after arriving at Moscow, against every impulse to collapse onto the fake-fur bedspread in my deluxe hotel room, I found myself seated in a gilded box in the first ring at the Bolshoi Theater, watching the most sentimental, the most extravagant, the most Russian of ballets. My attention wandered, as it always does in a theater, from the dancers to the music to the audience and back to myself; the theater can be better than therapy. All those strange faces and strange clothes. So many flowers. The box where the czar once sat. The dusty velvet curtain still decorated with hammers and sickles. Histrionic Russian bravas, as I have never heard bravas.

Palaces were the last thing on my mind.

A certain sort of traveler clings to the conceit that a guide gets between you and real life, but I am not one of them. A good guide, I would say, is real life. For three days and three nights, Natasha was the face of Moscow for me. She will always be. I think of her when I read the *New York Times* and watch Peter Jennings. How is she? Is she prospering in the New Russia? There was nothing our group could not ask to do, no aspect of her life about which we could not inquire. For someone with only a few days who doesn't speak the language, there was simply no getting closer to a real Russian.

And Natasha was not just a real Russian; she was a real Muscovite, which I quickly surmised is not unlike a real New Yorker. Here was someone who could take care of herself: quick-witted, aggressive, cynical, sardonic, proud to know everything about a city that seems strident and obnoxious to those who don't understand and love it.

Natasha showed us all the great sights: Red Square and Lenin's Tomb and St. Basil's and the various high points of the Kremlin, all of which you think you comprehend until you finally see them. There is no photograph of Red Square that can substitute for the rather chilly sensation of standing at the center of the center of this peculiar empire called Russia.

Natasha could aim high or low, touristically. You want pictures, she tells you exactly where to stand to get the best shot. You want nesting dolls, she tells you where to buy the better-quality tourist junk. You want to visit the Armory, that corner of the Kremlin with the gold-encrusted imperial carriages and the diamond-studded imperial crowns, and she escorts you past the mob being turned back at the entrance, then explains every case of treasures in such chatty detail that two hours hardly suffice for your tour.

On most days a few hours are unscheduled, and it is a little frightening to be kicked from the safety of Natasha's tour bus. Russia is macabre. Everywhere there is an air of menace. Each little exchange leads you to believe that you don't quite know the rules of the game you are playing.

Russia may be the greatest film noir ever made. It certainly does not hurt that the entire population of Moscow seems to be wearing three-quarter-length black leather jackets. But what you're picking up is more than a fashion signal. People do stare at you; you cannot disguise your Americanness. And the most unlikely and suspicious things do happen. You look down an alley and notice several grizzled men exchanging large amounts of cash. You visit Lenin's Tomb, and as you file past his embalmed body you are followed by a bride in her wedding dress and veil. You take a seat on empty bleachers in vast Red Square, where there is more than enough room for a military parade, and somebody sits down right next to you, but never says a word.

After a while you come to accept that nothing bad is going to happen to you, but that perhaps it is best to avoid eye contact, to look purposeful, and to get back to the security of the bus as soon as possible. It's a lovely luxury to be led.

Natasha led us to likely as well as unlikely places. Her Intourist script changes fairly often these days, as do Russian politics. Soviet landmarks are now considered dusty relics of a distant past, which was all of 10 years ago and could return tomorrow. In the course of an afternoon Natasha quite matter-of-factly pointed out the former headquarters of the KGB; the riverfront Art Deco apartment building favored by high-ranking comrades who had a tendency to vanish under Stalin; and the Russian parliament building, known as the White House, which Boris Yeltsin attacked with tanks just a few years ago in one of those peculiarly Russian counter-counter-putsch-coups that no outsider really understands. Perhaps you saw the flames on CNN. The speed with which things change in Russia leads you to wonder if things won't all have changed before your plane leaves.

And then Natasha, like a good parent, takes you to the Moscow Circus, where you would never take yourself. Everything is suddenly so normal; the parents and children are the same as parents and children everywhere. A dancing bear is a great equalizer.

For our last two hours in Moscow, between the 10 PM cossacks-on-horseback finale at the circus and the departure of the midnight train to St. Petersburg, Natasha has saved a special treat.

"One of our most beautiful metro stations is next to the railroad station," she says. "Who wants to see the metro?"

Who doesn't?

At 11 PM on Saturday, along with hordes of ragtag Muscovites, our group descends escalator after escalator through this great civic project begun under Stalin and adorned with chandeliers, Lenin statues, and red-

and-gold mosaics of comrades gathering sheaves of wheat. Natasha announces: "We still have a few minutes. Who would like to get on a train and see some other stations?"

Who wouldn't?

Finally it is time to let go. We take a long walk in a cold drizzle to car No. 1 on the overnight St. Petersburg express, an Anna Karenina moment if ever there was one. The car is all ours, except for the dour babushka attending us. Natasha demonstrates the correct way to lock the doors, for those of us who have been terrified by American reports of robberies on such trains, and assures us that everything will be fine. She shakes our hands and says goodbye. In eight hours, after we have glided through birch forests under a full moon, someone will be waiting for us on the platform in St. Petersburg.

As Car No. 1 rolls to a stop in St. Petersburg, there is a young woman in a billowing navy overcoat and another Hermès scarf who seems to know just where to stand to greet us. There is not even a moment to feel lost.

"Hello, hello," she purrs, averting her eyes. "My name is Marina."

Already I adore Marina. Just as Natasha personifies Moscow, Marina is St. Petersburg. She is no street fighter; she is reserved, decorous, with that aloof eastern European manner. She has long straw-colored hair, which she wears up like a Russian fur hat, and speaks in a mellifluous voice that comes to life over the microphone on our bus. Her passion is Bulgarian culture.

Marina's reserve camouflages her considerable energy. A couple of hours after arriving, our group is at the Hermitage, the former Winter Palace, for a two-hour tour of its highlights. I can now say I have seen the most famous Leonardo (the Benois Madonna) and Rembrandt (Flora, as modeled by his wife, Saskia) and van Gogh (Cottages) and Cézanne (Mont Saint-Victoire) and Picasso (The Absinthe Drinker) and Matisse (Dance) that the Hermitage has to offer, in the same detached way I vaguely recall once cruising past the Pietà as if on a conveyor belt.

But what do I really remember? The malachite urns that I could have hidden in. The eerie surgical-gown green that the Hermitage is painted, against the flat gray light of this northern city. The balcony overlooking Palace Square on which I have seen Nicholas and Alexandra greet their subjects in countless foxed photographs. This is the square where the October Revolution played out its final act in this very century.

City tours lay ahead, afternoons in which all I had to do was sit back and be taken to the various pieces of the St. Petersburg puzzle: to St. Isaac's Cathedral, the Fortress of Peter and Paul, the Admiralty, the Summer Garden. We shook hands with many an icon, but I often preferred the bus ride, listening to Marina narrate as we wound past the canals through Neoclassical streets painted in pastels.

For those of us who were inconsolable, Marina arranged a quick walk around the Summer Palace, too gold and too blue and absolutely shut tight, and then moved us on to a building that was open. She could not quite tell us with a straight face that Pavlovsk is an equally palatial palace, but it is an important one nonetheless. We visited many a ballroom and picture gallery and oohed and aahed on cue. And I forgot it all even before I was back on the bus.

A walk on Nevsky Prospekt, the city's main thoroughfare, isn't so easily forgotten. On this one street you come face-to-face with all the players in modern Russia: pensioners who haven't had a good day since perestroika, New Russians barking at cell phones in their Mercedes 600's, young people carrying shopping bags printed with pictures of the stars of the soap opera *Santa Barbara*, and foreign businessmen hungry for the Deal. Here, in a few short blocks, you can review current Russian fashions (bring your sense of irony) in the arcade called Passazh; walk through Dom Knigi, a bookshop where all the books are under glass; find a store selling very red posters of Lenin wagging his finger; and see tins of osetra caviar stacked like Bumble Bee in the Art Nouveau halls of the Yeliseev food shop.

Also on Nevsky Prospekt is the Grand Hotel Europe, where I stayed. It is the match of any of the world's great hotels and, for Russia, a miracle, really. It too is a theme park of New Russia, with metal detectors at its doors, and the Caviar Bar, and a disco where men pass out drunk on the tables, and maids who make themselves at home in your room while you are out, and ravishingly beautiful young women who sit for hours in the lobby, staring at any and all available men with impunity.

Marina rescued us from all this decadence with a "folkloric evening," that standard building block of the package tour. Such events invariably include attractive young singers, costumes suitable for photographing, a hearty meal served family-style, and a great deal of dancing and hand-clapping and mating ritual, all of which culminates in getting a few members of the loosened-up audience onstage and embarrassing them. This particular evening took place in a dacha reconstructed in a St. Petersburg basement, and as hard as I resisted, going so far as to refuse to perform a peasant courtship dance, I enjoyed it throughly. The vodka helped.

By our last day in Russia I only wanted to be escorted. Marina agreed to lead a tour of the Yusupov Palace, one of many owned by the richest family in Russia, and not usually on the short list. It was all ours, every ghostly bombastic room in it, from the marble staircase to the private theater to the basement where Rasputin, the mystic who virtually controlled Nicholas and Alexandra, was shot and clubbed before finally being tied up and thrown into the Neva River. For those who lack imagination, Rasputin is there, in wax.

The trip deserved to end on a higher place. We attended a concert at the Philharmonic Hall, and this being late April, when the sun sets around 11 PM, sunlight streamed in through the clerestories during the whole performance. I don't remember the program, but I do remember the face of the 20-year-old pianist as he attacked the keys, as well as the young woman who moved herself down from the balcony to the empty sixth-row seat next to me. Everything about her was achingly shabby. She borrowed a program, which cost pennies. But she clearly understood that music far better than I ever would. It was nice to have company.

We were tired, we were overstimulated, but on the ride to the airport Marina proved herself incapable of passing the new public library, or the old city hall, or the monument to those who died in the Great Patriotic War (World War II), without telling us all about them. And we were incapable of not listening.

She stayed with us until the very end, when our passports were stamped and our visas were seized and there was no chance of being turned back on Russian soil. And then came that awkward moment when there was nothing to do except shake hands with someone you don't really know at all, reflect on a somewhat new shade of the meaning of the word farewell, and hear your well-meaning self say, "Come visit us in America."

— Stephen Drucker

Stephen Drucker is the editor of *Martha Stewart Living*. This essay originally appeared in *Travel & Leisure* in 1997.

English-
Russian
Vocabulary

ENGLISH-RUSSIAN VOCABULARY

Although we have tried to be consistent about the spelling of Russian names in this book, we find the Russian authorities are not consistent about transliteration of the Cyrillic alphabet into our familiar Latin letters. In Moscow, for example, Intourist spells a street name "Chaikovsky," but in St. Petersburg it's "Tchaikovsky." We've tried to stick to internationally recognized U.S. and British systems of transliteration, but don't be surprised if you occasionally come across differences like Chekhov and Tchekov, Tolstoy and Tolstoi, Baykal and Baikal, Tartar and Tatar, rouble and ruble—to say nothing of icon and ikon!

We give here some hints on the vital matter of reading Russian signs and on pronunciation, as well as a general English-Russian tourist vocabulary. Reading street names is probably the most important use for even a small knowledge of the Cyrillic alphabet. To help you, a word or two about how they work in Russian. Many Russian streets and squares are named after *people,* but the people's names may appear in different spellings—often they are made into adjectives. Suppose we have a street called Pushkin Street, after the poet. The word street, ULITSA in Russian, is feminine (all Russian nouns have a gender; masculine nouns usually ending consonants, feminine in "a" and neuter in "o" or "e"). So you will see the street name as *Pushkinskaya ulitsa,* a feminine form of Pushkin. Pushkin Avenue would be *Pushkinsky Prospekt* in Russian (the word for avenue is masculine). Pushkin Chaussée would be *Pushkinskoye Shosse* (chaussée is neuter). Don't be worried if you see one of these signs when our guide tells you you are on *Pushkin* street, avenue, etc.—it's the same thing! As a general rule, once you have deciphered the first few letters, you will recognize the name—don't worry about the ending!

Another common way of naming streets is to say, for example, "Street of Pushkin," "Avenue of Tolstoy," etc.—*Ulitsa Pushkina, Prospekt Tolstovo* and so on. Here again, the *name* is easy to spot—its ending is not a spelling mistake, just a genitive case form of Pushkin, Tolstoy, etc. If you do get lost, most passers-by will understand if you ask for a street by its English name.

We owe a debt of gratitude to the Government Affairs Institute, Washington, D.C., for their permission to reproduce the Tables of the Russian Alphabet which follow.

THE RUSSIAN ALPHABET

А а	И и	С с	Ъ ъ
Б б	Й й	Т т	Ы ы
В в	К к	У у	Ь ь
Г г	Л л	Ф ф	Э э
Д д	М м	Х х	Ю ю
Е е	Н н	Ц ц	Я я
Ё ё	О о	Ч ч	
Ж ж	П п	Ш ш	
З з	Р р	Щ щ	

The Sound of Russian

Category 1:
Russian Consonants that Look and Sound like English

Russian Letter (Capital)	Russian Letter (Small)	English Letter
Б	б	b
К	к	k
М	м	m
Т	т	t
З	з	z

Category 2:
Russian Consonants that Look Different from Their English Equivalents

Russian Letter (Capital)	Russian Letter (Small)	English Letter
Д	д	d
Ф	ф	f
Г	г	g
Л	л	l
Н	н	n
П	п	p
Р	р	r
С	с	s
В	в	v
Й	й	y

Category 3:
Russian Consonants that Have No English Equivalents

Russian Letter (Capital)	Russian Letter (Small)	Sound
Ч	ч	ch
Х	х	kh
Ш	ш	sh
Щ	щ	shch
Ц	ц	ts
Ж	ж	zh
Ь	ь	soft sign

The Russian Vowels

Russian Letter (Capital)	Russian Letter (Small)	Sound
А	а	ah
Я	я	yah
Э	э	eh
Е	е	yeh
Ы	ы	ih
И	и	ī (ee)
О	о	oh
Ё	ё	yo
У	у	u (oo)
Ю	ю	yu

EVERYDAY WORDS AND PHRASES

The most important phrase to know (one that may make it unnecessary to know any others) is: "Do you speak English?" — *Gavaree'te lee vy pa anglee'skee?* If the answer is "Nyet," then you may have recourse to the lists below:

Please	Пожа́луйста	pazhah'lsta
Thank you	Спаси́бо	spasee'ba
Good	Хорошо́	kharasho'
Bad	Пло́хо	plo'kha
I	Я	ya
You	Вы	vy
He	Он	on
She	Она́	anah'
We	Мы	my
They	Они́	anee'
Yes	Да	da
No	Нет	nyet
Perhaps	Мо́жет быть	mo'zhet byt
I do not understand	Я не понима́ю	ya ne paneemah'yoo
Straight	Пря́мо	pryah'ma
Forward	Вперёд	fperyo't
Back	Наза́д	nazah't
To (on) the right	Напра́во	naprah'va
To (on) the left	Нале́во	nale'va
Hello!	Здра́вствуйте!	zdrah'stvooite!
Good morning!	До́брое у́тро!	do'braye oo'tra!
Good day (evening)!	До́брый день (ве́чер)!	do'bree den (ve'cher)!
Pleased to meet you!	Очень рад с ва́ми познако́миться!	o'chen rat s vah'mee paznako'meetsa!
I am from USA (Britain)	Я прие́хал из США (Англии)	ya preeye'khal eez sshah' (ah'nglee ee)
I speak only English	Я говорю́ то́лько по-англи́йски	ya gavaryoo' to'lka pa anglee'skee
Do you speak English?	Говори́те ли вы по-англи́йски?	gavaree'te lee vy pa anglee'skee?
Be so kind as to show (explain, translate)	Бу́дьте добры́ по-кажи́те (объясни́те, переведи́те)	boo'te dobry' paka-zhee'te (abyasnee'te, perevedee'te)
Excuse my poor pronunciation	Извини́те моё плохо́е произношéние	eezveenee'te mayo'pla-kho'ye praeeznashe'nye
I beg your pardon	Прости́те	prastee'te
I want to post a letter	Мне ну́жно отпра́вить письмо́	mne noo'zhna atprah'-veet peesmo'
Postcard	Почто́вая ка́рточка	pachto'vaya kah'rtachka

DAYS OF THE WEEK

Monday	Понеде́льник	panede'lneek
Tuesday	Вто́рник	fto'rneek
Wednesday	Среда́	sredah'
Thursday	Четве́рг	chetve'rk

Friday	Пя́тница	pyah'tneetsa
Saturday	Суббо́та	soobo'ta
Sunday	Воскресе́нье	vaskrese'nye
Holiday, feast	Пра́здник	prah'zneek
Today	Сего́дня	sevo'dnya
Tomorrow	За́втра	zah'ftra
Yesterday	Вчера́	vcherah'

NUMBERS

How many?	Ско́лько?	sko'lka?
1	оди́н	adee'n
2	два	dva
3	три	tree
4	четы́ре	chety're
5	пять	pyat
6	шесть	shest
7	семь	sem
8	во́семь	vo'sem
9	де́вять	de'vyat
10	де́сять	de'syat
11	оди́ннадцать	adee'natsat
12	двена́дцать	dvenah'tsat
13	трина́дцать	treenah'tsat
14	четы́рнадцать	chety'rnatsat
15	пятна́дцать	pyatnah'tsat
16	шестна́дцать	shesnah'tsat
17	семна́дцать	semnah'tsat
18	восемна́дцать	vasemnah'tsat
19	девятна́дцать	devyatnah'tsat
20	два́дцать	dvah'tsat
30	три́дцать	tree'tsat
40	со́рок	so'rak
50	пятьдеся́т	pyadesyah't
60	шестьдеся́т	shezdesyah't
70	се́мьдесят	se'mdesyat
80	во́семьдесят	vo'semdesyat
90	девяно́сто	deveno'sta
100	сто	sto
1000	ты́сяча	ty'syacha

INFORMATION SIGNS

Toilet (Gentlemen) (Ladies)	Туале́т (М) (Ж)	tooale't
No smoking!	Не кури́ть!	ne kooree't!
Taxi rank	Стоя́нка такси́	stayah'nka taksee'
Entrance	Вход	fkhot
Exit	Вы́ход	vy'khat
No exit	Вы́хода нет	vy'khada net
Emergency exit	Запасно́й вы́ход	zapasnoi' vy'khat
Stop!	Стоп!	stop!

Drinks

cold water	холо́дной воды́	khalo'dnoi vady'
mineral water	минера́льной воды́	meenerah'lnoi vady'
grape, tomato juice	виногра́дного, тома́тного со́ка	veenagrah'dnava, tamah'tnava so'ka
whisky, vodka	ви́ски, во́дка	vee'skee, vod'ka
liqueur	ликёр	leekyo'r
lemonade	лимона́д	leemanah't
beer	пи́во	pee'va
tea, coffee, cocoa, milk	чай, ко́фе, кака́о, молоко́	chai, ko'fe, kakah'o, malako'
fruit juice	сок	so'kee

Meat

steak	бифште́кс	beefshte'ks
roast beef	ро́стбиф	ro'stbeef
veal chops	отбивну́ю теля́чью котле́ту	atbeevnoo'yoo telyah-chyoo katle'too
pork chops	свину́ю котле́ту	sveenoo'yoo katle'too
ham	ветчину́	vecheenoo'
sausage	колбасу́	kalbasoo'

Poultry

chicken	цыплёнка	tsyplyo'nka
hazel-grouse	ря́бчика	ryah'pcheeka
partridge	куропа́тку	koorapah'tkoo
duck	у́тку	oo'tkoo

Fish

soft caviar	зерни́стой икры́	zernee'stoi eekry'
pressed caviar	па́юсной икры́	pah'yoosnoi eekry'
salmon	лососи́ны	lasasee'ny
cold sturgeon	холо́дной осетри́ны	khalo'dnoi asetree'ny

Vegetables

green peas	зелёный горо́шек	zelyo'nee garo'shek
radishes	реди́ску	redee'skoo
tomatoes	помидо́ры	pameedo'ry
potatoes	карто́шка	karto'shka

Desserts

cake	пиро́жное	peero'zhnaye
fruit	фру́ктов	froo'ktaf
pears	груш	groosh
mandarines	мандари́нов	mandaree'naf
grapes	виногра́ду	veenagrah'doo
bananas	бана́нов	banah'naf

white and rye bread	бе́лый и чёрный хлеб	be'lee ee cho'rnee khlep
butter	ма́сло	mah'sla
cheese	сыр	syr
soft-boiled eggs	яйца всмя́тку	yai'tsa fsmyah'tkoo
hard-boiled eggs	яйца вкруту́ю	yai'tsa fkrootoo'voo
an omelette	омле́т	amle't

SHOPPING

Description

good	хоро́ший	kharo'shee
bad	плохо́й	plakhoi'
beautiful	краси́вый	krasee'vee
dear	дорого́й	daragoi'
cheap	дешёвый	desho'vee
old	ста́рый	sta'ree
new	но́вый	no'vee

Colors

white	бе́лый	be'lee
black	чёрный	chyo'rnee
red	кра́сный	krah'snee
pink	ро́зовый	ro'zavee
orange	ора́нжевый	arah'nzhevee
yellow	жёлтый	zho'ltee
brown	кори́чневый	karee'chnevee
green	зелёный	zelyo'nee
light blue	голубо́й	galooboi'
blue	си́ний	see'nee
violet	фиоле́товый	feeale'tavee
grey	се́рый	se'ree
golden	золото́й	zalatoi'
silver	сере́бряный	sere'bryanee

In the shop

Baker's	Бу́лочная	boo'lachnaya
Confectioner's	Конди́терская	kandee'terskaya
Food Store	Гастроно́м	gastrano'm
Grocer's	Бакале́я	bakale'ya
Delivery Counter	Стол зака́зов	stol zakah'zaf
Wine and Spirits	Ви́на—коньяки́	vee'na — kanyakee'
Fruit and Vegetables	Овощи—фру́кты	o'vashshee — froo'kty

INDEX

NOTES

NOTES

NOTES

NOTES

NOTES

NOTES

NOTES

With guidebooks for every kind of travel—from weekend getaways to island hopping to adventures abroad—it's easy to understand why smart travelers go with **Fodor's**.

At bookstores everywhere.
www.fodors.com

Fodor's Travel Publications

Available at bookstores everywhere. For descriptions of all our titles and a key to Fodor's guidebook series, visit www.fodors.com/books

Gold Guides

U.S.

Alaska

Arizona

Boston

California

Cape Cod, Martha's Vineyard, Nantucket

The Carolinas & Georgia

Chicago

Colorado

Florida

Hawai'i

Las Vegas, Reno, Tahoe

Los Angeles

Maine, Vermont, New Hampshire

Maui & Lāna'i

Miami & the Keys

New England

New Orleans

New York City

Oregon

Pacific North Coast

Philadelphia & the Pennsylvania Dutch Country

The Rockies

San Diego

San Francisco

Santa Fe, Taos, Albuquerque

Seattle & Vancouver

The South

U.S. & British Virgin Islands

USA

Virginia & Maryland

Washington, D.C.

Foreign

Australia

Austria

The Bahamas

Belize & Guatemala

Bermuda

Canada

Cancún, Cozumel, Yucatán Peninsula

Caribbean

China

Costa Rica

Cuba

The Czech Republic & Slovakia

Denmark

Eastern & Central Europe

Europe

Florence, Tuscany & Umbria

France

Germany

Great Britain

Greece

Hong Kong

India

Ireland

Israel

Italy

Japan

London

Madrid & Barcelona

Mexico

Montréal & Québec City

Moscow, St. Petersburg, Kiev

The Netherlands, Belgium & Luxembourg

New Zealand

Norway

Nova Scotia, New Brunswick, Prince Edward Island

Paris

Portugal

Provence & the Riviera

Scandinavia

Scotland

Singapore

South Africa

South America

Southeast Asia

Spain

Sweden

Switzerland

Thailand

Toronto

Turkey

Vienna & the Danube Valley

Vietnam

Special-Interest Guides

Adventures to Imagine

Alaska Ports of Call

Ballpark Vacations

The Best Cruises

Caribbean Ports of Call

The Complete Guide to America's National Parks

Europe Ports of Call

Family Adventures

Fodor's Gay Guide to the USA

Fodor's How to Pack

Great American Learning Vacations

Great American Sports & Adventure Vacations

Great American Vacations

Great American Vacations for Travelers with Disabilities

Halliday's New Orleans Food Explorer

Healthy Escapes

Kodak Guide to Shooting Great Travel Pictures

National Parks and Seashores of the East

National Parks of the West

Nights to Imagine

Orlando Like a Pro

Rock & Roll Traveler Great Britain and Ireland

Rock & Roll Traveler USA

Sunday in San Francisco

Walt Disney World for Adults

Weekends in New York

Wendy Perrin's Secrets Every Smart Traveler Should Know

Worlds to Imagine

Fodor's Special Series

Fodor's Best Bed & Breakfasts
America
California
The Mid-Atlantic
New England
The Pacific Northwest
The South
The Southwest
The Upper Great Lakes

Compass American Guides
Alaska
Arizona
Boston
Chicago
Coastal California
Colorado
Florida
Hawai'i
Hollywood
Idaho
Las Vegas
Maine
Manhattan
Minnesota
Montana
New Mexico
New Orleans
Oregon
Pacific Northwest
San Francisco
Santa Fe
South Carolina
South Dakota
Southwest
Texas
Underwater Wonders of the National Parks
Utah
Virginia
Washington
Wine Country
Wisconsin
Wyoming

Citypacks
Amsterdam
Atlanta
Berlin
Boston
Chicago
Florence
Hong Kong
London
Los Angeles
Miami
Montréal
New York City
Paris

Prague
Rome
San Francisco
Sydney
Tokyo
Toronto
Venice
Washington, D.C.

Exploring Guides
Australia
Boston & New England
Britain
California
Canada
Caribbean
China
Costa Rica
Cuba
Egypt
Florence & Tuscany
Florida
France
Germany
Greek Islands
Hawai'i
India
Ireland
Israel
Italy
Japan
London
Mexico
Moscow & St. Petersburg
New York City
Paris
Portugal
Prague
Provence
Rome
San Francisco
Scotland
Singapore & Malaysia
South Africa
Spain
Thailand
Turkey
Venice
Vietnam

Flashmaps
Boston
New York
San Francisco
Washington, D.C.

Fodor's Cityguides
Boston
New York
San Francisco

Fodor's Gay Guides
Amsterdam
Los Angeles & Southern California
New York City
Pacific Northwest
San Francisco and the Bay Area
South Florida
USA

Karen Brown Guides
Austria
California
England B&Bs
England, Wales & Scotland
France B&Bs
France Inns
Germany
Ireland
Italy B&Bs
Italy Inns
Portugal
Spain
Switzerland

Languages for Travelers (Cassette & Phrasebook)
French
German
Italian
Spanish

Mobil Travel Guides
America's Best Hotels & Restaurants
Arizona
California and the West
Florida
Great Lakes
Major Cities
Mid-Atlantic
Northeast
Northwest and Great Plains
Southeast
Southern California
Southwest and South Central

Pocket Guides
Acapulco
Aruba
Atlanta
Barbados
Beijing
Berlin
Budapest
Dublin
Honolulu
Jamaica
London

Mexico City
New York City
Paris
Prague
Puerto Rico
Rome
San Francisco
Savannah & Charleston
Shanghai
Sydney
Washington, D.C.

Rivages Guides
Bed and Breakfasts of Character and Charm in France
Hotels and Country Inns of Character and Charm in France
Hotels and Country Inns of Character and Charm in Italy
Hotels of Character and Charm in Paris
Hotels of Character and Charm in Portugal
Hotels of Character and Charm in Spain
Wines & Vineyards of Character and Charm in France

Short Escapes
Britain
France
Near New York City
New England

Fodor's Sports
Golf Digest's Places to Play (USA)
Golf Digest's Places to Play in the Southeast
Golf Digest's Places to Play in the Southwest
Skiing USA
USA Today The Complete Four Sport Stadium Guide

Fodor's upCLOSE Guides
California
Europe
France
Great Britain
Ireland
Italy
London
Los Angeles
Mexico
New York City
Paris
San Francisco

WHEREVER YOU TRAVEL, *H*ELP IS NEVER FAR AWAY.

From planning your trip to providing travel assistance along the way, American Express® Travel Service Offices are always there to help you do more.

Moscow, St. Petersburg & Kiev

Moscow
American Express Travel Service
21A Sadovaya-Kudrinskaya
(7)(095) 7559000/7559001

St. Petersburg
American Express Travel Service
Grand Hotel Europe
1/7 Mikhailovskaya Ul
(7)(812) 3296060/3296070

Kiev
European Travel Services (Ukraine) (R)
Suite 2
36 Ivana Franka
(380)(44) 2465573

do more ® | AMERICAN EXPRESS

Travel

www.americanexpress.com/travel